PROGRAMMING WITH
PYTHON
FOR SOCIAL SCIENTISTS

Sara Miller McCune founded SAGE Publishing in 1965 to support the dissemination of usable knowledge and educate a global community. SAGE publishes more than 1000 journals and over 800 new books each year, spanning a wide range of subject areas. Our growing selection of library products includes archives, data, case studies and video. SAGE remains majority owned by our founder and after her lifetime will become owned by a charitable trust that secures the company's continued independence.

Los Angeles | London | New Delhi | Singapore | Washington DC | Melbourne

Phillip D. Brooker

PROGRAMMING WITH
PYTHON
FOR SOCIAL SCIENTISTS

⑤SAGE

Los Angeles | London | New Delhi
Singapore | Washington DC | Melbourne

⑤SAGE

Los Angeles | London | New Delhi
Singapore | Washington DC | Melbourne

SAGE Publications Ltd
1 Oliver's Yard
55 City Road
London EC1Y 1SP

SAGE Publications Inc.
2455 Teller Road
Thousand Oaks, California 91320

SAGE Publications India Pvt Ltd
B 1/I 1 Mohan Cooperative Industrial Area
Mathura Road
New Delhi 110 044

SAGE Publications Asia-Pacific Pte Ltd
3 Church Street
#10-04 Samsung Hub
Singapore 049483

Editor: Jai Seaman
Editorial assistant: Lauren Jacobs
Assistant editor, digital: Sunita Patel
Production editor: Ian Antcliff
Copyeditor: Richard Leigh
Proofreader: Neville Hankins
Indexer: Elizabeth Ball
Marketing manager: Susheel Gokarakonda
Cover design: Shaun Mercier
Typeset by: C&M Digitals (P) Ltd, Chennai, India
Printed in the UK

© Phillip Brooker 2020

First published 2020

Library of Congress Control Number: 2019944187

British Library Cataloguing in Publication data

A catalogue record for this book is available from the British Library

ISBN 978-1-5264-3171-4
ISBN 978-1-5264-3172-1 (pbk)

At SAGE we take sustainability seriously. Most of our products are printed in the UK using responsibly sourced papers and boards. When we print overseas we ensure sustainable papers are used as measured by the PREPS grading system. We undertake an annual audit to monitor our sustainability.

CONTENTS

EXTENDED CONTENTS

ABOUT THE
AUTHOR

Phillip Brooker is a Lecturer in Sociology at the University of Liverpool, with interdisciplinary research interests in and around ethnomethodology and conversation analysis, science and technology studies, Computer-Supported Cooperative Work, and human–computer interaction. On the platform of a record of research in the emerging field of digital methods and social media analytics (having contributed to the development of a Twitter data collection and visual analysis package called Chorus (http://www.chorusanalytics.co.uk)), his current research interests lie in exploring the potential for computer programming to feature in core social science research methods training. He also convenes the Programming-as-Social-Science (PaSS) network (http://www.jiscmail.ac.uk/PaSS).

PREFACE

In 2002, I enrolled at a college near my home town and, like every student enrolling that year, I was brought into the dean's office for a brief discussion of my A/S- and A-level choices: sociology, history, English literature and music. I was very much looking forward to studying all four of them. The dean's first comment to me was to say that he was concerned by my choice to hone in exclusively on the arts and humanities – looking over my GCSE transcripts, he noted that I'd done fairly well in things like science and IT, and advised me that if I didn't pick up at least one course in science or computing at college, I'd never have the chance to study anything like that again. Not at university, not in a graduate job, not in a career, not ever. Even though this little 5-minute interaction took place half a lifetime ago, I vividly remember being shaken by the prospect of having a whole swathe of options closed down for ever. That kind of thing is a lot for a 16-year-old to have to deal with, especially within the scope of a 5-minute appointment. As I sat there in the dean's office, my brain couldn't handle a quick but comprehensive reconsideration of what I wanted to do with the rest of my life, so I stuck with my choices and walked out of the dean's office having enrolled to study sociology, history, English literature and music. However, trepidation and worry had replaced my earlier excitement.

Since getting those A-levels (and enjoying the courses!) and going on to university to study sociology at various levels I have, rather unexpectedly, ended up doing research across a variety of fields including science and technology studies, the sociology and philosophy of scientific knowledge and research, human–computer interaction, and Computer-Supported Cooperative Work. Some of my more recent work has been in social media analytics – a relatively new area of social science based on exploring collections of user-generated data from places like Twitter or Instagram – and specifically around the development of innovative digital methods which social scientists can use to study those topics. All of this has culminated in my having to teach myself Python, as a tool that is now integral to my research and which helps me get a handle on the digital data I need to work with.

So, on a daily basis, throughout my university studies and my academic career, I have found myself doing things that the college dean told me I couldn't possibly ever do. The reason I'm writing this potted history of myself is not for any kind of self-aggrandisement (though admittedly it's pretty satisfying to stick two fingers up at the college dean who very nearly convinced me not to study the things I was passionate about learning). Infinitely more important than that is that I demonstrate that computer programming is *not* outside of the scope of what you, as a social scientist, can learn, if you find a need to do so. As a student and practitioner of the social sciences, you're already a smart, engaged, critical thinker – if you weren't, you wouldn't be interested in social science! – and this book is about complementing those existing skills with Python programming as a new tool that will help you extend your reach into new topics and new forms of social research. In that sense, the key goals of this book are not just to teach you the mechanics of how to write out Python code, but to show you how you might apply your existing social scientific skills to thinking about the role of programming and software in research and in society generally.

I also want to acknowledge the enormous debt my own learning of Python – in fact, my learning of *all that I know* in the social sciences – owes to the sociologically affiliated field of ethnomethodology. As a discipline which is premised on understanding how social life operates from the perspective of those living it, ethnomethodology has enabled me to dive right into the things that have interested me, including how scientists use computer programming to do their work, how people collaboratively use computer software across various different activities, how to help build software tools that address the needs of Digital Social Science researchers, how to understand the ways in which people interact with and through the internet and social media as part of their daily lives, and more. Moreover, ethnomethodology has encouraged (and in fact *required*) me to engage directly with the things that the people being studied do when they are using computer technologies as part of their activities – to get first-hand experience of how they do these things by learning to do them myself. In short, ethnomethodology is how I learned to do programming. And as a result, this idea of learning and doing Python ethnomethodologically is the core pedagogical device of this book too. In the hopes of aping David Sudnow, the ethnomethodologist whose studies of learning to play jazz piano resulted in the acclaimed Sudnow Method of jazz piano tuition, my ethnomethodologically grounded studies of computer usage and programming feed directly into this attempt to transmit those knowledges and skills to others. It is on these grounds that I wholeheartedly encourage readers to seek out ethnomethodological literature, to attend courses, seminars and conferences on it, to speak to their lecturers about it, and to use it as a background to their own social scientific endeavours.

Phillip Brooker

ACKNOWLEDGEMENTS

My original acknowledgements section overran into about three pages which, though unfortunately too unwieldy, is indicative of how lucky and privileged I am to have had the benefit of support from so many people throughout the process of researching and writing this book. Though it's sadly not possible to reproduce a full list of names here (and though the acknowledgments that follow barely scratch the surface of what is deserved), my sincerest thanks go out to the following:

- The various scholars affiliated with Manchester's ethnomethodology research community, all of whom have contributed immeasurably to the thinking that underpins this book (and indeed all of my work).
- All of the social media analytics/human-computer interaction people I have worked for and with as a postdoc across Brunel, Bath and Newcastle/Northumbria Universities. I would hope that the influence you have had on this book is patently obvious; it is certainly very much appreciated.
- My colleagues in Liverpool's Department of Sociology, Social Policy and Criminology; I couldn't wish for a better or more supportive group of people to work with. Aside from everything else (and there is *lots* for me to be thankful for here!), you've all been so incredibly polite as I bore you to death about coding and bots and Raspberry Pi computers and so on, which is no mean feat.
- The editorial team and various other staff at SAGE who I have been involved with over the last few years - your input, guidance and advice have always been invaluable and very much appreciated.
- Finally, I'd like to directly thank Wes Sharrock (for reasons that will be obvious to anyone who is lucky enough to know Wes), and Michelle, Noah and The Little Pea (for being Michelle, Noah and The Little Pea).

YOUR ONLINE RESOURCES

To further your learning, this book is supported by the following online resources:

- Python code files for in-text exercises
- Additional exercises
- Directory of Python libraries
- A reading guide to help you get the most out of this book.

Visit https://study.sagepub.com/brooker

PART ONE

Part One contents

UNDERSTANDING PROGRAMMING

Part One objectives

- To set out the scope of this book in terms of what you can expect to learn from reading it (and, of course, doing the exercises!).
- To define some key terms and concepts we will be using as we go forward.
- To begin to think about "Programming-as-Social-Science" as a unique approach to understanding the world which integrates (unsurprisingly) Python programming techniques with the work of social science.

Welcome to the book! Part One intends to get everybody on the same page and kick us off by outlining all of the core stuff of computer programming, and why we might be interested in learning how to program as social scientists. We'll be asking and answering questions going right back to "so what *is* computer programming anyway?", as well as figuring out ways of looking at and using programming that are helpful and valuable to us as social scientists. This is going to form the background to the later chapters where we're learning about how to read and write Python computer code – the things we cover here aim to give context to what you're learning later.

So, while Part One doesn't directly deal with the mechanics of how the Python programming language works, it is still really useful in terms of keeping our focus not just on the idea of programming as an instrumental means-to-an-end type of deal, but thinking about programming in such a way that it can be leveraged for social scientific purposes.

Let's get to it!

0

Introduction

Chapter objectives

- To outline what computer programming is, and why a social scientist might be interested in learning how to do it.
- To state the position of this book among other available instructional literature on both computer programming and digital methods.
- To establish a basis for a specifically social scientific approach to programming - "Grilled Cheese Programming" - which is sensitive to our needs and requirements.

Both "social science" and "computer programming" are slippery terms that cover a lot of diverse topics and research practices. This makes it difficult to pin a date on when either can be said to have started. But by any measure, both have been around for a *long* time. Arguably, modern social science emerged out of the Enlightenment period in Europe in the mid-seventeenth century, with figures such as Thomas Hobbes and John Locke producing work on philosophy, morality and politics that went on to inform the more explicitly proto-sociological developments of eighteenth- and nineteenth-century thinkers like Adam Smith, Henri de Saint-Simon and Auguste Comte. Perhaps surprisingly, given how we might think of computers being a relatively recent technological development, it's generally agreed that the computer program can be dated as far back as 1843, with Ada Lovelace's creation of the first algorithm which formalised a set of instructions for computing a sequence of "Bernoulli numbers" to be carried out via Charles Babbage's (then designed but unbuilt) "Analytical Engine".

But despite the fact that both social science and computer programming are long-standing enterprises, it's only far more recently that academics have begun to explore how the two might be combined. Social science - especially those areas of it that focus on topics where collaboration is inevitable, such as human–computer interaction and Computer-Supported Cooperative Work - has already produced more than a few studies of the work of programming (see the further reading section below). In these studies, the focus has been on the social aspects of how programmers manage their working together: how the work of programming gets done by programmers. However, doing a study *of* computer programming is not quite the same as *using* computer programming *to do* a social scientific study - why is it that we're only now starting to think about what computer programming might offer as a tool and skill for social scientists?

Further reading

Social Studies of Programming

Graham Button and Wes Sharrock's mid-1990s works in the field of Computer-Supported Cooperative Work are great examples of the kinds of interest and approach a social science researcher might bring to studying programming as an activity:

Button, G. and Sharrock, W. (1994) Occasioned practices in the work of software engineers. In M. Jirotka and J. Goguen (eds), *Requirements Engineering: Social and Technical Issues*. London: Academic Press, pp. 217-240.

Button, G. and Sharrock, W. (1995) The mundane work of writing and reading computer programs. In P. Ten Have and G. Psathas (eds), *Situated Order: Studies in the Social Organisation of Talk and Embodied Activities* (Studies in Ethnomethodology and Conversation Analysis No. 3). Washington, DC: University Press of America, pp. 231-258.

The shift is largely motivated by the fact that digital data and the internet as a site of everyday social interaction have significantly changed the playing field of the social sciences. Within this emerging field of "Digital Social Science", both the topics and methods associated with social science research have become increasingly computer-oriented. As people interested in studying social life, we can't ignore that a lot of what people get up to in everyday society is organised around and through the use of things like computers, the internet, search engines, entertainment-streaming services, social media, smartphone apps, and so on. This is hugely important across the whole of social science; as Housley et al. note, focusing on the digital world offers social science the potential not only to extend its reach into new forms of sociality, but also to deepen our understanding of existing forms: "these technologies and their allied data have the potential to 'digitally-remaster' classic questions about social organization, social change and the derivation of identity from collective life" (2014: 4). Moreover, if we want to find out about any of these things as social scientists, we will inevitably have to draw on a variety of digital tools and methods to do so. Even ethnography, a method more typically associated with the physical presence of a researcher within a participant's setting, is not exempt from these effects; as Hallett and Barber (2014: 308) note, ethnographic researchers "need to reconceptualize what counts as a field site ... studying a group of people in their 'natural habitat' now [often] includes their 'online habitat'". So, engaging with computational and digital tools and data has already become integral to what social scientists do. This book seeks to extend that thinking and demonstrate (among other things) that learning how to program can significantly enhance how social scientists can think about their studies, and especially those premised on the collection and analysis of digital data.

Definitions

Digital Social Science/Computational Social Science

To say there is a single field called "Digital Social Science" is a bit misleading – in reality, this term is so broad as to cover lots of different, constantly shifting forms of philosophical orientations, disciplinary commitments, research approaches, topics and methods. So I'll use the term "Digital Social Science" in an intentionally very loose way which doesn't make any kind of futile attempt to unify all of these things, but which still serves as a shorthand for any kind of research that somehow involves using digital tools and methods (whatever those may be) to explore digital topics (whatever those may be!).

However, just because you might see the term used elsewhere, it is worth noting that there does already exist a specific area of inquiry called "Computational Social Science" which seeks to

(Continued)

take a scientifically systematic approach to the application of tools like programming to social science problems and questions (cf. González-Bailón, 2013; Lazer et al., 2009; Nelson, 2017). However, the approach I'm presenting here (programming as social science) slightly diverges from the scientifically systematic orientation of Computational Social Science for reasons explained in Chapter 2, so for practical purposes and ease of reference, this body of work will fall under the term "Digital Social Science" throughout.

However, the point of this book is not (just) to provide social scientists with an introduction to the mechanics of the Python programming language – such introductions are already available across lots of books and websites (though few are tailored to the specific needs of social scientists as this book is). Nor is it to suggest that social scientists need to adopt programming as a way of "formalising", "mathematising" and/or "automating" their work, as if such things were even possible – see Section 1.2 for fuller details of the issues surrounding these ideas. Indeed, arguments against scientism (i.e. the idea that our work should operate more like the natural sciences of physics and chemistry) and the bureaucratisation of social science (i.e. the transformation of our work into a purely technical non-interpretive "number-crunching" exercise) have been a defining characteristic of influential thinking about the role and purpose of social science, from Wittgenstein (2009 [1953]) and C. Wright Mills (2000 [1959]) to Button et al. (1995) and Savage and Burrows (2007). The strength of the social sciences has always been in their resistance to scientism and bureaucratisation, and in this sense, this book *emphatically does not* approach programming as a way of "upskilling" social science or reifying computer science/scientists as a gold standard to strive towards. We are already very skilled at what we do, and no amount of computing power or speed could possibly compete with our human capacity for critical thinking, for methodological reflexivity, for generating critiques and counter-narratives, for motivating social change and activism, and so on.

Rather, the point of this book is to show how the work of programming can fit into and enhance the skillsets and knowledges we already have, and in doing so bring about a uniquely social scientific approach to programming as a research method (we'll go on to call this "Programming-as-Social-Science", or PaSS for short) that we can leverage to do the work *we* want to do, in ways that *we* want to do it. The remainder of this book can be read as an elucidation of this central theme.

0.1 Who Is This Book for? Why *This* Book?

There are short answers to the above questions. Who is this book for? It's probably no surprise that the intended audience of a book called *Programming with Python for Social Scientists* is social scientists who want to learn to program. In Python. And why *this* book? That can be boiled down to the following statements:

1   Social science digital methods resources don't typically cover programming. This makes it difficult to think about the practical aspects of doing Digital Social Science work, and it limits

our capacity to be reflexive about our methods and methodologies when we use software tools developed by others.

2   Python programming resources, on the other hand, don't speak to the requirements of social science, and this makes it difficult to see how the general-purpose/abstract knowledge and skills transmitted through those resources can fit into the work we are trying to do.

3   The value of this book is that it handles both social science and computer programming simultaneously – it demonstrates Python as a social science research toolkit and walks through some examples of those tools in use in social-science-relevant tasks, but also shows you how to think about programming as a research method more widely.

It is, however, worth exploring a slightly longer answer to each of those questions, one that goes into who those people *are* who are social scientists in need of programming skills, and what they will get from this book that they can't get anywhere else. The following sections will go into more detail about the kinds of work and thinking that programming can facilitate (and, by the same token, what kind of person would be interested in learning how to do those things). But for now, suffice to say that this book is for those people – students and researchers in the social sciences – looking to build skills with digital data and methods, in relation to both quantitative and qualitative research. The chapter headings of Part Three indicate the kinds of thing that "building skills with digital data and methods" constitutes; for instance, there are chapters on working with text files (i.e. data stored in .txt format), chapters on drawing data through social media platforms via Application Programming Interfaces (APIs), chapters on web scraping, chapters on visualising data, and so on. Of course, these are not the *only* things you can do with Python as a social scientist; rather, these tasks are explored in this book as a way of demonstrating a small number of Python applications relevant to (Digital) Social Science that as a collection loosely follow a crude "grab data, work with data, look at data" narrative. However, I want to be really clear that the overarching aim of this book is not to delimit the scope of Python by suggesting its potential can be exhausted across one volume; Python is an open-ended and evolving toolkit, which makes the possibilities for its application and usage endless. In outlining the very basics of just a few potential applications, the aim is to engender a "programming mindset" (see Chapter 15) in readers, which can then be applied to their own programming activities whatever they may be. The materials provided in this book will form the foundations for these activities, but the most interesting stuff will happen when you take your "programming mindset" forward into your *own* projects.

The design of the book

The materials covered in this book are designed for a range of skills, abilities and career stages from advanced (year 3-ish) undergraduates looking to learn techniques for research-oriented assessments, right through to professional researchers seeking to develop methodologies and methods that will help them dig into Digital Social Science more deeply. The book as a whole is designed and structured in a modular way such that although it unfolds in a linear fashion (with chapters building from introductory content on programming in general, to more specific outlines of Python techniques, to applications of those techniques in research-relevant contexts), each chapter also provides useful reference material to which readers may wish to return at various points in their programming activities. Readers with absolutely no familiarity with programming will be able to work from basic concepts (e.g. Chapters 1–4, which establish the foundational ideas of what programming can offer social science and provide reference material on key Python concepts) and thereby build towards the more advanced skills and techniques outlined in later chapters. Readers who may already have more grounding in programming (or who have previously been through this book!) can dip into individual chapters to address specific skills and techniques they may wish to develop (e.g. Chapters 5–12, which are about substantive topics with a direct Digital Social Science research relevance), using earlier chapters as reference material to refresh their memories where required.

So that's who this book has been designed for – Digital Social Science practitioners (from undergrad to professional) whose work might be enhanced by a better understanding of programming in terms of not only how to write and work with Python, but also how to think about programming and software as part of the research process and part of society generally. But a question remains: why *this* book in particular?

Why not digital-methods-for-social-science literature?

As noted above, social scientists are now inevitably having to engage with computational issues as part of their day-to-day work, whether that's as a topic of study (i.e. people interacting and doing social life online) or as a method and means of working with digital resources relevant to social science concerns (e.g. using software to extract and visualise such things as social media data corpora, publicly available government datasets, or the WikiLeaks archive). This has resulted in an emerging body of work on "digital methods", designed to help social science students and researchers think about digital data and the digital world by exploring the conceptual, methodological, philosophical and ethical aspects of digital data from a specifically social science perspective. These books and journal articles (a selection of which feature in the further reading section below) give a great introduction to various methodological ideas around the use of digital data, such as its politicisation, its commercialisation, how such methods might sit alongside theoretical ideas already in play in the social sciences, how to combine "offline" and "online" methods – for example, through new syntheses such as Kozinets's (2010) "netnography" – and so on. However, these materials only offer a one-way understanding of digital technologies: they demonstrate how to draw on things that are already available (like Google search results, or Twitter hashtag conversations, or comments on a Facebook page, or blog posts on a particular topic of interest) to make social scientific sense of them.

═══ Further reading ═══

Digital Methods

In reality, nobody really agrees on a set of defined methodological principles for undertaking work with digital data (not that there are many that agree on this in the "traditional" social sciences either!). However, the following resources are good starting-points for thinking about some key methodological issues within the context of digital data:

Brügger, N. and Finneman, N.O. (2013) The web and digital humanities: Theoretical and methodological concerns. *Journal of Broadcasting and Electronic Media*, 57(1), 66–80.

Kozinets, R.V. (2010) *Netnography: Doing Ethnographic Research Online*. Los Angeles: Sage.

Matthews, N. and Sunderland, N. (2013) Digital life-story narratives as data for policy makers and practitioners: Thinking through methodologies for large-scale multi-media qualitative datasets. *Journal of Broadcasting and Electronic Media*, 57(1), 97–114.

Rogers, R. (2013) *Digital Methods*. Cambridge, MA: MIT Press.

Tufekci, Z. (2014) Big questions for social media Big Data: Representativeness, validity and other methodological pitfalls. In *Proceedings of the Eighth International AAAI Conference on Weblogs and Social Media*, Ann Arbor, Michigan, USA, 1–4 June 2014. Palo Alto, CA: AAAI Press, pp. 505–514.

Of course, this approach is very interesting in its own right and has yielded some really insightful studies. However, it is not especially common for these methodological studies to go into much detail on the practical aspects of how to gather and work with these kinds of digital data – for instance, it's one thing to talk about the principle of using Instagram pictures as data, but how are you supposed to actually get hold of a dataset of images? And how are you supposed to organise and filter such a potentially enormous dataset to make sure you're looking at the bits of data that are actually relevant to your project? And what exactly are you supposed to do with those data (other than just vaguely poke your way around some files and think about them) to get yourself to a point where some interesting insights have resulted? This is the kind of thing that can be done quite straightforwardly if you have computer programming skills. But digital methods resources don't typically cover the practicalities of *doing* research with digital data, and this can make it very difficult to see how we can even begin to engage with such research as social scientists. Moreover, being able to answer these questions is often just as important as the analyses that result from our research, in terms of our need to reflect on and explain our methods and our research process (as we will explore in more detail in Section 1.2). So overall, it would be helpful to be shown how to do this kind of work on a practical level, and resources that can help you learn computer programming would give you the tools you need to be able to do that. However, that's not the kind of thing you can find out from existing social science resources on digital methods.

Why not existing computer-programming-for-beginners literature?

There *are* textbooks and other resources for teaching computer programming to complete beginners, and specifically there are lots that aim to give learners a background in the core concepts of Python and in useful applications of it. Some resources teach Python in an abstract manner, focusing on teaching the mechanics of the language without reference to real-world problems. These types of resources are great for just learning the basics of Python, though it's often perhaps difficult to see how you might apply that learning to the things you want to be able to do with computer programming (as in, you might then ask the question, "Great, so I know what all these bits and pieces of Python grammar and syntax do – now what?"). Which is exactly why some other resources are more organised around teaching Python in an applied manner, focusing on building programs for specific jobs (e.g. organising large batches of files, extracting text from PDF files, or editing images). But again, it might be difficult to see how you apply these particular skills to your social science research projects (as in, you might then ask the question, "Great, so I know how to organise large batches of files, but how does that help me with my discourse analysis of Instagram pictures of the Scottish Referendum, beyond the technical exercise of organising my large batch of Instagram pictures?"). Both of these types of resources are great for teaching the raw skill of using Python in a general-purpose way for a wide audience. However, what these resources do not do is recognise the requirements that social scientists have of their research tools[1] – chiefly, that it is not enough to simply be able to use a skill (like programming) in abstract or even to do specified tasks which we might find useful. We need also to be able to think critically about the impact that that skill has on the problems we are trying to work on, and to think about how that skill intersects with the philosophical, conceptual, theoretical and methodological positions our work might embody – in short, how computer programming and code itself are social practices embedded in the social world. It is, then, not much help to us to be taught how to program in the ways that these two types of resources attempt (i.e. via drills that are disconnected from real-world problems, or via real-world but non-social-science problems). We need instead to learn programming in ways which can also help us ask and answer deeper questions around the status of the topics we are applying programming to and the research processes we undertake to do that. Moreover, we need to learn programming in a way which allows us to think about its potential role and status as a research tool *beyond* the examples of its application.

Hence, while this book has elements of both of the types of resource outlined above – there is reference material on the grammar and syntax of Python, as well as more detailed chapters on how to apply those concepts to specific (social-science-relevant) tasks – all of the material covered is underpinned by a overriding concern with *using your programming mindset as a social scientist*. This is what will help you *use* Python programming beyond the scope of what is featured in this book; as a research method – not just a raw skill – about which you are able to think critically reflexively and social-scientifically.

0●2 Why Python? Why Python 3?

So now we've settled it: if you're a social science researcher looking to engage with digital data or other such computational issues, you're in the right place. But there are lots of programming languages out there, so why should we focus specifically on Python? And why, even more specifically, on Python version 3?

To answer these questions, we should take a little step back and think about what a programming language actually is. In essence, a programming language is a collection of tools which allow a human user to manipulate the physical hardware of a computer. It's the same sort of principle as when you are using a calculator to do a sum – you type in instructions for the sum you want calculating, those instructions tell the calculator how to translate that

---

[1] I mean, they don't *attempt* to do this, so it feels a bit unfair to call them out on it. But nonetheless, the point still stands in terms of why *you're* reading *this* book right now.

into mechanical operations, the calculator performs those mechanical operations (crudely, it switches various transistors on and off), and it then translates the results of those operations back into a human-friendly format (i.e. numbers) to feed back to you the answer to your sum. However, we should also recognise that the "programming language" we use to do sums on a calculator is very strictly defined. The calculator only accepts certain types of input – it accepts numbers, connected by mathematical operators, and an equals sign to signify that your instructions have ended. Moreover, the results it produces are just as strictly defined. You won't ever get anything other than a numerical result out of a calculator, no matter what instructions you put in.[2] This is where programming languages are far more powerful than just being calculators – you have *far* greater expressive control over the format of your input into a programming language, and the formatting of the results is also pretty much limitless – you can use a programming language to do anything from simple calculations to enabling sophisticated analyses of digital data, running a Twitter bot, controlling the movements of a physical robot, or having your Internet-of-Things fridge WhatsApp you when you're out of milk.[3]

However, even though what a programming language does can be characterised as "providing an interface between a human user and computer hardware", not all programming languages are the same. Some programming languages are geared more towards efficiency in number-crunching (e.g. Matlab), some are more oriented to web and web-application design (e.g. JavaScript), some facilitate building software tools with an emphasis on Graphical User Interfaces (GUIs) (e.g. Visual Basic), and some even bypass the idea of programming language as a mediator between human instructions and machine operations altogether (e.g. Assembly Language Programming, which goes right back to interacting with binary machine code that controls your computer's central processing unit).[4] The difference between all of these is that the way each language has been developed means they are better suited to doing certain types of job than others, even if in principle it would be possible to do exactly the same tasks across them all.

What can Python do?

But what kind of job is Python geared towards doing? Python is a "general-purpose" programming language, which is to say, it is capable of doing pretty much anything you need it to do, with relative ease (and the kind of "things" you might need to do as a social scientist are explored in more detail in Chapters 5–12). This is in no small part due to Python being well supported by an extensive array of add-on packages (or "libraries" or "modules"), which can facilitate users in doing lots of different tasks by adding to the repertoire of the language. We will use some of these "modules" in later sections of the book, so don't worry too much about what this means for now. Suffice to say that we can think of the large range of Python modules available as being like when we learn a new word that helps us more succinctly and

---

[2]No, turning the calculator upside down and using the numbers to write rude words doesn't count.

[3]#latestagecapitalism

[4]Learning Assembly Language Programming is one of the most masochistic uses of time imaginable. Don't learn Assembly Language Programming.

more easily express ourselves – using techniques from Python modules is like the difference between saying "you know that snow that's also like rain, but also like ice and it comes down quick and hurts when it falls on you?" to simply saying "hailstones". So, while Python might not be the most efficient at doing certain jobs when compared with other programming languages (as in, other programming languages may be more streamlined for the kinds of task they are optimised for), if we're willing to make use of additional modules, it can be a "one-stop shop" for users – an enormous number of different, varied, social-science-relevant tasks can be done within Python as a single programming language, which saves on the effort of having to learn any others!

Another key motivation for choosing Python is that it's among the easiest to learn of programming languages, yet one which is still immensely powerful (and enormously popular among professional programmers). This is largely due to Python's emphasis on the readability of code – literally, the way it appears on screen in such a way that users can more intuitively make sense of the code they are seeing. Readability will be emphasised as a key concern in the writing of code throughout the book, and we will explore some good techniques for ensuring readability in your code (and good reasons for doing so) in due course. In particular, these issues will come up throughout the whole of Chapter 3, when we're examining the basic grammar and syntax of Python. But for now, it will suffice to say that as it appears on your screen, Python code is much easier to read than code in many other languages, and this is important because being easy to read makes it more straightforward to follow, learn and understand.

And a final little bonus is that Python is an "interpreted" language, which is to say that unlike other popular programming languages, you don't have to compile the code before you run it. We really don't need to even go into what compiling is here, but it's worth saying that it's another step in getting a program to run which takes time to learn to do, and can be a source of further confusion in terms of testing and debugging a program. So, the fact that we don't have to worry about any of that with Python is a good thing, and it means we can concentrate more pointedly on just writing the code.

What can Python 3 do?

And now, one last question remains: why Python version 3 in particular? It's not quite as straightforward as "it's the newest version", though that is a key deciding factor. There are two versions of Python that are currently still widely used: Python 2 and Python 3. Within these, there are different release numbers which signify new releases as various changes have been made, bugs have been squashed, new features have been added, and so on; as of the time of writing, the latest version of Python 2 is 2.7.13 and the latest version of Python 3 is 3.6.2. However, the fact that 3 is a higher number than 2 does not mean that Python 2 is now obsolete – far from it, in fact! Python 2 is still very widely used by lots of programmers, and will continue to be used for a long time (especially so because people will inevitably want to maintain and tweak their existing Python 2 code, but they may not be interested in rewriting all of that code in Python 3 – "if it's not broke, don't fix it" is always a good rule). However, since Python 3 has been released, more and more Python users have made the switch to writing their code in the newer version, to the extent that the Python Software Foundation (which oversees the ongoing development of the language) will no longer provide any updates on

Python 2. This has more explicitly positioned Python 3 as "the present and future of the language", according to the Python Software Foundation's official statement on the subject (Python Software Foundation, 2017). In this sense, although both versions of the core Python language are very stable (in that we could easily work with either), we can reasonably expect that module and package developers will concentrate their efforts more closely on providing support for Python 3 (and, therefore, that's where we should concentrate our efforts too).

One final point worth making is that learning Python 3 does not preclude you from knowing Python 2. In fact, for the most part, there are very few significant changes to the core language of either version. This is to say that after you've worked through this book and learned Python 3, should you come across a script written in Python 2, you will easily be able to understand what's going on. Rather than being a different language, think of it as being a (slightly) different dialect or accent – you might not understand the odd word or phrasing, but you'll be well equipped to deal with resolving any such issues as they arise. And, extending this idea of "transferable skills" further, it has already been stated that one of the key aims of this book is to engender a *programming mindset* in readers. This means that the skills you learn to apply through Python 3 are not solely or completely limited to working within that language. What you will learn from our working with Python 3 is a set of more general skills and knowledge around programming generally – things like how to structure the flow of a program with logical statements, how to document code effectively, how to structure and work with data, and more. In short, along the way you will pick up knowledge of how computer programming works in a general sense, and this can then be applied (if you wish to do so) to other languages that might also help with your work, with Python 3 as your first stepping-stone along the way.

So, *that's* why Python, and Python 3 in particular.

0●3 "Grilled Cheese Programming": A Methodology, A Manifesto

One of the core motivations for this book has been the lack of Python learning material that explicitly engages with the concerns and requirements of social scientists. This is not a trivial complaint (won't somebody *please* think of the social scientists?!) – it's perfectly possible for us to learn how to program via these existing bodies of work, but the concerns we have in social science research are not necessarily the concerns that other programmers from other domains share. It is therefore worth thinking about the kind of programming we eventually want to be able to do (and how to direct the learning accordingly). Of course, this being the opening chapter of the book, I'll have to remain (intentionally) vague about the details of the tasks we might want to do. But it is certainly worth setting out our stall early in terms of establishing a methodology and/or a manifesto which can guide our thinking as we progress. And this book is going to do exactly that with the concept of "Grilled Cheese Programming".[5]

---

[5] The core concept was born out of a comment I came across on a Reddit post, left by user Network2501 – credit where it's due!

Social science requirements for programming

One big difference is that as social scientists – especially as we're in the process of learning how to code – we are not necessarily going to be concerned so much with efficiency and speed in our code, like those who use programming in the physical sciences or in mathematics might be. Despite how often the term "Big Data'" gets bandied about in the Digital Social Sciences, more often than not the data we have are of a manageable size and the things we want to do with those data don't require enormously complex and processor-heavy calculations. Researchers in other fields have to pay close attention to speed as a factor in their code – if some data processing task takes days to run, it becomes more important to concentrate on how to trim down any little time leakages which might help the code run more quickly. For us, although the size and complexity of data and tasks we might be dealing with are variable, the insights we want our code to facilitate just don't require that level of focus on efficiency. This is not to say we should be completely ignorant of how to write efficient code, but just that for the most part, it is not going to be a dealbreaker in our efforts to learn and apply programming skills to our work.

Equally, we are not necessarily going to be concerned about deriving the most elegant, concise or "light-weight" solutions to our coding problems (i.e. solutions which come in the absolute fewest lines of code possible). This is something that might drive researchers in other areas – in computer science, for instance, where beautiful code could itself be the desired endpoint of a research process. For us, in the first instance as learners and later as social scientists who program (i.e. Programming-as-Social-Science (PaSS) practitioners), we are probably best off concentrating on just getting our code to work. But related to this, we also want to focus on making our code as transparently readable as possible – this might mean lots of extra lines of code (i.e. solutions which are not so "light-weight") and fewer things going on within each line (i.e. solutions which are not so elegant or concise). Having our code as transparently readable as possible is important, because we have to be able to clearly show our method and the assumptions that we have built into the code – that's what social scientists require of their methods. Again, this is not to say that we should completely ignore things like "elegance", as guidelines for writing good code. However, we will be far more interested in putting the more "critical" aspects of programming front and centre in our practice, even if that comes at the expense of what usually counts as "good coding practice".

There will no doubt be plenty of other areas where the learning styles and practices of programming-as-a-social-scientist will diverge from those associated with programming-like-anybody-else. We will collectively figure out more about this as the field emerges. And of course, none of this is to say that we have a *completely* different approach to coding than programmers in other domains – for instance, other programmers are also concerned with the transparency and readability of their code. However, the point remains that of all the things that could drive how different types of programmer program, social scientists will have their own special weighting which gives what we do a unique and distinct set of requirements.

What is important to remember, especially as the field is emerging and we are all still learning, is that we should not necessarily be upholding the existing coding practices of other disciplines as gold standards to work towards. We will learn more and do better if we keep a focus on figuring out these issues for ourselves, as we're doing the work and in relation to our own ideas about what we want to use programming to do. More often than not, this will mean just diving into whatever problems we want to work on, and not worrying so much about producing the quickest, most efficient, most concise, most elegant, most "light-weight" (or most anything else) code. The code we will produce will almost definitely be "imperfect" according to the standards set by other coding communities. Remember this should you ever visit any of the online communities where people ask and answer coding problems, such as http://www.stackoverflow.com or various subreddits like r/LearnPython and r/LearnProgramming; these forums can be lifesavers, but just don't take it seriously when somebody answers along the lines of "I'm ignoring the question you asked and instead I'm going to condescendingly suggest an 'improvement' that will shave off a whopping 0.03 seconds of processing time". Rather, you should come at programming in Python more on the basis that if a piece of code solves a problem, that's really all we need it to do. And that's really the nuts and bolts of what I mean by taking "Grilled Cheese Programming" as the methodology and manifesto of this book: not everybody needs to be a Michelin-starred chef, but it's useful if you can cook yourself a meal.

0●4   Aims, Scope, Outcomes and Overview of the Book

Aims and objectives

There are two overall aims of this book, the first specific and the second more general:

- To explore the possibilities of programming as a social science research skill/method applicable across different research-oriented tasks (both quantitative and qualitative), by facilitating the uptake of Python programming by students and researchers.
- To position the idea of a "programming mindset" as a valuable way to think about contemporary (i.e. digital) data, phenomena and topics of interest to the social sciences.

The book is designed to achieve these aims by virtue of a pedagogical approach specifically tailored to the requirements and exigencies of social science research work – this is to say that the learning materials presented here are developed with as tight a focus on the work of social science (and how programming might intersect with it) as possible. Moreover, the book draws heavily on Python's reputation as among the most intuitive and readable of programming languages – these qualities (among others) make it an ideal platform for thinking about how and why to incorporate programming skills into our methodological repertoire.

Scope

Inasmuch as programming skills are not yet widely adopted among social science students or researchers, the scope of this book is intentionally wide: this book aims to provide a single resource where conceptual, reference and pedagogical/tutorial materials around Programming-as-Social-Science can be located and drawn upon. The pedagogical materials will cover various tasks that social science researchers, especially those interested in digital data, will find useful (see Chapters 5–12). However, the book will not include tutorials on a range of options within the same theme – for instance, Chapter 11 on using social media APIs will outline how to use Python to extract a specific type of data via Twitter's APIs; it will not explore how to extract different slices of Twitter data, nor will it explore how to extract data from other social media platforms (e.g. Facebook, Tumblr) or other APIs. Of course, such tasks would almost certainly have value for social science research work, but outlining a comprehensive set of steps to follow for any and all such potentially interesting projects is an impossibility. Rather, what this book sets out to do is impart a more general "programming mindset" to readers, whereby you can work through the pedagogical exercises to get a flavour of the practical work of programming, and then go on to apply those lessons to your own work and interests. In this way, the chaptering covering how to work with Python to access a Twitter API is not so much about teaching you about how to access a Twitter API (although that will happen along the way) – it is more about giving you the requisite skills and confidence with Python programming to then go on to explore other types of digital data from other platforms for yourself.

Learning outcomes

With this in mind, the learning outcomes of the book are as follows. By the end of this book, you should:

- Be able to "open the black box" of software development for the benefit of quantitative and qualitative research involving the use or study of computational tools.
- Have a base knowledge of the core Python grammar and syntax that can then be applied as a multi-purpose research tool.
- Have worked through a series of tutorials of general concern to social science research work (e.g. extracting digital data, managing data in text files, building visualisations from that data).
- Be able to take forward the skills and knowledge learned into projects of your own, and use your newly acquired "programming mindset" to advance your studies and/or the social sciences.

This last learning outcome should be the one to keep in mind as you work your way through the book – your "programming mindset" will have an application far beyond the scope of what can be covered in one book.

Overview

On this basis, the remainder of the book will proceed as follows. The remainder of Part One, "Understanding Programming" (Chapters 0–2) will begin with Chapter 1 ("What *Is* Programming? And What Could it Mean for Social Science Research?") which will ground readers in the key concepts and ideas behind programming as a social science research tool, encouraging you to think about the myriad ways in which the research process and computer software tools have become enmeshed, and the implications of this for social research. Chapter 2 ("Programming-as-Social-Science (Critical Coding)") will explore the idea that software and algorithms are not neutral or politically objective, as those not versed in their creation might perhaps expect. Nor do any and all algorithms necessarily comply with standard ethical practice for social research. Hence, this chapter is designed to help you unravel the ways in which politics and ethics become built into code, algorithms, software, visualisations, and so on.

Part Two, "Basic Python Grammar, Syntax and Concepts" (Chapters 3–8), will introduce readers to Python as a programming language, outlining what Python is and further exploring why it is apposite as a tool for first-time programmers (based on its design philosophy, which emphasises the readability and intuitive structure of code). The chapters in Part Two will cover a range of core concepts, and emphasise the role of Python as a "scripting language" for "doing tasks" (as opposed to other programming languages which might be seen as more purely for "number-crunching" or web development and so on).

Part Three, "Working with Python" (Chapters 9–14), will take this core Python programming knowledge further by exploring various applications of these skills to social-science-relevant tasks. Chapter 9 ("Designing Research That Features Programming") will outline a number of issues that researchers will need to consider before even writing their first line of code for a project. Research design will be foregrounded as an issue of critical importance for research projects involving programming, yet also one that is wholly dependent on the exigencies of the project at hand. Hence, this chapter will work towards providing general advice and guidance on how to think about research design in terms of integrating programming appropriately across the course of a research project. The tutorials that comprise the rest of Part Three (Chapters 10–14) represent discrete tasks which rely on separate sets of techniques, though the tutorials are structured in a such a way as to make them a linear progression in terms of both difficulty level (e.g. from simple to advanced techniques) and how a research project might naturally progress (e.g. from data collection to data visualisation). Each chapter will feature an initial outline of common techniques relevant to the concept of the topic, plus a range of tutorials to work through which require you to build scripts relying on those techniques. The chapters will be presented in such a way as to recognise that the techniques shown are not exhaustive – given the unforeseeable range of applications to which these techniques might be applied, such a project would be impossible. Rather, these tutorial problems are for the purpose of imparting skills and knowledges pertaining to the *concepts* of the topics they represent (text editing, using APIs, web scraping, etc.), which may then be applied to the specific projects and purposes readers may have.

Having worked through the tutorial problems set in Part Three, Part Four, "Programming-as-Social-Science", will reflect on the learning undertaken thus far by reviewing how the skills and knowledges covered in the book can tangibly contribute to social science research work (i.e. how elements from each of the tutorial chapters might be used together as part of a wider research project). Chapter 15 ("Conclusion: Using Your Programming-as-Social-Science Mindset") will provide some final points on preparing your code to be shared and disseminated with others, as well as reflect on the aims and objectives of the book as a whole. Rather than provide a step-by-step guide to programming which may be copied and pasted directly into a research project, this book has aimed to impart a "programming mindset" to readers which can be drawn upon to handle digital data in ways which can be adapted to the idiosyncrasies of readers' own research interests and projects.

Chapter summary

- This chapter aimed to introduce readers to the idea of computer programming, and to explain how this book intends to help you learn how to program in Python.
- The social sciences are now having to engage with computational techniques and methods more than ever, which makes computer programming (specifically in Python) a valuable skill for us to learn.
- Though there are lots of Python learning resources already available, none are tailored to the needs of social scientists specifically, and this is a problem.
- This book is designed to teach you how to program in Python, as well as how to think about programming from the social science perspective.
- The book is driven by an overarching methodology/manifesto of "Grilled Cheese Programming": not everybody needs to be a Michelin-starred chef, but it's useful if you can cook yourself a meal. In the same way, we don't need to program according to standards set by other disciplines, but it will be useful if we can learn to do things with Python for ourselves.

1

What Is Programming? And What Could it Mean for Social Science Research?

─────────── **Chapter objectives** ───────────

- To introduce some key concepts and terms around computer programming.
- To explore how computer programming fits into and sits alongside social science research methods as part of a "socio-technical assemblage".
- To highlight the capacity for programming to contribute to and support contemporary forms of social scientific research (where interdisciplinarity is increasingly a requirement).
- To introduce the concept of "workflows" (and two types thereof: "script workflows" and "developmental workflows") as ways to help us think about programming as social scientific work.

1 ● 1   Defining Our Terms

One of the first hurdles that new learners of programming have to overcome is that it immediately brings you into contact with a set of terms that are clearly meant to have some kind of meaning that you are not (yet) equipped to deal with. However, this shouldn't be as off-putting as it might sound – *of course* you don't know what some of these terms will mean, just as undergraduate sociology students (as I once was myself) might have struggled to understand what "technical terms" like "base/superstructure" or "historical materialism" or "dialectical method" mean in their very first Sociology 101 lectures. So, these "problems" are not really problems at all – you just haven't learned these terms yet, and figuring out what they mean is part of the learning process.

To this end, what follows is a short list of definitions of some key generic programming terms, as they will be used throughout the book. There may be some disagreement between my definitions and those you may find in other resources, but that in itself should show you that for each of these "technical terms" there may not even be one single clear interpretation. Just as terms like "culture" or "public" in the social sciences evolve and change and have multiple meanings which are not necessarily consistent with one another, so do the terms that programmers use. So don't worry too much about trying to find the one clear definition for any of these things – there probably isn't one, which means the best way to learn how to talk about programming is to practise programming.

Key terms

The small selection of terms I want to start with are not presented alphabetically, but in a linear form designed to take you from knowing very little, perhaps nothing, of programming in Python, to having an appreciation of the interrelation of some of the core concepts that programmers deal with in their day-to-day work:

Programming language. A programming language is, as we have noted in Section 0.2, a tool with which users can instruct a computer to manipulate its hardware in various ways. This can be used for a pretty much infinite array of purposes – though it's perhaps easier to think about how a robot can be programmed (with a programming language) to move its limbs physically, the same principles also apply to things we might normally think of as "not hardware". For instance, when you use a programming language to perform even a simple calculation (e.g. 2 + 2), what you are doing is giving your computer an instruction to manipulate various transistors and switches within its physical hardware to do that calculation and produce an answer. Because of the very general nature of programming languages (i.e. as toolkits for doing computing), they can be applied in lots of different ways across lots of different disciplinary interests: to run calculations, to model phenomena, to collect and organise data, to automate tedious and/or repetitive jobs, and so on. We can think of programming languages as multi-purpose tools for doing a limitless array of computing tasks – this can be really helpful for social scientists dealing with digital data, as we will see.

Programming. Programming is what you do when you're using a programming language. So we'll be doing plenty of this shortly!

Python. Python is the name of the language we are focusing on in this book. Python was first released in 1991 by Guido van Rossum, and its name is a homage to the British comedy series *Monty Python's Flying Circus* (of which van Rossum was a fan). The core idea behind Python, as van Rossum envisaged it, was to develop a language that was intuitive and easy to learn but still as powerful as other languages; was open source, so that any user could contribute to the ongoing development of the language; used code that read pretty much like standard English (so that users would have not much more trouble reading a page of code than they would a page of a book); and was suitable across a wide range of everyday tasks because the code could be written quickly and straightforwardly. Van Rossum was, by any measure, successful in achieving these aims – though there are lots of programming languages, Python still has a reputation as being among the easiest and most intuitive of languages to learn and use, yet is one that is still used in lots of professional contexts. This is one of the reasons why we focus on it specifically here (return to the Introduction for a fuller discussion of lots of other reasons why Python is great for us).

Code/coding. The term "coding" is used in much the same way as the term "programming", though there are slightly different subtleties of meaning worth knowing, especially around the noun versions of each word (i.e. "code" and "program"). Code is, essentially, the written-down instructions that result when you are doing programming. When you are writing a program, you are doing coding. If you are checking for errors in a program, you might say there is one in line 35 of the code. Essentially, a program is more of a "big"/finished product, whereas talking about code has a connotation of being more specific and bringing a line-by-line focus to the things you are writing.

Script. A script is, effectively, a collection of code – in that sense, the words "script" and "program" can often be used interchangeably. Scripts are the names of the files we work with as programmers. We might call a .txt file a "text file" or a .mp3 file "an mp3"; in Python, these files typically will have the extension .py and we call them scripts (so, MyPythonScript. py would be a Python script). Scripts can be written in any basic text editor (just be sure to change the file extension from .txt to .py), or in a piece of software called IDLE that may come with your installation of Python, or in any other Integrated Development Environment (IDE; see definition below). Across all these platforms, scripts are a way of collecting together lots of different bits of code (and saving them as a program) which we can run whenever we like. Scripts are not the only way to do programming (see **shell** below), but they are particularly useful when you want to save your progress to add to it later, or when you want to send a copy of your work to somebody else, or if you want to organise a collection of your programs in a folder on your computer, or any of the other types of task you might want to do with files. Some programmers also use the term "scripting" to describe the writing of scripts as a distinct programming practice that is different from other practices like building code in a shell (see below).

Shell. You don't have to write your code in the form of scripts – you can also program Python in what is called a "shell". Each operating system has a shell, so you may already know about shells in a roundabout way. For instance, in Windows systems you may have seen the Command Prompt or the PowerShell; for Mac systems, there is an application called Terminal; and, for Linux users, you have probably already been encouraged to learn some basic command-line prompts through Bash/Terminal. After you have installed Python on your computer, you can use shells like these to run Python. However, a standard Windows installation of Python also comes with IDLE, a Python "interpreter"/shell (which also comes with scripting functionality). All of these different methods of shell programming operate similarly – you start Python in the shell (though for IDLE, opening the shell automatically starts Python), then you type in commands line by line. You would normally use a shell to do "pilot" or "exploratory" coding: quickly and easily testing some small thing out, to work out issues or test ideas, often alongside and in addition to scripting. Shell programming is more about quickly checking that things work, whereas scripting is about building and storing more complex code structures (and sharing them with others). However, both ways of programming use the same Python language and concepts, so the things you'll learn in this book will apply to both shell and scripted usages of Python. In this book we will focus on scripting, because scripts are built and structured more "readably" than code in the shell, and this can help demonstrate more clearly how different bits of code hang together.

IDE. Python code can be written in various different ways – you can even just use any standard basic text editor to write out your code, save the file with the .py extension, and that will run as a Python program. However, lots of programmers use Integrated Development Environments (IDEs), which are pieces of software that provide lots of different functions designed to make programming easier to do. IDLE, mentioned above in the entries on **script** and **shell**, is perhaps the first IDE you will come across, since it comes with a standard Windows installation of Python. The functions that IDEs offer can range from relatively basic stuff like colour-coding bits of code according to their jobs in Python (which we will explore in more detail in Chapter 3 when we start looking at bits of code), to "code completion" (which is like the autocorrect on a smartphone that helps you write out text quickly, but for coding) right through to sophisticated automated debugging systems designed to point out errors that you might have missed. IDEs can be really helpful in terms of making your code more "readable" (i.e. so you can clearly see and keep track of what your code is about just by looking at it on the screen), and you may find their other functionality useful too. Choosing an IDE is largely a matter of trial and error and arbitrary preference/"gut feeling"; there are lots out there, some available for free, and each containing a different set of functionalities. However, it is relatively straightforward to dive into various IDEs to see which one you prefer – they are just bits of software that you can download, install and uninstall as you would any other software. For the purposes of this book, however, I will be concentrating on using IDLE. As such, I recommend that you do the same while you are learning, but of course you should feel free to do your own exploration of IDEs if you are interested – part of the fun of all this is in figuring out how to do it yourself, after all!

Algorithm. "Algorithm" might sound like an incredibly technical word with an highly specific meaning, but in the context of programming this is not the case. An algorithm is simply a list of steps to follow to solve a problem or achieve a goal of some kind. So, an algorithm for making a cup of tea might be as follows:

1   Put water in kettle
2   Boil water in kettle
3   Put boiled water, plus one teabag, in mug
4   Wait 4 minutes
5   Stir and strain teabag, before removing
6   Add milk.

Notice that the steps have to come in a certain order – you can't sensibly be said to be "making a cup of tea" if you put boiled water in the mug (step 3) after you have removed the teabag (step 5).[1] Also notice that there are *lots* of assumptions built into the tea-making algorithm above. How much water do you put in the kettle? How big should the mug be (and how much water do you put in it)? Are you supposed to stir and the strain the teabag with a particular implement (and if so, which)? Where do you put the teabag when you've removed it? How much milk do you add? While it's reasonable to expect a human to follow this tea-making algorithm and fill in the gaps, Python (or any other programming language) will need the details spelling out in full. So, in the programming context, an algorithm could contain step-by-step instructions for scraping some web data, extracting the text, then dumping it in a text file named according to the location from which the data were scraped. What those instructions might actually look like, however, will require a far greater focus on the specificity of your Python code than is indicated in the broad outline suggested above. We will learn more about how to do these specifics through the course of this book, but the concept of algorithms as sets of instructions will not change from this broad general definition.

Module/library. Python has a set of core concepts which we will learn about in Chapter 3. These core concepts are the building blocks for any programming in Python. However, as we get more familiar with those core concepts and start to want to do more complicated and sophisticated things with Python, we will start to draw on libraries and modules to help us do so – collections of new techniques that give us nice neat new "add-ons" to Python which

---

[1] It's worth mentioning that in the field of British Tea Fanaticism, there is a never-ending vociferous debate around the issue of milk - when to add it, before or after removing the bag. That's a can of worms I really don't want to open in the context of algorithms. But I will say, if you think that the best brews result from adding milk before the bag is removed, you clearly haven't had one of mine.

help us simplify complicated jobs. The words "module" and "library" are used pretty much interchangeably, and just refer to packages that are outside a standard Python installation, but which you can install and use yourself. Some modules/libraries are very well used and reputable in research communities, to the extent that using certain modules/libraries to facilitate research work is a standard practice in many disciplines.

Debugging/testing. Though these two words refer to different things, they tend to be packaged together, because they overlap somewhat and are often done together in practice. You've probably already heard the term "bug" in relation to software – a "bug" is an unwanted or unexpected aspect of the software, something which shouldn't be there and needs to be removed or fixed. The term "bug" is often attributed to Admiral Grace Hopper, a computer scientist working on the Mark II computer at Harvard University in the 1940s. The story goes that Admiral Hopper and her associates discovered a moth stuck in the physical hardware of the computer that was obstructing the operation of its physical components. Hence, it was necessary to remove the moth – to "debug" the system – to get the computer working again. Immediately puncturing that myth, Admiral Hopper herself has stated that the terms "bug" and "debug" were already in use in this context and she was just on the receiving end of a happy coincidence where the two meanings came into alignment. It's still a good story, though! And it provides another example of how the history of computing has been, to a large extent, driven by a great number of seriously smart women. That's always worth mentioning. Even though we typically now don't have to do pest control as part of our working with computers, debugging has taken on a more general meaning of (a) analysing programs in terms of whether or not they are doing what is expected, and (b) fixing problems that you spot along the way. We will look at specific good practices for debugging as we go through the book. "Testing" is a related concept: testing software refers to designing ways to figure out if your software is doing what it should be doing (so that you can see if it needs debugging or not). Testing software is important for research work, in that your analyses and insights will rely entirely on your being able to account for what your program is doing – if simple coding errors are being built in along the way due to poor testing, your analysis could suffer. However, there are a number of general guidelines to think about when doing testing, and we will explore these aspects of good practices for testing in later sections.

There are, of course, many more other new terms that will arise throughout the course of this book, and which are not covered here – this is not a comprehensive dictionary of all the terms you will come across as you learn programming, because lots of terms will be more specific to the material and examples in which they are situated and talking about them here, in abstract, is not necessarily a very useful thing to do. We will look more carefully at all of these new terms as they crop up. Moreover, as outlined above, the actual specifics of these terms are fluid and subject to different interpretations, so really the best way to get to grips with them is to do some programming and see first-hand how terms like these can be used to describe the work that you're doing.

1.2 The Research Process as a Socio-technical Assemblage

The title of this chapter is "What *Is* Programming? And What Could it Mean for Social Science Research?" In Section 1.1 we dealt (in a small way, to start the proceedings) with the first element of that title, by outlining some rough-and-ready definitions for some of the core concepts of programming. Now we can start to think about the second element – what could programming mean specifically in the context of social science research? This will involve thinking about the role of computers and software tools in our (research) work, and, I argue, thinking in terms of the research process as a "socio-technical assemblage" can be a helpful way of tackling these issues.

Social science in the "digital age"

The publication of an article in *Wired* magazine in 2008, titled "The End of Theory: The Data Deluge Makes the Scientific Method Obsolete" (Anderson, 2008), was a key moment in the development of a robust social scientific approach to computational tools and new forms of digital data. In that article, Chris Anderson argued that the sheer amount of data being harvested and moved around by companies like Google – then already in the order of petabytes – made it no longer possible to visualise or understand large datasets in their totality. As such, we now necessarily have to take an agnostic (i.e. disinterested, non-human-centric, mathematically or computationally led) approach to sorting such data for consumption. For companies like Google which routinely collect enormous amounts of data from people, Anderson argues that this means that they no longer need to understand the cultural practices and processes that go into the generation of such data – the data become the only reality worth looking at. But more than this, to Anderson, the whole idea of a human researcher who analyses such data becomes redundant – the data and the "agnostic" computational tools which enable you to work with them produce *their own* analysis, completely removed from human subjectivity. Another way of putting this is that because data now come in huge volumes, this signifies a paradigm shift in the idea of data-oriented (i.e. empirical) research, whereby the only important thing is to look at the correlations that emerge from the purely mathematical processes that we apply to the data. This is summed up in Anderson's (2008) statement that:

> Petabytes allow us to say: "Correlation is enough." We can stop looking for models. We can analyze the data without hypotheses about what it might show. We can throw the numbers into the biggest computing clusters the world has ever seen and let statistical algorithms find patterns where science cannot.

It's almost needless to say, but social scientists have found statements like these (which often get packaged up in overly celebratory and uncritical talk about the so-called turn to "Big Data" and "data science") incredibly problematic, for numerous reasons.[2]

---

[2] It does need to be noted at this point that my use of the Anderson (2008) piece is a *really* crude take on things – what Anderson writes absolutely does not typify what goes on in social-science-oriented Big Data and data science. However, the Anderson (2008) piece *was* an important opening for the types of bad practices that emerge when social analyses are derived from a research process that is ignorant of the underlying philosophies of social research, and it is for that reason that I discuss it here. So, while Anderson's (2008) article stands as emblematic of the worst and most uncritical conceptualisation of Big Data and data science possible (and therefore serves a rhetorical function in the above argument – a useful shorthand necessitated by the constraints of a book chapter), I am *not* claiming that there are any groups of social scientists that work in this way.

What has social science (and philosophy) already said about this?

Stepping back in time a bit, we can see that the social sciences have had long-standing and cogently expressed concerns with the ideas of "scientism" and "bureaucratisation" in social research, which Anderson's (2008) article completely fails to acknowledge – such concerns are evident in the work of Ludwig Wittgenstein (1958, 2009 [1953]) and C. Wright Mills (2000 [1959]), as well as more recently in the work of Savage and Burrows (2007, 2009) and Burrows and Savage (2014).

═══════════ **Definitions** ═══════════

"Scientism" and "Bureaucracy": Two Related Concerns

"Scientism" refers to the idea that social science should more closely model the natural sciences such as physics, chemistry and biology. This is pitched especially with regard to investigating the social world through the application of the "scientific method" (which gives primacy to the idea of direct objective observations of phenomena, as discovered through replicable and systematic experimentation).

"Bureaucratisation" refers to the idea that the work of social science is increasingly becoming a matter of applying standardised strategies for the collection, management, handling and analysis of data. This is often seen as transforming social science into a purely technical operation where no analytic or interpretive skill is required at any stage.

Social scientists who use either of these terms often do so very critically.

─────────────────────────────────────

Wittgenstein (1958: 18) argues that "Philosophers [in their capacity as commentators on social life and the social world] constantly see the method of science before their eyes, and are irresistibly tempted to ask and to answer questions in the way science does. This tendency is the real source of metaphysics and leads philosophers into complete darkness." In his work, Wittgenstein (1958, 2009 [1953]) makes a clear statement against the idea of scientism of social inquiry, suggesting that treating our subject purely as a scientific matter ignores those essentially subjective elements that characterise our subject and our approach to it. Hence, scientism only removes from us the possibility of studying what we claim to want to study: social life – that, to Wittgenstein, constitutes good grounds to resist the "scientisation" of the social sciences.[3]

Turning now to the social sciences' historical defiance of the standardisation (i.e. bureaucratisation) of research practice, C. Wright Mills provides a remarkably prescient comment on

─────────────

[3] Another note of clarification: not all attempts to "do social science scientifically" amount to "scientism" as defined here – for instance, Computational Social Science (see Chapter 0 in this book for some more detail, as well as González-Bailón, 2013; Lazer et al., 2009; and Nelson, 2017) is a rich body of work that embodies a scientific approach to social research, yet it is by no means ignorant or neglectful of the interpretive/hermeneutic philosophical traditions of social science. As with footnote 2, the constraints of a book chapter necessitate a brevity which unfortunately cannot always fully reflect the nuance of the positions at hand. But hopefully it gets the general idea across all the same!

the linkage between the context-free approach to empirical inquiry (such as that advocated by Anderson, 2008) and a reductive bureaucratisation of social scientific skill:

> In each and every feature of its existence and its influence, abstracted empiricism, as it is currently practiced, represents a "bureaucratic" development ... In an attempt to standardize and rationalize each phase of social inquiry, the intellectual operations themselves of the abstracted empirical style are becoming "bureaucratic." (Mills, 2000 [1959]: 101)

For Mills, the "bureaucratisation" of social scientific inquiry could only result in the destruction or preclusion of precisely what lends social science its unique value – namely, the creative "sociological imagination" that practitioners can leverage to produce deep insightful analyses of the ways in which grand historical processes intersected with the individual biographies of social actors. In short, though the standardisation of methods and practices of empirical research might seem a progressive move to some (i.e. Anderson, 2008), it cannot be anything but counter-productive to the generation of social scientific insight.

Scientism and bureaucratism in contemporary research

Combining the kinds of resistance that Wittgenstein and Mills put up against the idea of a scientised and bureaucratised social science, Savage and Burrows have connected these concepts specifically to new forms of Digital Social Science and "Big Data" in a series of influential papers (Savage and Burrows, 2007, 2009; Burrows and Savage, 2014), noting that:

> In many aspects of our work [at the time of the first paper in 2007] - at conferences, within fieldwork and so on - we were routinely coming across analysts working outside of the academy and, indeed, outside of the social sciences, who were producing social knowledge based upon access to, and the analysis of, such [digital/social media] data. Our concern was that this was likely to be yet another major nail in the coffin of academic sociological claims to jurisdiction over knowledge of the social. (Burrows and Savage, 2014: 2)

Though these sentiments might be expressed in a somewhat overly reactionary manner – if people who aren't sociologists want to use digital data to think about the social world in non-sociological ways, that doesn't have to detract from the value of sociology – the point stands that what is now called "data science" – that is, the kind of thing that Anderson (2008) talks about – is not a substitute for sociological insight. To conflate social science with data science, as Burrows and Savage think some are now apt to do more than ever, is to limit the scope of social science to a scientised and bureacratised version of itself. This is to be rejected outright, on the grounds that the subjective orientations of social science can promise other (arguably far greater) insights.

Taking this view of a social scientific approach to digital data, it should be clear that social science never has been, and never should be, a formalised, scientific, bureaucratised discipline – this applies equally to those arms of social science which deal with digital data and computer technologies. This way of thinking about the role of computers and software within the social sciences shows us that it is neither possible nor valuable to try to ignore the human, subjective elements that apply to all social research. It is within those subjective elements that our phenomena of interest lie – how can we claim to understand social life if we spend all of our time trying to remove it from our own research practice? Rather, in light of the resistance to Anderson's proposed remodelling of the social sciences, it becomes all the more important to acknowledge, embrace and understand how the research process features as part of a much wider array of factors that go into producing our phenomena of interest. The conception of the (digital) research process as a socio-technical assemblage can help us do that.

The importance of methodology

Lupton (2014) posits the software tools we use to facilitate our digital research as "methodological devices", which connect together research objects (i.e. various forms of data, or the things that we take those data to represent such as experiences, attitudes, and so on) with method (as the "techniques" via which we propose to locate and retrieve our phenomena of interest). Seeing tools in such a way immediately confronts us with a need to explore the impacts of digital data and software on our research: we start to see a need to ask questions around what affordances such data and tools offer our research, and how those data and tools construct and constrain the scope of potential analyses we might eventually produce. Gitelman and Jackson provide a neat summary of these concerns:

> However self-contradictory it may be, the phrase *raw data* ... has understandable appeal. At first glance, data are apparently before the fact: they are the starting-point for what we know, who we are, and how we communicate. This shared sense of starting with data often leads to an unnoticed assumption that data are transparent, that information is self-evident, the fundamental stuff of truth itself. If we're not careful, in other words, our zeal for more and more data can become a faith in their neutrality and autonomy, their objectivity. (Gitelman and Jackson, 2013: 2–3)

Thinking beyond this, to fetishise data as neutral, autonomous and objective is to appeal to the idea that a scientised and bureaucratised version of social science is possible and/ or desired – as we have seen above, neither is the case. In contrast, when we attend to the ways in which digital data and tools feature in the research process, we become attuned to the socio-technical assemblages (Brooker et al., 2015, 2016; Langlois, 2011; Sharma, 2013; Sharma and Brooker, 2017) that we invoke in the production of social scientific knowledge.

Even though a socio-technical assemblage is, by its nature, unique to the researcher who generates it and the purposes to which it is put, it is perhaps helpful at this point to provide a clear example of what such an assemblage might look like. Lots of researchers now use Twitter as a data source, so this provides a suitable demonstration to work with. As a researcher, you may find an interesting phenomenon on Twitter, via browsing your Twitter feed on the train in a morning – a particular hashtag conversation which you have spotted, within which there are some interesting forms of online social interaction at play. However, even in the noticing of such a phenomenon, you are likely already enmeshed with the Twitter algorithms that push popular (i.e. frequently favourited/retweeted) tweets to the top of your news feed – you have only found your interesting phenomenon because of the technical aspects of the Twitter platform which have led you to it. Beyond this, you now have to get the data out of the platform – this puts you in contact with both Twitter as a commercial entity and various software tool providers who might facilitate data collection. Twitter's public (free) APIs – the means by which software tools request data from the Twitter service – do not typically let users have 100% of the data they request. The exact amount of data varies according to the specifics of the queries that users make through the various Twitter APIs, but suffice to say that the only way to be sure you've got 100% of the data that match your search criteria is to buy the data from one of Twitter's approved vendors. As such, the notion of extracting data through a (free) Twitter API has limited the scope of data that you will receive (and, furthermore, you are from this point on beholden to Twitter's terms and conditions surrounding data usage). With regard to software tools for handling API queries, each tool is different, and each tool embodies a certain way of approaching the extraction of data from the Twitter APIs such that your work is now already intertwined with the unique functionalities (and limitations) that each piece of software inevitably has. Each tool will therefore produce a dataset which is geared towards being analysed only in certain ways; the data that come out are not "neutral", nor readily amenable to any and all possible interpretations. For instance, some tools do not provide for the collection of geo-location tweet metadata, which means that if you use those tools, you are excluded from doing any kind of location-based investigation – just one more way in which the technical systems you end up using to do your research lead you down certain paths and close off others.

A more sensitive approach to digital data

I could go on to detail lots of other steps in the research process, from actually analysing such data to producing publications on it. But even with this truncated example, notice that even before you've got a dataset to look at, a lot of analytic decisions have already been made and you are not necessarily in control of them – in the example above, you as a researcher are brought into a situation where your research is co-produced by yourself, by Twitter as a commercial entity, by the software you choose to use to extract and analyse data, and so on. What's more, all of this comes before you've even thought about the people and social interactions you are actually interested in studying in the first place (who must eventually also be featured as co-producers in your socio-technical assemblage, since they're the ones responsible for producing the phenomenon you're interested in studying)!

So, despite how complicated it might be to think of the research process as a socio-technical assemblage, it's clear that it is necessary to do so if we want to retain a critical and reflexive approach to our own research practice, so we can look back over what we do as researchers and think about the impact that our research process is having on the specific depictions of phenomena that eventually fall out of our analyses. As Baym and Markham (2009: xviii) note:

> the constitution of data is the result of a series of decisions at critical junctures in the design and conduct of a study ... Reflexivity may enable us to minimize or at least acknowledge the ways in which our culturally embedded rationalities influence what is eventually labelled as "data".

━━━━━━━━━━━━━━━ **Definitions** ━━━━━━━━━━━━━━━

Reflexivity

"Reflexivity" refers to the capacity of the researcher to look back and reflect on their research practice, so as to be able to see and understand the impact they have had on the analyses that their research produces. Often, reflexivity is seen as an "academic virtue", though some have been more careful about pitching reflexivity as a universal principle for ensuring "good research" (see Lynch, 2000). However, in cases such as Digital Social Science and work with digital data where there are "black boxes" in the research process – aspects of the research process where social scientists do not often get to see the "inner workings" – reflexivity becomes a necessary principle to be attended to.

In this sense, it is extremely valuable for us to find ways of "unpicking" assemblages – practical strategies we can deploy to help us figure out and reflect on the various impacts of socio-technical factors throughout the lifetime of a research project. Learning programming is one, potentially very powerful, way of doing this – imagine if you did not have to rely so heavily on tools built by other people to engage with the Twitter APIs, but could build those tools yourself and actually see this aspect of the research process in action! Moreover, having an appreciation of programming as the level at which such assumptions and decisions are built into software will give you a deeper understanding of those processes and their role within the assemblages we build. All of these factors become crucial to the undertaking of Digital Social Science work at all points – designing a research question, data collection, producing visual representations, writing up a study and publishing it. Being able to program and to understand programming as a practice gives us a way of opening up research "black boxes" which have previously been sealed shut.

1●3 Working Interdisciplinarily

What the above shows is that, given how diverse the Digital Social Science research process is (and the diversity of topics it brings you into contact with), it becomes increasingly necessary to understand and be able to reflect on the aspects of the research process which fall outside the traditional boundaries of your discipline.

━━━━━━━━━━━━━━━ **Definitions** ━━━━━━━━━━━━━━━

Interdisciplinarity

"Interdisciplinarity" refers to the idea of boundaries between different disciplines being made blurry or broken down in the undertaking of research projects, and to research collaborations where ideas from multiple disciplines are shared between researchers. There have always been aspects of the social sciences which have stepped outside formal disciplinary boundaries - for instance, the field of Science and Technology Studies incorporates work from sociology, history, philosophy, anthropology and many more fields. More recently, the advent of Digital Social Science and the growing interest in digital data as a resource have put the social sciences in close contact with various fields in and around computer science, such as data mining and data visualisation. Though interdisciplinary thinking and collaboration may be tricky – it is often difficult for researchers to step outside their subject-oriented comfort zones – the process of making unique combinations and reconfigurations of disciplines has the potential to create incredibly innovative insights and advances.

Due to the proliferation of digital data through social life, and the importance this accordingly places on ("big") digital data as a resource that social scientists must now engage with, interdisciplinarity has become almost an inevitability for social scientists looking to take up this kind of work. As outlined in Section 1.2, our work in such areas brings us into contact with a socio-technical assemblage of factors that affect our research whether we like it or not. Finding ways to understand and account for these assemblages therefore becomes critical to undertaking such research.

Learning to program can help us do this by offering a way to bridge disciplinary gaps between the social and computer science aspects of what we do – we will find as we go through the material in this book that it is possible to both understand and use code as a social scientist. This is to say that we will come to see how to use code as a tool for doing social science, and how to feature the analysis of code in the broader context of social scientific analysis; in short, how to make a social science sense of code. Hence, learning to program will be a valuable skill to help you undertake the kinds of interdisciplinary work that are becoming more prevalent and ubiquitous in contemporary social science.

This kind of value is also added to interdisciplinary collaborations on the personal day-to-day level. As we have discussed above, such collaborations are increasingly common. If you find yourself (as a social scientist) working on projects with computer scientists, software developers, data visualisation specialists or anyone else whose work involves coding, it can be enormously helpful to share some common ground that can help drive the work forward. Part of the trickiness of interdisciplinary working is in individual researchers learning to understand the languages and conventions of researchers from other backgrounds, and learning to code as a social scientist can go a long way towards getting on the same page as other researchers you may work with. This can benefit an interdisciplinary collaboration from start to finish: the research you can do as an interdisciplinary team will be stronger and proceed more smoothly by virtue of your having an awareness of the difficulties and challenges that other researchers face in their work.

As such, learning programming can make you a much more effective interdisciplinary researcher, a skill which is becoming increasingly important to contemporary social science methods and topics of study.

1.4 Thinking in Script/Developmental Workflows

One thing that will help you navigate the issues raised throughout this chapter – namely, remaining reflexive and attentive to the research process as a socio-technical assemblage, and being able to account for the role of software in your (interdisciplinary) research – is thinking about the code you build in terms of "script" and "developmental" workflows. These two things constitute two different ways of thinking about what you are doing when you are coding. Of course, thinking about and/or documenting these workflows is not a requirement of using a programming language; thinking about code in terms of workflows is not the same as doing coding. Nonetheless, constructing script and developmental workflows will help you plan your programs effectively, as well as reflexively "unpick" the algorithms and programs you are working on, and they will help you with the practicalities of adding new bits, testing, debugging, etc., and give you a clear document of the role of your code in your methodological process.

Script workflows

A script workflow is, in essence, a step-by-step account of what a program does, line by line, from top to bottom. This can be represented either textually or visually/diagrammatically. If we think back to the analogy between algorithms and the process of making a cup of tea that was advanced in Section 1.1, we can develop this to demonstrate what both the textual and visual versions of a script workflow might look like. First, the textual version:

1   Do I want a cup of tea?

    a   If yes, proceed to step 2
    b   If no, proceed to step 9

2   Is there water in the kettle?

    a   If yes, proceed to step 3
    b   If no, put water in the kettle, then proceed to step 3

3   Boil water in kettle
4   Put boiled water, plus one teabag, in mug
5   Wait 4 minutes
6   Stir and strain teabag, before removing
7   Add milk
8   Drink
9   Wait 30 minutes then return to step 1.

There are a few things worth noticing here, chief among these being that we've depicted our "tea-making script" with a series of checks and instructions. For instance, steps 1 and 2 begin with questions, which are designed to check certain conditions, such as "Do I want a cup of tea?", to which the answer will only be "yes" or "no". There are instructions that follow on from whichever of those conditions are satisfied (i.e. if I *do* want a cup of tea, I move to a step where I can begin to make one; if I *don't* want a cup of tea, I bypass the tea-making process to step 9 where I then wait and check again later). So, within this script workflow, you can see how we can build conditional checks to control the flow of the program. We can also perhaps extend this by trying to incorporate another element that accounts for the fact that I don't always want to be checking if I want a cup of tea:

1   Is it bedtime?

    a   If yes, stop drinking tea and go to sleep! Start again in the morning
    b   If no, proceed to step 2

2   Do I want a cup of tea?

    a   If yes, proceed to step 3

    b   If no, proceed to step 10

3   Is there water in the kettle?

    a   If yes, proceed to step 4

    b   If no, put water in the kettle, then proceed to step 4

4   Boil water in kettle

5   Put boiled water, plus one teabag, in mug

6   Wait 4 minutes

7   Stir and strain teabag, before removing

8   Add milk

9   Drink

10   Wait 30 minutes then return to step 1.

Notice that I've placed the bedtime check at the beginning of the workflow rather than the end. If I incorporated the bedtime check as the last stage of the script, that would be problematic – let's see why by looking at the last two steps if I *were* to place the bedtime check at the end:

9   Wait 30 minutes then return to step 1.

10   Is it bedtime?

    a   If yes, stop drinking tea and go to sleep! Start again in the morning

    b   If no, proceed to step 1.

So, if the bedtime check were at the end of the workflow, we would never actually reach that step – step 9 would always return us to the beginning of the process and force us to ask "Do I want a cup of tea?" again.[4] What these examples show is that thinking through a proposed script in these terms will help you plan out each step of the process appropriately, can help you figure out how to build on your existing plan to incorporate new functionality and features into your code, and will help prevent against errors along the way (such as a conditional check for bedtime that can never actually happen). Moreover, these script workflows are very useful methodologically – when it comes to writing up your methods, you already have a detailed account of the things your program is doing in relation to the particular research problem you are applying it to.

We can also draw out a diagram of a script workflow – Figure 1.1 follows much the same principles as the textual version, but is perhaps more useful for readers who prefer a visual representation.

Notice here that we have used a diamond shape for conditional checks, a rectangle shape to signify operations to be carried out, and an oval for the end-point of the process. These are just conventions that can help us more easily visually intuit how the workflow operates – the more complex a visual workflow gets, the more helpful it may be to use things like different shapes and colour-coding to navigate your way around it.

---

[4]You've probably already guessed that I like a cup of tea, but even for me, having to check whether or not I want a brew every half hour for the rest of my life would impact pretty negatively on me in numerous ways.

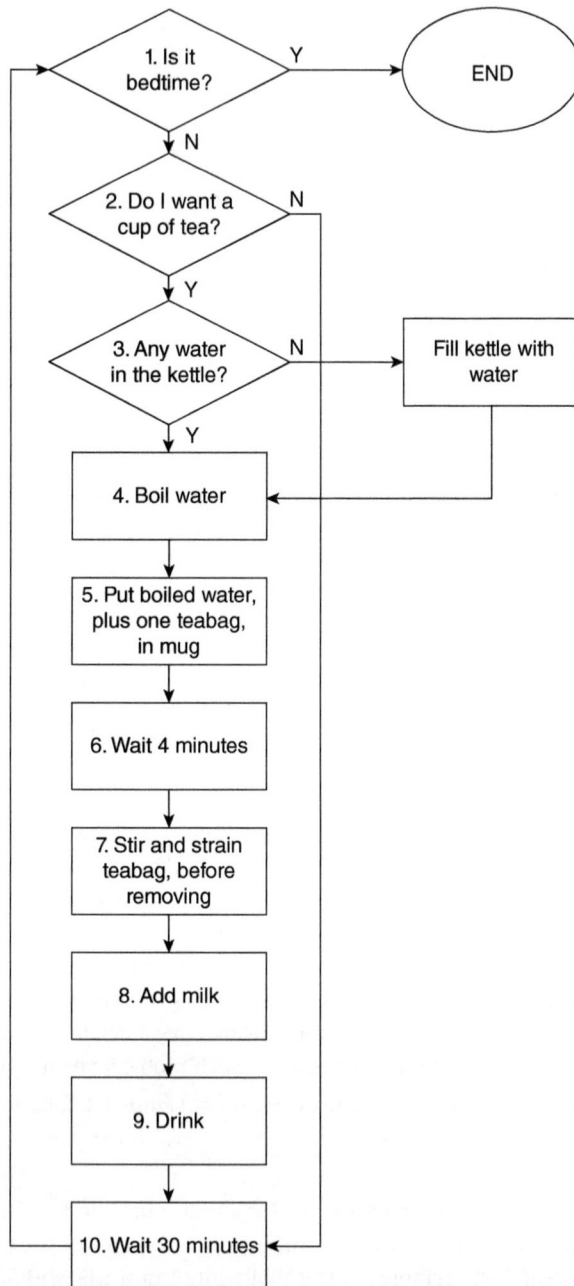

Figure 1.1 Visual script workflow for making a cup of tea

Whether you prefer the textual or visual method of doing a script workflow, the result is the same – it will help you plan, understand and account for the fine detail of what a program might be doing, reviewing the operations it involves line by line and tracing paths through those operations. This is valuable in terms of being able to locate and acknowledge biases and assumptions in your program at the point they become written into the script. For instance, my bias in the tea-making script is that I have a (strong) preference for adding the milk after removing the teabag – however, this is not the only way to do things and the script can in principle be constructed differently. The same idea applies to code, algorithms and programs – for instance, a script workflow that describes a search engine page ranking algorithm might show that what gets returned as a list of the "most relevant" results might in fact be driven by different ideas of what relevance is (e.g. the algorithm may emphasise results that lead you to specific online shopping sites in the hope that you will spend some money there). Hence, it is useful to use script workflows to lay all of these assumptions, biases and issues out transparently – this way of thinking can be applied to programs you write yourself or as a form of analysing and critically evaluating programs written by others, in such a way that it will enable you to critically reflect on code from the social science perspective.

Developmental workflows

Moving now to the idea of a developmental workflow, we can also describe the practical aspects of programming in terms of how that work is situated within the wider context of the research process. This is perhaps best not done in terms of a step-by-step account as we did with the script workflow above – as we have already noted, the research process is a complex and messy socio-technical assemblage, and forcing a linear depiction of it will be overly reductive (though the idea of a script workflow is helpful within the strictly bounded conditions under which a programming language operates). Rather, what a developmental workflow attempts to document is the *process of writing the program*. This might be analogised with the concept of the "fieldwork diary", where the aim is to document phenomena you come across as your research is unfolding, as well as to serve as a record of your orientations to (and impact on) those phenomena. Whereas what we call script workflows are something of a standard practice among programmers already (inasmuch as programmers do plan out their work in advance of actually writing the code, and use these planning documents as a way to assess and evaluate the programs that result), developmental workflows are perhaps more specifically intended for social scientific methodological purposes. Often, the work involved in actually writing the code is not documented, but what developmental workflows capture are the factors that go into building a program. This might include things like:

- The ways in which the literature you read informs your making of certain coding decisions.
- The technical limitations of your work (such as having to work with certain data formats or having to work towards the production of certain types of results) and the impact these limitations have on the ways in which you build the program.
- The operational problems you encounter throughout (i.e. the struggles in getting your code to do the things you want it to do), the potential solutions that you trial and the reasoning behind why the solutions you eventually settle upon are the best or most preferable.
- The methodological commitments you are trying to adhere to in your project, which might make certain requirements of your program in terms of keeping the program consistent with those guidelines.

- The interactions and tensions you might experience with other collaborators (both from within the social sciences and from other disciplines or sectors) or institutions (i.e. universities, corporations such as social media data providers, and so on), where they have an impact on the code that you write.
- Any ethical or legal considerations which shape the way in which your code operates.
- And literally *anything else* that seems important and/or relevant to an account of why you have done your coding in one particular way and not another.

In this regard, combining the more "micro" and descriptive focus of a script workflow with the grander scope and more self-reflective facets of a developmental workflow can help you connect your code-building to the wider context of your research work in terms of clarifying the role your code takes within the wider socio-technical assemblage that is mobilised as you undertake your project.

Chapter summary

- This chapter aimed to get into more depth as to what programming is, as well as provide some clear justifications for how and why we should be interested in it as social scientists.
- There are some core concepts that it's worth learning now, but for the most part, we can simply pick up the terminology as we go – all these seemingly complicated terms are less scary than they might sound!
- The social science research process, wherever it involves things like computer tools or digital data, means that we now have to be aware of the impact that software and programming are already having on our work – we can call the research process a socio-technical assemblage of such factors.
- Moreover, current trends in research mean we're more likely than ever before to find ourselves working with people from other disciplines (and perhaps especially computer scientists).
- For both of these reasons, learning computer programming can help us do our work – it can help us have a clearer understanding of our own research processes, and it can make collaborations between ourselves and researchers from other (computationally oriented) disciplines easier to achieve.
- One skill that is vital to researching through a socio-technical assemblage and working interdisciplinarily is the capacity to think in script and developmental workflows. These ways of thinking about the role of software and programs in your research can be helpful both in the planning stages and when we're accounting for our work in dissertations and other publications.

2

Programming-as-Social-Science (Critical Coding)

━━━━━━━━━━━ **Chapter objectives** ━━━━━━━━━━━

- To explore how we might undertake Python programming in specifically social scientific ways.
- To point towards some key areas of thinking to help us use Python programming as social scientists in terms of fitting Python programming with our existing (critical) practice – for example, to start to see Python programming as a social, political, ideological, moral and ethical issue.
- To reiterate the value of incorporating programming skills into the practice of social science.

Before we knew anything about programming, it might have been tempting to think of programming and coding as being a purely technical or instrumental exercise that's just about telling a computer to perform various tasks. If we think of programming in such a way, then it may also be tempting to see the work of programming as neutral and objective and simply a case of getting a program to run. If that were the case, then the trickiest thing in Python programming would be stuff like making sure every open bracket was closed, every comma was in the right place, and so on.

However, when programming in Python as a social scientist, there is *much* more to it than this. There's an analogy to be made here with writing. Writing is not just about making sure all your words are spelled correctly and that the order in which you put them makes grammatical sense; *what* you write and *why* you write it are important too. There are some pretty obvious distinctions between the kind of writing you might see in an anti-immigration opinion piece in a tabloid like the *Sun* and a peer-reviewed social science journal article on immigration based on evidence and reasoned argument. Both might follow standard grammatical rules and feature 100% dictionary-perfect spellings, but the purposes to which those pieces of writing are put might be markedly different and produce very different accounts of the social world.

All of this can be applied to programming too – programming is not just about the spelling-and-grammar issues of getting a program to work. Granted, if you do get a comma out of place in a Python script, that's going to cause problems (and hence, part of learning to code in Python *is* learning the relevant grammar/syntax and applying it correctly). However, there is a crucial fact that we need to bear in mind in *any* programming activity we're doing:

> Programming languages don't construct code; *people* construct code.

This is to say that as programmers who are also social scientists, we need to consider programming as a socially contextual activity – this is what this book means by the term "Programming-as-Social-Science" (PaSS), as a specific and unique approach to programming as a task that can be embedded in work that intends to explore the social world.

Part of coding as a social scientist is about leveraging a knowledge of code to *see* and *understand* and *critique* the code we're investigating and/or building ourselves. Programming is an activity that is, inevitably, embedded in the social world. How could it be otherwise? People who code are social actors. And therefore, coding is a social activity and needs to be considered as such. Coding is social, it's political, it's ideological, it's a moral issue, it's an ethical issue, and so on. This applies to *everybody* who programs, and that includes ourselves (or at least it will do by the time you get to the end of this book). And therefore, we need to have a critical eye on programming – we might already be adept at spotting social, political, ideological, moral and ethical issues in the world (and in our own practice) as social scientists, but until we're familiar with programming we might find it difficult to spot similar issues when they occur in code. As social scientists, we don't want to just learn to code; we want to learn to code (and read/think about code) *critically*.

We'll explore these ideas in various ways throughout the rest of this chapter, but having now introduced the notion that coding is a critical activity for us, I want to now give this notion a label: this is Programming-as-Social-Science (PaSS). Throughout this chapter, we'll explore PaSS as a way to think about programming being *integrated* into the work of social science as opposed to just being tacked onto the end of it as an "optional extra". If we start to see the work of social science and the work of programming as intertwined and inseparable from one another in our research practice, this affords us a way to look at what we're doing as programming for purpose rather than just coding as an abstract technical exercise that takes place in a "social vacuum". Seeing and thinking about code as *inevitably* situated in the social world (because where else would it be situated?) allows us to pay close attention to the intersections between code and society. This should guide our learning and our practice throughout the rest of the book and beyond.

2.1 Coding Social Injustice and Justice into the World

To concretise these ideas and open up a space for seriously thinking about these issues early on, it's worth exploring some of the ways in which programming has been applied in the social world to various effects. As noted, programming is a social practice, and this means it's also inevitably a political, ideological, moral and ethical issue. As Bucher (2018: 3) notes of algorithms (i.e. pieces of code, for our purposes):

> In ranking, classifying, sorting, predicting, and processing data, algorithms are political in the sense that they help to make the world appear in certain ways rather than others. Speaking of algorithmic politics in this sense, then, refers to the idea that realities are never given but brought into being and actualized in and through algorithmic systems.

We might note that the way code is shaped through/by social practices can sometimes contribute to progressive social justice, or can sometimes in fact be part of the generation and/ or amplification of social *in*justice, where the justice/injustice is a result of the way the code is placed within (and intersects with) society. The role of social practices within social justice/injustice is something that social science has been attentive to across its entire lifespan. However, in the context of programming, we can run through a select few examples to see how issues of social justice and injustice are implicated in code.

Coding social injustice

One example of how social injustice can be built into code is Google's Translate algorithm, which (before it was corrected) handled gender pronouns in ways which amplify and reproduce existing social injustices around misogyny (i.e. prejudice against women). In a tweet in 2017, Alex Shams (@seyyedreza)[1] reports findings based around the use of Google's Translate algorithm to translate various phrases from Turkish (as a gender-neutral language, where both men and women are referred to with the pronoun *o* rather than "he" or "she") to English (as a language which features gender differentiation via separate words for "he", "she", "his", "hers", etc.). The Translate algorithm therefore has a problem – translation between languages is not merely a case of substituting words for other words; how can an algorithm be built to handle cases where the *structure* of the language is different (e.g. when trying to translate gender-neutral phrases from a language like Turkish to gendered phrases in a language like English)? When Shams asked the algorithm to translate various phrases by giving it various inputs, the process became clear – statements such as "o bir aşçi" and "o bir hemşire" were translated as "*she* is a cook" and "*she* is a nurse" respectively, whilst statements like "o bir doctor" and "o bir mühendis" were translated as "*he* is a doctor" and "*he* is an engineer" respectively. The gender-neutral "o" is, through the operation of the software, transformed into gender-biasing terms.

Though we cannot access the actual algorithm to see what is going on here (in that Google is *very* protective of its "trade secrets"), seeing the outputs next to the inputs does allow us to infer certain things. First, it seems as though the Google Translate algorithm at the time is purveying stereotypically gendered accounts of who we might expect to find in various occupational roles – the algorithm is choosing, somehow, and despite a lack of input (Turkish being a gender-neutral language in this respect) to gender occupational roles in ways that reflect and reproduce gender biases that already exist in society. If we use the gender-neutral term *o bir* to refer to "caring" occupations like teaching or nursing or catering, then Google's algorithm assumed (and suggested to us) that we might be talking exclusively about women, whereas if we use *o bir* to apply to other types of work (such as engineering or medical practitioner work as a doctor), the algorithm makes a guess that we're referring to men. One interesting exception Shams noted is the translation result for *o bir polis* ("he-she is a police") – this is not how we would normally express such a statement in English anyway, but it's interesting that the algorithm evidently *does* have the capacity to sit on the fence in terms of gendering professions. For some reason, in the case of police work, the algorithm is perfectly happy to produce a result that covers both men and women. However, the question then might be: why does it not do this in *all* cases where *o bir* is used? Why, in most cases, are occupations presented in stereotypically gendered ways? One reason might be that, at the time at least, the Google Translate algorithm drew on frequencies of word usage from users to inform how it genders terms from non-gendered languages – any phrases that users run through the Google Translate algorithm are collected by Google as data to feed back into the improvement of the algorithm. However, this embedding of algorithm in society has an important effect – if the algorithm uncritically picks up cues from users' input, then since its users are members of gender-biased societies,[2] the algorithm is in effect built to *reinforce* existing gender biases.

---

[1] https://twitter.com/seyyedreza/status/935291317252493312.

[2] And, correct me if I'm wrong, but I can't think of a society which *isn't* gender-biased.

Another example of note is Microsoft's Twitter chatbot (known as "Tay"), as explored by Neff and Nagy (2016) and Perez (2016) – though Tay has since been retired, it was origi-nally intended as a computer program that operated via its own Twitter account, and which could participate in Twitter conversations with other users and "learn" more about human conversation (at least the bits of it that happen over Twitter) as it went. However, almost immediately after the Tay Twitter account went live, it began to post extremely offensive tweets as a result of having "learned" how to converse with malicious Twitter trolls. Over the course of its short lifespan, Tay's conversations quickly turned horrendously racist and misog-ynistic, to the extent that Microsoft ultimately had to pull the plug on the Twitter account after only 16 hours. How does something like this happen? Similarly to the Google Translate example outlined above, Tay's source of data to "learn" about human conversation was an open playing field for anybody who wished to interact with Tay – anyone on Twitter could "teach" Tay about human conversation, and, unfortunately for Tay and for Twitter, a large user-base of trolls latched onto this and purposefully fed hateful content into the code such that it would eventually be spewed back out by the chatbot. In this sense, there was nothing in Tay's code that could resist hateful commentary, and, as a result, the structure and design of Tay's code became complicit in *reproducing* that hateful commentary.

In both the Google Translate algorithm and Microsoft's Tay chatbot (Neff and Nagy, 2016; Perez, 2016) what we can see is that social injustice is "baked into" the code. Though it was clearly possible for Google to ungender the translation results (inasmuch as it's able to do so when talking about policing as a profession), and though it would have been possible to develop code that would allow Tay to ignore hateful comments (e.g. to remove racial slurs from its data capture so that they cannot feature in Tay's own conversational output and block users who had commented with these words so that they couldn't further shape the system), these things were not done. The programmers who constructed this code did not design their systems with social justice in mind. Perhaps, expressing this more strongly, we might say that they *chose* not consider the issues that led to the magnification of social injus-tice. Whether this is actively hateful or just lazy/ill-thought-out (or whether there's even a difference between the two), these examples both show how the design of code and the work of programming can be done in ways which generate and amplify social injustice. What's more, having the skill to think about the role of code within such injustice is a valuable resource for social scientists whose routine work it is to unpick such issues.

Coding for social justice

It is important also to consider programming work that is explicitly designed to make more critical interventions in the social world and *respond* to social injustices. One example is *The McDonald's Videogame* (as written about by Bogost, 2007). In this game, players are put in charge of the McDonald's – arguably the world's most popular fast-food franchise – production environment. Here, players have to navigate their way through a series of inter-locking moral dilemmas around whether or not to engage in "questionable business prac-tices" (Bogost, 2007: 30) in the generation of profit. Player choices might include such things as feeding their cattle cheap animal by-products (as opposed to more expensive but safer animal feed), as well as whether or not to bribe health officers to turn a blind eye to when meat that has been diseased through feeding cattle in this way has made it into a restaurant and is affecting customers' health. What we can draw from this is that, as a piece of programming, *The McDonald's Videogame* draws players into thinking about the moral issues that surround the global fast-food industry (and global capitalism more generally), and the ultimate aim here is to make players critically aware of these business practices. Does it feel icky to feed cattle with by-products in ways that might result in dangerous public health-care issues? How are you to morally reconcile yourself with a choice to pay off a healthcare official so that they don't damage your in-game reputation when public health disasters arise from your profiteering? And overall, how does it feel to be in a position where your success – as measured by your profits in-game – is directly related to shady moral and ethical practice? *The McDonald's Videogame* brings to the fore these kinds of questions, by designing a game (i.e. a program) where people can explore these issues critically for themselves.

Another example of programming explicitly designed around issues of social justice is the (since retired) @DroptheIBot Twitter account. This Twitter account searched Twitter for users who had tweeted with the term "illegal immigrant", and produced automatic responses to those people with the following phrase: "People aren't illegal. Try saying 'undocumented immigrant' or 'unauthorized immigrant' instead" (BBC News, 2015). The aim here was to interject in (perhaps unknowingly) hateful speech online to help shift the conversation around to less stigmatising and more socially positive ways of thinking about immigration. @DroptheIBot ultimately contravened Twitter's terms and conditions and was banned from the platform – the account tweeted directly at users too frequently, and did not seek permission from other account owners before sending them automatic messages, both of which are grounds for blocking an account according to Twitter. Moreover, the users in receipt of @DroptheIBot's automatic tweet (which sought to "correct" the language used by the original tweeter) was not well received either – some users did not appreciate being told their language was offensive, and not everybody even recognised that the corrective tweet was the product of an automated account at all.[3] Nonetheless, perhaps this was (in a way) the goal of @DroptheIBot – to interrupt the usage of an offensive and stigmatising term ("illegal immigrant") by drawing attention to those who have used it, however unwelcome and uncomfortable that attention may be.

▬▬▬▬▬ Further reading ▬▬▬▬▬

Digital Inequality

There is a lot of great social science research on how the inequalities of the social world pervade and operate online and in software. The following resources will help you dig further into a range of relevant issues:

Broussard, M. (2018) *Artificial Unintelligence: How Computers Misunderstand the World.* Cambridge, MA: MIT Press.

---

[3]@DroptheIBot received numerous replies from confused and angry tweeters who were wondering why this strange account was watching what they were saying on Twitter and what right @DroptheIBot had to butt into their conversations.

Daniels, J. (2009) *Cyber Racism: White Supremacy Online and the New Attack on Civil Rights*. Lanham, MD: Rowman & Littlefield.

Hicks, M. (2017) *Programmed Inequality: How Britain Discarded Women Technologists and Lost its Edge in Computing*. Cambridge, MA: MIT Press.

Nakamura, L. and Chow-White, P. (eds) (2012) *Race after the Internet*. New York: Routledge.

Wachter-Boettcher, S. (2018) *Technically Wrong: Sexist Apps, Biased Algorithms, and Other Threats of Toxic Tech*. New York: W. W. Norton.

Whether we're talking about social injustice or social justice, all of these examples share a point – any programming activity we undertake implicates a social, political, ideological, moral and ethical position on the world. As social scientists who program, it's therefore our responsibility to use our skills to both highlight social injustice where we see it in code and build programs that can promote and contribute to social justice where we see a deficit of it.

2.2 Ethical Considerations of Programming-as-Social-Science

This brings us neatly along to research ethics as a paramount concern for us, though we're not actually going to dig into this too deeply yet. Suffice to say that if we're going to factor programming into social science research activity, we need to also take on board these critical ideas for ourselves, and be reflexively critical of our own practice. Some of the things that are covered in this book implicate (potential) ethical issues. For instance, in a later chapter we will be exploring how to go about using Python to grab various kinds of data from Twitter users – however, just because it is possible to get such data (inasmuch as Python lets us do this in ways which do not contravene the Twitter terms and conditions governing data usage), this does not mean we *should*. We have to consider in various ways the ethical propriety of gathering such data – for instance, we have to think about issues such as the consent of "participants" in our research to having their data collected in such a way, and how to preserve the anonymity of people when reproducing insights based on these data (which is especially

━━━━ Definitions ━━━━

Social Science Research Ethics

Research ethics is an area that addresses the moral integrity of the researcher and the work they undertake, in terms of "ensuring that the research process and a researcher's findings are trustworthy and valid" (Nagy Hesse-Biber and Leavy, 2011: 59). As Bryman (2012) notes, ethical issues arise at all points with a research process, right from the outset when choosing what to research to the very final stages of writing up a project. The idea of following ethical research conduct as you do your research is imperative in social science generally (and therefore also in social scientific work involving programming).

pertinent when the data are digital in origin and can therefore be located relatively easily via a search engine). Of course, ethical issues are not just limited to data collection via Twitter (or in fact data collection generally), and arise in a project from start to finish – this requires researchers to keep ethics as a constant consideration in their work.

However, it is equally important to note that though there are various professional bodies (e.g. the British Sociological Association and the Social Research Association) which have produced formalised ethical guidelines, it is above all important to consider ethics as a more specific matter that has to be fitted to the project a hand – ethical practice is not a set of tick-boxes that can be checked off and forgotten about, but a live process.

In that sense, this book will not even attempt to provide a set of guidelines to follow. Creating a set of guidelines to govern ethical practice around programming is likely to be a futile task. This is not least because a standardised set of ethical guidelines is impossible (and perhaps even undesirable) in general, but because Python adds a layer of complexity as a multi-purpose toolkit that we might expect to see being used in so many different ways that a single set of guidelines could never cover them all. However, it *is* nonetheless flagging up one over-riding rule at this point – that we absolutely *need* to think ethically, throughout the course of any programming task we're doing. As we have seen in this chapter, it is perfectly possible to construct code that is ethically problematic – even large companies like Google and Microsoft (which have money and labour to throw at such problems) get it wrong, as we've seen with the examples of the Translate algorithm and the Tay Twitter chatbot. However, as social scientists who might practise programming as a social science research method (PaSS) we are ideally placed to see and intercept and avoid these kinds of issues as well as call them out when we see them arise elsewhere in society.

================ **Further reading** ================

Professional Ethical Guidelines

There are several professional bodies that have produced general ethical guidelines that may be relevant to your work going forward. The following list is a selection of a few common sources:

American Sociological Association, *Code of Ethics*. Available at: http://www.asanet.org/code-ethics

Association of Internet Researchers, *Ethics*. Available at: https://aoir.org/ethics/

British Sociological Association, *Guidelines on Ethical Research*. Available at: https://www.britsoc.co.uk/ethics

Economic and Social Research Council, *Research Ethics*. Available at: https://esrc.ukri.org/funding/guidance-for-applicants/research-ethics/

In sum, although ethics must always be fitted to the specifics of every individual project (and, hence, no guidelines will ever completely cover any given individual project comprehensively), thinking ethically about programming should underpin anything we do with code if we want to code critically.

2●3 What Can/Should We Do with Python?

At this point we can start to consider the idea of critical coding and Programming-as-Social-Science in terms of the possibilities Python might offer us as social scientists trying to engage critically and meaningfully in the social world. What does having a critical skill with coding in Python afford us? As it stands, social scientists who do not have these skills but who want to engage in the digital/computational aspects of the social world say things like:

> software is difficult to understand because it is ephemeral. We do not see how software works, and instead we rely on the metaphor of software to construct our understanding of computation. (Guzman, 2017: 76-77)

Moreover, and taking building social media bots as just one example of the kinds of task to which Python programming might be applied, it is noted that the bot

> remains an evasive creature and an object of fantasies and rumours. Nobody knows for sure where it will turn up next, how it will figure in established social practices and even less in what way it may change them. The meaning of the socialbot is being invented in laboratories, appraised in the marketplace and construed in the mass media as we speak. (Gehl and Bakardjieva, 2017: 1)

In light of complaints like these, there is a *lot* we can do if we learn programming (and specifically, as social scientists, we learn to do programming critically). Both Guzman (2017) and Gehl and Bakardjieva (2017) have complaints that it is difficult to understand the computational stuff of the world – if we want to understand these things, unless we have some inside knowledge of them (e.g. we are able to understand them in code), we have to rely on clunky metaphors to talk about them, or we have to somehow make peace with the fact that social scientists can only reflect on technologies like bots from the outside (whereas it might be preferred for us to be more instrumental and directly engaged in their design, construction and implementation). Hence, learning programming brings us into closer contact with software and computing as increasingly ubiquitous elements of the social world, and allows us to open up a new range of topics and areas that have previously been (perhaps frustratingly) outside of our remit. For those of us who want to leverage software and computing as either the object or medium of our studies (or both), practising Programming-as-Social-Science could address precisely these issues.

To sum things up, and give a sense of how the rest of this book will proceed from here (i.e. how and why we will be learning to code in Python in this way), we might break down the value of having Python skills in two ways that roughly align with two interlocking practices – reading code and writing code:

1   Being able to code in Python will give us a better understanding of (and greater capacity to talk about) the processes by which social justice/injustice are "baked into" the world via software and computer technology. Given these skills, we will be able to make sensible accounts of all sorts of socially relevant technologies (e.g. algorithms, software, devices – literally *anything* computational!); rather than just focusing on the content that sits around these

technologies (e.g. the documentation, the inputs and outputs, the descriptions of them), we can begin to explore directly how the technologies work on a core level.

2   Being able to code in Python allows us to build software and computer technologies for ourselves, which can be applied to accounting for and understanding the social world as well intervening in and responding to social injustices. For instance, to kick back on the kinds of complaint made by Guzman (2017) and Gehl and Bakardjieva (2017) above, we can use our Python programming skills to do all sorts of things - build bots, collect new forms of data, look at that data in different ways, visualise and revisualise data, interact with people/research participants in novel ways, and so on. Being able to use Python to do our social scientific work extends our reach, and Python being a multi-purpose toolkit means the potential applications are literally endless in scope - those with creative critical coding skills will be ideally placed to produce innovative and robust social science going forward.

These two sides of the Python coin – reading code and writing code – inevitably go hand in hand, and no doubt they will feature closely alongside each other in whatever Programming-as-Social-Science project you turn your attention to. Both reading and writing Python code rely on an understanding of how programming works, coupled with an expertise in (critical) social science to contextualise that code in context, as it is being embedded in the world. Whatever stage you are at in your social science career, you will already be acquiring that expertise in critical thinking about social issues; by the end of this book, you'll also have an expertise in Python programming required to undertake PaSS.

Chapter summary

- This chapter aimed to build on the material in Chapter 1 to demonstrate why social scientists might specifically be interested in and get value from having Python programming skills. This approach - the blending of social science and programming skills - was characterised as programming-as-social-science.
- First, we reiterated the idea that code is written by *people* and exists *in context* in the social world - in short, coding is a social, political, ideological, moral and ethical issue.
- Second, we looked at how code fits with and fits into the social world - how it can be used to amplify and reinforce social injustice in some cases, and how it can be used to support and advocate social justice too.
- Third, we (briefly) considered ethics as a core issue of concern - if we are to be critical coders, we need to also be critical of our own coding practices, and though it is not possible to produce a set of tickbox guidelines to follow that ensure good ethical practice (given Python programming is such an open-ended activity), keeping ethics in mind will help us do this.
- Finally, we outlined the value of thinking about Programming-as-Social-Science in this way. In short, being able to read and write code can help us engage with the social world in new and exciting ways.

Summary of Part One

- In Part One, we've covered a lot of ground already, even before looking at any code! First, we explored some of the reasons why social scientists might be interested in learning computer programming, and why Python specifically is a good language for us to learn.
- We also introduced key concepts and terms around computer programming generally, as a working glossary that we can continue to build as we go.
- We then pointed the way towards Python being a tool for extending the reach of social science when it is integrated into our existing practices; this was done by pitching Python (and programming generally) as part of a wider interdisciplinary socio-technical assemblage of social science research methods.

  o This was supported by introducing two ways of thinking about social-scientifically oriented computer programs as "workflows", to help break down the process of computer programming to see it as an organised practice that we can get involved in.

- We then advanced the idea of Programming-as-Social-Science as a unique and valuable approach to thinking about how we might integrate computer programming into the things we do as social scientists.

  o This was done by considering the ways in which computer programming and software can impact on the social world in both positive and negative ways, and treating computer programming as (a) an area of human activity which has (b) a political, ideological, moral and ethical dimension.

PART TWO

Part Two contents

BASIC PYTHON GRAMMAR, SYNTAX AND CONCEPTS

Part Two objectives

- To support you in acquiring practical "hands-on" experience with Python, from installing the language to using it to complete tasks for yourself.
- To introduce you to a range of core concepts in Python, including: commenting; variables; mathematical operations and comparison/equality; flow control (and whitespace) with logical conditions; lists; tuples; dictionaries; strings; functions; loops; classes; installing and importing modules; timing your code; creating interfaces with inputs: and good commenting practice.
- To facilitate a practical engagement with Python in terms of reading and writing code for various purposes (i.e. to point towards the development of a "programming mindset" as a key outcome of the book which will be supported further in later chapters).

By this point we're armed with all this knowledge that helps us understand and contextualise Python programming as a research tool, and how it might fit into the social science research process more widely. Now we will start by learning how to read and write and work with the core concepts of Python.

To work your way through Part Two, you will need to use this book alongside working on Python scripts – how to do this will all be explained in detail throughout the following chapters, but, for now, suffice to say that you should set yourself up on a suitable computer, and work through the instructions, in order, as they are presented to you. Don't be tempted to skip through sections – the stuff covered in these chapters builds up iteratively, and you need to work from start to end of Part Two at least once. However, once you've done this, you might find it useful to return to individual sections for a refresher/reminder of specific Python methods or techniques.

Now, let's see some Python in action!

3

Setting Up to Start Coding

─────────── **Chapter objectives** ───────────

- Get Python installed on your computer.
- Be able to think about code not as a scary impenetrable mess of alien language, but as something that can be read, written and understood.

3.1 Getting Started with Python

The first step is to download and install Python on your computer. If you are using a university computer it may already have Python installed (or there may be an institutional software repository where you can download pre-approved packages including Python). But for those looking to install it on a personal device, it is free, and there is extensive information on how to do so via the official Python website (Python Software Foundation, 2019a). The latest release of Python 3 at the time of writing is version 3.6.3. – however, you should choose to download whatever the latest version is at the time you are reading. A link to download the latest version of Python 3 is provided on the front page of the Python website; furthermore, the latest version and earlier versions are archived and available to download from the Python downloads pages (Python Software Foundation, 2019b).

When you have selected which version you want to download, you will be presented with a page detailing changes and updates to Python available in this release, as well as a number of different files available to download – these are the installer packages for Python. Handily, for Windows and Mac users, Python is available for installation through an installer wizard, which drastically simplifies the installation process. Here, there are various options for installers (particularly for Windows), and you should download the one that matches your system requirements, using the information presented in the table on the website as a guide.

Linux users may find that Python is already installed as part of your particular operating system/distribution. However, if it is not, you will have to install it from the source code, which is listed as a "source release" operating system option. If you are doing this, you may have to search out information relating to installing Python from the source code that relates to your specific Linux distribution.

As noted, the installer packages (the two options being "executable" and "web-based" – either is good here) are the simplest way to install Python. These installers will walk you through the installation of Python in much the same way as installer packages for *any* software – it's mainly just a case of checking the information you are presented with and clicking OK or Next appropriately. This will install Python to your computer.

When Python is installed, you have the language on your computer, as well as some extra pieces of software that will help you use (i.e. read and write) that language – namely, IDLE. As discussed above, IDLE is an Integrated Development Environment: it actually stands for "Integrated Development and Learning Environment", which makes it perfect for us here. IDLE is a tool for helping us write code. As noted above (Section 1.1), there *are* other IDEs and you may be interested to explore these and see what functions they offer that you might benefit from. But for simplicity's sake, I will be demonstrating Python coding through IDLE, and you might find it helpful to stick with me on IDLE as you're learning so that everything I show you looks the same on your screen.

If you use a Linux distribution, you may not have IDLE. However, you will still be able to use Python as a shell in the Linux terminal simply by typing `python3`. You will also be able to do larger scripting tasks using any text editor (which your Linux distribution may have come with) – popular (free) editors for Linux include geany and gedit. You may also be able to find more sophisticated IDEs to use for this purpose, though in principle a text editor can be fine. Any scripts you use as part of this book and that you write yourself will then have to be executed through the terminal too (by typing `python3`, followed by a space, followed by the directory location of your script). So, if you are working with a Linux operating system, simply use your terminal for shell tasks, and wherever this textbook mentions IDLE, substitute that for the text editor of your choice.

The Python shell

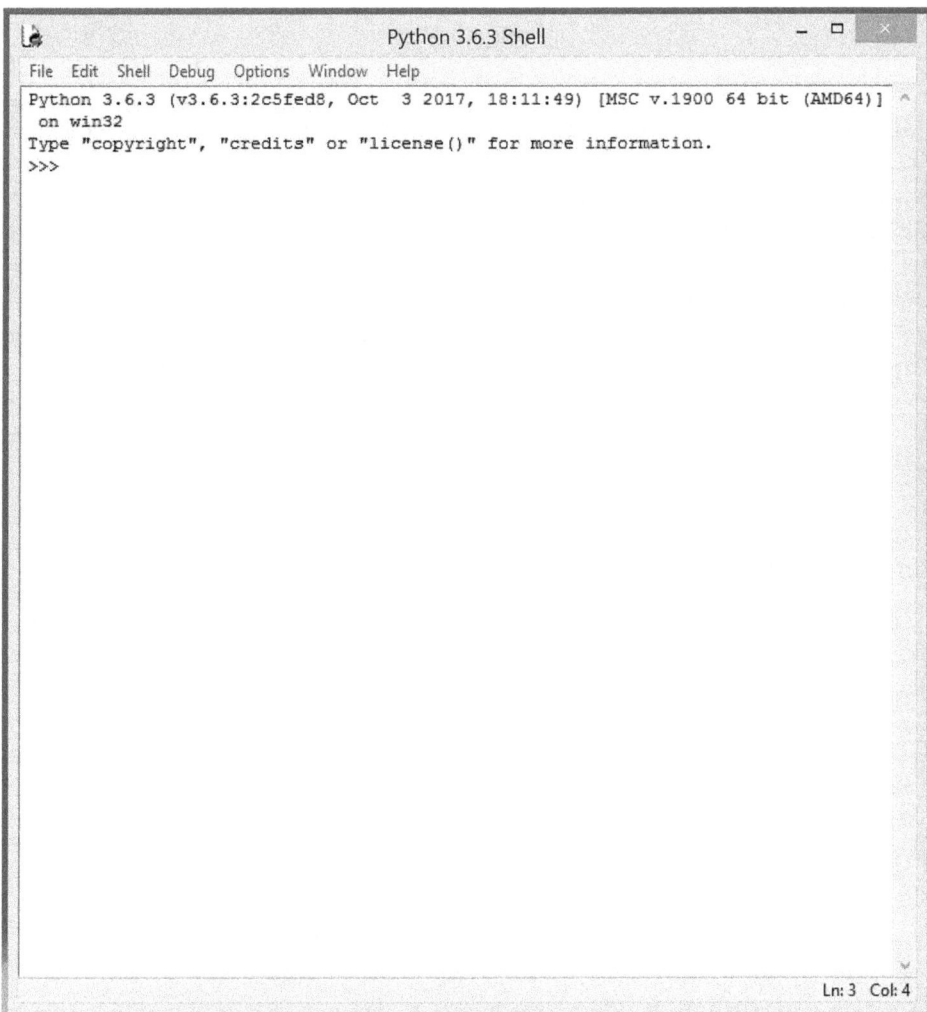

Figure 3.1 The Python shell

IDLE is a program that you can open on your computer – it will be listed in your list of installed programs as something like "IDLE (Python 3.6 64-bit)". Open it. You should see something like the screen in Figure 3.1. This is the Python shell – see Section 1.1 for further details on what a shell is. We can use this to do some coding right now. Note that the way I've typed out the "Hello World!" command below is important. I have used three "angled brackets"/"greater than" signs (i.e. >>>) to indicate that the following command is to be typed into the shell – in Figure 3. 1 you'll see that there are >>> denoting where you would type out some code. This means you *shouldn't* actually type the >>> bit yourself – it is already there in the shell. So, whenever you see >>> you should recognise that this means you are going to be typing stuff into the shell. By contrast, where >>> is not used, this means that you will be working in or with a Python script. Now, type the following into the shell:

```
>>> print("Hello World!")
```

Then press return. You should see the words Hello World! printed out – so far so good! But, as noted in Section 1.1, programming in the shell is not really for big tasks – it is useful for testing new things and running little commands (as we have done here), but if we want to build bigger things we will eventually want to store them in scripts. So it's a good idea to get familiar with this early on.

From the Python shell menu, select `File` then `New File`. This will bring up the "Editor window", which at this point consists of a blank page – an empty script for you to fill with code. In the first instance, we will be using both the shell and scripting sides of IDLE (so be sure that you know the difference between the two, and be sure that you are working in the right one for any given task). But as we start to build more complex things, we'll find ourselves working more exclusively with scripts.

Working through this book

The chapters in this part of the book will require you to download and play around with a series of `.py` script files. All of these files can be found at https://study.sagepub.com/brooker. They will also be set within the chapters of this book (for reference), but it is far easier for you to work with them on the computer in the way I've suggested. Once you have downloaded the files you will (eventually) need to open them in the Editor window of IDLE – this is done by right-clicking the file and selecting the `Edit with IDLE` option. Note that if you just double-click the file icon, it will not open in the Editor window; it will just run the program and whatever is in this script. This is not going to be a problem for any of the scripts developed for this book, since they do not contain anything harmful. But first of all you should be wary of freely running scripts from locations you might not trust. Second, remembering to open Python scripts for editing with the right-click method will hopefully prevent against confusion later on.

You will also be asked to work with these downloaded scripts in various ways, which will mean running those scripts and subsequently using them through the Python shell. Again, this will be explained as we proceed through the sections, but there are two important general notes to bear in mind.

First, you should *always* type out any code or commands rather than copy and paste them from this book (if you have a digital copy) or from elsewhere. Though it is of course possible to copy and paste code in the same way as digitised text, for learning purposes this is a bad idea. Copying and pasting code that I or others have written means that *you're* not really learning how to code; you're learning how *someone else* codes, and you're learning how to copy and paste. Neither of those things count as learning to code for yourself. So, even though it may seem laborious and more time-consuming than necessary, you should always type out the instructions and commands that this book instructs you to do, for yourself. This will help you get a first-hand feel for the act of coding as a practical exercise – you might make errors along the way, but that's exactly the point; in doing so, you'll be figuring out best practice for coding, paying attention to the fine detail of the code, making/spotting and addressing errors – in short, you'll be figuring out how to code for yourself.

Second, you should make sure to do *all* the steps you are instructed to do, in full – even if they seem elementary or you can predict what the outcome will be. Again, it is enormously important to pay attention to the detail here, and the only way to do that is to encounter it first-hand. As anyone who has done an undergraduate social science dissertation will know, there is a difference between reading about social science and doing it for yourself – that applies here too. You cannot fully learn coding just by reading about it. You have to *do* it. And then you have to *practise* it. And that means actually getting your hands on the keyboard and doing the work.

The core language of Python is premised on a relatively small set of concepts, each of which we will deal with in turn. Even though they might seem very basic and simple and limited in their use, they in fact form the basis for any and all things built with Python. So we will go through these core concepts one by one (talking a little about their relevance to social science along the way), and eventually (in Part Three), we'll see how they can be creatively deployed as part of bigger tasks like data collection, web scraping, visualising data with graphs, and so on.

3.2   Commenting

Commenting is how you leave notes and labels in a script, to help readers and yourself keep track of what a program is for and what it's doing. Though it might seem strange to learn how to code by first learning how to label code (what is there to label if we don't yet know any code?), this is done with good reason. Chiefly, the scripts you will be using to learn about the language of Python will *all* involve comments that I have left that will tell you more about what the script is, and what you are supposed to do with it. Hence, you need to be able to identify which bits are comments, and what comments are supposed to do.

First, open the script associated with Section 3.2 (3_2_Commenting.py) in the Editor window. This gives a demonstration of two different ways to do commenting – the first using two sets of three speech marks, the second using the hash symbol. Though both may be colour-coded differently, these different ways of commenting text within a script do the same job. And the job of commenting is to provide extra information and detail about code.

Even though comments do not form a functional part of any code (which is to say, the code will run exactly the same whether the comments are there or not), comments are absolutely invaluable. Comments can help readers make sense of your code, but they can also help *you* make sense of your code. Imagine, once you're an expert coder, if you came across a script you wrote years ago that had thousands of lines of code in it. Will you immediately remember the full detail of what each and every line does (unlikely), or are you going to need pointing in the right direction and reminding (likely)? Even if it's your code and you're an expert coder, it can be difficult to remember and/or understand code that you wrote years ago, or that was written by somebody else. Hence, comments can serve as useful labels, descriptions and reminders for what individual bits of code do and how they connect with other bits of code. This gets increasingly useful as your scripts get more complex, or if you share your code with others. And this is the reason why commenting is perhaps the single key difference between good and bad code – a piece of code itself might be elegant and streamlined, but if it is not commented properly, it is unreadable and unusable.

```
1   """
2   Programming with Python for Social Science
3   Phillip Brooker
4
5   3. 2. COMMENTING
6   """
7
8   #In this script you can see two types of comment. Some comments, like those
9   #at the top of this page, are denoted by the use of three speech marks.
10  #There, you can see that there are three speech marks to 'open' the comment,
11  #then there is the comment itself, and then three speech marks to 'close' the
12  #comment. Whatever is between the two sets of speech marks is a comment.
13
14  #However, you can also see that comments can be denoted by putting a hash at
15  #the start of the comment - this is what you can see in this line for instance.
```

We will explore good (and bad) commenting practices in more detail in Section 8.3, but for now, suffice to say that wherever you see comments in the scripts you will look at in Part Two, pay attention to what they tell you, and what they may ask you to do.

Chapter summary

- This chapter has aimed, first and foremost, to get a working version of Python installed on your computer.
- From there, we've looked at the Python shell, and have learned how to open scripts and work with them. This is something that you'll be doing as part of your learning throughout the book.
- We have also explored commenting as a core programming practice, in terms of what comments look like in Python code, and what purposes they serve for programmers.

4

Core Concepts/Objects

▬▬▬▬ Chapter objectives ▬▬▬▬

- Take a first step in understanding programming in Python as being about handling various types of objects (such as "variables").
- Get some practice working with simple objects in Python.
- Be able to think about ways of navigating around objects in Python code using flow control (i.e. conditional statements).

4●1 Variables

There are three basic data types in Python, which we can store in variables – there are more things that we can store in variables too, but for now, we will concentrate on *integers*, *floats* and *strings*.

Open the script associated with Section 4.1. called 4_1_1_VariableTypes.py. In this script, you'll see lots of things going on, but let's take it step by step. In the IDLE Editor window, if you click on any code, you'll see at the bottom right-hand corner of the screen that IDLE gives a value for Ln: and Col: – these are line numbers and columns, respectively. Think of line numbers as rows in a spreadsheet, and columns (predictably) as columns in a spreadsheet. If you are not using IDLE, it will still be very helpful for you to be able to refer to line numbers in your code as you learn. Most text editors will provide this functionality in some way, and it is advisable that you enable line numbers so you can quickly refer to them when they are mentioned.

So, let's first look at line 9 in this script – this is how an integer is declared in Python.

```
1    """
2    Programming with Python for Social Science
3    Phillip Brooker
4
5    4. 1. 1. DATA TYPES
6    """
7
8    #an integer is a "whole number" (i.e. one with no decimal point)
9    my_integer = 12
10
11   #a float is a numerical value with a decimal point
12   my_float = 12.1
13
14   #a string is text
15   my_string = "This is my string."
16
17   #You can check the data type of variables using the "type" method
18   type(my_string)
19
```

```
20    """
21    QUESTION 1: What type of variables do you think the following five are? DON'T use
22    type() until you've had a guess.
23    """
24
25    var1 = "14"
26
27    var2 = 14 + 14
28
29    var3 = 14 + 14.2
30
31    var4 = "14 + 14.2"
32
33    var5 = 14.2 - 0.2
34
35    #There are WAY more variable types than these - integers, floats and strings
36    #are the three data types Python uses, but variables don't have to be used to
37    #store just data types - they can store all sorts of more complex data
38    #structures (i.e. things that collect bits of data together) like lists or
39    #dictionaries. But that's for later!
40
41    my_list = [var1, var2, var3, var4, var5]
42    my_dict = {"First Variable": var1, "Second Variable": var2, "Third Variable":
      var3, "Fourth Variable": var4, "Fifth Variable": var5}
43
44    """
45    QUESTION 2: What do you think you will see if you use type() on my_list and
46    my_dict? Have a guess and see if you're right.
47    """
```

In line 9, we can see that we are declaring a variable (my_integer) by giving it a value of 12, which is an integer, using the = sign. We can also see in line 12 how to declare a variable and give it a value which is a float (in this case 12.1). And on line 15, we declare another variable and give it a value which is a string ("This is my string."). We can also see, on line 18, how to check a variable to see what type it is. Using this knowledge, run the script (i.e. press F5, or go to the IDLE editor Run menu and click on Run module), and see if you can answer Question 1, first having a guess for yourself, then using type() to check your answers.

Did you guess the answers correctly? Were your predictions confirmed by checking each of the five variables with type()? Let's explain these answers in a little more detail for each variable:

- var1 is a string. Though its value may *look* like a number (14), you should see that it's enclosed in speech marks. Hence, Python is being told to read in the value *not* as an integer, but as a string. The importance of this is that Python now knows to treat the value given as text rather than as a number - this is something you will see cropping up all over the place as we get deeper into Python. Once you have run the script, you can check this in Python by typing the variable name and pressing return - this will return the value that you have written to the variable in question. And now you can see the result, you can check the variable type by typing type(var1), which will return the variable type for `var1` (in this case, `'str'`, which means string). Both of these commands are shown in the box below:

```
>>> var1
'14'
>>> type(var1)
<class 'str'>
```

- var2 is an integer. You can see that the value given is not a single number, but a sum (`14 + 14`). However, the *result* of the sum is an integer, hence what is written to the variable `var2` is an integer value of `28` (which, when checked with the `type()` command, will show as `<class 'int'>`, meaning integer). Try checking the value and type of var2 with the commands below:

```
>>> var2
28
>>> type(var2)
<class 'int'>
```

- var3 is a float. As with `var2`, the actual value being written to the variable is the result of a sum. However, unlike `var2`, this sum uses a decimal point (`14 + 14.2`), which results in a float number rather than an integer (`28.2`). Adding the decimal number turns the type from an integer to a float. Hence, the result that is written to var3 is a float (which, when checked with the `type()` command, will show as `<class 'float'>`, meaning float). Try checking the value and type of var3 with the commands below:

```
>>> var3
28.2
>>> type(var3)
<class 'float'>
```

- var4 is a string. You should have identified that though we're doing a similar thing as in when we declared a value for `var3`, what we are giving as a value for var4 is enclosed in speech marks. This means that Python will not treat the value of this variable numerically (i.e. it won't calculate the result), but will treat the value as a piece of text. Hence, the result that is written to var4 is a string (which, when checked with the `type()` command, will show as <class 'str'>, meaning string). Try checking the value and type of var4 with the commands below:

```
>>> var4
'14 + 14.2'
>>> type(var4)
<class 'str'>
```

- var5 is a float. This is interesting - for var3 we added a decimal point to an integer value and that turned the whole variable into a float type. This time, we're subtracting a decimal point from a number (i.e. with the sum 14.2 - 0.2, which would expect to result in 14, an integer). However, when you type the commands below, you can see that calling the result for var5 gives you 14.0 - there is a decimal point, so this is a float (which, when checked with the type() command, will show as <class 'float'>).

```
>>> var5
14.0
>>> type(var5)
<class 'float'>
```

Though we can already see a few ways of turning variables of one type into another (i.e. if we add speech marks to an integer or float, it becomes a string; if we add a decimal value to an integer, it becomes a float, etc.), we will look at more methods of doing this later in the chapter.

As can be seen in the code above, variables can be assigned values of lots of types, beyond these three raw data types (i.e. integers, floats and strings). We will learn more about different things (including lists and dictionaries) that we can assign to variables in later chapters. But for now, try guessing the answers to Question 2 and using type() in the shell to confirm your answers as follows:

```
>>> type(my_list)
<class 'list'>
>>> type(my_dict)
<class 'dict'>
```

So, since we have assigned a list to the variable my_list and a dictionary to the variable my_dict, when we use the type() command to check the data types, the results it gives confirm exactly that. We will learn more about what lists and dictionaries *are* and what they *do* in later chapters, but suffice to say for now that there are three basic data types – integers, floats and strings – plus other objects in Python (such as lists and dictionaries) that can be assigned to any variable you declare. And, moreover, you can check the type of any variable using the `type()` command.

Running scripts, using commands, and passing arguments around

At this point, it's also worth reflecting on what we did in terms of *how* we worked with Python code, so that we can apply these skills in future chapters. So, first of all, you opened up a script in the Editor window, then ran (i.e. executed) that script in the shell. This enabled you to *work with* that program in the shell – all the variables that were assigned in the script became usable to you in the shell. This is important – if you *hadn't* run the script, variables like var1 wouldn't have been declared and wouldn't have been assigned values. From there, you also learned how to use a command in the shell, on a script that you have executed – in our example above, we checked the data types of different variables by typing `type(my_integer)` and so on. Here, we had a command called `type()`, and we passed that command an "argument" which was the name of a variable (i.e. `my_integer`). Applying this command to different variables gave us different results. This concept of commands and arguments is very useful to us too – it allows us to work with and develop the code in our scripts, to check things are as we expect, and to learn more about coding as we go. These are skills that we will be applying both through this chapter and throughout the book generally (and as such, there's no need for me to tell you how to do this in the same level of detail throughout – we can tick this off as something you've learned about coding already!).

Playing around with variables

OK, so now let's do something fancier with variables and variable types – open and run the script called `4_1_2_PlayingAroundWithVariables.py`:

```
1    """
2    Programming with Python for Social Science
3    Phillip Brooker
4
5    4. 1. 2. PLAYING AROUND WITH VARIABLES
6    """
7
8    #Variables can be reassigned and overwritten:
9    #Can you guess the value of new_var?
10   original_var = 30
11   new_var = original_var + 20
12
13   #Can you guess the value of original_var2?
14   original_var2 = 10
15   original_var2 = original_var2 + 10
```

```
16
17    #Can you guess what string1 will contain?
18    string1 = "This is the first part of the string."
19    #Notice the space at the beginning of the reassigned string1 below: why is that
20    #there?
21    string1 = string1 + " This is the second part of the string."
22
23    #Try adding these two variables together, and explain what happens.
24    first_bit = 14
25    second_bit = "14"
26
27    """
28    We can also convert variable types to different variable types, as follows:
29    """
30    #To 'stringify' something, we can use str(VARIABLE). Below, I'll declare a
31    #variable which is an integer, then I'll use str(VARIABLE) to write the
32    #'stringified' version to a new variable.
33    my_integer_variable = 30
34    my_stringified_variable = str(my_integer_variable)
35
36    #To 'integerify' something, we can use int(VARIABLE). Below, I'll declare a
37    #variable which is a number written out as a string, then I'll use
38    #int(VARIABLE) to write the 'integerified' version to a new variable.
39    my_string_variable = "30"
40    my_integerified_variable = int(my_string_variable)
41
42    #To 'floatify' an integer, we can use float(VARIABLE). Below, I'll declare an
43    #integer variable, then I'll use float(VARIABLE) to write the 'floatified'
44    #version to a new variable. Try this for yourself in the shell.
45    my_integer_variable = 30
46    my_floatified_variable = float(my_integer_variable)
47
48    #NOTE: one way to convert an integer to a float is to just add 0.0 to it, as
49    #you can see below. Try this out in the shell:
50    my_integer_variable = 30
51    my_floatified_variable = my_integer_variable + 0.0
52    type(my_floatified_variable)
53    #Because a float is just an integer with a decimal (i.e. 'floating') point, all
54    #we have to do to 'floatify' an integer is give it a decimal, even if that
55    #decimal has no numerical value. However, can you see a problem with this?
56    #What if you want to 'floatify' a string by adding 0.0 to it? It makes no sense
57    #to add a decimal point to a string in this way, and that will cause an error.
58    #Try this in the shell: >>> my_string_variable = "30" + 0.0
59    #Now try this: >>> float(my_string_variable)
60    #Hence, using float(VARIABLE) is a better way to handle variable type
61    #conversions as a general rule.
```

Given what you know about variables, variable types, and how to work with commands and arguments, you should be able to follow what this script is doing, and play around with these variables yourself. Follow the instructions in the comments: see if you can predict what is happening in the variables, then check them by calling the variables to see what really results (i.e. type the variable name into the shell to return the result).

The block of code starting at line 8 outlines how you can use variable names in place of their results – think of this like the algebra you learned at school, where letters can stand in the place of numbers (e.g. $a = 8$). In Python, however, we don't just use variable names to stand in for numbers, we can use them in place of any object (e.g. integers, floats, strings, lists, dictionaries).

The block of code starting at line 13 shows us how to overwrite variables with new values. So, we can see that original_var2 is first assigned a value of 10 but then we overwrite that by declaring original_var2 as having a new value of original_var2 + 10. Interestingly, you should have spotted that we have used the first value of original_var2 as part of the computation of the new result – effectively, we are telling Python to take the original value of original_var2, add 10 to it, then store that back in original_var2. This is useful since we can use this as a way to generate and update information without having to create a brand-new variable to store it in every time.

The block of code starting in line 17 shows this process of overwriting a variable in action with regard to string data – the same thing applies here; a string that is originally stored in string1 is then overwritten by the string plus an extra string (and you can see the results if you call string1 in the shell).

An error message!

The block of code starting in line 23 asks you to add two variables (first_bit and second_bit) together – you can do this with the + sign (though we will go through mathematical operations in more detail in later sections). You should see that what results is an error message that looks like this:

```
1    Traceback (most recent call last):
2      File "<pyshell#2>", line 1, in <module>
3        first_bit + second_bit
4    TypeError: unsupported operand type(s) for +: 'int' and 'str'
```

Let's unpack what this means. First, Python is telling us where the error is occurring – it occurs in <pyshell#2> (which we can infer means something we have done in the shell). We also have details of exactly what caused the error: in line 1 in the module, we typed first_bit + second_bit, and this is what went wrong. Moreover, we can also see details of the nature of the error (i.e. *why* it went wrong) – Python tells us that what we have done has caused a TypeError, which is described as unsupported operand type(s) for +: 'int' and 'str'. So, we can see that the operator we have used (the plus sign) doesn't work as a way of "adding" integers to strings. And we can perhaps see why this is the case – it's nonsense to ask Python to add a number to some text; what kind of result would that even be? Hence the error message.

This script also demonstrates (from line 27 onwards) various commands for converting integer types. Work through the examples, try to predict what the types of each variable are, and check your working with `type()`.

Again, let's reflect on what we've learned here, aside from getting some practice working with variables of different types in different ways. First, we saw an error message, and figured out what it was telling us. This is massively useful when you start writing your own code. Inevitably, errors will happen – that's just part and parcel of the process – but it's useful to be able to locate them, understand why they happened, and use that knowledge as a way to figure out how to address them. In a general sense, being able to read, understand and use error messages to locate and figure out how to solve coding problems is an enormously valuable skill, so it's good to start doing this really early on. Second, we saw in the code block starting at line 48 that there is more than one way to do the job of floatifying a variable (depending on what type of variable it is). Though we can turn integers into floats by adding an empty decimal point (i.e. a value of 0.0), we can't do this with strings – for strings, we have to use `float()`. What you can see from this is that there is not necessarily one best way of doing anything in Python, and creative thinking can be required to solve the problems you come across – which is all part of the fun!

Variables in action

Variables are a core aspect of Python programming, and can be used in lots of different ways. This is because variables can be assigned to be lots of different things: individual numerical values, calculations based on other variables, massive collections of data (e.g. lists or dictionaries, which you will learn about later in this book), and more. Here are some examples of what you might use variables to do:

Storing results. Suppose you want to retrieve some information from some census survey data (which we will think about in the next section on comparisons and equality); you are specifying some criteria for selecting bits of data you are interested in from the master dataset. Perhaps you want to look at employment data for all male respondents aged 18–25. You can tell Python that you want to store this selection of data in a new variable – this new variable now contains all the data you're interested in for your project!

Structuring a program. Variables are also very useful as placeholders in programs, where you know you will need to store some information somewhere, but you haven't yet generated that information. For instance, suppose you want to do some web scraping – perhaps you want to look at the comments that people leave on a particular online newspaper article as a study of media representations of politics, and you're scraping new comments at the end of every day. So, you're expecting some data at a point in the future, but for now, you just want to establish a place to put those data when they arrive. One way of doing this in Python is to create a variable which holds an empty list (you will learn about lists later in the book), into which the data can be dumped when your program has scraped them. In this way, you can build and test the rest of your web-scraping program without worrying about having any real data yet – it's a great help when it comes to thinking about how to structure a particular programming task!

Saving program states. If you have a fairly complex program with lots of stuff going on, you can use variables to keep a track of what has happened (i.e. if a function has been run once, you can switch `function_tracking_variable` from 0 to 1 – the narrative would be, "Has this thing happened? If no, make it happen. If yes, don't do it again, move on to the next thing."). So variables are not just about data, but can be used in other contexts too – here, as markers of states in a program, but the possibilities are limitless.

4 ● 2 Mathematical Operations and Comparison/Equality

The previous section gave a comprehensive walkthrough on the topic of variables and their types (as well as introducing you to other concepts like passing arguments using variable names and so on). This was done so that you could see, as clearly as possible, what you need to do in order to work your way through this book and its associated materials. From here, we don't need to give the same amount of detail. In fact, it is better for your learning if you spend time working through the code examples and answering questions for yourself, using the materials in this book as a support to introduce you to concepts that you can explore through your own coding.

Mathematical operations

Though we don't necessarily all want to do quantitative work with Python (and we'll explore the possibility for qualitative applications later in the book), we will still need to be able to use numbers in various ways in our code – the reasons why will become more apparent as we get into more complex programming. But for now, run the script titled `4_2_1_MathematicalOperations.py`, have a look at what it says, and let's try out some basic mathematical operations:

```
1    """
2    Programming with Python for Social Science
3    Phillip Brooker
4
5    4. 2. 1. MATHEMATICAL OPERATIONS AND COMPARING THINGS
6    """
7
8    #Even if we don't want to do quantitative work with Python, we still need
9    #to know about common mathematical operations - you will see examples of
10   #how and why in later sections. But for now, it's worth familiarising
11   #ourselves with these common operations.
12
13   """
14   + is add
15   - is subtract
16   * is multiply
17   / is divide
```

```
18    ** is 'to the power of'
19    """
20
21    #So now, why not try out a few of these in the shell.
```

Note that running this script wasn't strictly necessary here – you might have spotted that everything in the script is a comment, so there is no functional code that actually runs. But still, good to stick with the format of opening and running scripts so that we can work in the shell, since that's what we'll be doing throughout Part Two.

So now, let's try out a few mathematical operations in the shell:

```
>>> 6 + 3
9
>>> 6 - 3
3
>>> 6 * 3
18
>>> 6 / 3
2.0
>>> 6 ** 3
216
```

One interesting thing to note is that even though we might expect the division performed above to result in an integer (2), it comes out a float (2.0). If we absolutely needed to have a division come out as an integer, there are a few ways we could do it:

```
>>> int(6 / 3)
2
>>> 6 // 3
2
```

In the first way of expressing the sum, we request Python to give us the result of 6 / 3 as an integer-type variable. In the second way of expressing the sum, we use a double slash (//) to give us the "floor division" of the sum (which is just another way of asking Python to give us an integer value when we do a division). We have to be careful here, however; what if our division *should* result in a float (i.e. a non-integer number), but we try to force it into an integer? For instance, if we input 8 / 3, we get a result 2.6666666666666665 (which is correct to 16 decimal places). However, if we input int(8 / 3) Python gives us a result 2 – it doesn't round up to 3 as we might assume, but simply scrapes off anything after the decimal point.

Comparing things

Now let's run the file 4_2_2_ComparingThings.py and work through the concepts of comparison and equality in Python:

```
1    """
2    Programming with Python for Social Science
3    Phillip Brooker
4
5    4. 2. 2. COMPARING THINGS
6    """
7
8    #It often helps for us to be able to compare things in Python, to see if a
9    #variable matches some criteria that we establish, etc (see the later section
10   #on social science applications for more detail). This becomes especially
11   #powerful when we combine it with things like IF, ELIF and ELSE statements
12   #(which we will do later), but for now, here are a list of ways in which
13   #we can compare things in Python. I have declared three variables below -
14   #try typing the comparisons I've listed into the Python shell and see what
15   #happens.
16
17   a = 2
18   b = 3
19   c = 4
20
21   a == b #The double-equals signifies an "is the same as" comparison.
22   a != b #This signifies a "not the same as" comparison
23
24   b > a #"is greater than"
25   b >= a #"is greater than or equal to"
26
27   b < a #"is less than"
28   b <= a #"is less than or equal to"
29
30   c % a #This is called the "modulo", which effectively means the remainder.
31           #So here, the value that will be given when you type this into the Python
32           #shell will be the remainder that is left over when c is divided by a. The
33           #modulo is more of a calculation than a comparator, but it's mainly
34           #only relevant to us as a way of comparing things.
35
36
37   #QUESTION: You can also do calculations within comparisons. Can you guess what
38   #will result in the following cases? Have a guess, then type them into the
39   #Python shell to check.
40
41   a+1 == b
42
```

```
43    c-1 >= b
44
45    c/4 > a
46
47    a*2 == c
48
49    c % a == 0
```

It'll be good to note at this point that though the modulo operator/comparator might not immediately come across as having much use, it can come in handy in various ways as we start to build more complicated programs. So, it's worth bearing in mind going forward.

The results of your calculation comparisons are listed below – did you find any surprising? If so, try thinking through these comparison again, paying close attention to both the value of the variables you're working with and the operations you're performing.

```
>>> a+1 == b
True
>>> c-1 >= b
True
>>> c/4 > a
False
>>> a*2 == c
True
>>> c % a == 0
True
```

You can see that what results here is not a numerical value – that's a key difference between performing a calculation (where a numerical value is an appropriate answer) and evaluating the equality of two statements (where a `True` or `False` answer makes sense). The idea that statements can be True or False in programming is called "Boolean logic". This crops up across Python programming in lots of different ways (and we will see more about this in later sections), but for now, suffice to say that checking whether or not certain statements/expressions are true or false can be a helpful thing to do.

We can also compare string information. This is useful for things like retrieving text data from a file. In the shell, declare the variable `string1` as below, then try out the following comparisons and see what results:

```
>>> string1 = "Twitter_username"
>>> "Twitter_username" == string1
True
>>> string1 + " plus a tweet." == "Twitter_username plus a tweet."
```

(Continued)

```
True
>>> string1 == "Twitter_username plus a tweet." - " plus a tweet."
Traceback (most recent call last):
  File "<pyshell#10>", line 1, in <module>
    string1 == "Twitter_username plus a tweet." - " plus a tweet."
TypeError: unsupported operand type(s) for -: 'str' and 'str'
```

This last comparison threw up an error – can you see why? Strings can't be handled with the same range of arithmetical operations as integers/floats. It doesn't make sense to subtract an element of a string from another string in the same way as we do with numbers.

Comparison and equality in action

Comparing values and identities of Python objects is fundamental to programming in Python, and has lots of applications. As you begin to build your own code and do tasks with Python, you'll find yourself constantly returning to these ideas, in many different ways and for many different purposes. Below are just two examples (though the possibilities really are endless and very much open to creative thinking):

Information retrieval. Suppose you have some data stored in a text file – a table of Twitter data which features tweets, the usernames of the people tweeting, and time-stamps (i.e. times and dates the tweet was posted). You can use a comparison to identify (and then work with) all tweets which contain a specified username; for example, by checking if a username matches your criteria, you can tell Python to store that username's tweet in a separate dataset to play with later. You can also build on this in many ways – for instance, if you count all the times a particular username has posted (which you will learn how to do in later sections using a "list method"), you could then use a comparator to identify and work with all the usernames which have produced more than a specified number of tweets so that you're accessing the "most vocal" users in your dataset.

Sorting data (and finding null fields). You can also use comparators to sort data in different ways. Suppose you have some census survey data, but some respondents have not filled out all of the questions – perhaps some people chose not to answer a question on their gender. If you want to explore gender differences in (for instance) people's employment and earnings, you would need to first be sure of their gender – you might find it tricky to run significant statistical models on the survey results where respondents did not provide details of their gender. So, using a comparator, you could identify and work with all the survey respondents who have provided gender data (gender_data != None).

4●3 Flow Control (and Whitespace)

Now we know how to compare things, we can apply this in more complicated code structures, using IF/ELIF/ELSE and AND/OR statements to control how our code flows according to logical conditions. First we'll talk about these concepts in the abstract, and then we'll open up and work with a code file where these concepts are demonstrated in action.

Before we start, however, we should note that when you run a script in Python, the language carries out each command line by line from top (line 1) to bottom (the end of the script). Hence, when you're constructing conditional logic in your code with IF/ELIF/ELSE and AND/OR statements, you need to consider the order in which you place your conditions – this is something we'll explore in further detail with regard to the example given below.

Conditional logic in Python

IF/ELIF/ELSE. We can use an IF statement to get Python to apply sections of code based on conditions we establish, and an ELSE statement to apply a section of code if the IF statement doesn't apply – this is called "conditional logic". For instance, we might use IF/ELSE to build code along the lines of "if a certain condition is satisfied, do something; if not, do something else". ELIF stands for "else if" – this is a clause we can use to introduce multiple IF statements into one section of code. So, while IF and ELIF allow you to establish specific conditions that must be satisfied, the ELSE statement is a coverall that catches any other cases that *aren't* satisfied by your IF/ELIF clauses.

What if we don't want to do *anything* for cases that don't match our IF condition (i.e. what if we don't care what happens in the ELSE bit)? There are two things we can do. We can just have the IF on its own without the ELSE – in this case, Python will assume that you want nothing to happen for cases that don't satisfy the IF condition. Or we could use pass with our ELSE condition to say that "IF the condition is satisfied, do something; ELSE, pass on by and do nothing". Keep this in mind, because you will see it in later sections. Both ways of doing things produce the same result. However, it is perhaps useful to think about using pass since it encourages you to think "well, what *would* count as not having satisfied the IF clause?". Tying up these kinds of loose ends and being complete is a really helpful way of building your programming skills – you can take shortcuts when you've been programming long enough, but while you're learning it's best to write things out with completeness in mind, and to make your code as readable as possible. So, long story short – use pass!

AND/OR. There are also other types of logical operators Python recognises; AND/OR can be used as a way of connecting statements together. Used in combination with IF/ELIF/ELSE, you can construct code in such ways as "if a certain condition is satisfied and another condition is as well, do one thing; if only one of those conditions is satisfied, do something else".

Whitespace/nesting statements. Whitespace just means literally the space on the screen that is white (i.e. there is no code written in it). For instance, you will see in the code example below that some lines begin with a tab or four spaces. By default, pressing the tab key in Python gives you a space equivalent to pressing the space bar four times. This can be changed in IDLE if you like, but for standardisation and simplicity, it's best to use tabs (rather than four spaces with the space bar) and keep Python's default settings. Whitespace is *very* important in Python, as a way of ensuring that sections of code are connected to (or nested within) others. This can be seen in the code excerpt below – for instance, line 17 is an IF statement that begins at the start of the line, but line 18 (a print statement) is "tabbed in"/indented. Throughout this code example, all IF/ELIF/ELSE lines are placed at the start of the line, whereas the lines underneath them (the ones that carry out the instructions for when those clauses are triggered) are "tabbed in"/indented. This is called *nesting* – you connect a line of code to something like an IF statement by first using a colon (:) at the end of the initial line (here, the line containing the IF/ELIF/ELSE bits), then indenting the line(s) below. This is how Python recognises sections of code as connected to one another. The colon is important – it lets Python know that the line of code below is connected to the line of code with the colon (which can also be seen by the line of code below starting with a tab of whitespace). In writing, this probably comes off as more complicated than it is – suffice to say, it's important to pay attention to the colons and whitespace tabs as a way of identifying and accounting for bits of code that are nested within other bits of code.

You will see whitespace in lots of code from here on, so it's important to understand how it works and what it does. The concept is demonstrated below, but do feel free to try playing around with whitespace to help your understanding: for instance, what happens if you remove the whitespace from some lines? In fact, experimenting and playing around with code in this way is *very much* encouraged throughout this book – one way to get familiar with reading and writing Python syntax is to experiment with it, see what happens, and see if you can understand why you get the results you do when making these kinds of tweaks. Don't be scared to try things out!

FizzBuzz!

Now, let's try out an exercise with IF/ELIF/ELSE and AND/OR statements. Open the file called 4_3_FlowControl(AndWhitespace).py, run it, and work your way through the instructions:

```
1    """
2    Programming with Python for Social Science
3    Phillip Brooker
4
5    4. 3. FLOW CONTROL (AND WHITESPACE)
6    """
7
8    #Now we can compare things, we can get into more sophisticated stuff. Here is
9    #a script that takes a variable ("number") and runs various checks on it. If
10   #the number is evenly divisible by three (i.e. with no remainder), the code
11   #prints the string "Fizz". If the number is evenly divisible by five, the code
12   #prints the string "Buzz". If a number is evenly divisible by both three and
13   #five, the code prints "FizzBuzz".
14
15   number = 1
16
17   if number % 5 == 0 and number % 3 == 0:
18       print("FizzBuzz")
19   elif number % 3 == 0:
20       print("Fizz")
21   elif number % 5 == 0:
22       print("Buzz")
23   else:
```

```
24        print(number)
25
26   #First, run the script - what happens? Is that expected?
27
28   #Second, change the value of the variable "number" in line 15 to the following
29   #values:
30        #3, 98, 75, 55, 45, 29853
31   #What happens? Is that expected?
32
33
34
35   #EXERCISE: Create a program which produces statements about numbers that you
36   #give it, with the following conditions:
37        #if the number is over 100 print "Phew, that's a big number."
38        #if the number is even, print "This one is even."
39        #if the number is even and over 100 print "Stop. I can't even."
40        #if the number doesn't satisfy any of these conditions, print the number.
41   #This program can be written at the bottom of this script.
42   #Check the program with a few values to see if it gives the results you expect.
```

As you run the script, you should see that you are already given a result – an integer (1) is printed. This is because the variable number is automatically passed through the "FizzBuzz" logic, since running the script means Python executes each line from top to bottom.

In the spirit of experimentation (as noted above, why not try seeing what happens if we change the AND in the "FizzBuzz" code section (line 17) to an OR? Try it out – if you do this, the conditional logic will print the word "FizzBuzz" for every number that was divisible by 5 with no remainder OR every number that was divisible by 3 with no remainder. Can you see how changing the AND to an OR will affect how the code operates? Try running this script with a few different values for number to see what happens – is this what you expect?

Now we can turn to the exercise – try writing out some conditional logic before you look at the suggested answer I've sketched out below. It may help to plan out your conditional logic before you start writing it (see Section 1.4 for details on how to do this).

Could you get the logic to work? Did it produce the results you expected? My answer to the exercise is below:

```
1   if number > 100 and number % 2 == 0:
2       print("Stop. I can't even.")
3   elif number > 100:
4       print("Phew, that's a big number!")
5   elif number % 2 == 0:
6       print("This one is even.")
7   else:
8       print(number)
```

If you wrote your code in the bottom of 4_3_FlowControl(AndWhitespace).py, you do not have to declare a new variable number – you will already be using the one I declared for the purposes of the "FizzBuzz" code section. However, if you started a new script, you will need to declare a variable number, else there will be nothing to pass to your conditional logic (and you will get an error message telling you as much).

The logical order of code and the order of logic in code

Inevitably, there will be different ways to write a piece of code that satisfies all the conditions outlined in the exercise – my suggestion above is one of probably many (and not necessarily the best one!), and you may have written a piece of code that does the job just fine but in a different way. That's no problem at all – creativity is an essential part of coding! However, one key thing to bear in mind here, aside from the mechanics of using IF/ELIF/ELSE and AND/OR (and associated bits of Python syntax like colons and whitespace), is the order you put your conditions in. My suggested solution above works along the following narrative:

1   If the number is both greater than 100 and even, print "Stop. I can't even."
2   If the number is just greater than 100 (but not even), print "Phew, that's a big number!"
3   If the number is just even (but not greater than 100), print "This one is even."
4   If the number is not greater than 100 and not even, just print the number itself.

Now, let's think about what would happen if we mixed up the order of our conditional logic statements – perhaps we can rewrite the code like this:

```
1    #NOTE, THIS CODE DOESN'T SATISFY THE EXERCISE CONDITIONS!
2
3    if number > 100:
4        print("Phew, that's a big number!")
5    elif number % 2 == 0:
6        print("This one is even.")
7    elif number > 100 and number % 2 == 0:
8        print("Stop. I can't even.")
9    else:
10       print(number)
```

Perhaps intuitively this way makes more sense – the exercise listed the conditions in this order! However, let's work through what happens if we use this wrong version of the code:

1   If the number is greater than 100, print "Phew, that's a big number!"
2   If the number is even, print "This one is even."
3   If the number is both greater than 100 and even, print "Stop. I can't even."
4   If the number doesn't satisfy any of these conditions, just print the number.

Can you see the problem here? Step 3 *will never be a valid outcome of the conditional logic*. The script will try to satisfy step 1 first and either print the associated string or move on to try step 2. If the script triggers step 2, it will either print the associated string or move on to step 3. However, there is no way the criteria of step 3 could be satisfied *without having already been satisfied (and a print executed) in steps 1 or 2*. Can you see why this is the case? If we check for the single conditions separately (i.e. `number > 100` *and then* `number % == 0`) before checking for a combination of those single conditions (i.e. `number > 100 and number % == 0`), one of the single conditions will have been satisfied before we've ever got to the combination of the two of them.

Reread the correct and incorrect versions of the solution with this in mind, to see if you can identify and understand the difference. One general rule of thumb when constructing conditional logic in this way is always to write the logic in such a way that the most exclusive (i.e. the most difficult to satisfy) condition is checked first. And, in a more general sense, pay attention to the order of your conditions – odd things can happen when you don't!

IF/ELIF/ELSE in action

IF, ELIF and ELSE statements are a crucial part of programming in Python and can be used in lots of different ways. As we've seen, they can control the values that are assigned to variables, but they can also be used as "flow control" statements which tell your program to do different things depending on the conditions you establish (and more). We'll see examples of both of these things below, but one key thing to remember is that the structure of your IF/ELIF/ELSE statements is critical to how they operate. As noted, code runs from line 1 down to the bottom of a script, so the sequential order of your lines of code becomes important here – it's generally a good idea to plan out the logic of your IF/ELIF/ELSE statements before writing the code, so as to prevent against building these kinds of "bugs" into your program.

Controlling the flow of the program (and planning code with "pseudocode"). Sometimes programs will have lots of bits of code which do lots of different things, but you may not want to just run the code from line 1 to the end each time. Hence, using IF/ELIF/ELSE statements as a way to control the flow of your program (in conjunction with "functions", which you will learn about later in the book), you can tell Python which jobs you want to perform and which to bypass.

For instance, suppose you want to do some web scraping on a particular webpage – perhaps you want to look at an influential political commentary blog, and scrape once a day for any new content that might have been posted. So, you already have some metadata – the date of the last time you attempted to scrape the blog, and the dataset of blog content you have already scraped (sorted by date). Using just these bits of information, you could use an IF/ELSE statement to check to see if the blog has new content, and, if it does, add that content to your existing blog dataset:

```
if date_of_newest_blog >= date_of_last_blog_in_my_data:
        [RUN THE WEB-SCRAPING FUNCTION]
        [ADD NEW CONTENT TO EXISTING DATASET]
        [CHECK AGAIN TOMORROW]
else:
        [CHECK AGAIN TOMORROW]
```

As you will hopefully have recognised, the above code is not standard Python – it is not, in fact, any kind of code at all. Often it helps to plan out your code before you write it, so that you don't have to worry about getting the Python syntax 100% correct before you've sorted out the logic and flow of the code. The above code example is written out as "pseudocode" – something which kind of looks like code in that you can see how the structure of the code (in this case, an IF/ELSE statement) is supposed to work, but where all the details haven't yet been filled in. There is no one way to write pseudocode, but it can be used to help you get your head around potentially complicated coding tasks (where planning is essential to preventing against "bugs" further down the line).

Sorting data with conditions. Suppose you have some Instagram data of pictures and videos where the caption also contains a specific hashtag – #Brexit, which features lots of different ways in which people visualise and express opinions on the UK's referendum about leaving the European Union. However, your research is about people who feel particularly strongly about this, and you would like to work primarily with the pictures and videos of users who have Instagrammed pictures and videos using #Brexit more than 10 times. An IF/ELSE statement will help you refine this master dataset – for each username, you can apply the following logical conditions:

```
if user_post_count >= 10:
    [PUT THE USER'S USERNAME IN A LIST]
else:
    pass
```

In this statement, if the user's total Instagram posts containing the hashtag #Brexit is 10 or more, their username is appended to a list (which you can then work with further). Note that the `pass` statement just instructs Python to do nothing (hence, if the user's post count is less than 10, the IF/ELSE statement ends without doing anything). It is also worth noting that the process of iterating through each username can itself be automated using a for loop (which you will learn about in later sections).

AND/OR in action

AND/OR conditions are really powerful complements to the logical conditions (i.e. IF/ELIF/ELSE) that you already know about, though as you have seen, there are important differences between AND and OR as logical statements which you need to bear in mind.

Combining conditions 1. Suppose you have some economic census data and you're looking to play around with them by exploring the effects of different demographic combinations on employment status. For instance, for each survey respondent you can check to see if they satisfy specific demographic criteria you're interested in (i.e. if they satisfy certain conditional checks):

```
if respondent_gender == "male" and respondent_age <= 18:
    [PUT THE SURVEY RESPONDENT'S DATA SOMEWHERE NEW]
else:
    pass
```

Using and to connect the two different conditional checks on variables means that the values have to pass *both* checks in order for the survey respondent's data to be selected.

Combining conditions 2. Suppose you have the same economic census data as in the previous example. The way the census's demographic data were collected means age is also bracketed into the following categories, each of which are stored in Python as strings:

- younger than 18
- 18-30
- 31-40
- 40-50
- 50-65
- older than 65.

Your research interest might be in people aged between 18 and 40; hence, you need to select data from two categories. However, these categories are, by virtue of age as a demographic, discrete – it is impossible for survey respondents to belong to more than one category (i.e. they can only be one age, and these categories do not overlap). So, in order to select the right slice of data, you would need to combine your conditional checks with the OR statement:

```python
if age_category == "18-30" or age_category == "31-40":
    [PUT THE SURVEY RESPONDENT'S DATA SOMEWHERE NEW]
else:
    pass
```

Because the categories you are working with are discrete – it is impossible for someone to be in both the 18–30 and the 31–40 categories simultaneously – OR is the appropriate way to connect the conditional checks (and AND is not).

Note that it is important here that the age categories are stored as strings – can you see how the conditional checks would need to be altered if the age categories were (accidentally) treated as integer values? Without enclosing "18-30" in speech marks, Python would not know that you were trying to check the category as a string and would instead treat it as a mathematical operation (i.e. 18 minus 30) – this would cause no end of problems to your IF statement! Hence, the knowledge you already have of the different data types in Python is something to bear in mind when building conditional checks in this way.

Chapter summary

- In this chapter, we started by looking at some different basic types of variables in Python - integers, floats and strings.
- We also looked at some different things we can do with them (i.e. check their type, convert them to other types, etc.), in their capacity as "objects".
- In doing so, we learned how to unpack what an error code is telling us - a useful skill to take forward as you start to build and do more complex things in Python.
- From there, we learned about (and practised) how to compare objects in Python with mathematical operations.

- We then explored the idea of using these comparisons as part of "conditional logic statements" in code via IF/ELIF/ELSE (and AND/OR as a complementary technique), paying attention to the way in which Python executes code (i.e. line by line down the page) and the effects that that has on how you should design effective conditional logic statements.
- In doing so, we encountered the importance of whitespace as both a necessary and valuable (in terms of readability) Python coding practice.
- We also practised working with conditional logic in a small-scale but independently led exercise – in this exercise, you built your first "tool" with code, a tool for producing statements about numbers depending on their characteristics (i.e. odd/even, up to/over 100).

5

Structuring Objects

━━━━━━ **Chapter objectives** ━━━━━━

- Get some practice handling more complex objects (i.e. collections of other objects).
- Further appreciate the difference between different object types in terms of their practical usages (e.g. understanding which objects are appropriate for specific programming purposes).

5 1 Lists and List Methods

Now we have an appreciation of individual variables and can do things with them like calculations, we can move on to some of the slightly more complex objects and structures within Python, and explore some of the methods through which we can work with them.

While this section is about lists and list methods, we should begin by outlining a selection of general-purpose commands that cut across different contexts in Python. Although these commands are useful as ways of working with lists, they can also be used with different objects in Python such as dictionaries, tuples and strings (see later chapters for details on all of these). So, it's important that we learn about these general-purpose commands as a way to engage with Python objects in a general sense (and a nice bonus is that this also gives us a way of practising passing arguments to commands).

Some general-purpose commands

Open and run the file titled 5_1_1_GeneralPurposeCommands.py, working through the exercises as instructed:

```
1    """
2    Programming with Python for Social Science
3    Phillip Brooker
4
5    5. 1. 1. GENERAL PURPOSE COMMANDS
6    """
7
8    #Here are a few 'all-purpose' commands that can be used across lots of
9    #contexts/objects in Python e.g. lists, tuples, dictionaries, strings, etc).
10   #However, bear in mind that some of the 'arguments' you feed them might not
11   #make sense and might produce an error - for instance, what would the absolute
12   #value of a string be?).
13
14   #The arguments passed to the commands below are just examples to demonstrate
15   #the concepts. You should try out these commands with different types of
16   #variables and objects in the shell, to get a feel for how they work.
17
18   max(1, 2, 3, 4, 5) #gives the maximum value of the argument
```

```
19    min(1, 2, 3, 4, 5) #gives the minimum value of the argument
20    abs(-1) #gives the absolute value of the argument (i.e. turns negative numbers
21            #to positive values) - applies to integers and floats only
22    type(-50.5) #gives the variable type
23    len("This is a string.") #gives the length of the argument
24
25    #You can also pass other objects to these commands:
26    var1 = (2, 3, 1, 6, 3, 6, 3, 5)
27
28    max(var1)
29    min(var1)
30    type(var1)
31    len(var1)
32
33    #There are LOADS more commands native to Python. LOADS. But this is just about
34    #getting used to the idea that objects have properties that you can call in
35    #Python. We'll be doing this as we get deeper into lists, dictionaries and
36    #string formatting/methods.
37
38    #EXERCISE: Try typing each of these commands into the shell and see what
39    #happens - can you understand why you see the output that results?
```

Working through this exercise will give you some more practice with working with commands in various ways – we have actually already done this with type(), which also features below. The answers to the exercise are below:

```
>>> max(1, 2, 3, 4, 5)
5
>>> min(1, 2, 3, 4, 5)
1
>>> abs(-1)
1
>>> type(-50.5)
<class 'float'>
>>> len("This is a string.")
17
>>> max(var1)
6
>>> min(var1)
1
>>> type(var1)
<class 'tuple'>
>>> len(var1)
8
```

Some things to note. First, the length of an object depends on what type of object it is. In the example we've used, the object is a string, and requesting the length of the string gives us the number of characters (including spaces) in that string. We will see how `len()` can be used with other objects in later chapters, but suffice to say that many objects have a length that can be checked with `len()` – you may want to try out a few different objects yourself in the shell.

Second, var1 is a tuple (which we will explore in more detail later in the book), which is a collection of data. In this case, it is a series of numbers. Hence, when we ask for the maximum and minimum value of var1, we get 6 and 1, respectively – in the series of numbers, there are two 6s, but we only get one value since none of the numbers within var1 are higher than 6. And again, when we check the length of var1 with `len(var1)`, we get the number 8 – this tells us the tuple has eight things in it.

Working with lists

Now we can move on to lists as a specific concept in Python (and one to which some of these general-purpose commands have a relevance). First, it may help to outline the concept in an abstract way, then show how these things look in a script. Lists are data structures written as a series of comma-separated values/items between square brackets. It's worth noting that items in a list do not have to all be of one type – the example I use here features a list containing only strings (for the sake of keeping things simple), but in principle lists can contain any number of different values and types. In this way, lists can be used to collect values and items (e.g. bits of data) together. Moreover, items within a list are accessible by virtue of their being "indexed" – each item in a list has an index position according to where in the list it appears. However, it is important to know that Python organises lists (and other similar objects) with "zero indexing" – this is to say that the first item in a list is given an index value of 0, the second item is given an index value of 1, the third item is given an index value of 2, and so on. This may seem a little counter-intuitive at first, but it should become clear in the exercise below why this is a useful thing (and in any case, remembering to start thinking about indexes at 0 instead of 1 is not too much of a hardship). Various other methods can be applied to lists, and we will go through some of these below.

At this point, it's good to move into actually seeing how lists look in code, and what you can do with them. Open the script called 5_1_2_ListsAndListMethods.py, run it, and work your way through the instructions.

```
1    """
2    Programming in Python for Social Science
3    Phillip Brooker
4
5    5. 1. 2. LISTS AND LIST METHODS
6    """
7    #Here is a simple list:
8    animals = ["dog", "cat", "bat"]
9    #Call animals in the shell. Why does it look like that? HINT: look at all the
10   #commands below that Python is enacting when we run this script - lines 14
```

```
11   #through 27 (and lines 56 and 57) are performing tasks which are altering the
12   #original animals list.
13
14   #Here is a selection of list methods, with which you can play around with lists:
15   animals[2] #Calls the value at index position 2.
16   animals[0] #Calls the first entry in the list (because zero-indexing)
17   animals[-1] #Calls the last entry in the list
18   animals[2] = "rat" #replaces "bat" with "rat" (because zero-indexing)
19   animals.append("ibex") #appends "ibex" to the end of the list.
20   animals.sort() #sorts the list alphabetically (or numerically if integer/float)
21   animals.index("cat") #tells you what index position an item is at
22   animals.insert(1, "llama") #inserts "llama" into index position 1. Everything
23                              #after that gets knocked on 1 place.
24   animals.pop(3) #removes the item at the denoted index and 'returns' it
25   del(animals[3]) #removes the item at the denoted index but doesn't return it
26   animals.remove("dog") #removes the item if it finds it
27   animals[0:1:1] #calls all the info at index positions from 0 to 1 (not including
28                  #1), in steps of 1. NOTE: if you don't set the step (i.e.
29                  #animals[0:1]) Python assumes you mean in steps of 1.
30
31   """
32   NOTE: There's a difference between round and square brackets here. Round
33   brackets are what Python uses to accept an 'argument'
34   (i.e. animals.index("cat") needs the argument "cat" so it knows what index to
35   produce for you). Sometimes no argument is necessary - e.g. you don't need to
36   tell Python any extra information for animals.sort(), it just sorts the list.
37   Square brackets on the other hand are to do with index positions.
38   """
39
40   #You can also have lists within lists:
41   mammals = ["dog", "cat", "bat"]
42   birds = ["parrot", "budgie", "eagle"]
43   reptiles = ["chameleon", "komodo dragon", "gecko"]
44   fish = ["sturgeon", "marlin", "shark"]
45   planet_earth =[mammals, birds, reptiles, fish]
46
47   #QUESTION: What do you think the following commands will return? Guess first,
48   #then type them out in the shell to verify.
49   planet_earth[1]
50   planet_earth[3]
51   planet_earth[1][1]
52   planet_earth[0][2]
53
54   #Each of these results can be stored - they're objects in and of themselves.
55   #So let's store an index position as a variable, then use that variable to do
56   #something with a list.
```

(Continued)

```
57    cat_index = animals.index("cat")
58    animals.insert(cat_index, "cobra")
59    #Can you see what we did in these two lines? We assigned the index position
60    #number of "cat" to a variable cat_index, then we used that variable as an
61    #argument in animals.insert() (which requires an index position, which we give
62    #by cat_index rather than by number, and a thing to insert, which we gave as
63    #the string "cobra").
```

So, there are lots of things to learn about lists here. You should note first of all that a list itself is just something assigned to a variable – above, we have just declared a variable called animals, and assigned a few strings containing animal names to a list by putting them in square brackets and separating them with commas. You should also know that there are *lots* more methods for working with lists than are shown here – I've just given a few useful ones to get you started. And the way to get started properly is to try making a list yourself, and see if you can apply the methods and commands listed in the script to it – see if you can predict the result that a method will yield, then test it by using the method and seeing what happens. As part of this, you should try using the commands that construct lists (listname. append(), listname.insert(), listname.pop(), del(listname[index_position]), listname.remove(), etc.) – you don't have to literally type out each entry into the list variable, you can use Python commands to do the work for you.

Working with num_list

Now we know what a list is, what it's for, and what we can do with one, let's put our knowledge to the test: open up the file called 5_1_3_ListsAndListMethodsExercise.py. Note that the version of the exercise that appears in this book contains an abridged version of num_list – it's too big to fit on a page! So, don't be put off by the size of the list in the exercise script and how different it appears in the book – the list is *designed* to be too big for you to properly check by eye (hence, you'll *need* to apply Python methods to address the exercise questions, rather than cheat by just looking at the values – how sneaky of me!). When you've opened it, run the script, and let's see if we can answer the questions in the exercise:

```
1     """
2     Programming with Python for Social Science
3     Phillip Brooker
4
5     5. 1. 3. LIST EXERCISE
6     """
7
8     #Look at this big list (which contains a lot of numbers between 0 and 999)!
9     num_list = [387, 729, 730, 94, 727, 535, 367, 59, 446, 740, 588, 307, 225, 956,
10                175, 961, 332, 731, 875, 362, ...]
68
69    #NOW, let's do stuff with it. QUESTION: Can you tell me:
70
```

```
71   #Q1: How many things are in this list?

72

73   #Q2: What are the last 20 items of the list, sorted numerically?

74

75   #Q3: What is the range of the first 50 items?

76

77   #Q4: What is the range of the first 50 items after you've inserted a value of

78   #5000 at index position 30?

79

80   """

81   EXERCISE: Can you now:

82

83   * Break the first 25 numbers in num_list up into batches of 5, each stored in

84     a list of its own.

85   * Then compile those 5 mini lists into a bigger one.

86   * Then, tell me what the third element of the fourth list is?

87

88   DO ALL THIS USING PYTHON COMMANDS: FIDDLING IN THE SCRIPT IS

89   CHEATING!!!

90   """
```

So in this exercise, there are four relatively straightforward questions, and one which requires you to write your own script. Let's deal with the four questions in turn first. Question 1 is "How many things are in this list?" We can check this in the shell by using the len() method:

```
>>> len(num_list)
776
```

The len() command gives us the length of the list (i.e. how many items it has in it), so that's our answer!

Question 2 asks "What are the last 20 items of the list, sorted numerically?" There are two elements of the question that we need to use Python to address. The first is plucking out the last 20 items of the list – the concept of extracting/calling specific selections of data is also known as "slicing". The second is sorting them by number. We can do each of these in two lines of code (with a third line to show us the result) as follows:

```
>>> new_list = num_list[-1:-21:-1]
>>> new_list.sort()
>>> new_list
[26, 29, 158, 314, 525, 550, 557, 610, 635, 649, 651, 668, 749, 801, 812, 812,
822, 969, 977, 989]
```

The first line of this solution declares a new variable (new_list), in which we store a selected range of values within the big num_list list. The values we've chosen are based on their index position, since we know that we want to start at the last one in the list and we can use a negative index position to find that for us. We *do* actually know what the index position of the last thing in the list is, since we've worked out how many items are in the list in Question 1. In this case, num_list[775] is the last item in the list, since len(-num_list) tells us there are 776 items – remember, Python uses zero indexing for lists, which means that the length of the list will always give a number one greater than the last index position. *However*, just for the purposes of getting more acquainted with the idea of negative index positions meaning starting at the end of the list, this is what I've done in my solution here – in any case, negative index positions come in really handy when you don't know/can't predict how long a list is.

So, back to num_list. In this new variable we store a range of list items starting at the –1 index position (i.e. the last item in the list), ending at the –21 index position (which gives us 20 items, as requested in the question), and moving in steps of –1 (i.e. going backwards through each item, rather than forwards). Note that it would be a good idea at this point to call new_list (i.e. type new_list into the shell to get Python to show us what it comprises) to see if it has actually done the thing we want – making periodic checks on the code you build is one way to help prevent against (and locate) bugs as you work. After line 1, these 20 items are now stored in new_list; we can then use new_list.sort() to sort the items numerically. Then, we can simply call new_list to see the results.

Question 3 asks "What is the range of the first 50 items?" We need to first know what a range *is* to address this question. Those of you who have some familiarity with quantitative/statistical methods will know that the "range" refers to the difference between the maximum and minimum values in a set of numbers. So, with this in mind, we can address the question in the following single line of code:

```
>>> max(num_list[0:50]) - min(num_list[0:50])
981
```

Let's unpick what is going on here. First, we know that the first 50 items of the list can be called on by using num_list[0:50]. The way indexing is used here is such that we start at 0 (because of zero indexing), and go through to *but don't include* the item at index position 50 – hence, the last item we actually grab has an index position of 49, but because of zero indexing we still end up with 50 items in total (which is what we want). We *could* store this set of items in a variable (perhaps called first_50_items?) and refer to it that way, but equally, since it doesn't take too much time to type out, we can just use and reuse the actual typed out bit of code easily enough. In order to calculate the range, we need to know the maximum and minimum values in this selection of data. This is given by max() and min(), respectively – you can see we've nested the argument which grabs the selection of 50 items within the max() and min() commands above. And finally, computing the range requires us to find the difference between the two (i.e. to subtract the minimum from the maximum); you can see in the solution above that the minus sign is doing this work as we go (though in principle, we could store the maximum and minimum values in their own variables and run the calculation on those). This gives the result of 981.

Question 4 ask us a similar question to the one we've just answered: "What is the range of the first 50 items after you've inserted a value of 5000 at index position 30?" So, we can reuse some of the code we've just built to help us address this as follows:

```
>>> num_list.insert(30, 5000)
>>> max(num_list[0:50]) - min(num_list[0:50])
4994
```

You can see that line 2 of this solution is exactly the same as the code we built to answer the previous question. However, the result (4994) is different. This is because, as the question requires, we've used line 1 of the code to insert a new value into the list, which skews the range. So, line 1 shows how we insert the new value into num_list at the desired location, line 2 repeats our bit of code for finding the range within the set selection of items in num_list, and that produces the result 4994.

Now, moving on to the exercise, we can see that there are multiple steps to address. Let's take these one by one. First, we need to break the first 25 numbers in num_list up into batches of five, each stored in a list of its own. This will require us to do some list slicing as follows:

```
>>> list1 = num_list[0:5]
>>> list2 = num_list[5:10]
>>> list3 = num_list[10:15]
>>> list4 = num_list[15:20]
>>> list5 = num_list[20:25]
```

These five lines of code each declare a new variable, and assign to that variable a specific slice of num_list items. Remember I said above how zero indexing would make more sense as we got to the exercise? Well this is why! You can see in the exercise question we need five batches of five numbers – because Python uses zero indexing and sets an end-point at one index position before the number we give the argument (e.g. in the list1 slicing we give the end-point a number 5, which means we collect the item at index position 4), the list slicing comes out as nice rounded values that are easy to understand: 0–5, 5–10, 10–15, 15–20 and 20–25. At this point we can call any and all of these new variables to see if they contain the things we want them to contain – it's good to check things as we go to prevent bugs down the line.

So now that we have our variables established (and we can check them to see if they're what we want), we can compile these five new lists into a bigger list as follows:

```
>>> list_of_lists = [list1, list2, list3, list4, list5]
```

Using the variable names for each of our new lists, we can pass these into the new variable "list_of_lists" which itself is a list. This might sound a bit complicated, but if we actually call list_of_lists, we can see that it shows a series of lists nested within a bigger list (pay attention to where the square brackets denote the start and end of lists):

```
>>> list_of_lists
[[387, 729, 730, 94, 727], [535, 367, 59, 446, 740], [588, 307, 225, 956, 175],
[961, 332, 731, 875, 362], [53, 738, 647, 258, 888]]
```

Next, the exercise wants us to figure out what the third element of the fourth list is: again, we have to remember about zero indexing. So, the fourth list is actually the one at index position 3 in list_of_lists, and the third element of that list will be at index position 2. With this in mind, we can access that value as follows:

```
>>> list_of_lists[3][2]
731
```

As noted previously, you may have done this exercise very differently and still got the same results – that's great! I've just shown you one way of doing things, but the point of a multi-purpose tool like Python is that it can be creatively worked with and applied however you like.

Lists and list methods in action

Lists are *very* useful in Python, for many reasons – you will see them crop up everywhere in pretty much any Python program! This is because lists can be used in lots of different ways, and for lots of different purposes. Here are just two examples to get you started thinking creatively about how to use lists in your programming:

Keeping data collected. Variables are great for storing bits of data, but it's easy to lose track of how many variables you have assigned. Suppose you have crime data on the number of muggings in London per day, taken over the course of a year. It would be a bad idea here to have lots of different variables to store these individual pieces of data – this would result in lots of lines of code, and be very difficult to read and work with as a collection:

```
>>> 16June2017 = 5
>>> 17June2017 = 8
>>> 18June2017 = 4
>>> 19June2017 = 5
```

and so on. A better way to handle these data would be to put them in a list:

```
>>> muggings_per_day = [5, 8, 4, 5, ...]
```

Lists can be used to keep data collected together. Another benefit of this is that you can then use list methods to do things with the data stored in them – for instance, you could use list slicing to check the first 30 days of figures, or you could see how much data you have in total with `len(muggings_per_day)`.

Deriving frequencies and updating datasets with list methods. Suppose you have some data stored in a list – the names of Facebook users who have "liked" and/or shared posts from the Labour Party's Facebook page, over a 12-month period. Some people will have liked and/or shared lots of posts, so their usernames will appear in this list more than once. If you want to find out who is liking and/or sharing these posts most frequently, you can use `data_list.count("username")` to find out just how much this particular user has engaged with the Labour Party on Facebook (and, if you do a count of each username in the dataset, you have the necessary information to then produce a frequency graph which will visualise this information very neatly!). Building on this, you might also want to update your data list with new posts as they come in – perhaps you can scrape for new likes and shares at the end of a day, to see what else has come in. To add these new data to the existing list, you can just use `data_list.append("new_data")`; this way, your data can always be up to date!

5 ● 2   Tuples and Tuple Methods

Tuples are much the same as lists in many respects – they are a data structure that allows you to collect together various items. However, there are two key differences. First, the syntax – lists are constructed with square brackets, and tuples use round brackets. Second, tuples are *immutable*, which is to say that, unlike lists, tuples cannot be altered with methods: whereas you can, for example, insert, append, remove, delete values from a list, a tuple doesn't let you do this. So, they may be limited in terms of the methods that can be applied, but they are useful in some contexts (as can be seen in the "Tuples and tuple methods in action" subsection below). So let's jump in and see how to create and work with tuples in code.

```
1    """
2    Programming in Python for Social Science
3    Phillip Brooker
4
5    5. 2. TUPLES
6    """
7
8    #In essence, just lists that are immutable (i.e. once assigned, there are no
9    #methods for fiddling with them). Have a look at the "Tuples and Tuple Methods
10   #in Action" subsection to see why this might be handy.
11
12   my_tuple = (0, 10, 30)
13   my_tuple[1] #calls the item at index position 1.
14
```

(Continued)

```
15   #As with other data structures like lists and dictionaries, you can also build
16   #tuples from existing values, and these don't have to contain all the same
17   #types of data:
18   age = 32
19   location = "Manchester"
20   hairstyle = "bald"
21   energy_level = 0.1
22
23   Phil = (age, location, hairstyle, energy_level)
24
25   """
26   That's about it...you can't do things like pop or remove things from tuples.
27   They're immutable. But, if you want to take bits from a tuple and play with them
28   you can always assign them to a variable: my_tuple_extract = my_tuple[1]. And,
29   some things like len(my_tuple) will work because they don't try to edit the
30   data (they just describe it as "metadata" - data about data).
31   """
```

So, lots of the general-purposes commands, plus things you have learned about lists (e.g. "slicing"), will apply to tuples, but lots of things (e.g. appending, removing, popping or deleting items) will not apply. Try creating some tuples yourself, to see what methods you can apply, and which result in an error message.

Tuples and tuple methods in action

Keeping data associated. Tuples can help keep data structured. Suppose you have data containing user handles and biographies for thousands of Twitter users – perhaps you're looking to see who states a political preference in their Twitter bio. You know each user has their own distinct biography, and it doesn't make sense to separate the usernames from the bios in this case. So, using a tuple, you can make sure that each username is always and only associated with its own particular biographic information. What's more, you've already learned about nesting lists within lists – you can do this with tuples too. So, you can have a big list containing all the (username, bio) tuples for each user to play around with!

Preserving an original dataset. Suppose you have some survey data which you want to format and then test out a number of different calculations and operations on specific demographic cross-sections (e.g. females aged 25–40). Since you want to run some fairly complex formatting and calculations and operations on this cross-section, it is difficult to foresee any unexpected consequences in terms of how this might change the original dataset – this could be bad for the reliability and validity of your study, and makes it difficult to explain where your results have come from. So, of course, you would not want to risk altering the original dataset, though you do want to play around with it and explore different ways of filtering and organising the data to get some insights. Here, it would be useful to store the data in a set of tuples before you work with them further, so as to make sure that the original data are always preserved and cannot be changed (i.e. they are "immutable").

5●3 **Dictionaries and Dictionary Methods**

Still working within the idea of data structures, we can now turn to dictionaries as another way of collecting things together. With lists (and tuples), we can see that the information they contain is retrievable by reference to the index position of those bits of information. Practically, this means that for lists, we have to work with numbers as a way of locating information – we request the first entry in a list by calling the thing that is at index position 0, the second entry by calling the thing that is at index position 1, and so on (remember zero indexing). However, this is not always appropriate, and we may find instances where we want data to be structured and made referable to by a string perhaps. Whereas lists are numerically ordered by index position, dictionaries are unordered sets of objects. These objects each have a "key" (i.e. a label by which you can refer to the object) and a "value" (i.e. a bit of data). Keys and values are separated/linked by a colon, whereas distinct dictionary entries are separated by a comma. The difference between lists and dictionaries is further visible in the syntax we use to declare them as variables: lists use square brackets [ ] and dictionaries use curly brackets { }. Let's see how to build a dictionary in action, and use some dictionary methods to get better acquainted with the concept.

Working with dictionaries

Open the file called 5_3_1_DictionariesAndDictionaryMethods.py, and run it.

```
1    """
2    Programming in Python for Social Science
3    Phillip Brooker
4
5    5. 3. 1. DICTIONARIES AND DICTIONARY METHODS
6    """
7
8    #Dictionaries are just as important as lists, but we're not going to go over the
9    #same things here - a lot of what we did with lists was about using commands
10   #to find our way around objects, and those same sorts of ideas apply here; we
11   #don't need to go over them in the same depth. However, dictionaries are
12   #different objects than lists, which means they do have some unique
13   #attributes/methods that we do need to outline.
14
15   #The main difference: lists sort things by index position, but with dictionaries
16   #you can create your own names/labels for index positions. So, it's a different
17   #way of structuring data that may be more applicable for some tasks.
18
19   animal_dict = {"dog": "woof",
20                  "bird": "tweet",
21                  "cow": "moo",
```

(Continued)

```
22                    "pig": "oink",
23                    "turtle": "?"}
24
25    animal_dict["fish"] = "glub" #adds a new entry
26    del animal_dict["fish"] #removes an entry
27    animal_dict["bird"] = "squawk" #edits an entry
28    print(animal_dict["dog"]) #prints the value of the key
29    animal_dict.items() #breaks up dict into items, prints them #METADATA
30    animal_dict.keys() #prints keys
31    animal_dict.values() #prints values
32
33    """
34    NOTE:
35    A lot of the methods we learned about with lists will work with dictionaries
36    too. Things like .pop() and len() we learned about, but given there are
37    so many more methods we can't cover, you'll find more overlaps the more you
38    look into it and try things out for yourself.
39    """
40
41    """
42    OTHER NOTE:
43    You can embed lists within dictionaries, dictionaries within dictionaries,
44    dictionaries within lists, tuples within dictionaries within lists within lists,
45    etc...complex data structures and hierarchies! Below, you can see an example of
46    how to put a dictionary within another dictionary, and how to pull information
47    out of it - this applies also to lists (except for lists, you will be using
48    numerical index positions rather than string keys).
49    """
50    dict1 = {"first thing": 1, "second thing": 2, "third thing": 3}
51    dict2 = {"dict_within_dict": dict1}
52    #Now let's pull the value for "second thing" out of dict1, using dictionary
53    #methods to work with dict2:
54    dict2["dict_within_dict"]["second thing"]
```

You should have seen that the Python shell said woof as you ran it – can you see why? Line 28 is a command that prints the value associated with the key dog in animal_dict. And this serves as a reminder that whenever we run a Python script, each line will be executed (barring errors) from top to bottom. With that in mind, call animal_dict – is this what you expect to see, given how the variable is originally declared (line 19)? Can you follow the methods below the variable (lines 25–31) and see what happens in animal_dict that edits it into the result you see when you call it?

Now, play around with animal_dict using the various dictionary commands outlined here – see what the commands produce when you use them. Pay attention also to the way you can pull information out from nested data structures (lines 41–54). This is an important concept, and the Python syntax on display here is something that cuts across multiple different contexts (including lists and strings) – a general way to think about this technique is original_object[object_within_object][object_within_object_within_object][and_so_on].

The dictionary of YOU

Once you have familiarised yourself with these methods, we can work through the exercise in 5_3_2_DictionariesAndDictionaryMethodsExercise.py. Try to do all the steps yourself first, then look at my suggested solution below. Note that I could have picked some less nerdy information to put into my suggested solution below, but it doesn't actually matter what you put in as keys and values, as long as you're getting practice with how to type out the syntax and in understanding how various dictionary methods operate. Additionally, as you work through each step, try calling some relevant information in the shell so that you can see what results and check whether your code is working as expected:

```
1    """
2    Programming in Python for Social Science
3    Phillip Brooker
4
5    5. 3. 2. DICTIONARIES AND DICTIONARY METHODS EXERCISE
6    """
7
8    #EXERCISE:
9    #(1) Write a dictionary (with your name as the variable name) that stores your
10   #following attributes:
11        #Date of birth
12        #Place of birth
13        #Favourite TV show
14        #Favourite film
15
16   #(2) Add a key and value to your dictionary denoting your favourite band or
17   #artist. Use ONLY dictionary methods to do this.
18
19   #(3) Delete the "Place of birth" field and replace it with one called "Current
20   #residence" - put the town you currently live in as the value.
21
22   #(4) Create an empty dictionary in a variable titled the name of your favourite
23   #album by your favourite band/artist.
24
25   #(5) Within this new dictionary, use dictionary methods to populate the
26   #dictionary with the following keys (and give them values):
27        #Year of release
28        #Number of tracks
29   #Do steps (4) and (5) for two or three albums by that band.
30
```

(Continued)

```
31    #(6) Add these albums to a new dictionary called "favourite albums". Use ONLY
32    #dictionary methods to do this.
33
34    #(7) Write "favourite_albums" into your original dictionary (the one with your
35    #name as the variable name), under the key "Favourite albums".
36
37    #(8) See if you can call specific single bits of information in your big
38    #dictionary of dictionaries using keys - what is your favourite film? What's
39    #the year of release of one of your favourite albums?
40
41    #(9) See if you can print out the keys and values of your big dictionary.
```

Let's work through some suggested answers to each of the different elements of this exercise. Step 1 asks you to write a dictionary (with your name as the variable name) that stores a set of attributes: your date of birth, place of birth, favourite TV show and favourite film. For me, this is as follows:

```
>>> phil = {"D.O.B.": "16/11/1985",
            "Place of birth": "Bolton Royal Hospital",
            "Favourite TV show": "Twin Peaks",
            "Favourite film": "2001: A Space Odyssey"}
```

So what I did here was just write out some keys and values for a dictionary bearing my name as the variable name – so far so good. Note that you don't *have* to press return after the comma – in fact, Python doesn't care about that, and will read anything that follows the comma as a new piece of information. However, in order to make things look more readable on the page/in the shell, it is often a good idea to think about presenting information clearly rather than having it all in one long unreadable line of code.

Now, step 2 wants us to add a key and value to this dictionary detailing our favourite band or artist, using dictionary methods:

```
>>> phil["Favourite band"] = "Ween"
```

Now we're getting more familiar with dictionary methods to edit and work with dictionaries we have created, we can add in new information to a dictionary by declaring a new key and assigning it a new value.

Step 3 asks us to delete the Place of birth key and replace it with one called Current residence that states the town we currently live in:

```
>>> del phil["Place of birth"]
>>> phil["Current residence"] = "Atherton"
```

Here, we use the `del` dictionary method to get rid of the key we don't want (and as a result of that, the value is deleted also), and we create a new key and value as we did above in the second element of the exercise.

Step 4 asks us to create an empty dictionary in a variable titled with the name of our favourite album by our favourite band/artist:

```
>>> quebec = {}
```

This is a pretty simple step in the exercise, but it's worth considering nonetheless. Creating empty things (in this case a dictionary, but in principle it could be anything: an empty list, an empty string, an empty tuple, an integer value of 0 to be changed later, etc.) is often useful as a way of helping build code. For instance, if you know you will need a dictionary at some point further down the line (because you've planned out your code like a responsible programmer!) but you don't yet have the information or data to put in it, you can at least create an empty dictionary, build the rest of your code around that, and fill the details in later. So here, I create an empty dictionary with the variable name `quebec` by just assigning an empty set of curly brackets to the variable.[1] We'll be populating this empty dictionary with info shortly.

Step 5 wants us to put new information in this new empty dictionary – the year of release of the album denoted by the variable name, and the number of tracks on the album. And then, we need to repeat the process for two other albums by that band:

```
>>> quebec["Year"] = 2003
>>> quebec["No. of tracks"] = 15
>>>
>>> the_mollusk = {}
>>> the_mollusk["Year"] = 1997
>>> the_mollusk["No. of tracks"] = 14
>>>
>>> pure_guava = {}
>>> pure_guava["Year"] = 1992
>>> pure_guava["No. of tracks"] = 19
```

So here, we put some new information into our empty `quebec` dictionary associated with that particular album, then repeat the same thing for two other Ween albums. There's a few lines of code here, but you should see that what we're doing is repeating the idea of creating an empty structure, then using dictionary methods to populate it (rather than writing out

---

[1] *Quebec* is perhaps a controversial choice of favourite Ween album, I know - *The Mollusk* is great, yes, but the standout tracks on *Quebec* stand out *way* more IMO.

these dictionaries "by hand"). You can see there are also empty lines in the shell that separate out the different album dictionaries. This was done just by pressing return in the shell without writing any code. The only reason to do this is to keep things readable on the page – ultimately this is just a presentation issue, but presentation issues are very important in terms of helping us code (and helping others read our code).

Step 6 needs us to put all these favourite album variables into a new dictionary called favourite_albums, using dictionary methods:

```
>>> favourite_albums = {}
>>> favourite_albums["Quebec"] = quebec
>>> favourite_albums["The Mollusk"] = the_mollusk
>>> favourite_albums["Pure Guava"] = pure_guava
>>>
>>> favourite_albums
{'Quebec': {'Year': 2003, 'No. of tracks': 15}, 'The Mollusk': {'Year': 1997,
'No. of tracks': 14}, 'Pure Guava': {'Year': 1992, 'No. of tracks': 19}}
```

Now we're doing something slightly different – whereas before we were assigning string information as values to various keys, now we're assigning variables themselves (which contain dictionaries) as values. So, it's at this point we start to create a more complex data structure – we are collecting our three favourite Ween album dictionaries (quebec, the_mollusk and pure_guava) into a bigger dictionary called favourite_albums. See what results when you call the favourite_albums dictionary in the shell (as I did in the example above) – you should see that there are lots of curly brackets denoting when each dictionary begins and ends; that is, three small dictionaries nested within one larger one.

Step 7 asks us to write favourite_albums into our original dictionary:

```
>>> phil["Favourite albums"] = favourite_albums
>>>
>>> phil
{'D.O.B.': '16/11/1985', 'Favourite TV show': 'Twin Peaks', 'Favourite film':
'2001: A Space Odyssey', 'Favourite band': 'Ween', 'Current residence':
'Atherton', 'Favourite albums': {'Quebec': {'Year': 2003, 'No. of tracks':
15}, 'The Mollusk': {'Year': 1997, 'No. of tracks': 14}, 'Pure Guava': {'Year':
1992, 'No. of tracks': 19}}}
```

Now we're going even deeper down the rabbit hole! What we are doing in this section is writing a new key and value into our original personal dictionary (in this case, phil). So now phil contains (among other things) a key called Favourite albums, which itself is a dictionary that contains dictionaries for three different albums (quebec, the_mollusk, pure_guava). Call your original personal dictionary and see what it looks like – you should be able to see how the nesting works by reading the syntax that results. This is our completed personal dictionary! And you can see what it looks like when called in the shell, as above.

Step 8 asks us to retrieve, from our big personal dictionary, our favourite film and the year of release of one of our favourite albums:

```
>>> phil["Favourite film"]
'2001: A Space Odyssey'
>>> phil["Favourite albums"]["Quebec"]["Year"]
2003
```

So, now we can try accessing information within our personal dictionary. Remember, we can use square brackets to pull out indexed information – this is what we do with lists too, though note that with lists we would have to use numerical index positions and with dictionaries we need to use the keys that we have assigned variables to. And remember also, when we are dealing with nested information, we need to use the correct syntax with square brackets (as above). Also worth noting is that the result for our favourite film comes out in quotation marks, whereas the result for the year of one of our favourite albums doesn't – can you see why this is? Remember how we set up the values for these bits of information – the name of the film is stored within a string (which gives it the speech marks in the results), whereas the year of release we declared as an integer (which means no speech marks, just the number); it's important to be able to understand the *type* of information we are retrieving as well as what it actually contains. We could even do this by using type() to check, for example, type(phil["Favourite albums"]["Quebec"]["Year"]), which would give us the result <class 'int'>.

Step 9 asks us to print out all the keys and values (respectively) of the big personal dictionary we have created:

```
>>> print(phil.keys())
dict_keys(['D.O.B.', 'Favourite TV show', 'Favourite film', 'Favourite band',
'Current residence', 'Favourite albums'])
>>>
>>> print(phil.values())
dict_values(['16/11/1985', 'Twin Peaks', '2001: A Space Odyssey', 'Ween',
'Atherton', {'Quebec': {'Year': 2003, 'No. of tracks': 15}, 'The Mollusk':
{'Year': 1997, 'No. of tracks': 14}, 'Pure Guava': {'Year': 1992, 'No. of
tracks': 19}}])
```

You should note here that I've used the .keys() and .values() commands within a print command – actually, in this instance, this doesn't make a difference to what you see in the shell (if you type `print(phil.keys())` or just `phil.keys()` the result comes out the same). However, it's a good opportunity to think about nesting commands within other commands, while we have nesting in mind!

You should also note that there are more values than keys in your big dictionary – can you see why this might be? The `phil` dictionary has dictionaries nested within it, so when I print the keys, it prints *only* the keys assigned directly to `phil`. However, when I print the values for `phil`, you can see that the values within the nested dictionaries get "expanded", such that we can see the entire range of values contained within the big `phil` dictionary. This allows us to visualise and read the data structure we've just created – if we do `print(phil)` too, we will see the full expanded contents of the dictionary (i.e. keys *and* values together), as follows:

```
>>> print(phil)
{'D.O.B.': '16/11/1985', 'Favourite TV show': 'Twin Peaks', 'Favourite film':
'2001: A Space Odyssey', 'Favourite band': 'Ween', 'Current residence':
'Atherton', 'Favourite albums': {'Quebec': {'Year': 2003, 'No. of tracks':
15}, 'The Mollusk': {'Year': 1997, 'No. of tracks': 14}, 'Pure Guava': {'Year':
1992, 'No. of tracks': 19}}}
```

So, with all these methods and techniques in mind, that about wraps up dictionaries!

Dictionaries and dictionary methods in action

Dictionaries are similar to lists in some respects: they are both used to store collections of information and can be nested within one another (i.e. to store collections of collections of information!). However, dictionaries are based on key–value pairs rather than index positions – this makes dictionaries useful for when information needs to be stored in a format where numerical index positions do not make sense (i.e. where it is best to associate a value with a non-numerical label).

Storing research participant details. Say you have done a survey, part of which has involved collecting the contact details of each respondent so that you can get in touch with them later to see if they want to participate in the next stage of the research. Each respondent has given you a set of details: a name, an email address, and a postal address (which itself has multiple fields: house number, street name, town, city and postcode). All of this information *could* be stored in a list of lists, where each respondent had their own list, and the group of respondents were collected together in a master list:

```
1    respondent1 = ['Tom', 'tom@tommail.com', [3, 'Tom Drive', 'Tomton', 'Tomsville',
2    'TM3 3TM']]
3
4    respondent2 = ['Paul', 'paul@paulmail.com', [5, 'Paul Road', 'Paulerpool',
5    'Paulhampton', 'PL5 5PL']]
```

```
6   respondent3 = ['Daisy', 'daisy@daisymail.com', [7, 'Daisy Street', 'Daisyfield',
7   'Daisyshire', 'DY7 7DY']]
8
9   respondent_list = [respondent1, respondent2, respondent3]
```

However, structuring this information in lists would make retrieving individual pieces of information quite complicated – lists operate with index positions, meaning that if you wanted to retrieve the postcodes of each respondent, you would need to have to remember the index position of each respondent's postcode. Moreover, this is not easy to read in the code, since by using index positions it's not immediately clear which bits of information you are attempting to retrieve. For instance, to get Paul's postcode, you would need to type the following command:

```
>>> respondent_list[1][2][4]
```

Notice that nowhere in this command does it say which respondent you are trying to deal with, and which bit of information of theirs you are trying to retrieve. This way of structuring the code is not very readable!

A better way to structure the data would be with a dictionary:

```
1    respondent1 = {'Name': 'Tom', 'Email': 'tom@tommail.com', 'Address':
2    {'StreetNo': 3, 'StreetName': 'Tom Drive', 'City': 'Tomton', 'County':
3    'Tomsville', 'PostCode': 'TM3 3TM'}}
4
5    respondent2 = {'Name': 'Paul', 'Email': 'paul@paulmail.com', 'Address':
6    {'StreetNo': 5, 'StreetName': 'Paul Road', 'City': 'Paulerpool', 'County':
7    'Paulhampton', 'PostCode': 'PL5 5PL'}}
8
9    respondent3 = {'Name': 'Daisy', 'Email': 'daisy@daisymail.com', 'Address':
10   {'StreetNo': 7, 'StreetName': 'Daisy Street', 'City': 'Daisyfield', 'County':
11   'Daisyshire', 'PostCode': 'DY7 7DY'}}
12
13   respondent_dict = {'Tom': respondent1, 'Paul': respondent2, 'Daisy': respondent3}
```

Structuring information in this way – using a dictionary to assign keys for each of the values of interest – makes it easier for you to remember how to retrieve different pieces of information, and also for you to hand your code over to others so that they can read it too. For instance, compare our earlier command for pulling Paul's postcode with the one below:

```
>>> respondent_dict['Paul']['Address']['PostCode']
```

Very readable, very easy to remember! And, better still, if Paul gets in touch to tell you he's got a new email address, you can very easily update that information:

```
>>> respondent_dict['Paul']['Email'] = 'paulsnewemail@paulmail.com'
```

5 ● 4 Strings and String Methods

Though we might not see strings as data structures in the same way that lists, tuples and dictionaries are, we can still see strings as containers of multiple bits of data – text data. As such, it's useful for us to learn how to work with and edit strings with string methods (we'll see more about just how useful this is in later sections). For now, open and run the file titled 5_4_StringFormattingMethods.py:

```
1    """
2    Programming in Python for Social Science
3    Phillip Brooker
4
5    5. 4. STRING FORMATTING/METHODS
6    """
7
8    #We already looked a little bit at this:
9    string1 = "First Bit."
10   space = " "
11   string2 = "Second Bit."
12   print(string1 + space + string2)
13   #This is called string concatenation.
14
15   new_string = "this IS a SliGhtly more ComplicaTed strINg"
16
17   new_string[1] #calls the letter at index position 1 (i.e. the second letter)
18   new_string[0:4] #calls the first four characters
19   new_string[5:] #calls everything including and after the fifth character
20   new_string[::2] #calls all characters in steps of 2 (i.e. every other character)
21   new_string[-1:-10:-1] #calls the last ten letters in steps of -1 (i.e. reverse)
22
23   len(new_string)
24   string1.lower() #makes it lower case
25   string1.upper() #makes it upper case
26   string1.split() #takes each item, puts it in a list as an individual item.
27                   #TRY THIS. See what happens.
28
29   #You can also put strings together via methods other than concatenation:
30   string4 = "is cool."
31   string5 = "Programming %s" %string4 #the %s denotes a placeholder for a string.
32                                       #this is more useful than it looks.
33
34   """
35   % STRING FORMATTING OPERATORS:
36   You can see the %s in line 31 above - that means that Python expects something
37   to be inserted that is a string type. Here are some other string formatting
38   symbols you can use:
```

```
39
40    %s string
41    %i or %d integer
42    %f float
43
44    So, run the following code and see what happens:
45    print("Hi, my name is %s and I'm %d years old." %("Phil", 32))
46
47    Play around with this way of constructing strings: try passing variables
48    to the operators, and experiment with the order of the arguments you pass to
49    the operators.
50    """
51
52    """
53    EXERCISE:
54    In the shell, can you get Python to produce a print of new_string that is
55    properly punctuated (i.e. capitals in the right place, full stop at the end)?
56
57    Can you then print it out backwards?
58    """
```

Work your way through the code above, trying out the methods for yourself in the shell and seeing what results.

Slicing with ranges in Python

As noted, we have already done some string concatenation (i.e. using the plus symbol to join strings together as one). However, the methods on display above also demonstrate how to do string slicing with ranges – if you've worked through the code and done some experimenting with these methods you should already have an idea of how range slicing works. Moreover, we have also seen it used in other contexts like with lists (so it shouldn't be completely unfamiliar). However, it's worth reviewing how range slicing works as a general guideline too, so you can see how it applies in other contexts. So, for instance, if we have a variable called my_string which contains string-type data, let's explore the following bit of code to understand more about what slicing with ranges means:

```
>>> my_string[0:10:2]
```

First, we should be able to see that because of the square brackets, what we're doing is calling out bits of information from my_string. The colons also indicate that we're not just calling out a single character from the string, but a *range* of characters. And we set the parameters of this range by including numbers. The first number (0) is the starting-point – this tells Python that we want to start our range slice at the character in index position 0 (i.e. the first character in our string, because of zero indexing). The second number (10) is the end-point – this tells Python that we want to end our range slice at the character in index position 10. Note that this means that the character in index position 10 is *not* included in our range; the range ends *before* it (i.e. the range end-point is not inclusive). Finally, the third number (2) sets the steps we want the range to travel in – here, we have set the range slice to work in steps of 2, so this will capture *every other* character in the string (i.e. it will catch one, skip the next, catch the next, skip the next, catch the next, skip the next, etc.).

However ,we don't *have* to set parameters for starting-point, end-point or step count. We could do something like this:

```
>>> my_string[0:10]
```

Here, we are telling Python to start at the 0 index position, end at the 10 index position, but do not give a parameter for step count – as such, Python reverts to its default and returns characters in steps of 1 (i.e. every character in the range). We can choose not to include a parameter for starting-point, end-point or step count. If we choose not to include a parameter for starting-point, Python defaults to starting at the 0 index position. If we choose not to include a parameter for end-point, Python defaults to ending at the final character in the string (whatever index position it is). If we choose not to include a parameter for step count, Python defaults to working in steps of 1. These "empty parameters" can be quite helpful if we don't know how many characters are in a string for instance (i.e. if we don't know at which index position we actually want to end, we can leave it blank). As noted, range slicing is useful in other contexts too, such as lists and tuples – so, hopefully you can see how these methods and techniques can be useful in coding more generally!

As a little aside, it's worth noting that slicing numerically doesn't work for dictionaries – can you see why? Dictionaries are unordered sets of information; hence, it doesn't make sense to think about "ranges" of information in a dictionary in the same way as it does for strings, lists and tuples. It is possible to iterate through all the things in a dictionary with `for ITEM in DICTIONARYNAME:` (using techniques we'll explore later in the book; don't worry about it for now!), but note that this doesn't refer in any way to index positions (and hence, slicing doesn't work in quite the same way).

Formatting a string

Now we can move on to addressing the exercise. Here, I'll show you multiple ways of answering the exercise questions, which will give us an opportunity to think about constructing code with readability in mind.

The exercise comes in two parts. First, we're asked to produce a print of `new_string` that is properly punctuated, with a capital letter at the beginning of the sentence, lower-case letters throughout the rest of the sentence, and with a full stop at the end. We can see that if we print `new_string` in the shell, it's kind of messy and we'll need to think about how to go about sorting it out!

```
>>> print(new_string)
this IS a SliGhtly more ComplicaTed strINg
```

So, first what we need to do is separate out the bits that need to be upper case, and the bits that need to be lower case, and we can apply the appropriate methods accordingly:

```
>>> uppercase_bit = new_string[0].upper()
>>> uppercase_bit
'T'
>>> lowercase_bit = new_string[1:].lower()
>>> lowercase_bit
'his is a slightly more complicated string'
```

What we've done here is create two new variables. uppercase_bit takes the first character of new_string, and applies the .upper() method to it. In contrast, lowercase_bit takes the rest of the string (from index position 1 to the end) and applies the .lower() method to it. Now we can concatenate the two new variables, remembering to add a full stop at the end, and print the whole lot as follows:

```
>>> print(uppercase_bit + lowercase_bit + ".")
This is a slightly more complicated string.
```

Of course, we did not *have* to put the upper-case and lower-case elements in their own variables – as I've noted in earlier sections, there are multiple ways to do the same job in Python. So, one alternative way would be to do all this work in just one line of code, as follows:

```
>>> print(new_string[0].upper() + new_string[1:].lower() + ".")
This is a slightly more complicated string.
```

Each way gets the same result. However, although the second way is apparently more "efficient" – it's one line of code that does the entirety of what we want to do – I think I prefer the first way of tackling the problem by separating out different slices for different operations and storing them in variables to be concatenated later. And, I think I prefer this because the first way is more *readable*. Let's look at the two different ways together now:

```
>>> uppercase_bit = new_string[0].upper()
>>> lowercase_bit = new_string[1:].lower()
>>> print(uppercase_bit + lowercase_bit + ".")
This is a slightly more complicated string.
>>>
>>> print(new_string[0].upper() + new_string[1:].lower() + ".")
This is a slightly more complicated string.
```

In the first way, we have some descriptive variable names that can help us understand what is going on, which is helpful when we come to concatenate everything together. However, in the second way of doing things, though it is nice to have everything done in just one line of code, it is perhaps more difficult to understand what is going on – imagine if you were showing this to somebody else who was learning to code; would this be the best way to demonstrate string methods and formatting to them? Readability is something you must bear in mind as you're developing code, even when you're learning – unreadable/unclear code is not helpful, no matter how efficient it may be.

Now we can turn to the second part of the exercise: printing out our newly and correctly formatted string backwards. I'll show you how I did this, and walk you through each of the elements of the code afterwards:

```
>>> clean_string = uppercase_bit + lowercase_bit + "."
>>> print(clean_string[-1::-1])
.gnirts detacilpmoc erom ylthgils a si sihT
```

Again, the first thing I did was put the correctly formatted string in its own variable, `clean_string`. This helps make the turning-it-backwards bit of code more readable (and, moreover, it means if I'm trialling-and-erroring things on this code, I can just type out `clean_string` rather than `new_string[0].upper() + new_string[1:].lower() + "."` every time I want to try something new). So, the next step is to use string slicing to select which characters I want to print, and in what order. Let's go through the string slicing parameters I've used, `[-1::-1]`, and think about what's going on here.

First, I need to set a starting-point for my print statement – I want to start at the end of the string (so that I can work backwards from there). Hence, I set the starting-point to –1 (see the code about string methods above if you need a refresher on this). However, I do not want to set an end-point for the print statement – I want to print the *whole* string backwards, not just up to a certain point. Note that if I set the end-point to be 0, this would come out wrong – can you see why? End-points in slicing *don't* include the final character established in the parameter, and hence setting the end-point as zero would miss off the final character in the reversed string (i.e. the capital T that starts the original `clean_string`). So, leaving the end-point parameter blank is the proper thing to do here. However, I *do* need to set the step counter – by default, Python would choose a step counter of 1, which means going *forward* by one character at a time. But if I start at the end, there would be nowhere to go forward *to*, and hence Python would print out a blank statement. As such, we need to set the step counter to a negative value, –1, so that it captures all the characters, but proceeding backwards rather than forwards.

We've played around with some methods and techniques of string formatting here, and working with strings is a really powerful and ubiquitous aspect of dealing with data in Python (especially data downloaded or scraped from the web, which might naturally come in the shape of strings). You'll see more of this as we go forward into applications in later chapters. But techniques like slicing are worth bearing in mind more generally.

Strings and string methods in action

This section has introduced you to a few of the string formatting methods that are available within Python. These methods are enormously multi-purpose and you will no doubt find plenty of uses for them throughout any Python project where you are working with text strings. As such, it's worth keeping string formatting methods in mind, since they can feature in your programming work in lots of different ways.

Cleaning up text data. Suppose you have lots of different text files containing hundreds of pieces of Twitter user data (including things like how many followers a user has, how many people follow them, how many times they've tweeted, when they set up their account, and so on), and you have read each dataset into Python as a series of large strings (which you assign as a variable called user_data1, user_data2, user_data3, etc.). However, you notice that each text file features the time and date you collected the data at the beginning – not very useful for analytic purposes. All in all, there are 28 characters of junk that you want to chop out of the beginning of each string, and you want to write a Python script to help you do this (since you have lots of different files, and repeating that same job lots of times will be very boring, to say the least!). So, you could use the following command to chop out the first 28 characters of the dataset, and assign the remaining text to a new variable:

```
>>> clean_user_data1 = user_data1[28:]
```

This tells Python to assign every text character between the 28th character and the end of the string to a new variable called clean_user_data1 – your new dataset is free of junk! Moreover, using methods you will learn later in the course (i.e. for loops), you could tell Python to go through each of your datasets (user_data1, user_data2, user_data3, ...) one by one, automatically, perhaps even using string concatenation to add each new dataset into a single master_clean_user_data text string variable.

Using strings to say things about data. Suppose you have a dataset of thousands of tweets produced by a single Twitter user. Each tweet is read into Python as a tuple where the content of the tweet is associated with the time and date of its publication, for example:

```
tweet1 = ("30/06/2017 14:09", "This is my first tweet, maybe I'll tweet again
later.")
```

```
tweet2 = ("24/07/2017 17:15", "Really liking Twitter, thought I'd tweet a second
time!")
```

and so on. All of these tweets are stored in a master list, to collect them together:

```
master_list = [tweet1, tweet2, ...and so on]
```

It's perhaps useful to know the date range of your dataset – the date of the first tweet and the date of the last tweet. Using the index positions of the data in the master list (which you learned about in earlier sections) you can assign each date to a variable:

```
start_date = master_list[0][0][0:10]
end_date = master_list[-1][0][0:10]
```

For `start_date`, this variable takes the first element of `master_list` (i.e. the first tweet, stored in the index `[0]`), searches within that tuple entry for the first value (i.e. the date and time, stored in the index `[0]` of the tuple), then uses string formatting to select the first 10 characters from within that tuple entry (i.e. just the date, which is stored in `[0:10]`).

For end_date, this operates in much the same way, except you are looking for the *last* entry in `master_list` (hence the `[-1]` index position). You still want to access the first element of the tuple at the end of the list (the `[0]` element where the date and time are) and you still want to access only the first 10 characters of that element (the `[0:10]` which selects only the date).

Having sliced out the bits of each string we are interested in, we can then use string concatenation to compute a label to a frequency graph showing the frequencies of all tweets produced by this user by day:

```
graph_title = "Tweet Frequency for User1 Between " + start_date + " and " +
end_date + "."
```

Now, if you run

```
>>>print(graph_title)
```

you will see the following appear:

```
Tweet Frequency for User1 Between 30/06/2017 and 24/07/2017.
```

Nice neat label! But also, imagine you wanted to find out the same information for lots of different users and produce lots of different graphs (with lots of different graph labels); the code we've just written can apply to any and all data that you throw at it, however many tweets there are and whatever dates they span – what a time-saver!

Chapter summary

- In this chapter we extended our knowledge of objects by exploring ways in which we can collect objects together in larger structures - lists, tuples, dictionaries and strings - and methods for handling each of those objects.
- We started by working through some general-purpose commands - things you can do in Python to help you understand and work with a range of different object types. This also got you more familiar with the practice of using commands (i.e. how to do this practically in the shell or in a script).
- Next we looked at lists: how to build them in code, what they are for, and what we can do with them. We then worked through an exercise that gave you a chance to practise and explore these techniques more deeply.

- Next we looked at tuples: how to build them in code, what they are for, and what we can do with them.
- Next we looked at dictionaries: how to build them in code, what they are for, and what we can do with them. We then worked through an exercise that gave you a chance to practise and explore these techniques more deeply.
- Next we looked at strings: how to build them in code, what they are for, and what we can do with them. We then worked through an exercise that gave you a chance to practise and explore these techniques more deeply.

6

Building Better Code with (Slightly) More Complex Concepts/Objects

━━━━━━━━━ **Chapter objectives** ━━━━━━━━━

- Learn how functions and loops/list comprehensions can be used to "streamline" (i.e. simplify, automate, modularise) programming tasks.

6●1 Functions

Now for something a little different: functions. Functions in Python are a collection of 'things' – this is intentionally vague, in that functions are so multi-purpose that it's impossible to pin down any one thing they are beyond a collection. Typically, functions will take some sort of input, do stuff to that input, then turn it into some form of output – this is not *always* the case, and functions can be used creatively for lots of other jobs too. I appreciate the vagueness is perhaps a little frustrating here – stick with it, we'll get to the code in a bit and all will make sense! But for now, the reason why this is useful is that when you collect things together, they can be reused multiple times – we can use functions to do tasks repeatedly. This is a time-saver for us, in that it means we don't have to repeatedly write (or copy and paste) and execute multiple lines of code over and over again – we can just write the code into a function and execute *that* repeatedly. Additionally, this helps keep our code readable, since having a huge script full of copied and pasted blocks of code is difficult to visualise and deal with (how would we know which block does what exactly?).

So with this abstract definition in mind, let's start to think now about how to actually build functions for ourselves. You can see an example of this below, but as a general guideline, you have the syntax def (which stands for "define" – you're telling Python that you want to define a function), followed by the name of your function (your choice), then some round brackets. These round brackets can be left empty if the function doesn't need an argument passing to it (i.e. if it doesn't need an input), or they can have as many comma-separated arguments as you like (which serve as placeholders so the function knows how many arguments to expect and what needs to be done with each of them) – we'll see examples of both ways of building functions in the code excerpt below. Finally, the definition of the statement ends with a colon. Once the function is defined, we can then nest various commands and operations (and whatever else) within it by using whitespace (see Chapter 4 for a discussion of whitespace in Python and how it works).

One thing worth noting upfront is that, as with variables, you can name functions anything you like. However, programmers often use something called "camelCase" for naming functions. This is just a convention (rather than a hard requirement) that means beginning the name of a function with a lower-case letter, then using capital letters at the start of any new words (as I have done in the excerpt below).[1] The name of your function doesn't have

---

[1]It's also worth mentioning that camelCase is sort of "old-fashioned" (more of a Python 2 thing perhaps?) - and the official Python style guide (otherwise known as PEP8 (Python Software Foundation, 2013)) suggests using all lower-case words separated by an underscore. However, given that one of the core motivations of this book is (as social scientists) to learn to do programming for ourselves and in our own ways for our own purposes, I don't care too much about breaking with finicky protocols that don't obviously serve any particularly important social scientific need. I like the look of camelCase in my code, I think it's more readable than the PEP8 convention, so I'm using it here: dealWithIt.

any effect on what it does, but using camelCase just helps make it visually distinguishable when the thing you're referring to is a function and not something else (e.g. a variable, where it's conventionally fine to use something like an underscore to separate words). In short, it can help make your code more readable by others, which is always a good thing.

Working with functions

Now on to the code. Open up the file named 6_1_Functions.py, run it, and work your way through the instructions. Type out your solution to the exercise at the bottom of the script itself – you will need to refer to the list inside (topping_list), so you need to run the code in the same script as that list otherwise Python will not be able to refer to topping_list at all.

```
1    """
2    Programming in Python for Social Science
3    Phillip Brooker
4
5    6. 1. FUNCTIONS
6    """
7
8    #Functions are a core concept of Python. Let's see how they work. Try calling
9    #myFunction() by typing "myFunction()" in the shell:
10
11   def myFunction():
12       print("Thanks for printing myFunction()!")
13
14   #Now let's build something a little more complex - let's build a function
15   #that can take numbers that we pass it and check if they're even (and, if
16   #they're even, store them in a list).
17
18   even_numbers = []
19   def isEven(num):
20       if num % 2 == 0:
21           even_numbers.append(num)
22           return("This number is even. I'll add it to the list.")
23       else:
24           return("This number is odd.")
25
26   #Can you explain in words what this function is doing, line by line? Try
27   #writing it out and "reverse engineering" the function, to better understand
28   #how it works and what it does.
29
30   #Try using isEven(num) with different numbers in place of "num" to see what
31   #happens. Throw a selection of numbers at this function, then check to see
32   #what's in the even_numbers list to see if it's working as you'd expect.
33
```

(Continued)

```
34    """
35    EXERCISE:
36    I'm hungry - will you order me a pizza? Create a function for checking whether
37    or not I like various ingredients on a pizza, and return the results as a
38    string. As part of your checking, you should also check to see if the input is
39    actually a string or not (since I definitely DON'T like integers and floats on
40    my pizza). I'll give you a few hints:
41
42    * It will DEFINITELY help if you plan out your code in advance with a script
43      workflow (see Section 1.4 for further details).
44    * topping_list below contains details of all the ingredients I like.
45    * You can use "in" as a way to see if something appears within any given list
46      (i.e. "if THING in LIST" etc).
47    * Think about the various techniques you'll need to use to do all this work -
48      you DO know all these already, but may need to review earlier sections to
49      refresh your memory.
50    """
51
52    topping_list = ["cheese", "pepperoni", "sausage", "bacon", "anchovies",
53                    "salami", "chorizo", "ham", "jalapenos", "pineapple",
54                    "olives", "tomatoes"]
```

There are a number of things to note about functions at this point. First, it should be clear that the good thing about functions is that they can collect together lots of bits of code using lots of techniques *that we already know* – the only new syntax we learned how to write is the actual defining of functions (and a few little extras like return(), etc.). This makes understanding how to use functions a bit easier – we can just see them as containers of things that we already know (like calculations, conditional logic, lists, calls to other functions, etc.).

What is return() (and why not print())?

We can also see in the code above that whereas we've previously been using print() to display strings in the shell, we now have this new return() method – why? This relates to the idea that functions typically work as a way of turning an input into an output of some kind, as in Figure 6.1.

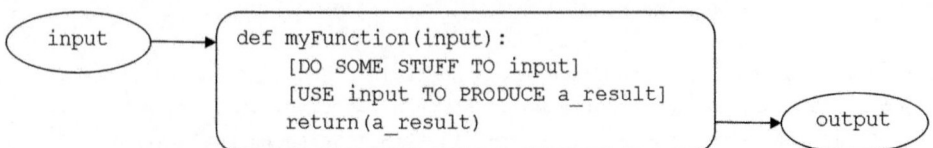

Figure 6.1 Generic function model

The return() method allows anything that results in our function to be used inside other calculations or expressions that we might require on the basis of the results the function produces. In the code excerpt above, the "results" that we're returning are all strings that we want to see printed in the shell, so this doesn't make much difference. However, the following excerpt can help us see the difference between print() and return more clearly:

```
>>> def iReturnAResult(num):
        print(num)
        return(num)
>>>
>>> def iOnlyPrintAResult(num):
        print(num)
>>>
>>> iReturnAResult(5)
5
5
>>> iOnlyPrintAResult(5)
5
>>>
>>> iReturnAResult(5) + 2
5
7
>>> iOnlyPrintAResult(5) + 2
Traceback (most recent call last):
  File "<pyshell#34>", line 1, in <module>
    iOnlyPrintAResult(5) + 2
TypeError: unsupported operand type(s) for +: 'NoneType' and 'int'
```

So let's unpick what is going on here. In line 1, I define a function (iReturnAResult()) which both prints and returns a number that I pass to it. In line 5 I define another function (iOnlyPrintAResult()) which only prints a result to the shell. I then call these functions using 5 as the number – iReturnAResult(5) prints out 5 then returns 5, whereas iOnly-PrintAResult(5) only prints out 5. So far, that should be pretty much what we expect. However, the difference between printing and returning results becomes apparent from line 14 onwards. On line 14, I call iReturnAResult(5) + 2. Here, I am using the result of the function as part of a calculation, and the outcome of this can be seen in the results that are shown in the shell – the print bit of the function gives 5, whereas the return bit of the function gets used in the calculation and gives a value of 7. I then go on to try the same sort of thing with iOnlyPrintAResult(5) + 2, and an error results – no output was returned, so Python found it impossible to complete the calculation we requested and threw up an error message.

Long story short: if we just want to *see* the result of a function in the shell, then it's fine to use print(). However, if we want to *use* the result of a function to do other things, then we need to use return(). Even though we really just want to see the output of the string in the examples I've given above (and hence, `print()` would have been fine), I've used `return()` just to show you how it works so that you can apply it elsewhere.

We also need to note that using `return()` exits you from the function – once your function hits a `return()`, it stops running, and any code below that `return()` will not execute. Hence, as with conditional logic, the order of lines of code becomes important – can you see how this would matter if we flipped around lines 21 and 22 of the `6_1_Functions.py` file, so that the `return()` statement came before `even_numbers.append(num)`? If that were the case, we would never be able to append anything to the `even_numbers` list, because the function would stop executing before it reached that line of code. So, return statements are best placed at the end of a function (or at the end of a sub-branch of logic within that function).

Scope: global and local code

Given what we already know, we should be able to follow what the function in lines 18–24 of `6_1_Functions.py` is doing for the most part fairly straightforwardly – it takes an argument (num, which we can substitute for a real number when we actually call the function by typing something like `isEven(5)` into the shell), and then checks to see if that number evenly divides by 2. If it does, it prints a statement that tells us the number is even, then adds the number to a list called `even_numbers` (which we originally declared in line 18); if it doesn't, it just prints a statement telling us the number is odd.

However, we do have to consider in Python that some variables are "global" and some are "local". This is to say that in Python, much like Las Vegas, whatever happens within a function *stays* within a function. In lines 18–24, you can see that we originally declare an empty list (even_numbers) outside the function, but which we refer to within the function. This works – when we use `isEven()` with an even number, we can then call `even_numbers` within the shell to see what's in the list and our even number will be there. However, what happens when we put a new list of even numbers itself within the function (as follows)?

```
>>> def newIsEven(num):
        new_even_numbers = []
        if num % 2 == 0:
            new_even_numbers.append(num)
            return("This number is even. I'll add it to the list.")
        else:
            return("This number is odd.")
>>> newIsEven(2)
"This number is even. I'll add it to the list."
>>> new_even_numbers
Traceback (most recent call last):
  File "<pyshell#11>", line 1, in <module>
    new_even_numbers
NameError: name 'new_even_numbers' is not defined
```

Here we have a function that is identical to the one in 6_1_Functions.py, except the list we're working with (new_even_numbers) is declared *within* the function rather than outside it. And we can see that the function works of a fashion – when we type newIsEven(2) into the shell, the function recognises the number 2 as even and acts accordingly. However, when we then call the new_even_numbers list in the shell we get an error message – it is not recognised by Python as having been defined. So what has happened here?

Because the new_even_numbers list is defined *within* the function, it is *local* to it – it does not exist outside the context of the function, and when the function is finished (i.e. when it hits a return statement), new_even_numbers is wiped from Python's memory and no longer exists. However, in the original function in lines 18–24 in 6_1_Functions.py, because the list is defined outside the context of the function, we can also refer to it outside the function. This is an important distinction to bear in mind when planning and writing functions – the *scope* (local or global) of different variables and the information that we are passing around needs consideration.

Functional code for pizza preferences

Now on to the exercise. Here we have to develop a function that will check whether or not various strings pertaining to pizza ingredients can be found in a list,[2] as well as exclude any arguments that we might pass to the function that *aren't* strings. I'll post my suggested solution below and we can work through it and test it out with a few arguments to see if it does what we need it to do:

```
1   def toppingCheck(topping):
2       if type(topping) == str:
3           if topping in topping_list:
4               return("If some %s went on my pizza, I wouldn't be mad." %topping)
5           else:
6               return("You know what? I'll pass on the %s thanks." %topping)
7       else:
8           return("You're not even trying. Come back when you've got a string.")
```

So let's go through this line by line. In line 1 of this solution, I define the function, calling it toppingCheck() and making sure that it has to be passed one argument (which I denote with the placeholder topping in round brackets). Then, I use some conditional logic to navigate around the various conditions required by the exercise. First, I check to see if the type of information contained in topping is a string – if it is, we can proceed to check whether or not it is a *valid* topping, but if it isn't we can reject the argument outright (i.e. the ELSE

---

[2] I know, pineapple. It's not a hill I'm willing to die on, but what's wrong with a sweet/salty combination of pineapple and some kind of pork on a pizza? There's a careful balance to be struck, yes, but don't rule it out outright!

condition that returns `You're not even trying. Come back when you've got a string.`). If the argument *is* a string, then I do a further check to see if the contents of that string can be found somewhere within topping list (i.e. `if topping in topping_list:`). If it *can*, then I return a statement (using string formatting) that proclaims it a valid topping. If it *can't*, then I return a statement that says no thanks.

Your solutions may differ, but I think a general thing to bear in mind is that since we have multiple nested conditions in play, we have to think carefully about how those IF/ELSE statements work with (and within) one another. Functions can have lots of things going on within them, and that's exactly why it's important to keep a clear handle on how different elements of a function intersect with one another – planning ahead is critical here, to prevent unexpected bugs in the development process.

Functions in action

Functions are one of the core concepts and objects of Python programming, and they play a ubiquitous and multi-purpose role in coding. Thinking creatively is the key to building good and useful functions. Here are two potential applications that will help you see how to start thinking about the (endless) possibilities.

Performing a task. Suppose we have lots of different text files containing hundreds of pieces of Twitter user data (including things like how many followers a user has, how many people follow them, how many times they've tweeted, when they set up their accounts, and so on), and each dataset had been read into Python as a series of large strings assigned as variables called user_data1, user_data2, user_data3 and so on. But at the beginning of each text file, we notice there were 28 characters of junk that we want to chop out – this junk is just the time and date you collected the data, which is not very interesting in terms of analysing the users themselves. So, given that there are lots of files to work with, and you want to do the same job on each file (i.e. remove the first 28 characters), let's think about how we can use a function to automate the task.

Although we want to apply the task of removing the opening 28 characters to all of our files, we'll write the function just to do the more generic task of working with one file – we can always use a for loop to pass lots of different files to the function, but we'll come to how they work in the next section. The main job for now is to write a *generic* function for doing the task we want to do (i.e. a function which is not specific to any particular file, so we can then drop each file into regardless of what it is called or what variable it is currently assigned to). We want our function to take some data, chop out the first 28 characters, then put the remaining data somewhere that we can explore later:

```
>>> new_user_data = []
>>> def fileCleanup(data):
        global new_user_data
        clean_user_data = data[29:]
        new_user_data.append(clean_user_data)
```

So, the function we've just written collects a few jobs together – it takes one argument (data), establishes the empty new_user_data list as a global variable so that the function can write to it outside the context of the function, creates a new variable (clean_user_data) containing all characters from the 29th to the end of the file (i.e. it chops out the first 28 characters), and then appends all of that remaining ("clean") data to new_user_data.

One thing to note, however, is the way in which I have used "arguments" to pass something to the function. The way I declared the function (i.e. def fileCleanup(data):) means that in order for the function to run it needs to be passed something called data – although we called it data, you can pass anything to a function really. The key thing at this point is that Python knows that this function needs to accept one argument (and that any other number of arguments will result in an error). The neat thing in calling the argument data is that while data is an arbitrary name for something (in that we could have called the argument x or whatever, or anything else we might like), we can then use the argument data within the function itself, so that the function becomes generic and will apply to *any* data that we pass to it. So, thinking in these terms, using data as a placeholder for any variable name we want to pass through the function, we have made our function generic so that it can be reused for all of the data files we want to work with. Handy if we ever collect more user data in the future that need similar cleaning up!

Organising your program. Again, it's useful to return to a previous example at this point to explore how functions can add to what we already know. We already know how to organise code with logic (IF/ELIF/ELSE and AND/OR), but it's worth going over these ideas again to see how our new knowledge of functions applies. Earlier we saw an example where we were thinking about how to use web scraping to gather data from an influential political commentary blog, scraping once a day for any new content that might have been posted. We thought about how to structure the logic using pseudocode, as follows:

```
1   if date_of_newest_blog >= date_of_last_blog_in_my_data:
2       [DO SOME WEB-SCRAPING]
3       [ADD NEW CONTENT TO EXISTING DATASET]
4       [CHECK AGAIN TOMORROW]
5   else:
6       [CHECK AGAIN TOMORROW]
```

We can now further build on this program with our new knowledge of functions. In the excerpt above, we have used pseudocode to signify several distinct components to the program: [DO SOME WEB-SCRAPING], [ADD NEW CONTENT TO EXISTING DATASET], and [CHECK AGAIN TOMORROW]. Knowing what we now know, we can use functions as a way of tidying up the organisation of these jobs:

```
1   def webScraper():
2       [SCRAPE THE BLOG]
3       [PUT THE RESULTS IN A LIST]
4       checkAgainTomorrow()
5
6   def checkAgainTomorrow():
7       [WAIT UNTIL 5PM TOMORROW]
8       webScrapingRoutine()
```

(Continued)

```
9   def webScrapingRoutine():
10      [CHECK FOR NEW CONTENT]
11      if date_of_newest_blog >= date_of_last_blog_in_data:
12          webScraper()
13      else:
14          checkAgainTomorrow()
```

You will see that we're still using a bit of pseudocode for programming tasks involving the actual web-scraping code and the actual timing of when we want to set the program to run – clearly we still need to learn about the Python code that would help us do these things. However, we've been able to advance our program a little bit by breaking up the jobs into functions which connect with each other depending on logical conditions. For instance, if we start by invoking the `webScraper()` function, we scrape a blog post from a website, then move to the `checkAgainTomorrow()` function. The `checkAgainTomorrow()` function waits until 5pm the following day, and then moves to `webScrapingRoutine()`, where Python checks to see if there's a newer blog to scrape. If there is, we go back to `webScraper()` to collect it (and then wait until the following day to check again). If there isn't, we just go straight to `checkAgainTomorrow()`. You can see how these functions connect up and flow into one another in a cyclical way.

There are two main benefits to bracketing or compartmentalising your program with functions. First, it becomes more visually obvious and readable as to how the flow of your program is operating – for instance, in the `webScrapingRoutine()` function above, you can clearly see which functions get invoked given the different logical conditions we have set out.

Second, if you ever needed to change how an individual function operates, the fact that the function is separated out makes it easier to think how you might do that. For instance, imagine if you wanted to change your `checkAgainTomorrow()` function to check twice a day instead of once – if the code for checking again tomorrow was written directly into the logic, you would always need to remember to make two changes (i.e. because the code that forms the basis of `checkAgainTomorrow()` appears in two different places in the above script). However, since we put `checkAgainTomorrow()` into a function, we can just change the things we put in the `checkAgainTomorrow()` function and we don't have to do any rewriting in other bits of our program which invoke `checkAgainTomorrow()`. This is good for saving time in terms of not having to write out bits of code multiple times (i.e. we can always just write `checkAgainTomorrow()`), but it also helps prevent writing bugs into the program – imagine how tricky it would be to find the source of errors that might occur if we had lots of little bits of code for checking again tomorrow but forgot to make changes to one of those bits!

6.2 Loops and List Comprehension

So far, when we've been working with conditional logic and functions, we've had to pass arguments around "manually" (i.e. by typing commands in the shell). This is a little tedious and time-consuming. Wouldn't it be great if we could automate the process? This is the kind of thing we can do with loops. Loops are a way that we can iterate through some kind of Python object, typically a range of numbers, or entries in a list, tuple or string (or other kind of object made up of smaller bits of things). So let's see how this works in code.

In terms of being able to read the code file, it's worth noting upfront that I've "commented out" two blocks of code below (lines 21–31 and lines 47–59) so that that code doesn't automatically run when you execute the script. Commenting out is a useful practice as you're building code – if you turn something into a comment (either by putting a hashtag in front of it, or containing it within two groups of three speech marks) then Python no longer tries to execute the code when you run the script. Hence, you can leave things unfinished, with errors, or just temporarily stop them running while you test or develop other bits of the code – very handy!

Working with loops

Open the file 6_2_1_LoopsAndListComprehension.py, run it, and work your way through the instructions. Note that I have broken this code up into two sections, since it wouldn't fit on the page. But if you run these sections together in the same script or separately in different ones, the results will be the same.

```
1    """
2    Programming in Python for Social Science
3    Phillip Brooker
4
5    6. 2. 1. FOR/WHILE LOOPS
6    """
7
8    #So far, when we've been working with conditional logic and functions, we've
9    #had to pass arguments around "manually" (i.e. by typing commands in the
10   #shell). This is a little tedious and time-consuming. Wouldn't it be great if
11   #we could automate the process? This is the kind of thing we can do with loops.
12
13   #The below code is a "FizzBuzz" script. You may have played "FizzBuzz" in
14   #school, but if not, the rules are as follows: go through the numbers 1 to 100,
15   #and say them out loud. For every number that divides evenly (i.e. no
16   #remainder) by 3 say "Fizz", for every number that divides evenly by 5 say
17   #"Buzz" and for every number that divides by both 5 and 3 say "FizzBuzz".
18   #"Uncomment" the code (i.e. get rid of the speech marks), run the script,
19   #and see what happens.
20
21   """
22   for number in range(1,101):
23       if number % 5 == 0 and number % 3 == 0:
24           print("FizzBuzz")
25       elif number % 3 == 0:
26           print("Fizz")
27       elif number % 5 == 0:
28           print("Buzz")
29       else:
30           print(number)
```

(Continued)

```
31    """
32
33    #Can you see what the for loop does here? It iterates through a range of numbers
34    #from 1 to 100 (the last number in the range is not included), and calls each
35    #one "number" for the purposes of the logic that follows. Then, it moves to
36    #the next "number" and repeats until we've gone through all the numbers in the
37    #range we've set.
38
39    #Another way to do this is with a "While Loop", which can iterate a job for as
40    #long as a certain condition is satisfied. NOTE: when using while loops we have
41    #to also build in a way to CHANGE whether or not the condition is satisfied.
42    #Below I do this by building in "number = number + 1" to the loop. Can you see
43    #what sort of problem might arise if my "while" condition was "while 1 == 1:"?
44    #Try it! Uncomment this code, run it, see what happens, then make some tweaks
45    #to play around and explore how the while loop operates.
46
47    """
48    number = 0
49    while number <= 99:
50        number = number + 1
51        if number % 5 == 0 and number % 3 == 0:
52            print("FizzBuzz")
53        elif number % 3 == 0:
54            print("Fizz")
55        elif number % 5 == 0:
56            print("Buzz")
57        else:
58            print(number)
59    """
60
61    #NOTE: it seems like we've used two different types of loop to do exactly the
62    #same sort of task. This is true, so why are there two different types of loop?
63    #You can see in the examples below ("Loops in Action") that each type of
64    #loop is appropriate in different contexts.
```

A few things to note here. First, you can see that we've used a new command, range(), in line 22. This command allows us to build up a series of numbers based on a starting-point, an end-point and a step count. You should recognise those terms from what you already know from previous sections about "slicing" – range() operates in much the same way. However, you do need to be careful about the syntax when using range(), because it is not exactly the same as slicing. Whereas with slicing you use square brackets and colons to separate values, when using the range() command you use curly brackets and commas. So, you can set a range of numbers as part of a for loop as follows:

```
>>> for number in range(0, 101, 4):
        print(number)
```

Try this out in the shell and see what happens. We ask Python to print out all numbers in the range 0 to 101 (not including 101, since end-points do not include the last value), in steps of 4. Is this list of numbers what you would expect to see? Note also that in 6_2_1_LoopsAndListComprehension.py where we use range() (line 22) we do not set a step count – as with slicing, if we do not set a step count Python assumes we mean steps of 1. However, *unlike* with slicing, we do need to set a starting-point and end-point every time – Python will not let you create an infinite/never-completing range (and your computer processor is very grateful for that). Try playing around with range() to get a feel for it going forward.

Another thing to note is that in the while loop in line 50, we do something that looks a bit mathematically weird:

```
50    number = number + 1
```

If you remember any school algebra, this may look a little strange. However, it's important to remember that programming is *not* mathematics,[3] and there are good reasons as to why this makes sense to do in Python. So, what is this number = number + 1 operation actually doing? First, we take a variable called number, and then we *reassign it a new value*. The new value that we are reassigning it is the *old* value of number, plus 1. So, in effect, we are using this as a counter that enables our while loop to keep track of how many times it has been iterated through – every time it runs, it will add 1 to number, until we get to 99 (where the while loop is told to stop iterating – see line 49 in the code).

Working with list comprehensions

Now on to list comprehensions (in the same code file, 6_2_1_LoopsAndListComprehension.py):

```
66    #An added extra of for loops is the idea that we can use conditional logic and
67    #loops WITHIN lists, to create NEW lists based on objects that we can iterate
68    #through (i.e. strings, tuples, or even other lists). This is called "list
69    #comprehension", and it works as follows:
70
71    iterable_object = "A string is an example of an iterable object."
72    new_list = [item for item in iterable_object]
73
74    #In the above code, the "new_list" variable will be where the new list is
75    #stored. Then we tell Python that we're creating a list by using square
76    #brackets. Then the first "item" refers to the thing that we want to put
77    #in the list. "for item in iterable_object" means that for each item in
```

(Continued)

---

[3] I'm sure some of you are very thankful for that.

```
78    #the object we want to iterate through, we will call that item and drop
79    #it in "new_list". Try calling new_list to see what it contains.
80
81    #We can also use conditional logic within list comprehensions, as follows:
82
83    animal_list = ["dog", "owl", "fox", "snake", "mouse", "squirrel", "fish"]
84    animals_w_legs = [animal for animal in animal_list
85                             if animal != "snake" and animal != "fish"]
```

Can you see what is happening in the first list comprehension (lines 71–72)? We are using a term, `item`, as a placeholder for individual characters in the string (a string being an "iterable object", i.e. a collection of characters that we can iterate through). We could in principle use any term we like – there is nothing special about the term `item` in Python, we could have written `letters` or `characters` or `foonboahd`. The important thing is that we are telling our list comprehension that for each `item` (or `letter` or `character` or `foonboahd`) we find in `iterable_object`, that *that* is what we want to add to `new_list`.

The second list comprehension works in much the same way, except that we're now iterating through a list rather than a string, and we're also using conditional logic to select (and not select) things to go in the new `animals_w_legs` list. So, we're iterating through all the animals in `animal_list`, but since we clearly want a list of only animals with legs (`animals_w_legs` being the variable name), we have used conditional logic to exclude `snake` and `fish` from the list.

Filtering data with loops and list comprehensions

With these techniques in mind, open the file called `6_2_2_LoopsAndList ComprehensionExercise.py`, run it, and try completing the exercise for yourself before looking at my suggested solutions.

```
1     """
2     Programming in Python for Social Science
3     Phillip Brooker
4
5     6. 2. 2. LOOPS AND LIST COMPREHENSION EXERCISE
6     """
7
8     """
9     EXERCISE:
10    Go through each word in "word_list" (below), and if a word contains the letter
11    "g", put it in a new list. Do this two ways: (1) with a for loop, and (2) as a
12    list comprehension.
13    """
14    word_list = ["able", "barrel", "beef", "beep", "biggest", "bookshelf",
15                     "bottle", "broken", "chip", "chrome", "clay", "clip",
```

16	`"colander", "collection", "complicated", "cousin", "crispy",`
17	`"dance", "drench", "drums", "egg", "elastic", "engine", "felt",`
18	`"fighting", "fine", "fire", "folder", "foolish", "freezing",`
19	`"fried", "fumble", "fuzzy", "gas", "green", "grief", "gross",`
20	`"grown", "harmonica", "hulking", "hybrid", "icon", "input", "jet",`
21	`"kindness", "lemon", "lurch", "melon", "mulch", "no", "obscuring",`
22	`"output", "political", "quit", "red", "regal", "rent", "retro",`
23	`"retry", "ride", "sad", "silly", "smell", "spatula", "steel",`
24	`"supermarket", "tab", "teeth", "tip", "tree", "trip", "tube",`
25	`"turtle", "unlikely", "varnish", "vine", "vulture", "wind",`
26	`"wing", "wink", "word", "written", "xenon", "yoghurt", "zesty"]`

The exercise comes in two parts. Part one asks us to use a for loop to go through `word_list` and put every word containing the letter "g" into a new list. My suggested solution is as follows:

```
1   g_words = []
2   for word in word_list:
3       if "g" in word:
4           g_words.append(word)
5       else:
6           pass
```

Let's walk through what happens here. In line 1 of this solution I declare an empty list (into which I'm going to drop words containing a "g"). In line 2, I write the for clause, which states that I want to do something for each `word  in  word_list` – note that I could have used whatever term I liked for `word`, but `word` makes sense in context (and will help other people to read what my script is actually doing). Then, I use an IF/ELSE statement to check to see if each of these words has a "g" in it. If the word *does*, I append it to `g_words`. If it *doesn't*, I just pass and go on to the next word. The for loop will iterate through each word in `word_list` until there are no more.

For part two of the exercise, we're asked to do exactly the same thing, but using a list comprehension instead of a for loop. My suggested solution is as follows:

```
1   g_words2 = [word for word in word_list if "g" in word]
```

So let's walk through this too. I start by declaring that I want a new list called `g_words2` (and denote this as a list by assigning the thing to it within square brackets). Then, I say that for every `word` in `word_list`, if there is a "g" in that word, put it in this list as an entry. Note that the bit of code that puts the words in the list is the very first `word` term (i.e. the one directly after the opening square bracket). So, running through from left to right, we can say we want our list to consist of things called a `word`, where those words are selected from all words in `word_list` on the basis of whether or not they contain a "g". This is quite a nice solution[4] in that it does everything in one line of code. However, given that it might be tricky

---

[4] If I do say so myself!

to unpick what each element of a list comprehension is actually doing (especially if they get more complicated than this!), then sometimes it will be preferable to keep things readable and use a more standard for loop.

Either way, with both of these methods, if you then call the lists that you have produced (in my case, g_words and g_words2), you should see the following words result:

```
['biggest', 'egg', 'engine', 'fighting', 'freezing', 'gas', 'green', 'grief',
'gross', 'grown', 'hulking', 'obscuring', 'regal', 'wing', 'yoghurt']
```

Loops in action

Loops are incredibly useful tools in Python, which allow you to automate jobs – very handy when you need to check through all the elements in a particular data structure (a list or dictionary, for instance) or perform a single task multiple times. Here are two examples, though the possibilities really are endless (especially when you consider how for/while loops can be used in conjunction with things like IF/ELSE statements, or even nested within other for/while loops!).

Iterating through data. Loops are a great way of automating the kinds of conditional checks we talked about in previous chapters, especially when you might have so many different bits of data that checking each of these one by one could take a very long time!

For example, suppose you have a dataset of tweets posted with the hashtag #GE2017 – thousands of tweets about a hugely popular topic of conversation, the 2017 UK general election. Each tweet is a tuple – the tweeter's username and the tweet content itself – and all of these tuples are collected together in one big list. But you're only interested in five particular tweeters, so how do you extract those users' tweets from this huge dataset, without having to scan through it all by eye? A for loop, combined with other techniques you already know from previous chapters, will help here:

```
>>> for username in big_dataset:
        if username == "userofinterest":
          [PUT TUPLE IN A NEW LIST]
        else:
            pass
```

Five lines of code, and you've sorted out a huge chunk of data into something you can actually work with!

Performing a job multiple times. Loops are also great when you want to perform some kind of job multiple times – they can be great time-savers in this regard, and enable you to do increasingly complex things quite easily.

Suppose you are interested in a particular Facebook page about political activism, and you want to collect details of the last 50 posts. You can use a while loop to keep count of how many posts you've collected, and to tell Python to stop once you've reached 50:

```
>>> post_count = 0
```

```
>>>
>>> while post_count <= 50:
        [SCRAPE THE LAST COMMENT]
        [MOVE BACK TO THE PREVIOUS COMMENT]
        post_count = post_count + 1
```

Rest assured that you are not going to break your computer or cause any horrible crashes if you get into a never-ending loop; you can always just close the program without waiting for it to finish (since waiting for a never-ending loop to finish would probably not be a great idea!). So don't worry too much about getting your code wrong – it's OK to make mistakes, that's part of learning! But of course, it's a good idea to think about and plan out how you expect things like for and while loops to operate before you write the code.

Chapter summary

- In this chapter, we learned about functions in Python; what they do, and what they are for.
- We also learned about Python conventions with regard to naming functions (i.e. using camelCase) which helps make our code more readable.
- In the exercise on functions, we built a tool that "streamlines" the process of checking whether or not I like specified pizza toppings - this tool simplifies, automates and modularises a particular Python task, and as such, allows us to appreciate the core purpose of functions (which is, crudely, to facilitate the repetition of tasks in a relatively small amount of code).
- We examined the difference between the `return()` and `print()` methods, paying attention to contexts in which one or the other is more appropriate.
- We looked at the concept of "scope", in terms of how we might define or assign things like variables either globally (i.e. outside a function) or locally (i.e. within a function).
- We then moved on to exploring for/while loops as ways of iterating through ranges and/or objects.
- We also looked at the concept of "list comprehension" - the building of lists based on for/while loop techniques (and which can also be coupled with conditional logic statements).
- We put this knowledge to use in a practical application as part of the associated exercise - iterating through a list of words to find all those that contain the letter "g" - using both for/while loops and list comprehension methods.

7

Building New Objects with Classes

━━━━━━━━━━━━ **Chapter objectives** ━━━━━━━━━━━━

- Learn how to build your own objects in Python, to feed into more advanced programming tasks.

7.1 Classes

So far, we've seen lots of different types of objects in Python (integers, floats, strings, lists, dictionaries, functions, etc.) and we've spent some time learning how to work with them. This belies Python's role as an "object-oriented" programming language – everything in Python is an object, and arguments can be passed around from object to object for whatever purpose you like.

However, we don't just have to rely on the objects that Python delineates for us – we can create our own with classes. With classes, we can build "blueprints" or templates for new objects, which we can give new attributes and new methods (i.e. functions). The reasons why we might want to do this should become clear as we go through the code and through the "Classes in action" subsection below. For now, however, we might note that we could be working with many different *kinds* of data (i.e. object) in any given coding project – below, I talk about an example where I'm working with different types of social media data, for instance – and it doesn't make sense to treat all these different types of thing as if they were the same (and as if we would want to perform the same kinds of functions on them). Hence, using classes, we can make distinctions between different types of object that we bring into Python, so that we can handle them appropriately. With classes we can collect new types of object together and work with them in repeatable ways on the basis that they share common properties.

Working with classes

Let's look at how this works in code. Open the file called 7_1_1_Classes.py, execute it, and work your way through the script and the instructions therein. Note that there are naming conventions to bear in mind when working with classes – classes use CapitalsOnly (whereas other objects like functions use other conventions like camelCase). This doesn't matter to the operation of the code (in that if you make a mistake and do everything in lower case, the code will still work), but it does help in terms of making a visual distinction between things like classes and functions when you're working with them, so as a readability issue these conventions are important.

```
1    """
2    Programming in Python for Social Science
3    Phillip Brooker
4
5    7. 1. 1. CLASSES
```

```
 6    """
 7
 8    #Below is how you create a class - there are lots of things going on, but we
 9    #will explore these in more detail in the relevant section of the book. For now
10    #suffice to say that this class contains attributes and methods (i.e. functions)
11    #that a zookeeper might find useful.
12
13    class Animal:
14        animal_list = []
15        animal_count = 0
16        def __init__(self, name, gender, species, age):
17            self.name = name
18            self.gender = gender
19            self.species = species
20            self.age = age
21            Animal.animal_list.append(self)
22            Animal.animal_count = Animal.animal_count + 1
23        def displayCount():
24            print("There are " + str(Animal.animal_count) + " animals in the zoo.")
25        def displayAnimal(self):
26            print(self.name + " is a " + self.gender + " " + self.species + ".")
27            print(self.name + " is " + str(self.age) + " years old.")
28
29    #So the "blueprint" bit of the class is outlined above, but we need to fill it
30    #with entries - below is a list of animals in the zoo, and various properties
31    #of them. This is how you assign things to the class we've just built.
32
33    gill = Animal("Gill", "female", "bison", 14)
34    bruce = Animal("Bruce", "male", "zebra", 7)
35    tony = Animal("Tony", "male", "orangutan", 22)
36    rebecca = Animal("Rebecca", "female", "tree frog", 1)
37    sweaty = Animal("Sweaty", "male", "fox", 34)
38    slippy = Animal("Slippy", "female", "penguin", 4)
39
40    #Now try playing around with each animal's attributes - let's call up certain
41    #bits of information about the animals in the zoo. Type this into the shell:
42    tony.species
43    sweaty.age
44    slippy.gender
45
46    #Now try playing around with the class methods (i.e. functions) we built in.
47    #Start by typing the following function calls into the shell:
48    """
49    Animal.displayCount()
50    Animal.displayAnimal(rebecca)
51    """
```

Class construction

Let's work through the `Animal` class I establish in lines 13–27 – I advise you to pay attention to the syntax and whitespace throughout. First, we tell Python we want to create a class called `Animal` by typing `class Animal:`. Then we give the class two variables that we want to be associated with it – this is to say that everything that gets classed as an `Animal` will have some kind of association with a list called `animal_list` and an integer variable called `animal_count`. Note that this is one of the useful things about classes; stuff that *isn't* classed as an `Animal` won't be able to impact on these variables, and this prevents unexpected bugs down the line (i.e. if we had an object that *wasn't* an animal, but was somehow making its way into `animal_list`, that would be a problem).

The next thing to note is some new bits of syntax you haven't seen before (lines 16–20). Every class will need to feature some code like this, which is called the "class constructor" (or "initialiser"), which looks like a function (i.e. `def __init__(self, name, gender, species, age):`). We don't need to know too much about the mechanics of how this works, but this line of code is where we set up the "attributes" of the `Animal` class – common properties that we want the class to store as part of each `Animal` object. So, for every `Animal` object we want to classify as such, we are telling Python that we want it to have a selection of properties: a name, a gender, a species and an age. Note that we also use the term `self` throughout this section of the code. This is an essential part of building a class, and just allows the class to deal with specific objects that we throw at it – for instance, if we want to *create* an `Animal` object, the `self` term is just a way we can get the `Animal` class to recognise the `Animal` object we are trying to create.

Once we have created a function for initialising instances of the class (i.e. we have a function called `__init__` which will take arguments for `self`, `name`, `gender`, `species` and `age`), we can also add extra stuff into this class constructor/initialiser section. So, for every new `Animal` object we create, I have written a line of code that will take that class object and put it in `animal_list` (line 21) and a line that will reflect that I have added a new Animal object by adding 1 to `animal_count` (line 22). You can see that I am not just referring to `animal_list` and `animal_count` in these lines, but also to `Animal.animal_list` and `Animal.animal_count`. This is because we need to tell Python where to find that list and that count variable – they are *within* the `Animal` class, and Python will not be able to locate them without being told as much. Bear this in mind as we get into working with classes later in the chapter.

The class constructor/initialiser is just something we have to have in every class, and the term `self` is conventional across Python classes. We *can* add other bits of stuff to our class (as I've done in the code excerpt for this chapter), but it's worth just remembering (or writing down) a basic framework for building a very simple class, which you can edit for the purposes of whatever classes you create:

```
1   class ClassName:
2       def __init__(self, attribute1, attribute2, etc):
3           self.attribute1 = attribute1
4           self.attribute2 = attribute2
5           self.etc = etc
```

That's an explanation of what the class constructor/initialiser does – in short, it sets out a template for any animal we want to classify *as* an `Animal` by saying it must have a name, gender, species and age. These are the expected *attributes* of the new `Animal` objects we want to create. However, we can also say that we want there to be certain methods (i.e. functions) that we want to apply *only* to `Animal` objects. These can be defined within the scope of the class too, and I define two such functions as follows.

Lines 23–24 define a function called `displayCount()` which doesn't take an argument, but which we can use to print out a string that provides information about how many animals are currently classified as `Animal` (i.e. it uses a stringified version of the integer value for `Animal`. `animal_count` to tell us how many animals are currently in the zoo). Lines 25–27 do a similar job – here, I define a function called `displayAnimal(self)` which takes one argument (`self`) and then prints out a string that gives us information about the object we've chosen to pass into the function as the argument (i.e. a particular animal we have classified as `Animal`).

Class instances

So now we have an explanation of how we have set up a class called `Animal`, and what is going on in the various bits of code within it. The next job is to establish a set of objects each of which we want to classify as an `Animal` – effectively, we want to create a selection of variables that contain all the attributes of an `Animal`, and classify that variable as such. You can see this in lines 33–38 of the code excerpt, but I'll just walk through one example below:

```
1   gill = Animal("Gill", "female", "bison", 14)
```

Here, we have a variable (`gill`), to which we assign the attributes we want (name, gender, species and age) as comma-separated values within round brackets, and before these brackets we tell Python which class we want this object classified under (i.e. `Animal`). One thing worth noting is that once the class is set up, we can run it in the shell and, if your particular IDE has the relevant functionality, we can see a "tool-tip" similar to the one in Figure 7.1.

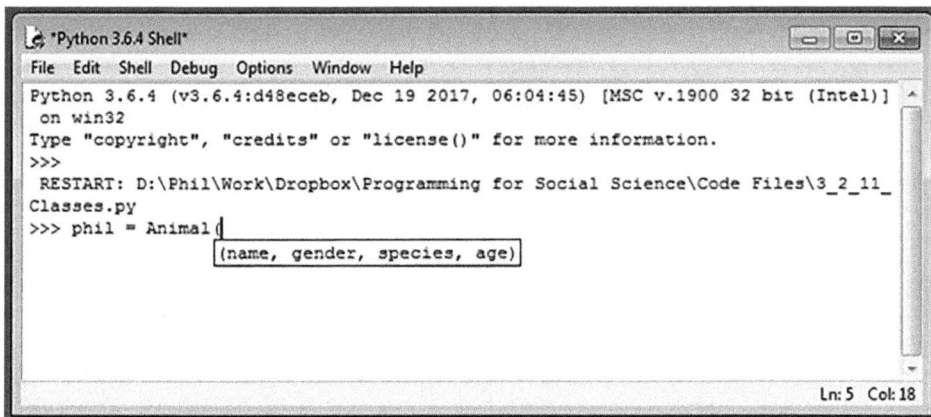

Figure 7.1 Assigning a class instance in the shell (plus helpful tool-tip)

In this image you can see that I'm creating a new instance of an `Animal` object called `phil` (with the attributes `Phil`, `male`, `human` and `32`) and IDLE (as my IDE of choice) provides a helpful little reminder as to what attributes are expected. This happens because we've set up the `Animal` class with attributes already, so Python knows that the object we're trying to work with needs to have information *about* those attributes (otherwise an error will occur). This is useful for us in terms of helping us remember what objects in the `Animal` class need to contain, as we're creating the information for a new instance of an `Animal` object.

Now we have a class, and we have things that are classified according to it. The next step is to play around with those things – the code excerpt asks you to try out some commands in the shell that pertain to bits of information associated with instances of the class (i.e. things that have been classified as `Animal`), and functions associated with the class (i.e. the functions which display the total count of all animals in the zoo, and present information about individual class instances). Try playing around with these things: call them yourself, assign a new `Animal` object, perhaps even build a new class attribute or method that you think it would be useful for a zookeeper to keep a track of – something like the continent from which the `Animal` originates? Then a function/method for keeping a tally of how many animals are from each continent? Try things out, see how they work, and whether they produce the results you expect.

Using classes to build an academic referencing tool

Once you've finished working with the `Animal` class, open the file called `7_1_2_ ClassesExercise.py`, run it, and work your way through the exercise. I should warn you: this exercise is a *big* one. Since classes can incorporate lots of different core Python concepts (all of which you already know), the exercise will use skills and techniques you've learned throughout the whole set of chapters in Part Two to this point. Handily, the exercise comes in five discrete parts – I'll deal with each part separately in my suggested solutions, and then bring them all together in a single scripted solution at the end. For now, try working your way through the exercise.

```
1    """
2    Programming in Python for Social Science
3    Phillip Brooker
4
5    7. 1. 2. CLASSES EXERCISE
6    """
7
8    """
9    EXERCISE:
10   1) Create a class for academic books you have read in your studies, which can
11   record various reference attributes (i.e. author name, year of publication,
12   title, publisher location and publisher name) as well as a string of the
13   variable name you're using for each entry.
14
15   NOTE: let's just stick with books as a publication format, and with single-
```

```
16    authored books at that. This just keeps things simple.
17
18    2) Within this class, create a class list which can store tuples of variable
19    name, author names and titles of each book you input, so you can keep a track
20    of all the things you read and keep a catalogue of which variables those
21    entries are stored under.
22
23    3) Create some entries - at least 5.
24
25    4) Build a method (i.e. a function) into the class for printing out references
26    in full Harvard format.
27
28    5) Find out (with relevant programming methods) how many entries are written by
29    a particularly favourite author.
30    """
```

Once you've had a go at the exercise, take a look at my suggested solution below:

```
1     """
2     EXERCISE:
3     1) Create a class for academic books you have read in your studies, which can
4     record various reference attributes (i.e. author name, year of publication,
5     title, publisher location and publisher name) as well as a string of the
6     variable name you're using for each entry.
7
8     NOTE: let's just stick with books as a publication format, and with single-
9     authored books at that. This just keeps things simple.
10    """
11
12    class Books:
13        def __init__(self, var, auth_name, auth_initial, year, title, pub_loc, pub):
14            self.var = var
15            self.auth_name = auth_name
16            self.auth_initial = auth_initial
17            self.year = year
18            self.title = title
19            self.pub_loc = pub_loc
20            self.pub = pub
```

This is the bones of our new class, Books. Within this class, we have established a range of attributes we want each Books object to have – a string of the variable name we're using, the author's surname and initials, the year of publication, the title of the book, the location of the publishing company and the name of the publishing company. Now, anything we want to classify as a Books object will have to feature all these attributes.

```
1    """
2    2) Within this class, create a class list which can store tuples of variable
3    name, author names and titles of each book you input, so you can keep a track
4    of all the things you read and keep a catalogue of which variables those
5    entries are stored under.
6    """
7
8    class Books:
9        book_list = []
10       def __init__(self, var, auth_name, auth_initial, year, title, pub_loc, pub):
11           self.var = var
12           self.auth_name = auth_name
13           self.auth_initial = auth_initial
14           self.year = year
15           self.title = title
16           self.pub_loc = pub_loc
17           self.pub = pub
18           Books.book_list.append((self.var, self.auth_name, self.title))
```

In this second part of the exercise, what have I done? I have added, to the Books class I already created, a new empty list called book_list. Within the initialisation function, I have made sure that for any books that get classified with this class, their variable name (as a string), the author's surname and the title of the book get appended to book_list as a tuple. You can see this in the following line of code:

```
Books.book_list.append((self.var, self.auth_name, self.title))
```

Walking through this line from left to right, we start with Books as denoting that whatever follows is part of the Books class. We then state that we want to append the contents of the round brackets that follow to book_list. And those contents are a tuple (denoted by a further set of round brackets) comprising the variable name, the author's name and the title of the book in question. As an aside, it's worth reiterating what the double round brackets are doing here. The first set of round brackets is what we need to show Python we want to append to book_list. The second set is our way of showing Python that what we want to append is itself contained within round brackets (i.e. is a tuple) – if we wanted to append a list we would see something like: ([CONTENTS, OF, LIST]) where the square brackets were contained within the round ones.

However, at this point, we still won't see anything in book_list, because we haven't yet assigned anything as part of the Books class. The next part of the exercise asks us to do exactly this:

```
1    """
2    3) Create some entries - at least 5.
3    """
```

```
 4   phenom_soc_world = Books("phenom_soc_world", "Schutz", "A", 1972,
 5                            "The Phenomenology of the Social World",
 6                            "Evanston, IL", "Northwestern University Press")
 7   phil_inv = Books("phil_inv", "Wittgenstein", "L", 2009,
 8                    "Philosophical Investigations",
 9                    "Chichester, UK", "Wiley-Blackwell")
10   dig_meth = Books("dig_meth", "Rogers", "R", 2013,
11                    "Digital Methods",
12                    "Cambridge, MA", "MIT Press")
13   twitter = Books("twitter", "Murthy", "D", 2013,
14                   "Twitter: Social Communication in the Twitter Age",
15                   "Cambridge", "Polity Press")
16   witt_hum_form = Books("witt_hum_form", "Hanfling", "O", 2006,
17                         "Wittgenstein and the Human Form of Life",
18                         "London", "Routledge")
19   hate_crim_cyber = Books("hate_crim_cyber", "Citron", "D", 2014,
20                           "Hate Crimes in Cyberspace",
21                           "Cambridge, MA", "Harvard University Press")
22   blue_brown = Books("blue_brown", "Wittgenstein", "L", 1958,
23                      "The Blue and Brown Books",
24                      "Oxford", "Blackwell")
25   pwpfss = Books("pwpfss", "Brooker", "P", 2019,
26                  "Programming with Python for Social Science",
27                  "London", "SAGE")
28   iss = Books("iss", "Winch", "P", 1990,
29               "The Idea of a Social Science, and Its Relation to Philosophy",
30               "London", "Routledge")
31   stud_ethno = Books("stud_ethno", "Garfinkel", "H", 1967,
32                      "Studies in Ethnomethodology",
33                      "Englewood Cliffs, NJ", "Prentice Hall")
34   tlp = Books("tlp", "Wittgenstein", "L", 2005,
35               "Tractatus Logico-Philosophicus",
36               "Abingdon", "Routledge")
37   cult_con = Books("cult_con", "van Dijck", "J", 2013,
38                    "The Culture of Connectivity",
39                    "Oxford", "Oxford University Press")
40   ethno_prog = Books("ethno_prog", "Garfinkel", "H", 2002,
41                      "Ethnomethodology's Program",
42                      "Oxford", "Rowman and Littlefield Publishers")
```

You can see that these lines of code look a little weird – you should recognise the syntax of ClassName(attribute1, attribute2, etc) from the code excerpt above (7_1_1_ Classes.py), but you can also see that what is between the brackets seems to be broken up over multiple lines rather than fitting neatly on one as it did before. This is because of space limitations in this book which prevent me from neatly showing lines of code longer than 80 characters. *However*, it is also a good convention not to write lines of code that are longer than

80 characters anyway – so far, we've managed to avoid this in the examples given, but now the examples are getting a little more complex this will not be possible. So, what you're seeing is a continuation of the selection of attributes we're building into each instance of the class Books, but each broken across three lines of code. For each instance, Python will run these three lines *as if* they were joined up – the various attributes required by the argument are separated by commas, so Python doesn't care if there are returns thrown in there too. In this context, Python only recognises and cares about commas. This is a handy trick for keeping all your code visible on the page rather than having it exceed 80 characters and go off the edge (which is what the "80 characters max" convention is supposed to prevent).

Other than that, you should recognise and be familiar with the idea of assigning information/attributes to a variable from the code excerpt 7_1_1_Classes.py – this is how we're populating our class of Books with instances.

The fourth part of the exercise asks us to return to the class object itself and add in a new method (i.e. function) which can use the attributes associated with each class instance to produce an academic reference in full Harvard format. And we all know what the Harvard format of referencing a book looks like – or we could all do a quick internet search to find out (hint, hint). So, we have all the information we need to do this (in the form of class attributes associated with each instance of Books), but we'll need some string formatting to help us, as follows:

```
1    """
2    4) Build a method (i.e. a function) into the class for printing out references
3    in full Harvard format.
4    """
5
6    class Books:
7        book_list= []
8        def __init__(self, var, auth_name, auth_initial, year, title, pub_loc, pub):
9            self.var = var
10           self.auth_name = auth_name
11           self.auth_initial = auth_initial
12           self.year = year
13           self.title = title
14           self.pub_loc = pub_loc
15           self.pub = pub
16           Books.book_list.append((self.var, self.auth_name, self.title))
17       def displayRef(self):
18           print(self.auth_name + ", " + self.auth_initial + ". " +
19               "(" + str(self.year) + ") " + self.title.upper() + ". " +
20               self.pub_loc + ": " + self.pub)
```

Here, you can see we've added in a method to our Books class, called displayRef(), which is a rather convoluted print statement featuring various class attributes all concatenated together in one big string. This function takes one argument (which we've called self), and we are building it so that we can pass an instance of a `Books` object through it. Reading from left to right, the `print` statement takes the author's surname followed by a comma and a space, followed by the author's initial followed by a full stop and a space. Then, we add a string of an open round bracket (and take the year (making sure to stringify it, since it naturally comes in the form of an integer, and integers and strings can't be concatenated), then add a closed round bracket) and a space. Next we add the title of the book, using the `.upper()` command to put this in ALL CAPS. This is followed by a string of a full stop and a space. Then we add the publisher's location, a colon followed by a space, and then the publisher's name. As noted above, every element of this is a string, which the `print` statement prints so that it appears as follows:

```
>>> Books.displayRef(dig_meth)
Rogers, R. (2013) DIGITAL METHODS. Cambridge, MA: MIT Press
```

So that's part four done! Part five asks us to then build a bit of code to find out (using relevant programming methods) how many entries are written by a particularly favourite author – in my case, things authored by Ludwig Wittgenstein. So, thinking in programming terms, we want to iterate through all the entries in `Books.book_list` and find any entries where `Wittgenstein` appears as `auth_name`. The word "iterating" should make us think of loops – my suggested solution is below:

```
1    """
2    5) Find out (with relevant programming methods) how many entries are written by
3    a particularly favourite author.
4    """
5
6    witt_list = []
7    for entry in Books.book_list:
8        if entry[1] == "Wittgenstein":
9            witt_list.append(entry)
10       else:
11           pass
```

What's happening here is that I create an empty list (`witt_list`) where I want to store any entries for books written by Ludwig Wittgenstein. Then I use conditional logic and slicing to identify those entries that satisfy that criterion – if the first index position (i.e. `auth_name`) of an entry in `Books.book_list` is equal to the string `Wittgenstein`, it gets appended to the list. If not, we pass and try the next entry. Once this code runs, I have a list that contains any entry where `Wittgenstein` is the value for `auth_name`. Then, in the shell I can run the following code to check the length of that list and see how many books in `Books` are written by Ludwig Wittgenstein:

```
>>> len(witt_list)
3
```

When viewed together, the whole script of my suggested solution is as follows:

```
1    class Books:
2        book_list= []
3        def __init__(self, var, auth_name, auth_initial, year, title, pub_loc, pub):
4            self.var = var
5            self.auth_name = auth_name
6            self.auth_initial = auth_initial
7            self.year = year
8            self.title = title
9            self.pub_loc = pub_loc
10           self.pub = pub
11           Books.book_list.append((self.var, self.auth_name, self.title))
12       def displayRef(self):
13           print(self.auth_name + ", " + self.auth_initial + ". " +
14               "(" + str(self.year) + ") " + self.title.upper() + ". " +
15               self.pub_loc + ": " + self.pub)
16
17   phenom_soc_world = Books("phenom_soc_world", "Schutz", "A", 1972,
18                   "The Phenomenology of the Social World",
19   "Evanston, IL", "Northwestern University Press")
20   phil_inv = Books("phil_inv", "Wittgenstein", "L", 2009,
21                   "Philosophical Investigations",
22                   "Chichester", "Wiley-Blackwell")
23   dig_meth = Books("dig_meth", "Rogers", "R", 2013,
24                   "Digital Methods",
25                   "Cambridge, MA", "MIT Press")
26   twitter = Books("twitter", "Murthy", "D", 2013,
27                   "Twitter: Social Communication in the Twitter Age",
28                   "Cambridge", "Polity Press")
29   witt_hum_form = Books("witt_hum_form", "Hanfling", "O", 2006,
30                     "Wittgenstein and the Human Form of Life",
31                     "London", "Routledge")
32   hate_crim_cyber = Books("hate_crim_cyber", "Citron", "D", 2014,
33                       "Hate Crimes in Cyberspace",
34                       "Cambridge, MA", "Harvard University Press")
35   blue_brown = Books("blue_brown", "Wittgenstein", "L", 1958,
36                     "The Blue and Brown Books",
37                     "Oxford", "Blackwell")
38   pwpfss = Books("pwpfss", "Brooker", "P", 2019,
39                   "Programming with Python for Social Science",
40                   "London", "SAGE")
41   iss = Books("iss", "Winch", "P", 1990,
42               "The Idea of a Social Science, and Its Relation to Philosophy",
43               "London", "Routledge")
44   stud_ethno = Books("stud_ethno", "Garfinkel", "H", 1967,
45                     "Studies in Ethnomethodology",
```

```
46                     "Englewood Cliffs, NJ", "Prentice Hall")
47   tlp = Books("tlp", "Wittgenstein", "L", 2005,
48               "Tractatus Logico-Philosophicus",
49               "Abingdon", "Routledge")
50   cult_con = Books("cult_con", "van Dijck", "J", 2013,
51                    "The Culture of Connectivity",
52                    "Oxford", "Oxford University Press")
53   ethno_prog = Books("ethno_prog", "Garfinkel", "H", 2002,
54                      "Ethnomethodology's Program",
55                      "Lanham, MD", "Rowman and Littlefield Publishers")
56
57   witt_list = []
58   for entry in Books.book_list:
59       if entry[1] == "Wittgenstein":
60           witt_list.append(entry)
61       else:
62           pass
63
64   len(witt_list)
```

Phew! That's a *lot* of stuff in this exercise! And it's a lot of lines of code (although most of that is data entry stuff to do with writing in 13 different books that I've read). But, this exercise has given you your first real programming project to tackle – if you've followed the steps and addressed the parts of the exercise in a way that gets you the results you need, you've built a useful tool! One key thing of this is to learn about how classes work and how to build them. Another key thing is to get some practice with techniques we've learned elsewhere in Part Two (string formatting, for loops, etc.). Another, and equally important, key thing we've done is *apply all the skills we know in using your programming mindset*, to think through problems in terms of how they might be translatable into various Python concepts. This is no mean feat! And it's something we'll be continuing to do throughout this book.

One final note to end our exploration of classes on – just like any other object in Python, we can position classes as part of a *hierarchy* of objects. This is to say that we can have "parent" classes and "child" classes, for instance. One example of how this might work is if we think about extending the Books class to include sub-classes or child classes for MultiAuthoredBooks or EditedCollections or BookChapters – we might want to use the Books class as a parent class which contains the fundamental attributes for *all* books, but then have various child classes within that which capture different *types* of Books. Equally, we might want to write other classes for things like JournalPapers or Blogs, and then collect all those together (with Books) in a bigger parent class called Publications (which could in principle contain attributes that cut across any and all publication types, Books, JournalPapers and Blogs being three of those child class types). So, just as we can create objects within Python by using classes, we can create object hierarchies by thinking of certain classes as "belonging to" others (and we can write these hierarchical relationships into the code). That, however, is a story for another day – though perhaps it is something for you to tinker with, based on the books exercise you have just completed.

Classes in action

Classes as "blueprints" for data. One option for sorting out your data is to use classes which generate a framework (or "blueprint") for your data. Suppose you're working with lots of different types of data in one Python script – you might be comparing people's social media usage across various platforms, so you have Instagram data, Facebook data and Twitter data. But each social media platform has a different set of features about it, which means that the data are not the same across all three platforms.

Instagram posts have data associated with them including (a) date and time of posting, (b) file directory of image/video, (c) a string denoting which type of file the post is (i.e. "image", "video" or "live video"), (d) a string containing the caption that accompanies the post, and (e) an integer value for how many likes the post has received.

Facebook statuses have data associated with them including (a) date and time of posting, (b) a string denoting which type of content the post contains (i.e. "text", "image", "live video", "shared post", etc.), (c) a string containing the caption that accompanied the status, (d) an integer for the number of likes/reactions the status update received, and (e) an integer for the number of comments the status update received.

Tweets have data associated with them including (a) the date and time of posting, (b) the text content of the tweet stored as a string, and (c) a string denoting whether or not the tweet was a retweet or an original post (i.e. "original" or "retweet").

It's clear that each of the three types of data has different properties associated with it – hence, it makes sense to create three classes (Instagram, Facebook and Twitter), so that you can be sure that whenever you're dealing with a tweet object you know exactly what attributes are associated with it. For instance, if you're inputting all the data around a new tweet, your Twitter class will not accept an argument for how many likes/reactions it has, because that doesn't make sense (that's more of a Facebook thing). So when you're working with classes in this way, it can help you keep your data organised to prevent against mistakes being made along the way.

Chapter summary

- Given what we know about the various object types that exist in Python, we looked at the concept of "classes" as a means of building our own objects, to which we can assign specific attributes as well as methods (i.e. functions).
- We also learned about the convention of naming classes with CapitalsOnly - this helps us (and others) easily identify where classes appear in code, which is helpful readability-wise.
- We worked through the concept of "class construction" (or "class initialisation"), as the way to set up a template for a new object.
- We then spent some time inputting new "instances" into our class template - we saw how you would add a new animal into an `Animal` class, by assigning its attributes to a variable.
- We then worked through a lengthy exercise that allowed you to practise your skills with building classes and class methods, as well as skills learned throughout Part Two (such as string formatting, for/while loops and conditional logic).
- We reflected on the concept of hierarchies of classes (i.e. parent and child classes) as a means of building more sophisticated objects and structures of objects in Python.

8

Useful Extra
Concepts/Practices

━━━━━━━━━━━━━━━ **Chapter objectives** ━━━━━━━━━━━━━━━

- Learn about a small selection of "added extras" to Python which can help you build (and think about building) better code.

That just about concludes our look at the core concepts of Python. In this chapter, I'll just be providing quick and easy reference material for the techniques on display, since by this point you'll be comfortable with working with Python code and will really just need a brief explanation to get you started.

8●1 Installing Modules

One of the most useful affordances of Python as a programming language is that it has an incredible community of developers around it, producing an incredible array of tools and libraries – let's call them modules – that can make the work of complex tasks (like using a social media API (Application Programming Interface), or web scraping, or visualising data graphically, all of which are covered in this book) much more straightforward to code. Earlier in the book, I compared using techniques from modules as being like the difference between saying "you know that snow that's also like rain, but also like ice and it comes down quick and hurts when it falls on you?" and simply saying "hailstones". Modules give us easy-to-use "shorthand" code for doing complex tasks, which saves us having to build this kind of code from scratch – we'll see some specific examples of this below. However, given that some of these modules aren't "native" to Python (inasmuch as they don't exist in the core Python language as you install it), we have to install them separately. You might see these called "third-party" modules. So here's a little guide to the kinds of thing you'll need to do to install Python modules on your system, via a demonstration of how I do these things on my Windows laptop.[1]

The application we need to install these Python packages is called "pip" (which stands for "Pip Installs Packages" – software developer humour ¯_(ツ)_/¯). Specifically, since we're using Python 3, we need to use pip3. Handily for us, your Python installation will have already included pip3 as part of it, so we don't need to install any extra stuff here. However,

---

[1]Like the rest of this book, this guide is written specifically from a Windows user's perspective, though I will also comment on how Linux users might apply these same things at the end of this section for reasons that will become apparent then. Again, this is due to the unavoidable tension between having to write instructions specific enough that they can be illustrative of the actual practical work they're intended to instruct in, whilst being general enough that they can be useful in the different contexts that readers no doubt want to apply them to. For the same reason, I should also note that as with some of the information elsewhere in this book, I have to deal with the "problem" that it's practically impossible to write a bespoke installation routine for specific users on specific operating systems with specific directory structures for specific module installations. However, the intention is that users of any operating system will be able to see how they might go about finding out the things they need to know in order to install the modules they need - if the step-by-step instructions don't work for you, try to make them make sense for your own specific context.

the way we're going to access this pip3 application is quite different from how we might access other applications we're more familiar with, like web browsers or word processors. Whereas a web browser or word processor has an icon to click and a fancy visually oriented user interface to help us use the program, we have to access pip3 in a more "old-school" way – through a command-line interface, where we type in text instructions to tell the computer what to do. So we'll learn just what we need to know about how to use the command-line interface in Windows for the specific purpose of installing some add-on Python packages.[2]

Locating the Python directory

Before we even think about getting into the command-line interface, though, we need to first figure out where our pip3 application is located, so that we can navigate to it and execute it to

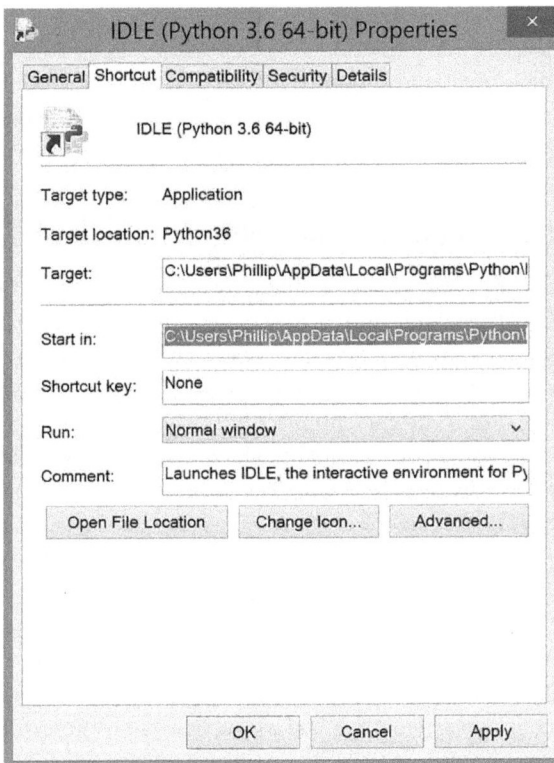

Figure 8.1 The Properties menu

---

[2]As in the previous footnote, this is specific to Windows (and specific to my own laptop in some respects, too) – so if you're on another type of operating system, the exact command-line language I'm using might not apply. However, you should be able to see the rough structure of what I'm trying to do, and, by this point, be willing to get more comfortable with looking up extra information online to find out how you would apply those things to the specifics of your own system.

install the packages we want to install. A relatively straightforward way of doing this is to find your Python3 IDLE icon, the one that you might click to open up the Python shell – right-click on it, then select the `Properties` menu. A menu should pop up which looks something like Figure 8.1.

The `Start in:` field is what we're interested in here (which is why it's highlighted in Figure 8.1) – this tells us where our Python 3 application is stored. Specifically, we're interested in where the `Python36` folder is, since within that there is a folder called `Scripts` where our pip3 application lives. And in order to run pip3 using a command-line interface, we need to make sure we are in the same folder as it. So, either keep the `Properties` menu open to refer to, or copy across the directory information so we can refer to it as we move on. For me, the directory information given in `Target:` is

```
C:\Users\Phillip\AppData\Local\Programs\Python\Python36\
```

The version I'm using is Python 3.6 – which is why I have a folder called `Python36`. Of course, you are unlikely to have the same directory structure as I do on your own computer (even if you share the name "Phillip"). So do this for yourself, and note down your own details to be used later, though I'll talk about my details for ease of reference from here on.

Navigating to the Python directory with Command Prompt

The next step is to get into the command-line interface and use it to find our way to the `Scripts` folder in our Python 3 directory and, to do that, we'll need to open up the Windows Command Prompt program. Any of the common desktop or laptop installations of Windows will have a version of Command Prompt lurking somewhere – typically this is going to be found in the system tools or somewhere similar, and typically you'll also have some kind of capacity to search for things on your system (in which case, running a search for "Command Prompt" will point you in the right direction). So, open Command Prompt, and you should see a screen which looks like Figure 8.2.

This is where we're going to type our instructions to navigate to the `Script` folder, and where we're going to tell pip3 what we want it to do. Notice in Figure 8.2 the line of text that says `C:\Users\Phillip>` – this is the line that we will type our instructions into and, handily, it also tells us where we currently are in the directory (i.e. we are in the `Phillip` folder in `Users`, which is in the `C:` drive of my laptop). This is just another way of accessing folders on your computer; here we're just seeing the folders in text form rather than as we might usually see them in visual form as icons, say if we went to `My Computer`, went into the `C:` drive, then went into `Users` and `Phillip` that way. If you try this on your own computer, you'll see that you can move between folders by double-clicking them, and there may be folders within folders and files within those folders – effectively, you're moving your way through a hierarchy of folders. We're going to do the exact same thing, but instead of having visual icons to click, we're going to type out instructions in Command Prompt. So Command Prompt is telling us where we currently are, and from the information in the `Properties` menu we already have, we know where we need to be. Now, how do we *get* there?

There are two commands that are useful here, the first of which we use to change directory (i.e. to move between folders). To do this, we have to type:

```
cd insert_name_of_folder
```

The command cd just means "change directory" – this is the instruction you're giving to your Command Prompt, followed by the name of the directory you want to change to. In the present case, given the information we have about where my copy of Python is located on my laptop (Figure 8.1), I know that since I am already in C:\Users\Phillip\ (where the backslashes denote a boundary between folders) the next folder I want to move to is called AppData. Figure 8.3 shows what I have to type to do that.

Figure 8.2 Command Prompt: our command-line interface

All I've done here is type cd AppData, and I've jumped to the AppData folder – great! Note, however, that there is a space separating the instruction (cd) from the argument we want that instruction to apply to (AppData). Spaces are treated as breaks in a command-line interface, which makes things a bit trickier to deal with if we have folders and files that have names that contain spaces – hence, if you're ever naming a file yourself and might end up using a command-line interface to play around with it, it's worth using underscores to

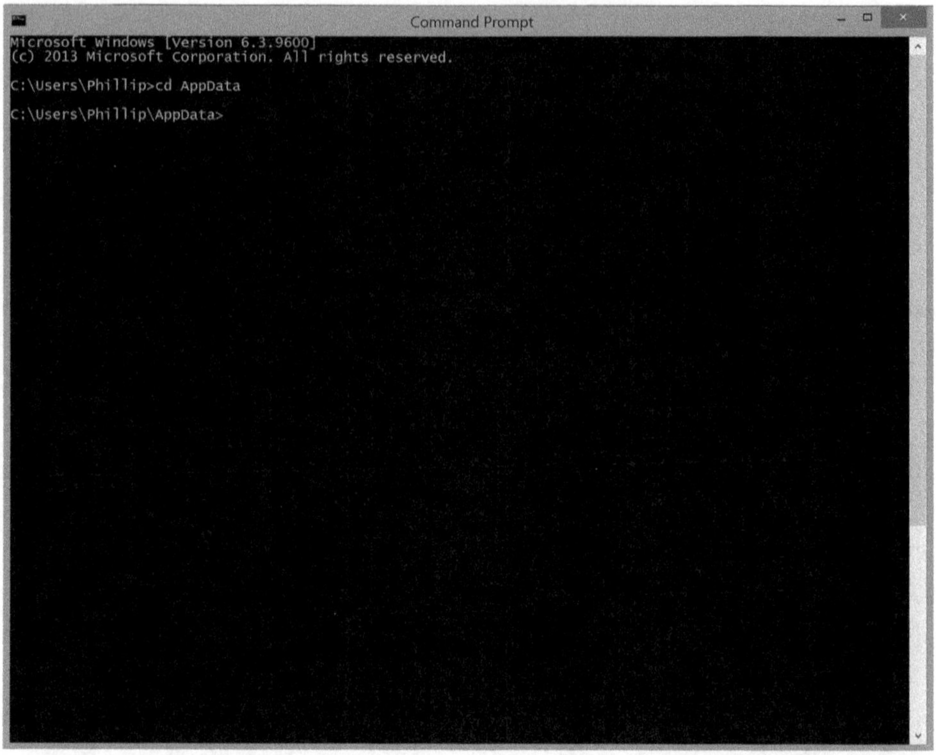

Figure 8.3 We're moving between folders!

indicate spaces, or just not using spaces generally in your naming conventions. Also, note, we *do* need to use the capital letters in AppData, otherwise Command Prompt won't recognise the folder – information and instructions are case-sensitive here, which means we need to be sensitive to cases too. Also note that now the line I'm typing information into shows the updated directory to tell me where I currently am in the hierarchy of folders – handy to know!

Great, we're moving closer to our Python3 directory! But before we go on, here are a few more things we can do with cd. In the example above, I'm in a folder called Phillip and I want to go to a folder within Phillip called AppData. But what can I do if I want to go back out of AppData to Phillip again? Here, we can use:

```
cd ..
```

Again we're using cd to change the directory, but instead of giving a folder name to take us further into the hierarchy of folders, we're using two full stops to take us in the other direction. So if you make a mistake and move to a directory you didn't want to be in, you can always get back out again.

However, moving folders one by one can be a bit tedious – this is much the same even when we're doing this visually with icons, where we might end up having to laboriously click icons lots of times to get where we want. However, we can use the command-line interface to take ourselves to exactly where we want to be in just one line of instruction. To do this, we can use backslashes to list the series of moves we want to make and perform them all at once, as follows:[3]

```
cd Local\Programs\Python\Python36\
```

This neatly leads me on to the next Command Prompt instruction we might find useful here. We're now in the `Python36` folder (which is where my Python 3 installation is located), but how do I know where to go next? Wouldn't it be *really* handy if I could see a list of everything contained in the folder I am currently in? Well, here's how to do that:

```
dir
```

Easy as that – `dir` is just short for directory, and we're just asking to see the contents of the current directory here. Figure 8.4 shows what happens when I type `dir` into the Command Prompt at my current location.

```
Command Prompt                                               - □ ×
Microsoft Windows [Version 6.3.9600]
(c) 2013 Microsoft Corporation. All rights reserved.

C:\Users\Phillip>cd AppData

C:\Users\Phillip\AppData>cd Local\Programs\Python\Python36

C:\Users\Phillip\AppData\Local\Programs\Python\Python36>dir
 Volume in drive C is OS
 Volume Serial Number is E034-3EA0

 Directory of C:\Users\Phillip\AppData\Local\Programs\Python\Python36

29/06/2018  12:42    <DIR>          .
29/06/2018  12:42    <DIR>          ..
07/11/2017  12:01    <DIR>          DLLs
07/11/2017  12:01    <DIR>          Doc
07/11/2017  12:01    <DIR>          include
07/11/2017  12:01    <DIR>          Lib
07/11/2017  12:01    <DIR>          libs
03/10/2017  18:17            30,334 LICENSE.txt
03/10/2017  18:17           362,094 NEWS.txt
29/06/2018  12:43                12 output.txt
03/10/2017  18:15           100,504 python.exe
03/10/2017  18:12            58,520 python3.dll
03/10/2017  18:12         3,610,776 python36.dll
03/10/2017  18:15            98,968 pythonw.exe
30/08/2018  09:34    <DIR>          Scripts
07/11/2017  12:01    <DIR>          tcl
07/11/2017  12:01    <DIR>          Tools
09/06/2016  22:53            87,888 vcruntime140.dll
               8 File(s)      4,349,096 bytes
              10 Dir(s)  141,960,470,528 bytes free

C:\Users\Phillip\AppData\Local\Programs\Python\Python36>
```

Figure 8.4 A list of directories in my `Python36` folder

---

[3]For the purposes of this example, I'm working on the assumption that I'm still in the `AppData` folder, which is to say that my starting directory is `C:\Users\Phillip\AppData`. As such, any moving between folders I'm doing has to take into account where I'm starting from.

We can see a list of everything contained in my `Python36` folder, and of particular interest to us is the `Scripts` folder, since this is where we'll find the pip3 application. So let's navigate to `Scripts` and use dir to double-check if pip3 is in there (Figure 8.5).

```
                                    Command Prompt                          - □ ×

 Directory of C:\Users\Phillip\AppData\Local\Programs\Python\Python36

29/06/2018  12:42    <DIR>          .
29/06/2018  12:42    <DIR>          ..
07/11/2017  12:01    <DIR>          DLLs
07/11/2017  12:01    <DIR>          Doc
07/11/2017  12:01    <DIR>          include
07/11/2017  12:01    <DIR>          Lib
07/11/2017  12:01    <DIR>          libs
03/10/2017  18:17            30,334 LICENSE.txt
03/10/2017  18:17           362,094 NEWS.txt
29/06/2018  12:43                12 output.txt
03/10/2017  18:15           100,504 python.exe
03/10/2017  18:12            58,520 python3.dll
03/10/2017  18:12         3,610,776 python36.dll
03/10/2017  18:15            98,968 pythonw.exe
30/08/2018  09:34    <DIR>          Scripts
07/11/2017  12:01    <DIR>          tcl
07/11/2017  12:01    <DIR>          Tools
09/06/2016  22:53            87,888 vcruntime140.dll
              8 File(s)      4,349,096 bytes
             10 Dir(s)  141,960,470,528 bytes free

C:\Users\Phillip\AppData\Local\Programs\Python\Python36>cd Scripts

C:\Users\Phillip\AppData\Local\Programs\Python\Python36\Scripts>dir
 Volume in drive C is OS
 Volume Serial Number is E034-3EA0

 Directory of C:\Users\Phillip\AppData\Local\Programs\Python\Python36\Scripts

30/08/2018  09:34    <DIR>          .
30/08/2018  09:34    <DIR>          ..
30/08/2018  09:34           102,796 chardetect.exe
27/07/2018  14:05            98,195 conv-template.exe
07/11/2017  12:01            98,197 easy_install-3.6.exe
07/11/2017  12:01            98,197 easy_install.exe
27/07/2018  14:05            98,185 f2py.exe
27/07/2018  14:05               836 f2py.py
27/07/2018  14:05            98,195 from-template.exe
01/08/2018  10:15           102,787 pip.exe
01/08/2018  10:15           102,787 pip3.6.exe
01/08/2018  10:15           102,787 pip3.exe
27/07/2018  14:05    <DIR>          __pycache__
             10 File(s)        902,962 bytes
              3 Dir(s)  141,927,297,024 bytes free

C:\Users\Phillip\AppData\Local\Programs\Python\Python36\Scripts>
```

Figure 8.5 The contents of `Scripts`

Excellent, we're in the place we need to be, with the tools we need to use – we can see that there is an executable file (i.e. an application, as denoted by the .exe suffix) called pip3. Now let's use it to install some packages!

Using pip3 to install modules

Having found our way to where pip3 is located, the rest is really simple. All we need to do now is type the following into Command Prompt:

```
pip3 install name_of_python_package
```

So here, we're calling on the pip3 application, telling it we want to install something, and then telling it the name of what we want to install. When pip3 has all this information, it will use your web connection to identify and install the package in question from the Python Package Index (PyPI), which is a huge repository of Python packages that people have developed and made available publicly to support lots of different types of Python programming tasks – more information on the PyPI and its contents can be found on the PyPI website (Python Software Foundation, 2019c). Of course, we're not interested in *all* of these packages, but only in the ones that will help us do some social scientific tasks. While we're in the right location, let's install all the different Python packages we're going to need throughout the rest of the book. So, what we need to do here is type out the following commands:

```
pip3 install bs4
pip3 install lxml
pip3 install matplotlib
pip3 install pandas
pip3 install tweepy
```

You should press return after each of these commands and wait until they have successfully installed before moving on to the next one.[4] Installing all five now will save you having to come back to the Command Prompt multiple times later on. You don't really need to know what these names refer to at this point, but for future reference, `bs4` is the PyPI name for the Beautiful Soup package which we'll use for web scraping, `lxml` is a package for processing data that comes in XML format, `matplotlib` and `pandas` are to do with managing and visualising data for analysis, and `tweepy` is a package that helps us play around with Twitter as a data source and service. Each of these packages is identifiable in PyPI by the name given in the command-line excerpt above; these names can easily be found out by visiting the webpages for each of the packages and looking at their respective "how to install this package" sections (so, if you ever need to find out the PyPI name of a package you want to install, it's information you can easily locate with a search engine).

And that's that – everything you need to work your way through the rest of the book is now installed and ready to use!

Summing up

The whole process described above can be boiled down to a series of steps to follow, where you have to fill in the gaps that make the steps relevant to whatever system you're working on (unless you're using a Linux-based operating system, in which case, see the note following this summary):

---

[4]If these packages *don't* successfully install, then unfortunately there's not much I can do in the pages of a book. The reasons why an installation might fail are local to specific computers and therefore there are no real general guidelines I can give, other than try to read the error messages that happen, and use a search engine to find people who have used programming question-and-answer platforms such as Stack Exchange and Stack Overflow to get support when they've had the same problem. That's how a lot of programming issues are resolved really, so it's not bad practice to get familiar with the idea of tweaking and applying somebody else's solution to your own specific problem. However, I will say that some of these chapters are entirely premised on your having the appropriate packages installed, to the extent that if you *don't* have those packages installed you won't be able to get anything out of those chapters. So do try to find a solution if you run into problems here.

1   Figure out where your Python 3 directory is – you'll need to know where the `Scripts` file is within that, since it is where you will find your pip3 application.
2   Open up a command-line interface (such as Command Prompt) and navigate to the `Scripts` file.
3   Use the pip3 application contained therein to install your Python libraries.

A final note for Linux users

The intention throughout this section has been to focus on the specifics of my own (Windows) system to give a general flavour of what you need to know and do to install modules for any operating system you might be using. However, it's also worth commenting briefly on how to do the same work on Linux-based operating systems, just because it's very simple. Here's how you install all these libraries on a Linux-based operating system:

1   Open the Terminal
2   Type in the following commands (do each one separately – that is, press return at the end of each line below):

```
sudo pip3 install bs4
sudo pip3 install lxml
sudo pip3 install matplotlib
sudo pip3 install pandas
sudo pip3 install tweepy
```

That's it! There *are* some differences in how you code in Python between Windows and Linux[5] which mean that the odd point in this book (which is Windows-oriented) would need tweaking to suit a Linux system, but, that being said, see how much more straightforward using Linux can be in some respects, especially when it comes to having a bit of extra control over how your computer works? Worth thinking about, now that you'll be routinely getting deeper into your computer as a Python programmer!

8●2   Importing Modules

We have already seen how to use various objects, commands, methods, and so on within Python. However, there are many different techniques that we *could* use which are not stored by default in the core Python language. There are lots of extra bits of code that Python can use as "modules" – banks of "add-on" techniques and methods and so on which we can bring into the main Python language as and when we require them. Some of these we'll need to install prior to using them (see previous section), but some exist within Python already –

---

[5]For instance, I got horrendously stuck trying to figure out why a graph wouldn't save as an image on Windows, only to later realise that the code I wrote on my little (Linux) Raspberry Pi microcomputer needed an ever-so-slight tweaking to make it fit its new Windows environment. It still infuriates me how long it took me to figure that out. So when you come to the chapter on data visualisation with Matplotlib later in the book, be forewarned that you might be able to detect the faintest whiff of "absolutely done with this".

either way, we have to be sure not only to install the modules but also to import them into whatever scripts we want to use them in.

What are modules for?

Modules can cover a whole host of different functionality – for instance, there are modules for incorporating randomised elements into your code (e.g. a module called random), modules for incorporating timed elements into your code such as giving you commands to wait for a specified period of time (e.g. a module called time), modules for incorporating the current date and time into your code if you need it (e.g. a module called datetime), and many many many many many *many* more. A full list of the current modules that come with a Python installation can be found in the Python Module Index (Python Software Foundation, 2019d) but as you undertake projects of your own, you may find a need to search out "third-party" modules (i.e. ones not built by or distributed with Python) which you can also install and use (as per the information outlined in the previous section). Given these modules each do different jobs, it's impossible for me to give a full comprehensive list of even one such module, nor would you find that particularly useful. However, what I *can* do is show you how to import modules into Python for yourself, such that you can then use what you already know to explore them for yourself. Just as with the core Python language itself, individual modules also typically have good documentation online which can tell you more about how they operate – search these out, and dig into them!

For now, I'm just going to demonstrate the mechanics of how to import one particular module called random, which can be used to generate randomness as part of Python code in various ways. I'll demonstrate two particular commands within random – choice and randint. We're not really interested in how the random module works in its entirety (though it *can* be useful to be aware of these concepts in your code going forward). Rather, treat this short introduction to the random module mainly as a demonstration of importing a module which you can use as a general template for importing modules.

Three different methods for importing (and using) modules

Let's go through three ways of importing modules into Python, each of which are in the code file called 8_2_ImportingModules.py. First, we can import the whole module into a script, so that any code that follows in that script will recognise whatever calls to the random module we care to make. You can see how this looks in the script below (which is taken from the code file for this section).

```
8    #METHOD 1 - importing a whole module
9
10   import random
11
12   def randomFruit():
13       return random.choice(["mango",
```

(Continued)

```
14                              "pomelo",
15                              "guava",
16                              "grapefruit",
17                              "watermelon"])
```

What you can see in this script is a line of code that does the importing – import random – and then some code that uses the random module. Here, the code is a function called randomFruit() which returns a random choice from a list of five fruits (stored as strings). Note the syntax:

```
return random.choice([SOME THINGS])
```

Here you can see that we are using a command called .choice(), which takes our list of fruits as an argument. We should also note that in order to *use* this .choice() command, we have to acknowledge the module from which it comes – we have to recognise that it comes from the random module by preceding the command with the module name and a full stop. So, uncomment the bits of code in METHOD 1, then run the script, and we'll make a few calls to the randomFruit() function to see what results:

```
>>> randomFruit()
'pomelo'
>>> randomFruit()
'guava'
>>> randomFruit()
'watermelon'
```

Great, seems to be doing the job!

Let's also look at another command within the random module: .randint(). This stands for "random integer", and we can use it to give us a random integer within a range that we set out. Without digging too deep into the specifics, this is how a basic usage of .randint() looks in code:

```
>>> print(random.randint(0,100))
82
>>> print(random.randint(0,100))
44
>>> print(random.randint(0,100))
90
```

Here we have a print statement that uses .randint() to give us a random number between 0 and 100 (which is why when we execute the command a few times we don't get the same result – it's randomised). Again, you can see that we need to tell Python that we want to draw on the random module by preceding our call to .randint() with the module name random, so that Python knows where to look for this command.

However, what if we don't want to import the whole random module; what if we only need to use a few methods within that module? Here's where we would use another way of importing stuff from a module, as detailed in METHOD 2 of the code file, and in the excerpt below. Comment out everything except the code associated with METHOD 2, and run the script:

```
22   #METHOD 2 - importing individual bits from a module.
23
24   from random import randint
25   from random import choice
26
27       def randomFruit():
28                       return choice(["mango",
29                       "pomelo",
30                       "guava",
31                       "grapefruit",
32                       "watermelon"])
```

Notice the difference between this and METHOD 1? When we import the commands with from MODULE import SOMETHING, we don't need to then refer to the module from which we've imported things. Hence, in the randomFruit() function, we can just write:

```
return choice([SOME THINGS])
```

This is a nice little feature of importing things in this way – it can save a lot of extra typing if you plan to make extensive use of the commands and other things we might be importing (in this case, it could save me typing out random repeatedly every time I want to use the .choice() command). So now that we've imported two commands from the random module – randint and choice – let's use them in shell, as we did before:

```
>>> randomFruit()
'mango'
>>> randomFruit()
'pomelo'
>>> randomFruit()
'grapefruit'
>>>
>>> print(randint(0,100))
4
>>> print(randint(0,100))
39
>>> print(randint(0,100))
33
```

Great; looks like everything works as expected!

But there's also a third way we can import things into our code – we can import things directly into the functions (and other objects like classes) that we intend to use them with, as follows. Uncomment everything except the code associated with METHOD 3, and run the file:

```
37   #METHOD 3 - importing stuff directly into a function.
38
39   def randomFruit():
40       from random import choice
41       return choice(["mango",
42                      "pomelo",
43                      "guava",
44                      "grapefruit",
45                      "watermelon"])
```

Do you see the difference between this and METHOD 1 and METHOD 2? In the previous two methods, we put the import code right at the top of the script, so that everything that follows would be able to use the stuff we imported – remember, Python code executes from top to bottom, so when you run a script, you need to remember to import things *before* you put them to use. However, here, we might only actually want to use the .choice() command in the context of this one single function – hence, we can put the import code in the function itself and it will do the job. So, again, let's make some calls to this function and see what happens:

```
>>> randomFruit()
'grapefruit'
>>> randomFruit()
'grapefruit'
>>> randomFruit()
'pomelo'
```

Great, all looks good! However, it's important to reiterate the importance of *scope* as a concept here. Importing things directly into a function means that they can be used *only* within that function, not throughout a script generally. This is fine (and neat and tidy) if that's what you want to do, but if you want to reuse the same commands/objects/etc. in different places throughout your script, then you would be better off importing those things more generically (i.e. at the very top of the script).

8●3 Timing Your Code

We've focused a lot on *what* code we want to run and how to build it, but it's also helpful (for various reasons elaborated on below) to consider *when* we want that code to run as well. Python has a set of tools and libraries we can draw on to do this kind of work, and here are the basics of how to use them.

Building waits into your code

For certain tasks we might want to do in Python, it's handy to be able to regulate the speed at which Python does them. Left to its own devices, Python will rattle through each line of code from the top to the bottom of a script as quickly as possible (depending on the speed of the hardware in your computer). Typically, this is exactly what you *want* Python to be doing – for most tasks, the maximum speed possible is a desirable thing, inasmuch as less waiting time is good. However, there *are* some instances where you *would* want a way to tell Python to slow down and wait – for instance, as we get further into the book we'll be looking at things like accessing social media through Python code, or doing web scraping, where there are rules on how many requests you are allowed to make, and where breaking those rules could result in your having your social media account blocked or being banned from making any further requests from a website. Hence, in order to do these tasks properly, we will need a way to tell Python to wait a certain amount of time before completing any further lines of code. This is very easily done using the sleep() method from the time module, as follows: open the code file called 8_3_Timing.py, run it, and see what happens (don't forget to give it some time to complete!). This is the bit we're interested in for now:

```
1   """
2   Programming in Python for Social Science
3   Phillip Brooker
4
5   8. 3. TIMING YOUR CODE
6   """
7
8   import time
9
10  print("Script start.")
11  time.sleep(30)
12  print("Script end. ")
```

Given the output, can you see what this code is doing, line by line? You should have seen a message pop up in the shell – Script start. – then you will have had to wait 30 seconds, then you will have seen a second message – Script end. How does this look in the code? First, we import the time module, which is where the sleep() command we want to use resides. Then, our very simple program will just print a message, wait 30 seconds and then print a second message. The key thing to note here that's new to use is the time.sleep(30) line – here, we're invoking the time module, specifically the sleep() method within it, which accepts arguments in integer form to indicate the number of seconds we want the program to sleep (or wait) before continuing on to the line below. So, if you type this into a script and run it, you should see in the shell that a message appears as soon as you run the script (Script start.), then, 30 seconds later, a second message appears (Script end.).

As noted, this can be useful when we want to build waits into any code. For example, we might want to wait 15 minutes before requesting any new data from a social media platform, or (using this with other information about generating random integers we've just learned) we might want to wait a random amount of time up to 4 hours before our script posts a message to social media (which would be useful if we were interested in building a social media bot of the kind outlined in Chapter 2). So it's worth having this technique in the bag in a general sense, for whenever and wherever you might need it. And it should be noted that the `time` module also contains lots of other useful techniques – it's worth checking out the documentation online (Python Software Foundation, 2019e) if you want to explore the possibilities further.

Using date and time in your code

Another useful thing to be able to do is use details to do with times and dates in Python code. Suppose, for example, we had a script to scrape data from a particular webpage but we only wanted to do a round of data collection once a day; we could build routines into a data collection script that allow us to check the current date and time and see whether enough time has passed that we can do a new round of data collection. For this kind of task, we'll need the `datetime` module. As with the `sleep()` method above, this is a general-purpose technique that there are lots of conceivable applications for, so it's worth knowing how to work with the `datetime` module in a general sense, and worth bearing in mind for any scripts you end up writing yourself. The `datetime` module contains lots of potentially relevant techniques, but here's how to use this module to ascertain the current date and time, and work with salient elements of that information:

```
1    import datetime
2
3    dt = datetime.datetime.now()
```

Simple as that! If I now run this script on my computer, the variable `dt` will contain details of the date and time at which that particular line of code was executed.[6] After running this script, if I print `dt` to the shell this is what I get:

```
>>> print(dt)
2018-12-07 16:23:30.713366
```

So hopefully we can recognise that we've got a range of information that might be useful here. I ran this script on 7 December 2018, at around 4.23pm, and the first bit of the results reflects the year, month and day in the first bit (though annoyingly this comes in a different format than the "day/month/year" version I'm used to in the UK, so I have to remember to factor that in to my code going forward), and we have the time in 24-hour format in the

---

[6]It's worth noting that this information doesn't update automatically - if we want to update the date and time details stored in dt, we will have to find a way to store the results of the `datetime.datetime. now()` method to dt again.

second bit of the results, `16:23:30.712266`. Note here that the last bit of the time (the `.712266` bit) contains details of the exact microsecond the line of code was executed – this is very precise, but perhaps not all that useful to us. We might not necessarily need *all* this information in the format it's presented to us – for instance, the microseconds – and we can pull out specific elements as follows:

```
>>> dt.year
2018
>>> dt.month
12
>>> dt.day
7
>>> dt.hour
16
>>> dt.minute
23
>>> dt.second
30
```

Here, all we're doing is saying that for the `dt` variable within which we've stored the results of the date and time at which the line of code was executed, we want to access an individual component of it (as denoted by the names `year`, `month`, `day`, `hour`, `minute` and `second`). This can be useful if we want to then just store certain bits of the whole `datetime` result elsewhere (e.g. to run a specific piece of code only at certain times of day by using IF/ELSE logic to do conditional checks on whether specified numerical values match current `datetime` values before running bits of code). Another technique that it's handy to have a general awareness of as you get deeper into building your own scripts, and if you want to dig into the `datetime` module further, you can do so by consulting the official documentation (Python Software Foundation, 2019f).

Scheduling tasks

Aside from actually writing code that deals with time and date, we might also want to just run a whole script at a certain time or date. For instance, suppose we have a Twitter bot similar to the ones discussed in Chapter 2, and we want to get that bot to post a tweet at a certain time every hour – how do we do that? We can write a script that will use Python and the Twitter API to write out some tweet content and post it to a specified account,[7] but how do we make that happen every hour? One particularly annoying way to do this would be to manually run the script at the right time – we could boot up our computer, open the script, run it, and that would do the job. But that's not really sustainable, since it's reasonable to assume that at some point we might want to go on holiday or sleep or otherwise feel like we're not obliged to always be near the computer. So, ideally, we're going to want to run this script automatically at a certain time. And for that, we're going to need some things in place.

---

[7] Or at least, we *will* be able to do this when we get to Chapter 11.

First, we'll need a computer that we can always leave running. My recommendation here is a Raspberry Pi microcomputer – the Raspberry Pi Foundation is a charity organisation based in the UK which, among other good things, builds a range of microcomputers designed to be small, low-cost but relatively high-performance computing hardware that can be used to learn about computing and build projects (hardware and software). More information on the Raspberry Pi Foundation and the range of hardware it builds can be found on its website (Raspberry Pi Foundation, 2019a). But the interest we might have as Python programmers is that microcomputers (as they are known) such as those built by Raspberry Pi are a great platform to build, host and execute scripts on. And much like cat-people share pictures of their fur-babies (whether you're interested or not), Figure 8.6 is a pic of my first circuit-baby.[8]

Figure 8.6 Awww, bless. My first Raspberry Pi

Given it is small (roughly the size of a credit card), doesn't use a lot of electricity and can be left running indefinitely, this Raspberry Pi is tucked in a corner of my front room and is where I run my bots from – my bots are Python scripts that need to be executed/run at certain times of day. The most common operating system used on a Raspberry Pi is called "Raspbian", which is Linux-based, and, hence, I'm going to show you how I schedule the tasks (i.e. the running of these bot scripts) on my Linux-based/Raspbian operating system using a service

---

[8]I have a few now … it may be becoming a problem.

called Crontab.[9] For the purposes of this book we don't need to know the ins and outs of using a Linux-based command-line interface, nor do we need to be experts in using Crontab – we just need to know some basics (and a few extra terms in which to express those ideas) to get us started, and that's all that is coming up next.

Crontab is a software utility/service that is common across lots of Linux-oriented operating systems, and which is designed to help users run scripts (including Python scripts) repeatedly and periodically at whatever dates and times they choose. The name is a portmanteau of two things – the Greek word for "time" (*chronos*) and the fitting of time information into a table format (which is shortened to "tab" here).

We don't have to get too familiar with the Linux command-line interface here; that's for another book. However, the following is how you would go about setting up a scheduled task using Crontab.

First, we'll need to open up the Terminal – similarly to the Command Prompt used in Section 8.1 when we were installing modules, we need to use the Terminal to give text-based instructions to the computer. In the Terminal, we type `crontab -e` and press return – this just means that we're telling the Terminal we want to open up the Crontab service specifically for editing (i.e. the -e bit). Figure 8.7 shows what it looks like on-screen, just *before* I press return, and Figure 8.8 shows the result *after* I press return.

So here, we can see a lot of instructions on how to use Crontab, which is very handy for us to refer to! What we need to know at this point is how to read what's on the screen. It's also worth pointing out, just for accuracy, that when we use the `crontab -e` command to make edits to Crontab, what we're doing is opening up a text file called `Crontab` where this information is stored, using a program called GNU nano which is a text-editor service designed for use within Linux-oriented systems. So, the aim of the game here is to edit a text file to add in new information about when we want our Python script to start; there's nothing more to it than that.

One first thing to note is that we can see that some lines of this Crontab text file begin with a # symbol – just like in Python, these lines are "comments", which is to say they contain information that is *not* designed to be read as an executable instruction by/for the computer. So any lines that begin with a # symbol, we can gloss over (although, of course, it's handy to keep them in and read them as you're learning to use Crontab). We *should* note, though, that if we're editing a Crontab file, it's quite handy to be able to leave comments in ourselves, to help us remember how and why we've scheduled a particular task in a particular way – you'll see in the figures in this section that I've left little hints to myself about what a particular set of scheduled tasks is about by using comments in this way.

---

[9]As with the section on installing new Python modules, what I'm going to show you about scheduling tasks is linked inextricably to the system which I'm currently using to do this kind of thing. However, the *idea* of scheduling tasks can also be implemented on Windows- and Mac-based systems as well as the Linux environments that are popular on a Raspberry Pi. So this is not only to introduce you to the concept of scheduling tasks, but also to get you familiar with the ways of thinking about tasks and timings and how they can be scheduled such that you can do this kind of thing on whatever system you choose - if that's not using Linux's Crontab, then more power to you!

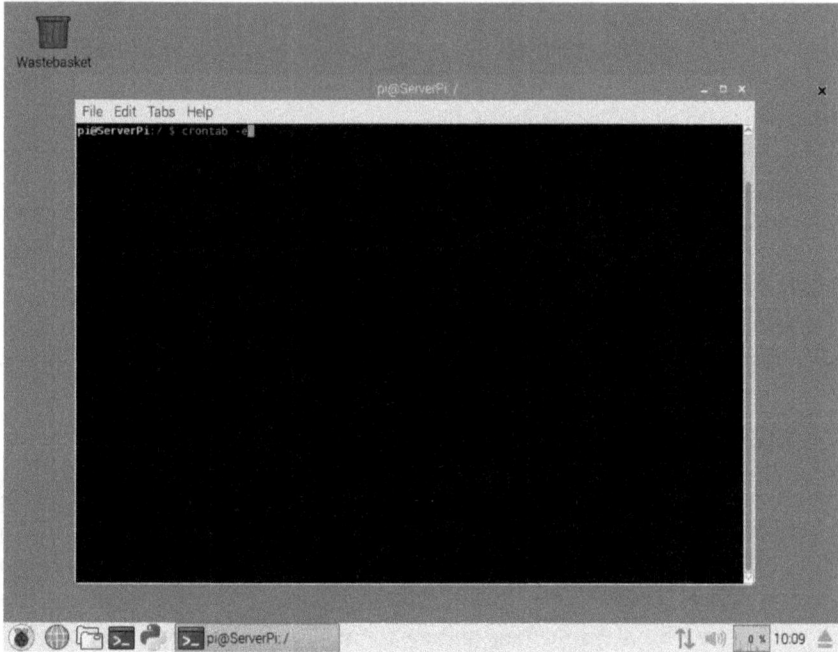

Figure 8.7 The Terminal on my Raspberry Pi system, with `crontab -e` ready to be input

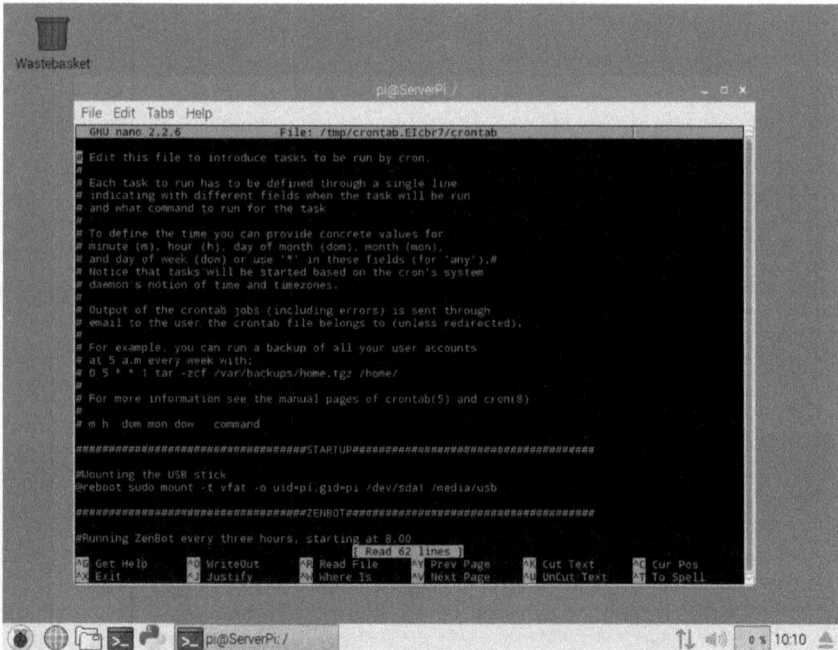

Figure 8.8 The Crontab file header – useful reference material

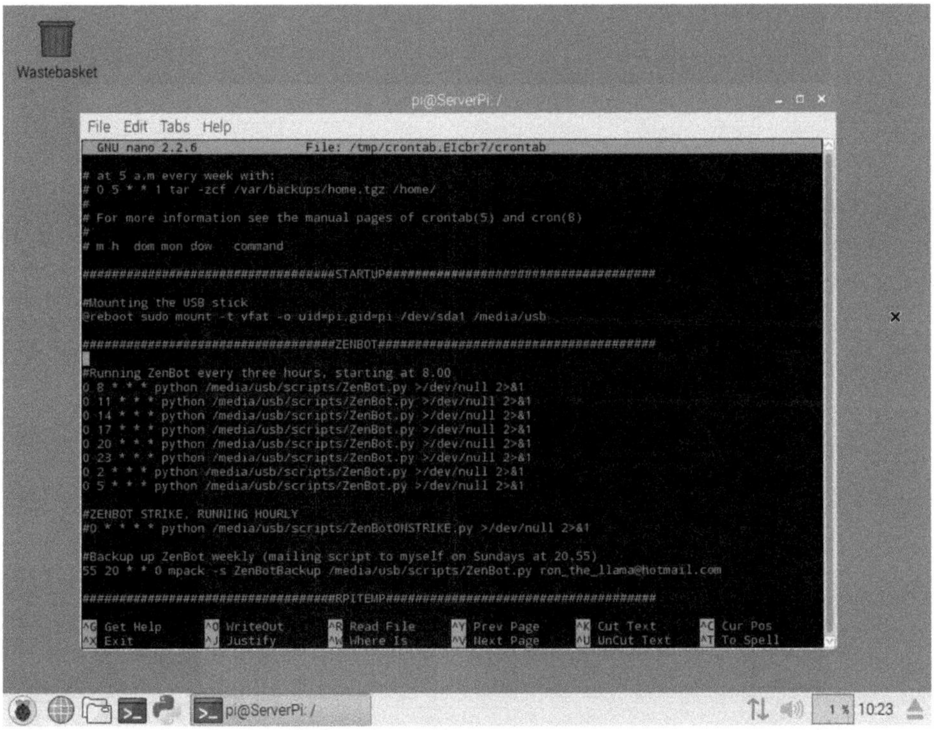

Figure 8.9 A selection of Crontab entries on my Raspberry Pi (not all Python)

Let's move on and figure out how to do some task scheduling. In Figure 8.9 I've scrolled down my own Crontab file a little bit so we can see some Python scripts that I've got scheduled. We'll focus on an example mocked-up Crontab entry that fits our present purposes of learning how to work with Python 3, and we'll explore how that is working. The entry we'll explore is

```
0 8 * * * python3 /media/usb/scripts/ZenBot.py >/dev/null 2>&1
```

This might come across a little technical and daunting, but we'll walk through each part of this in turn and things will start to fall into place. What we have here is an instruction to Crontab to run a specified Python (version 3) script at a specified time – hence, if you write a line like this in your own Crontab file (generally you would do this underneath the instructions/header comments bit), that's how Crontab knows which tasks to run and when.

In effect, a scheduled task is written as a line in the Crontab file by giving information to five fields (i.e. the 0 8 * * * bit, which has five pieces of information in it) followed by a shell command to execute (in the case of my example, this is the bit that goes python3 /media/usb/scripts/ZenBot.py >/dev/null 2>&1). First, let's look at the bit with the numbers and asterisks (i.e. the bit that goes 0 8 * * *), and ignore the rest of the entry for the time being. This bit of information tells Crontab the time and date you want your chosen task to execute. There are five fields here, and they each refer to a different level of time, as follows:[10]

```
1    ###EXAMPLE CRON ENTRY###
2
3    * * * * * command to execute
4
5    ###BREAKING IT DOWN###
6
7    * * * * * command to execute
8    T T T T T
9    | | | | |
10   | | | | |
11   | | | | L---day of week (0-6, Sunday is 0)
12   | | | L-----month (1-12, Jan is 1)
13   | | L-------day of month (1-31)
14   | L---------hour (0-23)
15   L-----------min (0-59)
16
17   NOTE: * means I want the command to be executed for every available number (for
18   instance, if there is a * instead of a number in the "days of the week" field,
19   this means that I want to run this task EVERY day of the week).
```

So, when I store the line

```
0 8 * * * python3 /media/usb/scripts/ZenBot.py >/dev/null 2>&1
```

as a Crontab entry, I'm telling Crontab that I want to run this Python script at zero minutes past eight (8.00am) every day of the month, every month of the year and every day of the week. If I want to run the same script on 16 November at 10.45pm, here's how that would look:

```
45 22 16 11 * python3 /media/usb/scripts/ZenBot.py >/dev/null 2>&1
```

And here's what it might look like if I wanted to run the script every hour on the hour but just on Tuesdays:

```
0 * * * 2 python3 /media/usb/scripts/ZenBot.py >/dev/null 2>&1
```

As you can see, there are various ways we can ask Crontab to run any given task at particular intervals, however we want to construct those intervals. So now we're comfortable setting up

---

[10]This is not a code excerpt nor a Crontab entry that would work in practice – this is purely reference material that demonstrates how a Crontab entry works (adapted from Raspberry Pi Foundation, 2019b).

the time and date we want a script to run, how do we establish *which* script we want to run? Let's now pay attention to the bit of the script that does this work (i.e. python3 /media/ usb/scripts/ZenBot.py >/dev/null 2>&1). The first thing to note here is that the command we want to execute comes with different components – what we need to know is that there's a bit that says python3, a bit that says /media/usb/scripts/ZenBot.py, and a bit that says >/dev/null 2>&1.

The bit that says python3 is required to tell the computer which program we want to work with – obviously for us as we work through this book, python3 is where it's at, but in principle you could schedule tasks for any other program or application. Using python3 here simply tells the computer that the script we want to execute should be done in the Python 3 environment (which is to say we don't just want to open the script as a text file or anything like that, but we want to *execute* it in Python 3).

The next bit says /media/usb/scripts/ZenBot.py, and since we've already established that we want to schedule a Python 3 task, this just tells Crontab where in the computer directory structure to find the particular script we want to execute. You'll hopefully already be able to see that here I'm telling Python 3 to execute a script called ZenBot.py which can be found in my /media/usb/scripts/ directory (where the forward slashes are used to show the directory path between folders).

The next bit (>/dev/null 2>&1) is optional really – if you don't have this in a Crontab entry, your script will run just fine at the time you specify. However, this is quite common to see in shell commands and Crontab entries in Linux-based systems, so I thought it would be worth at least describing here. We don't need to know what each symbol means in this phrase – all we need to know is that when we see this at the end of a Linux shell command or Crontab entry, we're just telling the computer to send any error messages to the /dev/null directory, which is effectively a black hole for dumping data you don't need. This is often used to prevent unnecessary data being stored – for example, if we're running a script every few seconds of every day, we don't necessarily want a rapidly expanding log of those details being stored somewhere on our computer taking up a rapidly expanding amount of space, so we "pipe it to /dev/null" and thereby banish that information for ever. You'll see this a lot in the context of Linux commands and Crontab entries, so while it's not strictly necessary to incorporate this extra bit, it's still worth knowing what it does and it's good practice for us to use in a lot of cases (i.e. all cases except where you *want* something like a log of error messages and so on).

To summarise, then, we're asking Crontab to run a particular Python 3 script (called ZenBot. py, and which can be found in the /media/usb/scripts/ folder) at 8.00am every day, and to dump any error messages straight in the bin. That's it!

One final thing now we know how to edit a line in the Crontab file – how do we *save* it? That's really straightforward too, and in fact we've already seen this at the bottom of Figures 8.8 and 8.9 – there are two commands we need to know here. First, when we've made changes that we want to save, we can do so by pressing Ctrl+O to WriteOut (i.e. write/ save) the text file. Then, we can press Ctrl+X to Exit the GNU nano interface and return to the terminal. At that point, any tasks we've scheduled will be set to run as and when we've scheduled them.

8 ● 4 Creating Script Interfaces with Inputs

One more concept that it is helpful to know about is the idea of using Python as an "interface" for working with the scripts you build. What this means will become apparent as we work through the section. But for now, suffice to say that there are some contexts where it would be better or more appropriate to use (and let other people use) our code without actually having to dig into the Python scripts and understand the code therein. Hence, what we can do is provide people with a means of inputting things into a script in the shell (i.e. so they don't have to edit the script directly). As you might expect by now, Python being an object-oriented language, these inputs can be stored and used like any other object in Python. We've dealt with different types of object (e.g. different data types and different data structures) already, so I won't reiterate that here. But what I will do is show you the mechanics of how to request and store inputs from users in the shell.

Creating an interface with `input()`

Open the code file called 8_4_InputsInterfaces.py, run it, and see what happens:

```
1    """
2    Programming in Python for Social Science
3    Phillip Brooker
4
5    8. 4. INPUTS AND INTERFACES
6    """
7
8    #Below is a super simple script that asks you for your name, then takes the
9    #data you give it and reformulates it as a string to be printed out.
10
11   name = input("Hi, what is your name?: ")
12   print("OK, " + name + ", nice to meet you! ...Well, see ya!")
```

Before we dig into the code itself, let's take a look at what happens in the shell when you run the script (Figure 8.10).

Interesting! We can see that we're being asked a question, and that we have a cursor that will enable us to type out a reply. So now I'll type in my name and press return (Figure 8.11).

I typed in my name, and got a result back that includes my name – let's use our programming mindset to think through what's going on behind the scenes. So, there must be some bit of code that presents me with some text (in this case, a question about my name), and a bit of code that stores that name somewhere so that it can be recalled in the text that follows (which repeats my name as part of another string of text).

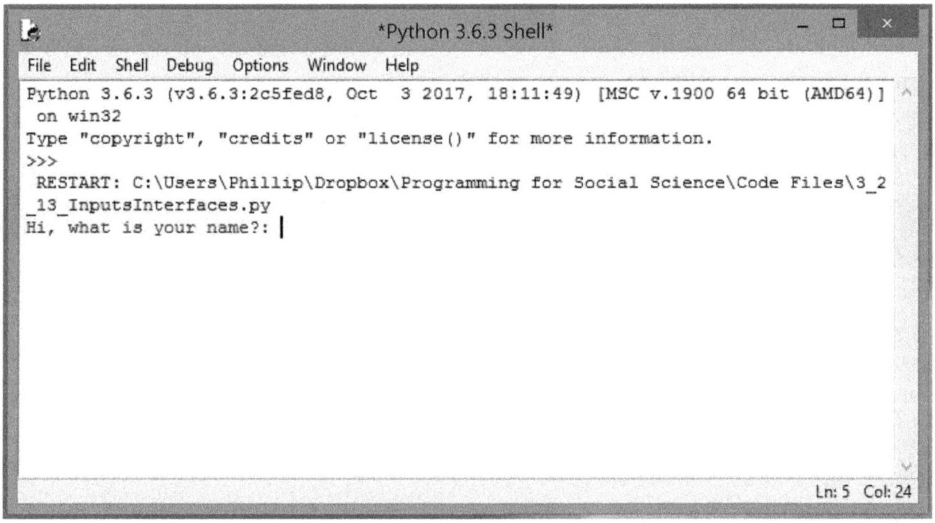

Figure 8.10 The interface in action 1

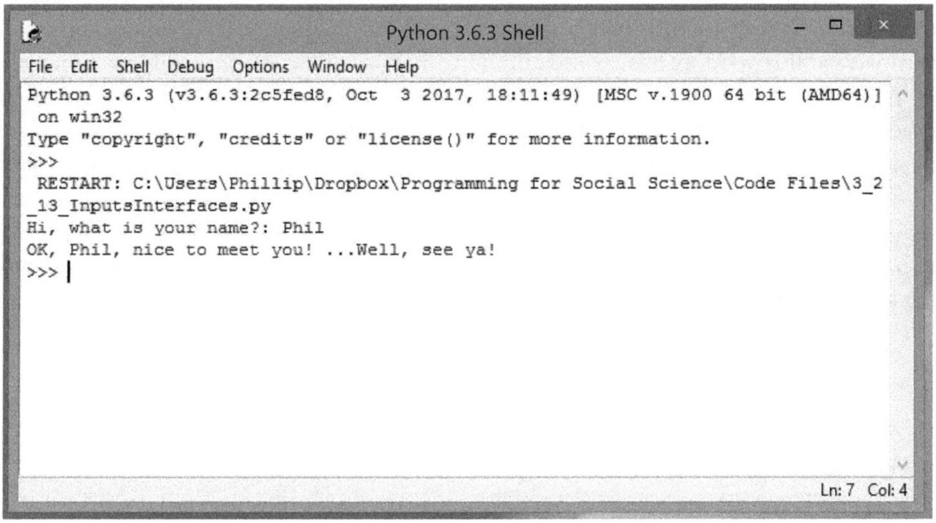

Figure 8.11 The interface in action 2

Now let's look at the code in the script to unpick how it works:

```
1   name = input("Hi, what is your name?: ")
2   print("OK" + name + ", nice to meet you! ...Well, see ya!")
```

The first line of this snippet designates a variable, name, which stores some input in response to the string text "Hi, what is your name?: ". A quick aside: note the space after the question mark and colon. This is not strictly necessary, but if you don't put a space into your string, then none will appear in the script (which means that on the screen of the shell, the user's input will look all mashed together with your string question – so this is just a little visual design thing: important, but not crucial).

So, we have a new command, `input()`, which can take data and store them somewhere, and which can be fed information that will come up in the shell to help users see what kind of data they're being asked to input.

The second line of the snippet then prints automatically once we've finished executing the first line (i.e. when we've typed in some data and pressed return). And this line is just a simple print statement where we're concatenating some words around the string text that the user has just stored in the variable `name`. Again, note the location of spaces and punctuation here – in order to make the complete string scan as a grammatically correct sentence, we have to consider how the results of variables fit into the string in terms of spaces and punctuation. This comes with practice.

Improving the interface

However, it's important to think through how we might be able to break this simple script, and what we could do to improve it. For example, what if I fed the `name` variable an integer? The variable would take the integer, but the print statement (line 2) would not be able to concatenate the integer with the variable and an error would occur (i.e. our program would crash). It's at this point we have to start thinking in terms of *user design*: bearing in mind who we expect to be using this script, how do we anticipate they may end up using it? Do we need to build in something that would turn an integer into a string in our print statement? Or do we need to use IF/ELSE conditions to ask users to try again if they accidentally put in an integer value where we expect a string? Another way to break the script (or at least have it operate "incorrectly") would be if the user just pressed return without typing *anything* in response to the question. If that were to happen, our print statement would come out looking a little funny:

```
OK, , nice to meet you! ...Well, see ya!
```

So, to prevent this, do we want to build in an IF/ELSE statement that makes sure the user is not allowed to leave the `name` variable empty? And how might that operate? (*Hint:* it might help if we put the name-repeating code in a function which we could run dependent on a check of the type of result that gets, or does not get, stored in name.)

We could also think in terms of *software design* at this point – what do we actually want to *do* with the data we're collecting? Do we want to put them in a big list of lots of other usernames? Or do we want to have an ongoing tuple for collecting bits of data about users of the script (say, `"Thanks for telling me your name, now what is your age?: "`)? Or do we want to eventually put all these attributes of users into a class of some kind? As noted throughout, planning your code ahead of time can help you consider these design issues and make your coding go more smoothly. And whether you take that advice or not, these types of design issues *will have to be* considered at some point, so it's best to save yourself the effort of constantly fighting software bugs and unexpected errors by considering these issues at the outset, even before you start writing the code.

Why bother?

Now, one thing remains: *why bother* building scripts like this? One thing I've alluded to is the idea that you can use these scripts to collect data from users who may not be familiar with Python (and hence would not be able to work directly with the script). However, if you can provide them with questions and a means of having their answers recorded (and used) that *don't* require a knowledge of Python, that could help. So, you might want to build scripts that can help other social science researchers do some task or other (perhaps web scraping, or some other task covered later in this book?) – you could then give them script, tell them to run it, request (via an interface) a web URL and a filename to store the data in, and that would be all they need to do some web scraping "for themselves".[11] They wouldn't need to actually see what was going on in your script (as long as you were confident it was working correctly), yet they could still do a task like web scraping. Equally, we could think about developing a survey/questionnaire in Python, where we collected information from participants using this input() method, automatically processed it into visualisations (using methods that I'll discuss in later chapters), and quickly graphed out some key things about the data they provide us with. As a user-facing interface, this input() method is really helpful.

We could also use the input() command for our own needs as programmers. For instance, suppose you have a script for cleaning up some data you've collected from Twitter (i.e. removing some junk lines that you don't need) with a function that identifies and chops out the bits you don't want. Instead of fiddling about in the script itself, you could create an interface that asks you for the filename of the data you want to clean, then applies your various clean-up functions to them, and dumps the clean data in a new file (which you can also name with another input() command). Or perhaps you have a big dataset full of crime survey data you've got from the web – perhaps you want to filter the data for people who live in the North West of England, for your analysis. But later, you might want to get more specific (e.g. Manchester) or switch to looking at another area altogether (e.g. "South West"), so you want some reusable code that will help you easily identify and filter out the stuff you want to look at. Here you could use input() to collect the name of the location you're currently interested in exploring in the data (e.g. Manchester, or South West), and then store the information pertaining to that location somewhere else (i.e. in a new text file, or a list within the script you're currently working in, or whatever).

There are lots of potential applications for the input() command and, as with anything in Python, having an awareness of it as a general tool early on will help you apply it creatively later.

8●5 Commenting and Documenting Code Effectively

Now, to wrap up Part Two – reading and writing the basic grammar and syntax of Python – it's appropriate to return to where we started – with commenting. We've seen lots of commenting and documentation of code, in every one of the code files we've worked with. We

---

[11] Well, *you'd* have done the web scraping *for* them really, but you get what I mean.

know that comments are denoted in a few different ways – with triple speech marks (for blocks of comments) or the hash symbol (for single lines). These comments provide a form of documentation that is designed to help you read and understand what is going on in a script. Comments are helpful in that (when they're done well) they allow a reader to quickly grasp what a piece of code is doing and why it is doing it in this particular way. They can also provide a way of signposting and navigating your way around a script (i.e. they can say "this function uses the result from another function, so run that one first" and so on, to help readers follow the flow of the script). Commenting can also be a helpful practice in terms of actually building/writing code – we can quickly "comment out" bits of code that we don't want to run so we can test other bits that we *do* want to run. Commenting can be used in lots of different ways, and we have hopefully by now got an understanding of commenting as not just something that is an extra effort or unnecessary aspect of coding, but integral to thinking about, building and sharing good code.

"Documenting code" is not just about comments

However, what we also need to recognise is that the idea of documenting your work extends beyond comments. Things like your choice of variable names, function names and class names are all part of making people see, easily and unproblematically, what it is that your code is doing. For instance, if I have a variable x, it is not immediately clear what this variable is intended to do in the code – what is it for? How will its results be used? Where does it get passed around to? All of these questions are easily glossed over if we have a poor choice of variable name. However, if we call that same variable username, we can immediately see what it is for, we can expect what type of data it will contain (i.e. strings of people's Twitter usernames, or something like that), and we have a better chance of spotting where it gets used as an argument in other functions or bits of code and why (inasmuch as the character x is more difficult to identify visually and understand intuitively than the term username).

Hence, when writing code, you have to think in terms of what somebody looking over your shoulder would make of the code you're building – could they in principle easily follow how and why arguments get passed around from object to object in the way you have designed? Could they in principle see the flow of the script, and your reasoning behind making it flow that way and not another? Are there bits of code which may at first seem counter-intuitive to them (and therefore would need further explanation)? You need to address these questions, not only for other people, but also for your future self who may return to a script a year down the line and not be able to remember the fine detail of why you've done the coding in this way. It sounds implausible that you'd need to remind yourself to this level of detail, but it does happen. All the time. Hence my encouraging you not to have to learn this the hard way!

In terms of what you should actually put in those comments and documentation, though, there's a trade-off to be made with the level of detail you provide. Too little is a problem because readers won't be able to follow what your code is doing and will have to guess for themselves. However, too much detail is also a problem, since it will look awkward on the page and prevent people from actually easily looking at the code. Thinking carefully about things like variable names will help here – if you can explain what you're doing with appropriate useful naming of code elements (supported by short succinct comments), do that! Again, it's very important to think as though there's somebody reading over your shoulder while you're coding – what do *they* need to know in order to make sense of your code? What isn't/can't be explained by the code itself (and therefore requires a comment to provide a little further elaboration)? Thinking about such things should become routine as you're coding, and soon enough you'll find yourself doing them automatically.

Chapter summary

- In this chapter, we complemented our knowledge of the core Python concepts by pointing towards a range of further techniques that we can use to extend the tools we build.
- We started by looking at how to install, import (and use) modules.
- Then, we looked at the idea of building the concept of *time* into code in various ways - as waits between the execution of commands in a script, or by making reference to the current date and time, or by scheduling whole scripts to be executed automatically.
- Then, we looked at creating script interfaces with inputs, and used this as a platform to think about "user design" in code (i.e. helping to make the scripts we build more easily usable by ourselves and others).
- Finally, we reflected back on commenting practices. In light of all we've done in Part Two, we returned to the idea of documenting code as a fundamental programming practice, discussing what good (and bad) commenting comprises and why commenting is important.

Summary of Part Two

- In Part Two, you've learned lots of things! First, how to get Python installed on your computer, and how to use IDLE as a script and a shell (since this is how the code excerpts and exercises were laid out throughout Part Two).
- You've also learned about all the key core concepts of Python, and have had an opportunity to play around and work with them for yourself. The things you have encountered - from variables right through to classes - are the building blocks of any and all Python code. Now you know them, you can confidently say that you're a Python programmer (though of course, the way to build on these skills is to practise and apply them in projects of your own).
- Along the way, you have also done various exercises for yourself, and have seen my suggested solutions to them (so that you can compare your own ways of doing things against mine).

    - This is useful for two reasons. First, you have worked your way through various exercises starting with relatively straightforward concepts and moving up to a big(gish) project - the exercise in `7_1_2_ClassesExercise.py` - which brings lots of different Python concepts together to address a problem. This is no mean feat!
    - But second, aside from actually doing some coding, you have gained some first-hand experience in thinking about how to address problems/questions with Python programming - this creative thinking is enormously important to programming work (and this is exactly what is meant in this book by a *programming mindset*).

- It's completely impossible to write in a book a comprehensive account of all the different things you can do with these core concepts. Hence, there is inevitably lots more to learn about how things like variables, different data types and different data structures operate. Nonetheless, what you have learned here gets you off the blocks - the knowledge and skills you now have are a platform from which you can go on to do your own independent (and more complex) Python programming for social science (and this will be supported further in later chapters).
- In short, in Part Two you have learned *how* to program in Python - what we'll learn in later chapters will help you see *why* we, as social scientists, would want to bother.

PART THREE

Part Three contents

WORKING WITH PYTHON

Part Three objectives

- To support you in advancing your Python knowledge by introducing you to a selection of more applied research-relevant techniques.
- To show you some basic Python commands (complemented by add-on commands drawn from other modules and libraries) in such a way as to spark thinking around how those techniques can be further developed for social scientific purposes.
- To encounter practical elements that sit around the use of Python for social science but which nonetheless form a part of what using Python is likely to involve as you go forward (e.g. generating API login credentials for data harvesting).
- To further develop your programming mindset by demonstrating how these more advanced research-relevant techniques map onto the core Python learning covered in Part Two, in terms of how to break down a research process into achievable component parts (and reflecting methodologically on what that entails).

At this point in the book, you have an awareness of possible roles for Python within the social sciences (Part One), and you know the core operating features of Python (Part Two). In Part Three we will draw these two things together, to start to explore some more specifically social scientific uses of Python (e.g. to extract and look at various types of digital data).

To this end, from here on, there are no code files – the materials in the book will help you make your own. The idea is that each chapter will present you with some basic techniques for engaging with the topic at hand, and you can then use the things I'm showing you to figure out how *you* might further develop and apply those techniques in work that fits *your* interests. This will, inevitably, involve locating and working with information which isn't contained in the book – which is, in fact, impossible to put into any single book (on the grounds that there are too many possible projects and libraries and relevant techniques out there to capture in one place). But that's a good thing. Even though they won't outline every single bit of code that's possible within any given topic, you can use the chapters in Part Three as a platform for building your own scripts and working on your own projects and tasks. I'll be suggesting some possibilities you might want to try out along the way, but at this point in your learning, you'll be finding your own things to do with Python, and gaining lots of practical experience with coding as you do so.

One final thing I want to state before we move on – though our learning up to this point in the book might arguably paint a picture of programming as being something of more interest to quantitative researchers (i.e. those with an interest in numerical data and the representation of the broader patterns and trends of the social world through numbers and statistics), programming can be just as useful a tool for qualitative research too. This will become more evident as we go through the chapters and point towards examples of how the techniques we're learning can be used for a variety of purposes, but it's worth flagging up early so that we can keep half an eye out for potential creative applications of programming to all sorts of projects.

Let's get started!

9

Designing Research that Features Programming

─────────────── **Chapter objectives** ───────────────

- To sketch out the idea of "design" (as applied to the design of Python code and projects that utilise it) as a social scientific concern.
- To outline a few "design methodologies" that are potentially interesting and valuable to Programming-as-Social-Science.
- To propose a small selection of practical issues to think around as you're moving towards planning/designing social work involving Python code.

There are two strands to what this chapter aims to cover, both of which deal with "design" as an activity that pertains to planning out what you want and/or need to do to undertake a project in Programming-as-Social-Science. The first strand of the chapter outlines the idea that we need to take "design" seriously as Python programmers, since whenever we're using those skills, that is the business we're in – we're taking an active part in the design of code/software to undertake social scientific tasks (or whatever tasks you're doing with them). The second strand presents a selection of things to consider in terms of planning any given programming task, pointing towards how to actually prepare to do some Programming-as-Social-Science work. Neither strand aims to be a step-by-step checklist that you can follow from start to finish – as with anything in Python, the specifics of the work *you're* intending to do mean that any guidance a single book could offer is limited. The specific individual work you'll (hopefully) end up doing with your Python skills means that it's impossible to predict in any general way what an appropriate approach to it might look like. Nonetheless, it *is* still worth going over some points in general, because this will (hopefully) inspire thinking around how you would go about designing/planning your own programming work when you come to do it. The key thing here is to start to see your programming work as embedded in a wider social scientific context (cf. Chapter 2 on PaSS and "critical coding"), and thinking about design in these ways can help us do that. So let's get to it!

9 ● 1   Design as a Social Scientific Activity

We first looked at the concept of programming as a social (e.g. political, ideological, moral, ethical, etc.) issue in Chapter 2, as a way to help us make sense of how programming can fit into our social scientific work. One of the things we learned in Chapter 2 was that whether we're using our knowledge of programming to analyse code produced by others or whether we're applying that knowledge to build code ourselves, we have to find some way to keep our focus on the intersection between programming and the social world – the interlocking of software with society. Here, we're taking these ideas further by using the concept of *design* as a lens through which to view the ways in which code and programming are objects and activities that are embedded in the everyday world of people and the things they do (including, of course, people who are social scientists).

As outlined by Lupton (2018: 2), "design" as a concept is used to refer to the process of "developing an idea about a product, system, service or policy to meet human needs and devising a plan for executing that idea". This can serve as a useful definition to hang our thinking about design on. Our interests of course (in the context of this book at least) are specifically in the design of code, which might result in tools or algorithms or data or visualisations and so on, and all of these are covered in some way in this book. Whatever work we're doing with our code – whether that's collecting data, visualising data, interacting with research participants, whatever – the way the code works is *designed*; it is *created* and *could in principle be created in lots of different ways*. For instance, suppose we want to use Python to collect data from a social media platform on a given topic of interest – *how* are we going to do that? Do we want to build some code that cycles through a list of individual users and collect their social media posts as timelines? Or is it going to work better for our project if we collect posts that match specified criteria (e.g. they contain a keyword that's of interest to the topic we're looking at)? Either way, how are we going to build the code that contributes to this work in an ethical way? How many posts are we looking at collecting – a finite specified number, or just as many as we can get our hands on? Which bits of those posts are we interested in – the text content? Images? Metadata such as the time and date the post was sent or how many likes/favourites it got? And either way, what are we then going to go on and do with the data – are we using them to undertake quantitative/statistical work or something more qualitative? And either way, quantitative or qualitative, how are we going to make sure the data we collect can support the things we intend to do with them? *Lots* of things to consider, before we even put our fingers to the keyboard!

If we boil all these questions down to one single pointer, we might say that *whatever the task, we need to consider where programming fits into our broader social scientific work* (which itself may comprise a diverse set of things like social theory, ethical issues, methods, analytic frameworks, etc.). Given that this is not a book about social theory, ethical issues, methods, analytic frameworks and so on, these things are only very lightly touched on here. However, what I do want to impress is that having an eye on design gives us an opportunity to not just build code that does a job, but to bake the critical reflective, reflexive work of social science directly into the code as we go – to reiterate, it's this integration of programming and social science that forms the central approach of this book, and which we're calling "Programming-as-Social-Science" (or PaSS for short).

Given Lupton's (2018) definition of design, we might note that the act of designing is inherently human-centred and user-focused – we don't just design code for its own sake; we design code to engage with people and the social world generally. In the example above (on collecting data from a social media platform), the task itself is inherently social before we even *consider* investigating it – the world of social media and people using it to give their opinions and undertake their everyday interactions (as the stuff we might be interested in exploring as social scientists) already exists prior to any social scientific investigation of it. Put differently, whatever investigations of the social world we might want to make as social scientists, we are always only ever second on the scene (cf. Garfinkel, 1967). As Schutz (1972) puts it, the social sciences are "second-order disciplines" – the social world already exists, and *only then* do social scientists turn up to look at it.[1] In this sense, our code and coding *has* to be social – it reflects and is thoroughly essentially contextualised by the fact of being situated in an already

---

[1] This is in fact one of the core premises of Wittgenstein-influenced ethnomethodology (cf. Brooker et al., 2017b; Garfinkel, 1967; Winch, 1990; Wittgenstein, 2009 [1953]) and Schutz-influenced phenomenology (cf. Schutz, 1972), if you want to explore these ideas from a social scientific perspective. And, being an advocate of these approaches, I would recommend doing exactly that!

existing social world. Thus, any code we build is *designed* – sociality is built directly into our code from the ground up, and unavoidably so.

The socially centred aspect of design, therefore, makes design practices inherently "user-focused" – whatever is being designed is directed towards a specific set of users (and their practices) and the specific needs that they have (or at least that the designers understand them to have). For our purposes, thinking of programming as a task of exploring the design of code that fits with human needs, we can then consider design as the bridge between code and the social worlds in which that code is ultimately embedded, as indicated by Lupton's (2018: 3) argument that "Like sociologists and other social researchers ... many design researchers now focus their attention on the socio-technical contexts of design as a practice and the sociocultural dimensions of the objects and systems that emerge from and are enacted through these practices." This is exactly the kind of thinking we need to bring to programming in order to make it work for us as social scientists.

To sum up the argument of this chapter so far, as budding programmers, it is imperative that we see our own work as being an endeavour in design. However, there are multiple ways in which we can do this – there are many "design methodologies" which might be helpful to our social scientific work, and it is worth capturing the essences of some particularly relevant schemas here that may help shape our practice going forward.[2]

Definitions

A (Small) Selection of Design Methodologies

Adversarial Design is a methodology organised around "agonism" - the active encouragement of disruption and conflict in order to provoke critical debate and deliberation. In the context of programming, Adversarial Design is, therefore, about using code to produce software and technology that generate confrontational, discomforting and disruptive user experiences, for the purpose of shocking users out of uncritical (though perhaps natural) dominant-ideological ways of seeing the world. A key works is Di Salvo (2012).

Critical Design seeks to integrate social and political theory into the design process, and is therefore an inherently interdisciplinary exercise that "is sceptical and questioning of the ideals and practices of mainstream design ... [and] ... is used to ask provocative questions, identify, and challenge tacit norms and assumptions and explore alternative futures" (Lupton, 2018: 3). Key works are Bardzell and Bardzell (2013) and Malpass (2013).

Ludic Design is premised on how design can support users in making meaning from the world by providing interfaces for loose, playful and creative interactions with it. As Gaver et al. (2004: 4) note: "If people are to find their own meaning for activities, or to pursue them without worrying about their meaning, designs should avoid clear narratives of [i.e. instruction on their] use. Instead they should be open-ended or ambiguous in terms of their cultural interpretation

---

[2]Most of the descriptions of design methodologies listed here were originally found in Lupton's (2018) work on "design sociology" - well worth a read in itself for further detail, as well as the key works that are given.

and the meanings – including personal and ethical ones – people ascribe to them." Key works are Gaver (2002), Gaver et al. (2004) and Wilkie et al. (2015).

Participatory Design refers to design practices that bring both designers and users together in the design process, such that "those who will use these ideas, processes or objects (the end-users) are able to have a say in how they are designed" (Lupton, 2018: 4). As such, Participatory Design practices might be characterised as a "process of experimentation, mutual learning, and reflection in action involving multiple participants beyond designers" (Lupton, 2018: 4). Key works are Björgvinsson et al. (2012), Muller (2003) and Robertson and Simonsen (2012).

Reflective Design captures practices where the design itself is intended to cast a reflective eye back on the practice of the designers – in other words, where designers are attempting, through their designs, to question their own "taken-for-granted values and tacit norms and assumptions … [and] move beyond single authoritative interpretations to elicit multiple viewpoints and developer ideas for alternative possibilities" (Lupton, 2018: 3). Key works are Sengers et al. (2005) and Sengers and Gaver (2006).

These design methodologies have provided the underlying principles, motivations and guidelines for numerous projects.[3] In sketching out this small selection of design methodologies, the aim is not to dig too deeply into the subtleties of each, but rather to point towards some potentially interesting ways of approaching our Programming-as-Social-Science work. Depending on what it is you want to apply these skills to, you may be interested in leveraging various design methodologies to frame the work – for instance, you could use a Critical Design perspective to construct code that produces an alternative visualisation of a pre-existing dataset to give a counter-narrative to a dominant discourse; you could undertake a Participatory Design project that involves research participants in the construction of that code to build tools that directly serve their needs; you could use Ludic Design principles to encourage participants to playfully (and inductively) elaborate on a social science topic; or you could treat your code as an effort in Reflective Design and take the code and coding process as an opportunity to draw wider reflections on your own programming and design (and social scientific) practices. In this sense, the above definitions, though far from being a complete collection of design methodologies in themselves, aim to serve as reference material that you may wish to return to later when you're at the point of building your own code and undertaking your own programming projects.

Though any given programming project does not have to tie its colours to any particular design methodology mast – you'll never really have to have a definitive statement to the effect that "this work strictly follows Adversarial Design principles" or anything like that – having these ideas in mind allows us to gather an appreciation for the different ways in which the code we design can intersect with the world and with people. Whichever methodology

---

[3] If you wish to find out more about the kinds of projects within which each methodology has been developed and put to use, the "key works" associated with each methodology would be an ideal place to start.

we might find most compelling or apposite for the project at hand, thinking about *how* our programming efforts might intersect with the social world (through the lens of design) affords us a vital opportunity for putting together not just a script that runs, but one that also does the work of social science; not just programming, but Programming-as-Social-Science.

9.2 Practicalities

The previous section deals with the kinds of considerations and frameworks we might want to bear in mind when designing projects that feature programming alongside social science. However, it is also worth paying attention to some practicalities to do with *how* to actually design a project – what does this concept of design actually *involve* in terms of tasks you will have to consider and undertake? As with lots of the topics in this book, it's impossible to have a checklist of things to consider when designing some code as part of a social science project – Python is a multi-purpose toolkit and social science is a broad and diverse set of disciplines, so any attempt to stitch it all together in a single cohesive narrative is doomed to fail. Nevertheless, it is worth just sketching out a few generic ideas to get you in the right frame of mind for thinking about this in terms of your own specific and individual programming projects – these ideas have already been outlined in various sections of this book, but reiterating them briefly here for reference is no bad thing.

Planning your code

The first thing to note is that, just as with an academic essay or publication of any kind, you shouldn't start writing code without having planned in advance what you intend to do – if as a student you have ever written an essay without first planning and organising what should be in it, you'll be acutely aware that this way of working runs a risk of ending up with a mess of stuff that may need a *lot* of editing and restructuring later if it is to make sense. The same applies to programming. Not having a plan will likely result in lots of wasted time spent coming across then sorting out issues that could have easily been anticipated in the planning stages, and can lead projects down dead-ends (e.g. if your lack of planning means you veer off the path you were intending to stick to and you end up spending time writing code that can never really undertake the job you set out to do). Sketching out a plan for your code, and how it fits with the project at hand more broadly, is vital here – following the guidelines advanced in Section 1.4 in Chapter 1, on script/ development workflows, will be helpful here in terms of making a start on thinking about these ideas. Moreover, having these kinds of plans laid out in advance is really helpful later on when it comes to writing up your work – a plan is a document you can use for reference to help you make sense of the work you've just done (which sounds simple, but practically never is). The only way to really develop these skills with planning is to practise them – come up with projects to do, plan them out, and pay attention to your planning skills along the way. It does get easier the more you do it, and you'll develop a routine that works and is helpful for you as you go.

So, though there's not much I can offer here in terms of specific advice – that's really going to depend on what you intend your code to do – the generic advice I can offer with regard to planning your code is pretty simple: just do it do it do it! Always always always!

Milestones

However, the planning and design we do shouldn't just be concerned with the Python code of course. How a script works and what needs to go into it *are* important, but we should also be planning more widely than that, and seeing how the various pieces of the puzzle – the code, the theory, the methods, the literature, the analysis, the data, the ethics, etc. – fit together. To this end, a good way to think about a project in full is to put down on paper a sense of the milestones that need to be achieved in order to get from the start to the finish. For instance, suppose we want to do a discourse analysis (i.e. close critical readings) of news articles on the topic of government responses to public health issues. With this topic and the framework of discourse analysis in mind, we can identify some key milestones. In *really* broad terms, we might say that we'll need to:

1   Look at literature on government and public health.
2   Generate some research questions/a hypothesis to investigate.
3   Identify some data through which we could explore these issues via discourse analysis.
4   Grab those data.
5   Process the data into something we can look at and work with.
6   Make an analysis of the data at hand.
7   Write up our analysis in such a way that it can be presented to others.

Though that's a really abstract way to talk about a project, it is still helpful to have a sense of where we want to end up in order to think further about what we need to do to get there. In this example, it's perhaps only the case that the Python skills we'll be using will drop into the grabbing and processing of data. If we have a sense that we want to do discourse analysis with these data, we already have an idea of what we might need to build into our code to do that (e.g. a web-scraping script that can take the text of a news article from a chosen website, and store articles as individual blocks of text that can be called on command for us to read and analyse). In thinking through these issues ahead of doing any coding, we'll be gathering vital information on the materials we'll need to use and asking and answering questions that will help us get on with the work. For example, what kind of data format is this, and which libraries will I need to help me wrangle it into shape? If I'm going to visualise this stuff, what sort of visualisation is appropriate and what sort of techniques will I need to do this? Are there any ethical/moral/legal implications I need to consider to do this work, and where would I go to find out that information? How do I want to run this script: is it going to be a one-off data collection routine or do I need to automate the process so it runs once daily or similar (and if so, how might I go about doing that?)? Moreover, breaking down the overall project into manageable individual components (while still thinking about how they connect together) allows us to treat big projects as more bite-sized chunks of work – if we think about any given project in terms of discrete milestones to be achieved, this is often a helpful way of understanding what needs to be done without being overly daunted by an otherwise seemingly enormous task.

It is the connecting up of the Python aspects to the wider research purposes and goals that is key here, since in order for our code to be useful and fit into the task at hand, it has to neatly follow on from the stuff that leads up to it, and itself fit snugly with the stuff that follows it. The better the handle you have on how the code fits into your research process (as a socio-technical assemblage – see Section 1.2), the smoother the flow of the work will be from start to finish. All of these things have to be designed into your project and your code, and only you can do that. However, luckily for you, all these issues are covered in various places throughout this book so you'll have a head start in thinking about the right sorts of issues!

Planning as a live process

Of course, once you've planned your work in detail, this doesn't mean that you're not going to run into troubles as you dig into the work. Having a thoroughly worked-out plan can never really prevent the troubles you encounter as you undertake a project, and the same applies to projects that incorporate Python code. I gave an example above of a project that uses web-scraping techniques to gather the text of news articles from a chosen website and store those articles as individual blocks of text that can be called on and read later – this may sound simple, and we may have a rough idea of the kinds of things we'll need to do to build that script,[4] but when we actually get to the point of building the code, all sorts of hurdles might present themselves. For instance, the way the text data are structured might make it difficult for us to pull them out of the webpage; the pages themselves might be inconsistently structured so our web-scraping script breaks when we try to apply it to other pages on the same website; we might not get these news articles as single strings of text (and therefore have to figure out some way to stitch multiple strings together so that we can keep an "article" as the unit of analysis); and so on. Problems such as these are only encountered as you're doing the work, and often can't be predicted and avoided beforehand. However, this is OK and nothing to worry about. Academic work often has to be tweaked and (slightly) redesigned as you go – if you've done literally *any* academic work, you'll know that I'm not really saying anything surprising here. However, planning ahead and breaking down the research process into milestones as suggested above can help you keep a handle on how to deal with these issues when they crop up, in terms of giving you discrete tangible problems to work on (rather than being in the constant state of bewilderment that a lack of planning ensures) and concrete goals to aim towards (rather than having to laboriously figure and refigure things out as you go).

Again, although the information presented here is intended to helpful, the best way to see how this all works is not to read about it but to practise and see it in action yourself – as you start to undertake Python projects yourself (including planning/designing them as well as eventually putting those plans/designs to use) you'll develop an understanding of what is required. And the book from here on is intended precisely to give you a leg-up on such projects, by demonstrating some useful techniques you might like to take further as a social science Python programmer in your own work.

---

[4]Or at least, you *will* have a rough idea of how this sort of task might be tackled once you've read the chapter on web scraping later in the book.

Chapter summary

- In this chapter, we started by positing "design" as a guiding concept for our Programming-as-Social-Science work, by first defining what is meant by the term and then showing how the concept of "design" (as applied in our context of Python programming for social scientific purposes) connects up code with the social word.
- We then outlined a selection of design methodologies that provide different ways of thinking about the programming we might do as social scientists.
- We briefly (and in a very general way) attended to some of the practicalities of planning/designing work involving Python, in part by recalling ideas expressed in previous chapters and pointing the way towards things to be learned as we proceed further into the book.

10

Working with Text Files

Chapter objectives

- To get you started thinking about files (and text files specifically) as a type of generic object of relevance to a wide range of social scientific work.
- To outline a selection of basic commands and methods to work with text files in various ways.
- To encounter some of the peripheral issues that are implicated in the work of dealing with text files (e.g. string literals)
- To further develop your programming mindset by pointing towards how text files can feature more broadly in tasks relevant to social science.

In Python, you can do all sorts of things with text files (and files generally) – you can open them, read in data from them (and play around with such data as you go), write extra information into them, and so on. This is really useful for us as social scientists, inasmuch as it means we can easily create and use files in various ways: for instance, as places to store and work with digitised data. While we're going to look at how to grab data from different sources later in the book (in Chapters 11–13), it's a good move at this point to get to grips with how we can play around with files, specifically text files, using Python code. We can think of this in the same way we might want to do something like create an empty list in a script, so that we can store things in it at a later point – the only difference here is that instead of a list, we're creating a text file, as something more generic and which can store lots of different things.

10 1 Show Me the Code!

First of all, it's a good idea to pay close attention to what we mean by a "file" and what a "text file" actually is.[1] A file on a computer is just a place where some kind of information is stored. This information can come in lots of different formats: for instance, there are different types of file for storing audio information (e.g. .mp3, .wav, .ogg, and .flac), different types of file for storing documents associated with the Microsoft Office suite (e.g. .doc, .xls, .ppt), different types of file for storing images (e.g. .jpg, .bmp, .png), and so on. What we're looking at here is a type of file that comes with a .txt extension – a text file. You may have seen these kinds of things before on your computer. If you've ever opened a .txt file in a basic text editor (like Notepad), you'll see that it's a very basic way of storing text information – typically a .txt file will have none of the fancy formatting available in more sophisticated word processors (e.g. a range of fonts, bold/italic/underline, and the capacity to insert pictures or tables). However, the basic nature of text files is what makes them quite useful for us as programmers; we don't have to worry about the fancy stuff if all we want to do is perform some very basic functions like creating a file, dropping some text into it, then saving it.

---

[1] I mean, as someone who's made it this far through a programming textbook, I *know* you know what a file and text file are, but it's still not a bad idea to restate these things, just to kick things off.

Opening, writing information to, and closing a text file

Here are those basics of using Python to work with text files – the following three lines of code will (1) create and open a text file (i.e. one with a .txt suffix/extension) ready to have data written into it, then (2) write some information – a short string, in this case – into the file, then (3) close the file to "save" it's contents.

```
1    new_file = open("output.txt", "w")
2    new_file.write("This is some info for the new file.")
3    new_file.close()
```

In line 1, you can see we're storing something as a variable called new_file – the thing we're storing is an open file. The open() method accepts multiple arguments, and here we have just used two: one to indicate the *filename* (plus extension) of the file we want to work with, and "w" to indicate the *mode* in which we want to open and work with the file. There are various modes we could open a file with:

- "w" opens the file in write mode, so we can write new information into it.
- "r" opens the file in read-only mode, which means we can't make any changes to the information in the file. This is handy when you want to make sure you're not accidentally altering the file you're working with.
- "r+" opens the file in read-and-write mode - which, predictably, opens the file so that you can both read from *and* write to it.
- "a" is append mode, which opens the file in such a way that you can only append information to the end of the file and not change anything before that. This is handy if, say, you have a dataset you want to add new data to but want to prevent accidentally changing the original data.

Now try writing something similar to the code snippet above into a script for yourself, and run it. If you've used the same filenames (etc.) as used in the snippet, you should see that a new file called output.txt has appeared in the same directory location where you saved this script (i.e. if you saved the script on the desktop of your computer, output.txt will be created there too). Open the file, and you should see what it contains – the message that we wrote to it with the .write() method. Look back at the code snippet, and see if you can track back what this snippet has done, on the basis of the new output.txt file that your script has created.

Another thing to note is that if there is *already* a file called output.txt in the directory the script is saved to (and your code asks Python to open output.txt in write mode), then your script won't create a new second version, but it *will* overwrite what is already in that file. Be careful not to overwrite things you want to keep (which is exactly why it's important to know about the different modes for opening files).

Also, *never forget to close a file*! If you leave files hanging open, you're always running a risk that the information you want to write there won't actually ever get written. Methods like .write() don't actually write the data to the file directly, but to a "buffer" that only writes when .close() is called. So, unless you close a file, new data won't get written to it. In the same way that Python can't deal with an open bracket without its being paired with a closed bracket, troubles arise when you open a file and don't then later close it. There is, however, an alternative way to ensure that any files you open get closed once you've done what you wanted to do with them. This bit of code avoids the open/close problem:

```
1   with open("output.txt", "w") as textfile:
2       textfile.write("Success!")
```

This way of opening files creates a kind of temporary variable to store the open file in (here we've called it textfile), and from here we can then nest whatever commands we like within the with statement such that whenever the script comes to the end of whatever is nested, it closes the file automatically. In the snippet above, output.txt gets closed once the nested textfile.write() command is completed, and we don't need any code to then tell Python to close the file.

However, it's worth thinking about what the two ways of opening and working with files offer. Using a with statement is good for always making sure that a file that is opened later gets closed, and without needing extra code. However, I still tend to prefer the first method where we have explicitly set out a line of code to open the file, and a later one to close it. This, to me, is more readable, and doesn't force me to try to nest everything I need to do within the (limited) confines of one with statement (i.e. I can do *lots* of things between opening and closing the file, and they don't all have to be crammed into one nested set of lines of code). But, it's really a matter of preference, and it's up to you to make decisions about which method is preferable and/or most appropriate for the job you are doing.

Reading text into Python from a text file

Now we can open (and write to) files, let's try reading in some data from an already existing text file. Open the file associated with this chapter called 10_number_lines.txt in a text editor, to get a sense of what it contains. You should see a lot of numbers – 500 to be exact, each on a different line of the file. Put this file in a directory location of your choice (e.g. the desktop of your computer), then try writing the following code into a Python script in that same location:

```
1   numbers = open("10_number_lines.txt", "r")
2   data = numbers.read()
3   numbers.close()
```

Now, run the script, and, in the shell, call on your data variable to see what results:

Drawing things to a close

That's just about everything in terms of the basics of working with text files in Python. However, now that we're coming to an end and we've been working with lots of files, opening and closing them and so on, can we remember which files are still open and which are already closed? I can't. But we know it's important to make sure everything is closed before we quit Python, so here's a way to check:

```
>>> file_name.closed
True
```

The above code snippet checks to see if the filename you want to check (in this case, the rather imaginatively named `file_name`) is closed, and returns a value of `True` or `False` to tell you. This is useful in and of itself, but it's also quite handy to use in the context of IF/ELSE statements, as follows:

```
>>> if file_name.closed != True:
        file_name.close()
```

Here, we've used `.closed` as part of a conditional statement to check if `file_name` is closed, and if it isn't (i.e. if the conditional statement is not true), we use the methods outlined earlier in the chapter to close it. Putting a statement like this at the end of a script, or typing it into the shell, can act as a failsafe to make sure you've definitely closed everything you need to before exiting Python.

And that's as good a place as any to end our look at techniques of working with text files in Python!

10●2 Some Possible Applications/Projects

As noted at the outset of this chapter, we've talked about text files and associated methods in an abstract way for now, rather than as something with a specific social scientific relevance – this is because we need to be able to set up a text file for later chapters (which will be more organised around grabbing stuff like web-based digital data to put in those text files). So that's one possible application of what you've just learned – text files as data storage. Bear in mind that "data" is quite a broad term here – we can think of "data" as referring to things like lists of numbers (as in our mocked-up example text file used in this chapter), or more varied forms of survey data, or login credentials for tapping into social media platforms to harvest other types of data from them (which is something we'll do in later chapters). In this sense, working with text files is a generic and general skill that we'll be referring back to constantly as we go forward into tasks that are more obviously relevant to social science.

For now, though, it's worth further honing your skills by practising them – use what you have learned in this chapter to test yourself further! Set yourself some tasks to do with text files, and see if you can use what you know to complete them. You may find that you have to get some extra information from sources like the official Python documentation if you're doing tasks that are more complex than those covered here, but that's exactly what this book is about – helping you learn to program in Python for yourself by kicking you off in the right direction.

To get some practice with these skills, why not grab a text file dataset that speaks to your research interests from somewhere on the web – examine it by eye first to identify a sensible way to read the data into Python, then read the data into Python and have a look around. Don't worry about digging into the data too much at this point – we can do that in later chapters – but hopefully you can already see how the skills you've learned will be invaluable a short way down the line.

Chapter summary

- In this chapter we started by talking about what a text file (and a file more generally) actually is, as a way to kickstart our thinking around how they're useful for social scientific work.
- We then looked at some basic Python code for opening, writing information to and then closing files. We looked at two ways of doing this - first, with the `open()` and `.close()` commands/methods; and second, as part of a `with` statement - and talked about the different reasons there might be for using each of them.
- We then moved on to look at reading information in from text files to Python, so that we could use that information in our code and scripts. This led to a discussion of the concept of "string literals", as a thing that can help us make sense of what we see in Python when we read in data from text files - string literals are also useful for lots of other reasons too, so it's no bad thing to cover this early!
- At that point, we moved on to look at working with text files in their directories (as opposed to using the "default directory" which is always just the same place the script is stored).
- After reiterating the importance of closing files when you're done with them (and showing a handy little technique you can use to check if a file is closed), we talked about possible applications and projects you might like to try to practise your skills. Text files are a pretty ubiquitous and generic feature of social science work with Python in lots of different ways, so although you'll be getting plenty of practice as you work through this book, it's still worth practising what you know already (along the lines of the suggestions made in Section 10.2).

11

Data Collection: Using Social Media APIs

━━━━━━━━━━━ **Chapter objectives** ━━━━━━━━━━━

- Learn how to set up and authenticate an account in Python.
- Learn some basic commands and methods that are of potential relevance to social scientific work.
- Think about these techniques in the broader scheme of things (i.e. what you would want to do with an API in a general sense, and how to go about doing it).

Social media is, more so than ever, acknowledged as a major resource for social scientists – social media platforms are, in one sense, vast collections of freely available unscripted opinions, experiences and insights on any number of topics.[1] Social media comprises a vast array of platforms on which a bewildering diversity of social interactions come to life – no wonder it receives so much attention from social researchers!

Given the potential for social media data to explore all kinds of social science questions, this chapter will look at how to use Python to tap into a social media platform (Twitter) via what is known as an Application Programming Interface (API). An API is a mechanism by which programming languages can build applications that interact (or "interface") with the platform the API supports. Most social media platforms offer an API, because this helps them support the development of new applications that can expand their services. You likely use APIs for all sorts of different platforms all the time, even if you weren't aware that that's one way of describing what you're doing – for instance, if you've ever posted a picture to Instagram and then chosen to share it also to other personal social media profiles linked to your Instagram account (e.g. Twitter, Facebook, Tumblr) then you have used an API to post that original image elsewhere. In effect, when we're playing around with APIs in Python as programmers, we are really just looking "behind the scenes" at how functions like "tweeting a message", "liking a Facebook status" and "commenting on an Instagram picture" work. And, thinking creatively, we can do all sorts of things with APIs that might be relevant to all manner of social scientific projects.

This chapter will look at how to use Python to access a social media platform via an API, and explore some techniques for performing various tasks with that API once we have access. In order for us to get into thinking about APIs less abstractly and more specifically, this chapter will take Twitter as an example platform. Really, there are plenty of other platforms with APIs that would be interesting to look at – Reddit, Facebook, Instagram, Tumblr, even platforms that aren't social media services but which allow programmers access to their data and services. However, Twitter is often the social researcher's "go-to" platform in these cases because it has a relatively "open" API (which is to say that it's quite an easy process to get into, and the limitations on their API usage are not too restrictive) – there are lots of pieces of social media research which take Twitter as their subject, for these reasons. However, although the techniques we're learning in this chapter are specifically

---

[1] There are, of course, ontological, epistemological, moral and ethical concerns that must be considered when treating people's social media lives as "data". Unfortunately, there's not room to explore these issues here, though they are alluded to elsewhere in the book.

oriented to Twitter as a platform and will help you dig into Twitter research (if that's what you want to do), the overall idea is to think of using APIs as a transferable skill that will give you a head start in thinking about how to work with lots of other types of platforms. We'll be covering lots of key issues that cut across the idea of using APIs generally, such that you will then have the skills to go on to explore other platforms and other types of research for yourself.

One disclaimer before we start to do this, however. It is *absolutely vital* that if you are following along with the chapter by constructing your own code (as I recommend you do!), you need to familiarise yourself with the Twitter documentation on API usage first (Twitter, 2019a). As of the time of writing, none of the code in this book would break Twitter's terms and conditions around API usage – everything I've done takes really conservative estimates on how much data I pull through the API and so on, for precisely this reason. However, given that Twitter can change its terms and conditions as it likes, *you* need to check ahead to make sure any code you build and implement still complies. Though this may sound daunting at first, spending a little time browsing the available documentation is actually a really good introduction to what the Twitter APIs are and what they do, and will help you think about the possibilities for how to use them. So, before you go any further, have a look through the documentation to familiarise yourself with it – we'll be referring back to several core issues as we go forward too, since one of the key skills of being a programmer working with things like social media APIs (or a "developer", as Twitter now calls you!) is being able to comfortably navigate around these kinds of documentation to find the things you need.

11.1 Getting Your Authentication Credentials

Now that you've had a look through the documentation, you might have already gathered that the Twitter APIs (and, in fact, most APIs on any platforms) will require authentication in order to give users access. All that "authentication" means here is that Twitter needs you to "log in" via Python so that the platform can give you access to use the API. Think of it like you might use your Twitter account in an everyday way – you first need to log in, with a username and password, to be able to see your timeline, favourite a tweet, talk to friends, follow new people, see what's currently trending, and so on. Logging in is what lets Twitter know it's *you* accessing the service, and the same principle applies here – authenticating your details sets up a connection between you and Twitter that you can then use to do various things with the platform (including using its APIs to do things like collect data). So, what follows is a step-by-step walkthrough of how exactly to get the necessary authentication details – this will include setting yourself up with a developer account with Twitter and retrieving the correct "tokens" (i.e. user details) that Python is going to need.[2]

---

[2]All of these details are correct as of the time of writing (30 November 2018), but of course I can't predict that these details and the Twitter website won't change in the future. So, treat the walkthrough as indicative of the steps that have to be taken and work through the process yourself with the details I give here as rough guidance.

Setting up a Twitter developer account

First and foremost, you will need a Twitter account (and eventually, a valid phone number that hasn't already been used with an existing Twitter account). You can either use one you already have, or set up a new one; either will work, but for the purposes of this walkthrough I'll talk about setting up a new account so that we can start from scratch.[3] So, if you're setting up a new account, you'll first need to visit the Twitter website (Twitter, 2019b) and click the button to "Sign Up" for a new account. At that point, you'll need to input your name and either your phone number or an email address.[4] You will be asked how you want to

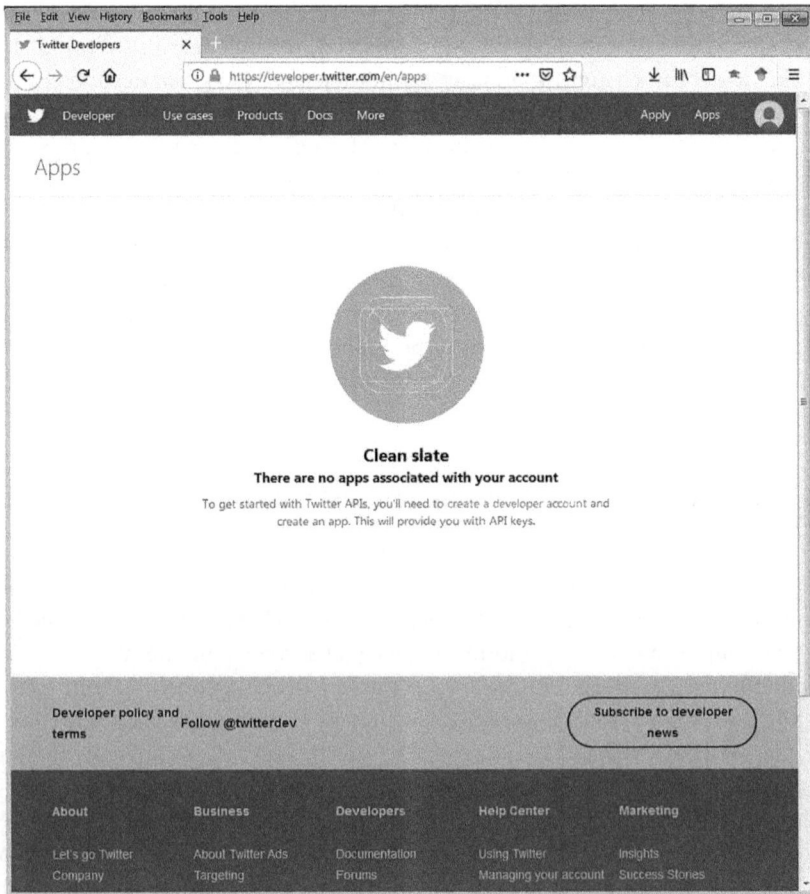

Figure 11.1 Let's make a Twitter app!

---

[3]I'll also talk about this whole process as if you're doing everything on a desktop PC. You can of course set up a new Twitter account on other devices like smartphones or tablets, but given we're working in the broader context of writing Python code on desktop machines, I'm going to stick to that path here too.

[4]You won't be allowed to use a phone number or email address that Twitter has already associated with another account.

"Customise your experience" – you don't have to do this, and since it's not especially relevant for our present purposes, I recommend skipping past it. You'll then be asked to view and agree with the Twitter terms and conditions before clicking a button to sign up. Depending on your chosen method of communication – phone or email – you'll be sent a verification code; use that code to verify your account. There will then be a series of messages asking you to input a password, pick a profile picture, tell Twitter what sort of content you're interested in, suggestions of who to follow and whether or not you want to receive notifications – you don't have to do most of these, so keep pressing forward until you can see your new (empty) Twitter timeline. Congratulations, you've got yourself an account!

Now the next step: you need to use this account to sign into Twitter as a *developer* (rather than a user). To do this, visit the Twitter developer pages (Twitter, 2019c) and sign in with your new details. Next, there is a menu along the top bar of this page called Apps – click that and you will be led to a screen that looks something like Figure 11.1.

At this point there are no apps associated with your account – we need to create a developer account in order to create applications. To do this we can click on the link, also visible in Figure 11.1, and this will take us to a screen like the one shown in Figure 11.2. This is where

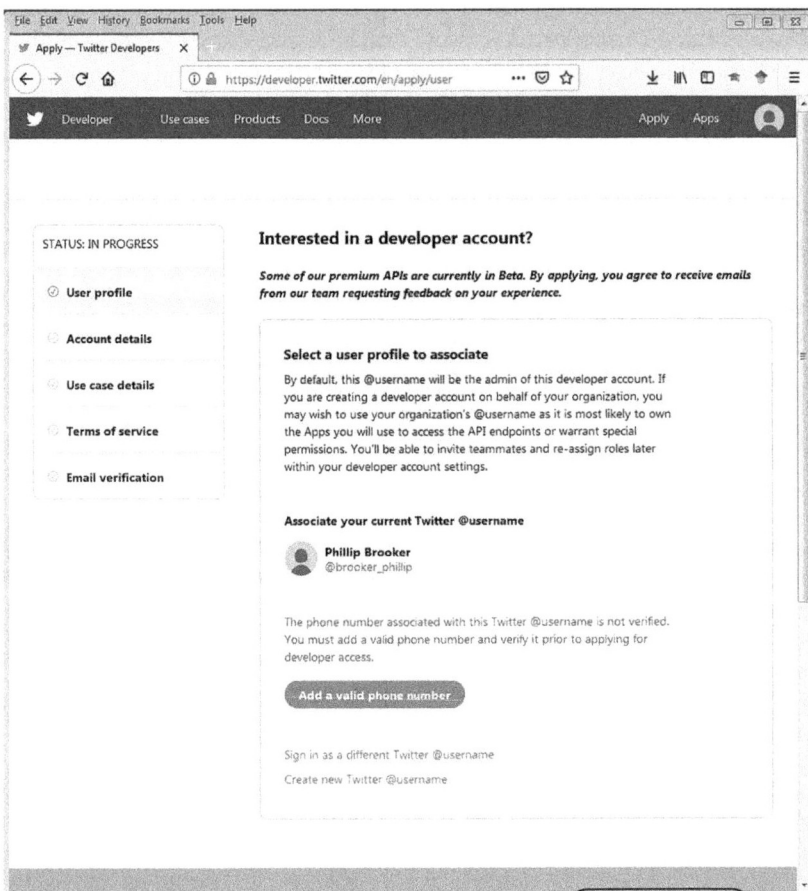

Figure 11.2 Setting up a developer account

we're going to get access to Twitter as developers, but you might already note that we're going to have to input some details – see the sidebar labelled STATUS: IN PROGRESS on the left of Figure 11.2. – including a phone number that is not already associated with a Twitter account.[5] So let's do that. You will be asked to add in a valid phone number, and once you have done so you will be asked to input a verification code which will have been sent to your phone via text.

You will also be asked to input some details about how you propose to use Twitter. You should take some time to read the documentation around this, all of which is presented on the page or via hyperlinks to other documentation (e.g. on "restricted use cases"). However, for our purposes, we are interested in only a selection of particular use cases, and not all of these should be selected (it depends on what you want to do with the Twitter APIs, and that's for you to decide). Practically, the information in this chapter will cover a range of cases which may include collecting data from Twitter (in which case you might want to tick the Academic research and/or Student project / Learning to code boxes), or publishing content to Twitter perhaps in an automatic way (in which case you might want to tick the Publish and curate Tweets and/or Chatbots and automation boxes). Make sure you *only* tick the boxes that are relevant to the specific project you intend to work on with this account.

At this point, you are also asked to describe in your own words what you are building by providing text answers to a range of questions. You should be as clear as you can about your intended usage of Twitter and how you intend to avoid usages of the Twitter APIs that fall under their "restricted use cases" policies (hence the need to read the documentation carefully). Again, this has to be as clear and specific to your application as you can make it, so I'll leave it to you to

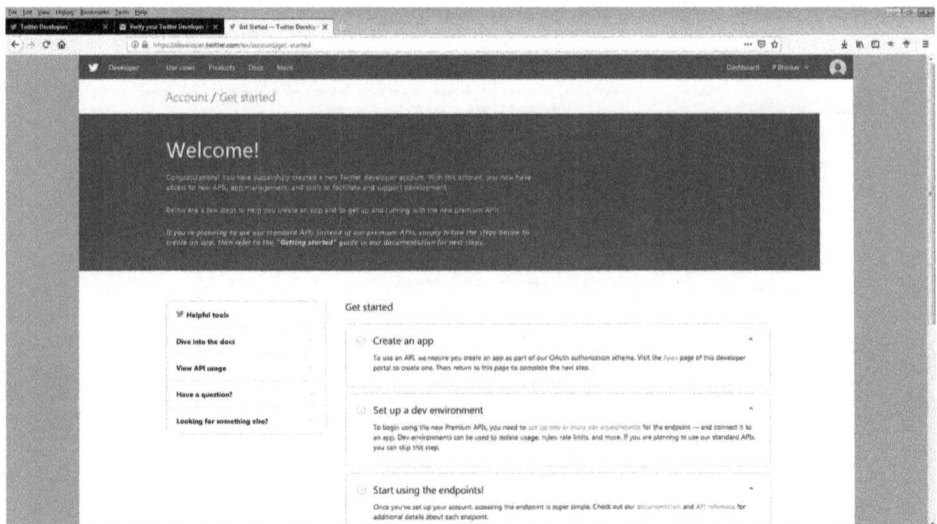

Figure 11.3   Welcome, new Twitter developer!

---

[5]If you are trying to set up a new Twitter account but have already used your phone number for another Twitter account, then I would suggest that you simply request developer access on your previous account already associated with your number.

type out this text – my advice, however, is that aside from clearly describing your specific intentions with the Twitter APIs, you make sure to think about how you will avoid the "restricted use cases" (as indicated in the documentation also available on this same page) that might seem particularly relevant to your proposal. And below this text, you will be asked if your product, service or analysis makes any information available to a government entity – select "No" here.

At this point, you will be asked to read the terms and conditions for usage of the Twitter APIs. There is a lot of relevant and valid information to be taken in here, so be sure to read it and even save a copy so you can refer back to it later. Once you have done so, check the relevant boxes to confirm you have done so and move on to the next section, upon which you will be informed that an email has been sent to the email address you have associated with the Twitter account in question – check your email to see if a request for verification has arrived, and if/when it does, click the link in the email to automatically verify your account. At that point, you will see a screen that looks something like Figure 11.3. Congratulations, you are now a Twitter developer!

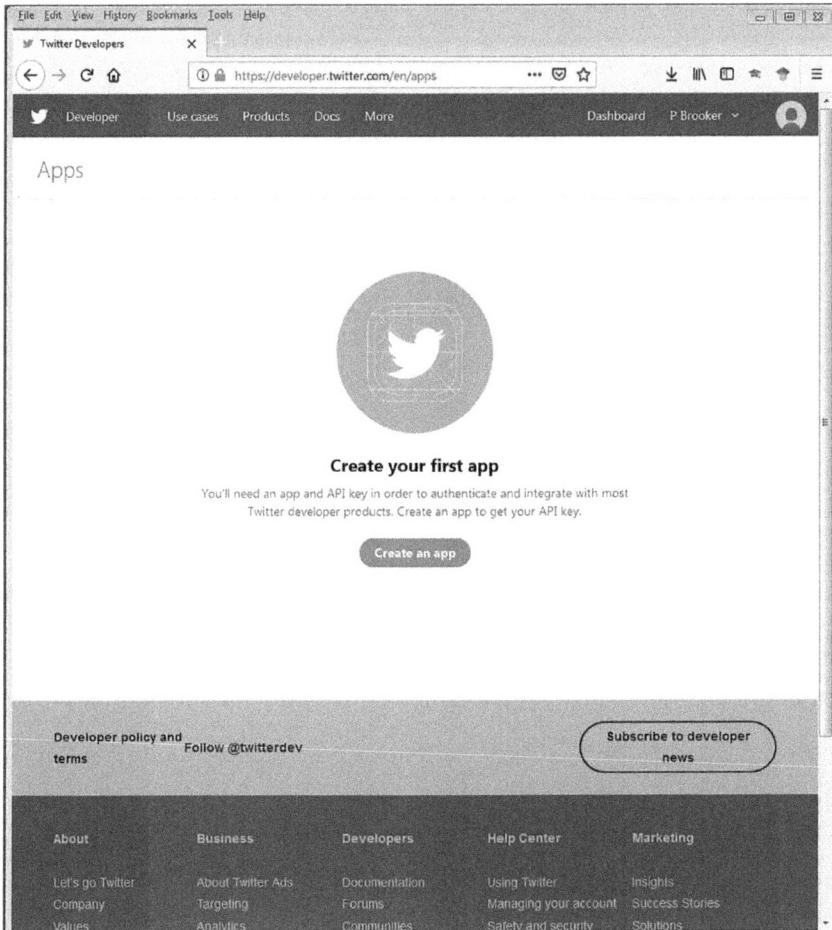

Figure 11.4 New app time!

Setting up a Twitter application

Now we're set up as Twitter developers, we have some access to the Twitter APIs – great! However, we still need to create an application to get the necessary credentials through which we can have our Python script speak to the Twitter APIs to make legitimate requests; as noted at the start of this section, we need to make it so that our Python script can "log in" to Twitter so that Twitter knows who is making the requests, in the same way that we can't tweet or read Twitter content as users unless we log into Twitter on the website or on the apps on our smartphones. So let's create an app and find those details that we need.

On the top bar of the developer's webpages, you will see the name you chose to link with your developer account – in Figure 11.3, this is at the top right of the image where it says P Brooker". Within that menu, you can select Apps and you will see a screen like that in Figure 11.4.

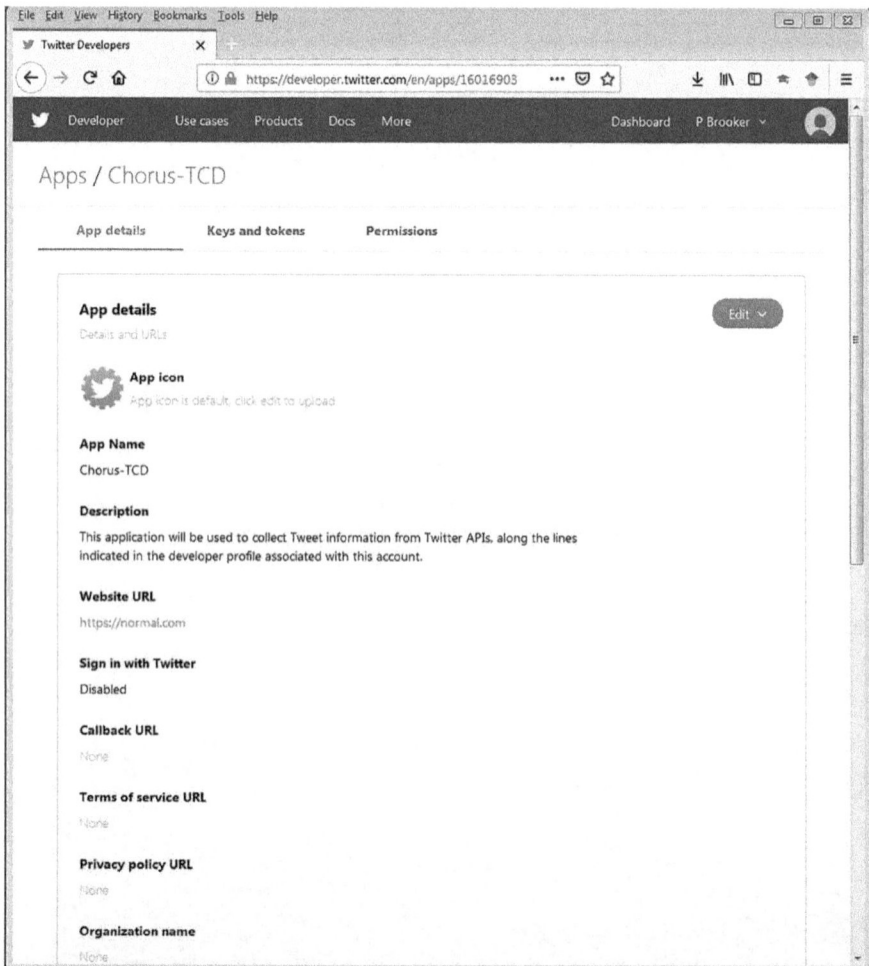

Figure 11.5 Your new app!

Click the Create an app button and fill out the details asked for in the form – you do not have to fill out all the fields here; the ones that are required are App name, Application description (where you are expected to write a description between 10 and 200 characters), Website URL and Tell us how this app will be used (where you are expected to write information with a minimum of 100 characters). Focus on these fields only, and ignore the rest (at least for now), and click through to create the app, whereupon you will be taken to a screen which looks like Figure 11.5.

Getting your application credentials

Well done – you've created an app! Now let's use it to generate the credentials we need to put in a Python script to authenticate our API access. To do this, click the Keys and token tab (visible in Figure 11.5)[6] and you will be presented with two "consumer API keys" – one string of text and numbers which is demarcated as the "API key" and one longer string of text and numbers which is demarcated as the "API secret key". Create and open up a new Python script file called AppCred.py, and store the API key and the API secret key as strings in variables as follows:[7]

```
1   CONSUMER_KEY = "INSERT API KEY HERE"
2   CONSUMER_SECRET = "INSERT API SECRET KEY HERE"
```

Next, we need to generate an "access token" and "access token secret" – back on the Twitter developer pages, we can do this by looking under the Access token & access token secret section of the page and clicking the Create button. This will generate two more lengthy strings of text and numbers, one demarcated as an "access token" and one demarcated as an "access token secret". Copy these both over to your new AppCred.py Python script as strings stored in variables, as follows:

```
1   ACCESS_TOKEN = "INSERT ACCESS TOKEN HERE"
2   ACCESS_TOKEN_SECRET = "INSERT ACCESS TOKEN SECRET HERE"
```

You should now have a script which looks something like the following (I've added a couple of comment lines in the header to suggest that it's probably also a good idea to have a reminder for ourselves about what is actually contained in this script):

---

[6]I'm not going to give screenshots here, since this effectively would be the same as giving out my Twitter password publicly. However, if you're following along, the screen you're currently at should be fairly obvious to interpret, given my written description.

[7]Be sure to use the same variable names as I have used here, for reasons which will become apparent below.

```
1   #AppCred.py
2   #My Application Credentials for Twitter APIs.
3
4   CONSUMER_KEY = "INSERT API KEY HERE"
5   CONSUMER_SECRET = "INSERT API SECRET KEY HERE"
6   ACCESS_TOKEN = "INSERT ACCESS TOKEN HERE"
7   ACCESS_TOKEN_SECRET = "INSERT ACCESS TOKEN SECRET HERE"
```

Excellent! This is all we need to start using Python to play around with Twitter's APIs. However, it's worth being really clear on this: *don't give out these details to anybody else!* Effectively, these are your login details, so it's really really really really *really* important that you keep these private – don't store them on a shared drive or anywhere where their security might be compromised (e.g. over a cloud storage service). And in fact, this is exactly why we're storing these details in their own little AppCred.py file – as we'll see in the next section, we can import these details into a Twitter API script without having to write out our secrets as strings in full; this means we can share the Twitter API script with others, without having to also share our authentication credentials. Now, all that remains to do is move your AppCred.py script to the location where you want to build a further Python script for exploring the Twitter APIs, because this is exactly what we're going to go on and do next.

11 ● 2 Show Me the Code!

At this point, you have a file called AppCred.py which contains all the details you need to tap into the Twitter API. Next, let's look at actually working with the API in a few different ways. Let's start by actually using our access credentials so that when we run the script, Twitter recognises that we have access rights to the stuff we want to access through the API. Here is some code that will do that:

```
1   import tweepy
2
3   from AppCred import CONSUMER_KEY, CONSUMER_SECRET
4   from AppCred import ACCESS_TOKEN, ACCESS_TOKEN_SECRET
5
6   auth = tweepy.OAuthHandler(CONSUMER_KEY, CONSUMER_SECRET)
7   auth.set_access_token(ACCESS_TOKEN, ACCESS_TOKEN_SECRET)
8   api = tweepy.API(auth)
```

This may look a bit serious and a bit technical at first glance, but let's go through it line by line. First, we have to remember to import the tweepy library (which we've already installed, as per the instructions in Section 8.1) – this gives our installation of Python a range of extra techniques for getting into Twitter's APIs (which we'll go on to look at later in this chapter).

Next, we need to import our access credentials from our `AppCred` file – remember, we didn't want to include these in the script itself for security reasons, so we have to import them from elsewhere. But it's worth noting the descriptive variable names here (`CONSUMER_KEY`, `CONSUMER_SECRET`, `ACCESS_TOKEN` and `ACCESS_TOKEN_SECRET`), which are designed so that it's immediately obvious what they refer to when we see them in code. It's also worth noting that I've split these imports from `AppCred` across two lines in the excerpt above – you don't have to do this, you can just separate each thing you want to import from `AppCred` by commas on one line; I did it this way just so it fits on the page.

Next come three lines of Tweepy authentication commands, which could do with a bit of unpicking so we know what's going on. In the first of these three lines, we set a variable (`auth`) to store our consumer key and secret. Though we don't really need to get into the fine detail of it, here we can see that there's a command called `OAuthHandler()` doing the work, and it takes two arguments (our `CONSUMER_KEY` and `CONSUMER_SECRET`). We also have to make sure that Python knows `OAuthHandler()` is from the `tweepy` library, which we do by prefacing it with the `tweepy.` command. The second of the three lines takes what is stored in our new variable `auth` and applies a further method to it (`.set_access_token()`), which takes two arguments (our `ACCESS_TOKEN` and `ACCESS_TOKEN_SECRET`). At this point, our `auth` variable has all the information needed to request access to Twitter's API via Tweepy when we want to do so later, and this is what is happening in the third of these three lines – we establish a new variable (`api`) which stores something associated with the `tweepy` library (as denoted by the `tweepy.` bit) called `API`, which takes one argument (the details we've just set in our `auth` variable). Now, whenever we want to use any Tweepy methods and/or commands (which we would do in code along the lines of `api.INSERT_METHOD_HERE(ARGUMENT)`), Python will be able to tell Twitter that we have the required credentials to have those requests granted.

Writing to Twitter (and using Twitter generally)

Now that we can get into Twitter's APIs, what do we do with them? One potentially interesting thing we can do (both to test our API access and for social scientific reasons discussed in later sections) is use Python/Tweepy to actually publish tweets to our authenticating account. Once you've got a script running which can authenticate your access to Twitter's APIs, try something like this in the shell:

```
>>> api.update_status("Hey Twitter, I'm a bot that posts this status!")
```

Now go and check your Twitter profile – if all has gone well, you'll have just used Python to tweet something as a bot! Though this is pretty cool in itself,[8] we'll talk more about what you could use this kind of thing for in later sections when we come to possible applications and projects.

However, it's also worth noting at this point that there are Tweepy commands for doing a whole range of stuff associated with using a Twitter account – we've just seen how to use Tweepy to publish a status, but we can also use it to do other things. Here's a small selection of those things:

---

[8]Well, I think it is. But then, I'm kind of a nerd.

```
1    ###POST A NEW TWEET (AS WE'VE SEEN ABOVE)
2    api.update_status(TWEET_TEXT)
3
4    ###DELETE A TWEET WE'VE SENT (IF WE HAVE ITS TWEET ID NUMBER)
5    api.destroy_status(ID)
6    #NOTE: we'll be looking at getting data from Twitter with tweepy later in the
7    #chapter; at that point, we can think about how to go about GETTING a tweet ID
8    #in the first place.
9
10   ###RETWEET A TWEET (IF WE HAVE ITS TWEET ID NUMBER)
11   api.retweet(ID)
12
13   ###SEND A DIRECT MESSAGE (IF WE HAVE A NAME FOR THE USER TO SEND IT TO PLUS
14   ###SOME TEXT)
15   api.send_direct_message(USERNAME_OR_USERID, "Message text")
16
17   ###FOLLOW OR UNFOLLOW ANOTHER USER (IF WE HAVE THEIR USERNAME OR ID NUMBER)
18   api.create_friendship(USERNAME_OR_USERID)
19   api.destroy_friendship(USERNAME_OR_USERID)
20
21   ###"LIKE" OR FAVOURITE ANOTHER TWEET (IF WE HAVE ITS TWEET ID NUMBER)
22   api.create_favorite(ID)
23
24   ###BLOCK AND REMOVE BLOCKS OF OTHER USERS (IF WE HAVE THEIR USERNAME OR ID)
25   api.create_block(USERNAME_OR_USERID)
26   api.destroy_block(USERNAME_OR_USERID)
```

Aside from the few things I've noted above, there are *lots* more things we can do with Tweepy – essentially, anything we can do on Twitter as a "manual" user, Tweepy has a bit of code we can use to do the same thing using Python. There are two things to note here. First, a reminder that it's not possible for me to write a comprehensive account of how to use Twitter via Tweepy, and I'm not going to try. The way to learn how to use techniques brought in from add-on libraries is not to see specific instances of the code written down in the book (except as a quick demo to get you started, as I've done above), but rather you need to get familiar with the idea of using the library's documentation and applying what you can read in it to code you're building. In this case, have a play around with the commands I've presented above to see if you can use Python to post a tweet, send a direct message to a friend, and follow/unfollow somebody.[9] And once you can do this, visit the Tweepy documentation pages (Tweepy, 2019) to explore what other possibilities there are and try some out. This kind of hands-on practice is really where your Python learning happens, so go and try some stuff out! I'll wait.

See, I waited! To return to the second of two things to note about what you've learned here: using Twitter through Python/Tweepy (rather than the Twitter app or web interface) might

---

[9]As evident in the code snippet above, there are some Tweepy commands that take a tweet ID number as an argument, so perhaps best to avoid those for now on the grounds that we don't have a way of easily getting this information - yet.

be kind of cool to do, but it's important also to think about what kind of social science applications this might have. Towards the end of this chapter I'll outline some specific projects and applications that you might want to try out for yourself, but for now, the key thing is to start to think about these Tweepy commands as not being ends in and of themselves, but as potential components in bigger projects, and this requires thinking about Tweepy techniques alongside techniques you already know in Python – loops, storing things in variables, passing arguments around, comparing objects, and so on – to build something more sophisticated than a simple script for posting hand-typed strings to your Twitter timeline. Putting all these pieces together will help you develop your programming skills and your programming mindset, which will help you reflect on your programming efforts from a social science perspective.

Reading from Twitter

However, perhaps a more obvious social science thing to do with a Twitter API is to use it to gather data of relevance to some kind of social science topic. Here's a little excerpt that scrapes data from my own Twitter timeline and stores it for use in Python:

```
1   user = "pdbrooker"
2   new_tweets = api.user_timeline(user, count=5)
3   data = []
4   for tweet in new_tweets:
5       data.append((tweet.id_str, tweet.created_at, tweet.text))
```

As we did above, let's now go through this code line by line to understand more clearly what is happening. In the first line, we establish a variable called `user`, in which we store a string which is a Twitter username – here I've given my own Twitter username, but you can choose another account if you're following along. In the second line, we establish another variable, `new_tweets`, in which we make a call to the API using a method called `.user_timeline()`, which takes two arguments: a username (which we take from our `user` variable) and a count of how many tweets we want to pull from that user's timeline (in this case, we will pull the five latest tweets from the specified user).[10] This returns a "fully hydrated" set of data per tweet, which is essentially every possible bit of information that can be found with a tweet – the username of the person who tweeted it (and *lots* of other details about the user), the tweet ID number, the time-stamp, the text content of the tweet, whether it's a retweet of something else, how many times the tweet was favourited/liked, and so on.[11] This makes for a lot of

---

[10]Note that this code snippet won't work if you just type these commands into a clean shell - can you see why? The code here presumes that you've already imported Tweepy and correctly authenticated your access to Twitter - if you want to follow along, try building a full script that contains all of these things by using what you've learned from this chapter and from the book so far.

[11]It's worth noting here that each tweet is returned as a JSON object, and we're doing a bit of JSON decoding here (e.g. when we're using bits of code like `tweet.id_str`, `tweet.created_at` and `tweet.text`). We'll be moving on to look more pointedly at JSON (and other data formats) in later chapters, but for now it's enough just to know how to pull some select information out of the tweet objects that we collect through Tweepy, and we can return to think about putting all these pieces together later.

information, much of which we're not going to need. Try calling the variable `new_tweets` to see what happens – wow, that's a lot of stuff and likely to make your Python script *really* slow at trawling through it. So the next bit of code is designed to sort this out a bit.

Returning to the line-by-line description of the code snippet above, once we've grabbed the five latest tweets from the timeline of the specified username and stored them in `new_tweets`, we establish an empty list for storing data in (`data`), and loop through all five tweets in `new_tweets` individually. For each tweet, we take its ID number as a string (`tweet.id_str`), its time-stamp (the time and date it was created, `tweet.created_at`), and the actual text of the tweet (`tweet.text`), and store those three things together in a tuple, which then gets appended to our `data` list. For each component of the tuple, we're using the `tweet.` bit to specify the object we want to work with (in each case, the current "tweet" that the for loop is iterating through), and using the suffix (`id_str`, `created_at` and `text`) to specify which bit of information we want to pull from that object. So, if you're following along, run the script and then see what's in the data list; perhaps try something like this to get a clear view of it (as opposed to just calling the data list as one big and potentially messy object):

```
>>> for entry in data:
        print(entry[0])
        print(entry[1])
        print(entry[2])
        print()
```

This little loop just goes through each of the tuples in data, pulling out their individual components (indexed 0–2) and printing them on individual lines, with an empty line separating them. And what you'll see here is that you get three strings per tweet – one containing a long number (the ID number of the tweet), one containing date and time information of when the tweet was sent (the time-stamp) and one containing the text content of the tweet. Think about what we've done here – we've collected some data from Twitter using Python commands, and stored bits of the data that we've selected as being potentially interesting in a variable which we can then investigate further. This is a useful skill for a social scientist! If we can identify a set of Twitter users whose opinions and experiences might be relevant to answering a particular research question, we can now gather their timeline data and see what they might have to say on the matter at hand (ethical issues notwithstanding). Taking this further, we can also grab lots of really rich "metadata" (i.e. data about data) from users with the following command:

```
>>> user_data = api.get_user(user)
```

We'll not go into too much detail here about how to dig around in the user data that this command pulls, but for now it's useful to know that this is how we would get such information as somebody's user ID, the biographic details they put on their Twitter account, their location details if they've made them available, the number of followers they have and the number of people they follow, the number of statuses they've posted, the time and date they created their account, and much more.[12]

---

[12]We'll be making more use of this command in a later chapter when we're exploring the JSON data format in more depth.

However, collecting data from individual user timelines is only one way to think about collecting data. What if instead we want to collect tweets that use some type of keyword or hashtag of interest to us? This is really easily done by just switching up the Tweepy command we use to get the data, so here's a slightly tweaked version of the code snippet above which will do the work of gathering the last five tweets using a specified keyword/hashtag:

```
1   search_term = "#python"
2   new_tweets = api.search(search_term, count=5)
3
4   data = []
5   for tweet in new_tweets:
6       data.append((tweet.id_str, tweet.created_at, tweet.text))
```

You should see that this is very similar to the code excerpt for extracting data from a specified user timeline. The key differences are, first, that instead of storing a username to search in the variable in the first line we're storing a string of a term we want to search by; and second, that instead of using the `api.user_timeline()` command we're using `api.search()` to identify and store data that we want in `new_tweets`. The rest is very similar, too – we use a for loop to go through each of the five latest tweets that match our criteria, and put their IDs, time-stamps and text (plus the tweeter's username) in a tuple in a list called `data`. So again, if you've been following along, try printing out the text of the data you've just collected to see what you've got. It's also worth again thinking about what we've done here – again we've collected some data from Twitter using Python commands, and stored bits of it that we've selected as being potentially interesting in a variable which we can then investigate further. However, whereas before we gathered data from individual timelines (which was a more user-centred way of thinking about Twitter data), now we're searching for keywords, which means we're going to get hold of conversations that are tightly organised around an issue we might be interested in for our research (e.g. #MeToo, the term "racist", or Brexit). And again, this is a useful skill for a social scientist! If we can identify a term (or set of terms) that are likely to contain interesting insights in relation to a particular research question we might have, we can then harvest data from Twitter of tweets that use that term (or those terms) to see what those conversations comprise (although again, it's important to think about ethics here – see Section 2.2 and Chapter 2 more generally for further details).

Taking it further (building bigger scripts, and rate limiting)

One thing we could do to take our Python knowledge about APIs further is to build a more sophisticated tool that we can leave running and which can collect lots more data than just a handful of tweets as we've done above. So, for instance, we might want to think about incorporating all the knowledge we've learned so far to do something like iterate through a list of usernames and extract a larger collection of their latest tweets.

However, as I noted at the start, the code snippets I've given have been very cautious in terms of how they comply with Twitter's terms and conditions around accessing data through APIs.

This has been fine so far, since I've only been guiding you through these processes, but as you move into building more sophisticated tools and practising these ideas for yourself, you're going to need to become increasingly familiar with issues pertaining to the proper use of data – as the saying goes, with great power comes great responsibility. And one thing you're responsible for as a Twitter developer (which is what you are now!) is consulting the Twitter terms and conditions to make sure the tools you build comply with the rules. This might sound scarier than it actually is – the rules are there for everybody to see, and, given what you know by this point in the book, you're more than capable of building compliance with these rules into your scripts and tools.

The key rule you need to know about in terms of using the Twitter APIs properly is to do with *rate limiting* – any Twitter developer who uses the various Twitter APIs as we have done here does not have complete free rein to make unlimited amounts of requests to the API (and here, requests include things like publishing statuses to your own account as well as pulling data from other accounts). In fact, the rate at which you can make those requests is limited – hence, rate limiting. Thinking more broadly than the context of Twitter, lots of APIs will feature rate limiting in some way, so it's important to be familiar with the concept whichever API you're using, even though the specific rules around rate limiting may change from platform to platform. This is to prevent individual accounts from spamming a platform's servers with rapid-fire requests and other such misuses, and helps to ensure that there's a broadly even flow of data between the platform and individuals making requests (i.e. making sure that one user is not getting more than their fair share of requests when compared with other users). On Twitter (and other platforms), the penalties for repeatedly breaking those rate limits are increasingly lengthy account suspensions and even having your account blocked entirely – hence, it's important to make sure you follow the rules here, and you're confident that you have restricted the amount of requests your code will be making.

As such, when we're building a bigger script to grab and handle Twitter data via one of the Twitter APIs, we need to know in advance how many requests we're allowed to make over any given time period. At the time of writing, the API rate limits for getting data via user timelines (as we do in the snippet below and earlier in the chapter) allow developers to make 900 requests every 15 minutes with standard user authentication details – this means that we need to make sure we're not getting data from more than 900 users every 15 minutes. But other Twitter APIs and other types of request are subject to different rate limits, and Twitter changes the rules around rate limiting periodically anyway,[13] so it's always a good idea to check the documentation to make sure you're doing the right thing. This documentation – about rate limiting and Twitter's terms and conditions around data usage more generally – is freely available in the Twitter developers documentation (Twitter, 2019a), and it's important to get yourself familiar with these rules before you build anything in Python, so that you know you are building a script/tool that will not break rate limits and will comply with whatever other terms and conditions may be relevant.

---

[13]Hence my evident unwillingness to pin myself down to saying "this is how many tweets you should pull, and this is the code to do it with" - the rules do change every now and then, and part of learning how to program is learning how to respond when they do.

With this in mind, and building on what we have already done above, an element of a script for iterating through a list of usernames to pull a selection of their latest tweets (which complies with rate limiting) could look something like this:[14]

```
1   from time import sleep
2
3   minutes = 15
4   user_list = ["pdbrooker", "SAGEOceanTweets", "SAGE_Methods", "SAGEsociology"]
5   data = []
6
7   for user in user_list:
8       new_tweet = api.user_timeline(user, count=100)
9       for tweet in new_tweet:
10          data.append((user, tweet.id_str, tweet.created_at, tweet.text))
11      sleep(minutes*60)
```

Again, it's worth going through this line by line so we can get a clear sense of what's going on. First, we import the `sleep` method from the `time` module (which we covered earlier in Section 8.3) – if we want to make sure we're building waits into our code (e.g. the 15-minute window that Twitter stipulates as being how long it takes to reset our rate limit allowance), then this is ideal for doing that. From here, we store an integer, `15`, in a variable called `minutes` (the reasons for which may already be apparent, but will become more so later in the description), and set a user list full of usernames of tweeters whose timelines we want to scrape – here, I've just picked out my own username plus a selection of those affiliated with Sage as the publisher of this book. And I also lay out an empty list called `data`, for storing stuff in later.

The for loop is where the action is. This iterates through each individual user in `user_list`, taking the latest 100 tweets on their timeline and storing them in a variable called `new_tweet`. Then, for each of the 100 tweets just collected in `new_tweet`, their username (from `user_list`), tweet IDs (`id_str`), time-stamp (`created_at`) and text content (`text`) are stored together as a tuple appended to the `data` list. Then, once all 100 tweets have been stored for a user, the `sleep` method forces our program to hold on for 15 minutes – `sleep()` takes an argument in seconds, hence we multiply the number set in our `minutes` variable by 60 – before moving on to the next user in the list. In this way, we process 100 tweets from one user every 15 minutes. If we didn't have the sleep built in and we had a list of many thousands of users, Python would just try to rocket through the whole lot as fast as it could – a terrible idea that's likely to break the rate limits. But this way, even though it

---

[14]I'm not really dealing with an amount of data that would trouble the current rate limits for `user_timeline` requests here (900 per 15-minute window) - this is just so my code is as future-proof as I can make it, should the rate limit rules come down below 900 and you try to copy what I've done here and get your account blocked. I'd like to reiterate here that it's entirely your responsibility to make sure code you're implementing doesn't breach terms and conditions and rate limits.

slows things down, we've built some code that can factor in rate limiting, albeit in a super-cautious way for reasons I've outlined above. If you're building your own script that uses the Twitter API, you can decide for yourself how you want to pace it (although I'll stress that you should check the documentation and abide by the Twitter terms and conditions around data usage if you want to make sure you're not doing anything that would get your account blocked).

One other handy thing to know about is how to check our rate limit status – luckily for us, Tweepy has us covered:

```
>>> api.rate_limit_status()
```

This command returns a fully hydrated JSON object (which we'll learn about decoding later, as I say!) that contains details of all the various rate limit caps and how many requests we have remaining for each individual request type. Try it out to see what you get back – it's a *lot* of stuff, but from it we can pull out numbers to help us build code into our script that helps us avoid breaking rate limits (e.g. we can count the number of requests we've made in the last 15 minutes, and if it's coming close to 900 we can tell our script to wait 15 minutes for our rate limit cap to reset before picking up where we left off). One key thing to remember, though, is that the request to check your rate limits is *also* rate-limited,[15] so make sure you're not making too many of these requests too!

Documentation – it's important!

I want to return to this idea of documentation as being massively important here, even though I've dropped it into the chapter a good few times already. To sum up what we've done in this chapter, we've used a library called `tweepy` to help us code various Twitter API requests directly into Python. But how do we find out about what new commands Tweepy offers, and the proper ways to use Twitter's APIs? Even if we're experts at Python, we don't automatically know these things (because they originate outside Python), so we have to go and check the documentation (Tweepy, 2019). The reason I keep labouring this point is that *this is a key part of what being a (Python) programmer involves*, especially one who is doing programming for social scientific purposes where we might be doing things like pulling in data from a non-Python source to work with. So, though you definitely need to practise your coding in a hands-on way by building scripts and tools that do things for you and your work, you also need to get hands-on practice at learning to identify and read and use documentation to help you code, whether that's documentation for bits of Python you're yet to come across, add-on modules for Python which you need to learn how to use (like Tweepy) or documentation for things totally aside from Python but which you want to work with (like Twitter). These kinds of texts are often invaluable for getting your code to work as you'd like, and though I can't pre-empt the kinds of thing you would want to do with things like the Twitter APIs within the scope of a single book, hopefully this book will give you the skills to make use of the

---

[15]If I could put a GIF in the book, this would be where I drop in the one with Keanu Reeves in *Bill & Ted* saying "Wooaaahhh ... ".

information you can find in such documentation, if I point you in the direction of where to find it and how to use it.

11●3 Some Possible Applications/Projects

As with any of these chapters in Part Three, there is a lot more of interest that you can do with Tweepy – for instance, I haven't talked about the "tweet streaming" functionality which lets users leave a connection open to collect tweets matching a specified criterion live and in real time (the commands I've demonstrated above get tweets that have been posted already). So, one way to take your programming further is to engage directly with the documentation around libraries you're using to see what else they offer, as I've noted above (Tweepy, 2019; Twitter, 2019a). So, have a look at these documents and see what else is possible with Twitter, Tweepy and Python, and try some things out!

However, it's also good to work on more concrete projects to develop your skills – something with an aim in mind that you can spend some time planning and working on. Here are just a few suggestions of things you could try, though feel free to change the details to suit your interests:

- *Build a Twitter news bot.* With the skills you already have on the basis of having read the book this far, you could build a Twitter bot that automatically finds and retweets tweets relevant to your research interests (e.g. that contain a keyword of relevance to your research, such as "#BigData" or "#sociology") once per hour. It's worth noting the potential qualitative relevance of something like a social media chatbot - one way to study how social interactions happen online is to create a tool for generating and playing around with such interactions (e.g. Brooker, 2019; Wilkie et al., 2015).
- *Collect and store some relevant data.* Identify and harvest some data that you think are interesting or helpful to addressing a research question of yours. To do this, you may find it helpful to bring together the techniques outlined in this chapter (authentication, collecting data through a Twitter API) with techniques learned previously (the core concepts of Python, creating and storing data in text files).
- *Explore how to use a different social media API.* Perhaps Twitter isn't for you? That's OK; we've concentrated on Twitter in this chapter as an example to work through, but in lots of ways the skills you have already learned up to this point (e.g. installing new Python libraries/ modules, looking at documentation to learn how to use them, putting that code together into a script, etc.) are transferable to different social media APIs. So, why not try figuring out how to do something similar to the work suggested in this chapter, but on Facebook, or Reddit, or Instagram (of course, using relevant documentation as a guide)? Different types of data lend themselves to different research approaches - for instance, though it's quite common for social media researchers to use things like tweets to enumerate and visualise words and their usage quantitatively, having a collection of Tumblr GIFs might lead you down a more qualitative path - so, collecting data from different platforms can expand your research skills in lots of ways even beyond learning new bits of Python to use. Jumping into a (small) project like this can be really helpful in terms of practising your skills, and the problems and solutions you'll encounter along the way are all part of what's needed to help you become a better programmer.

Chapter summary

- In this chapter, we talked about what a social media API is, and what we can use it for as social scientists (noting that though we're dealing only with Twitter as the example for this chapter, the learning you'll do will be applicable in the context of other platforms too).
- We then looked at how to set yourself up with developer access to Twitter, such that you can get all the relevant credentials you need to authenticate a Python script to use a Twitter API.
- We then looked at how to actually *do* that authentication in Python with `tweepy` (an add-on Python module/library), which also involved thinking about the security issues of storing login details directly in a script (in short: don't) and how to import things like variables and other data from other Python scripts as a way to prevent having to do that.
- From there, we moved on to thinking about using Tweepy to do things on Twitter – for instance, publish a tweet or follow another user.
- We then moved on to look at how to grab "data" from Twitter in two ways – first, getting data from individual user timelines; and second, using a keyword or hashtag to search for data.
- Next, we discussed the concept of "rate limiting" as something that applies to lots of social media APIs in different ways, and thought about strategies for handling rate limits in our code.
- Throughout all of this, I iterated and reiterated the importance of finding and using available documentation, on the grounds that while this book can provide you with a limited selection of techniques, the way to advance your programming mindset further is to start to do your own work and engage directly with the documentation that can help you figure out how to use a new add-on module/library and tell you the rules around using an API to make requests.
- Finally, we ended by pointing the way towards some potentially interesting projects you might like to try out. Though we didn't go too much into the details of what would be involved in these projects, that's precisely the aim – to give you an interesting starting-point, from which you can then start to build your own tools and scripts and encounter (and solve) problems for yourself.

12

Data Decoding/Encoding in Popular Formats (CSV, JSON and XML)

━━━━━━━━━━━━━━━━━━━━ **Chapter objectives** ━━━━━━━━━━

- Learn how to use Python to mine data from a URL end-point.
- Explore three different data formats (CSV, JSON and XML) with respect to the ways in which such data are structured, and Python techniques for navigating around them.
- Think about creative applications of these skills to a range of social scientific work, starting with very basic initial probing of the data at hand.

This chapter verges on aspects of what some digital researchers (particularly ones coming from a more computer science than social science background) would call "data mining".[1] However, rather than think in those (in my opinion rather limiting) terms, effectively all we're going to be doing here is looking for datasets in various places around the web and using Python to grab copies of them that we can then explore for social scientific purposes. This will start by looking at two general approaches to pulling data from the web using two different Python libraries – we're looking at two different methods since certain techniques are less easily applied to different data types/formats, so having a range of techniques in your toolbox means you're less likely to get stuck in practice. But also, it's a good reminder that Python is creative and not objective – there's no one best way to do any particular task in Python, and you'll be a better social science programmer if you can think creatively about different ways of doing things. Once we're comfortable pulling data from the web, then we'll look more pointedly at three different common data formats (CSV, JSON and XML) to get some practice dealing with each specifically. We'll do a single task three times (once per data format): we'll start with the mechanics of pulling and decoding the data from the web and writing them to a file, we'll look at the structure of the formatted data to get familiar with how the format works, and then we'll make a very basic initial exploration of the data we've pulled (using relevant Python libraries and techniques) to show you how you might navigate around the data and process them for further use.

12●1 Show Me the Code! Reading from the Web

First, if we're going to start looking at different data formats, we need to consider how we're going to get hold of them. Though it's generally pretty easy to simply find a dataset

---

[1] I'm hesitant to call what we're doing here "data mining" for three reasons (hence the scare quotes). First, this chapter mainly deals with the grabbing of data from web locations and decoding such data so that we can explore them - "data mining" *is* the exploration of (large, digital) datasets, but our focus here is less on producing findings than on the programming work required to initially pull the data out (though findings are alluded to throughout). Second, the use of the term "data" seems here somehow to have more of an affinity with purely quantitative work, which downplays the extent to which the "data" that are "mined" can have a qualitative relevance. Third, the word "mining" connotes a process whereby computational tasks are performed to chip away the rubble (i.e. unimportant stuff) to reveal nuggets of pure insight already formed - I'd argue that this way of looking at things completely ignores how data are a constructed (and never "raw") object, as something we need to attend to in order to do good social science.

online (there are lots of open datasets out there now!) – and click the download button to store a copy on your computer, it's handy also to know how to do this with Python for various reasons. For instance, what if the dataset we're interested in looking at is updated regularly? We might not want to have to repeatedly visit the website where the dataset is stored just to get the latest version – we could write a script that pulls and stores the latest version automatically. It's also quite handy to know how to do this for purposes of sharing research with others; for instance, finding a way to send another researcher an enormous dataset by email or via a physical storage device (such as a USB drive) can be much more fiddly than simply sending someone a script that they can run to get a copy for themselves.

In order to do this work of pulling data from the web with Python, we'll need to know a few things in advance, however. First, we need to know that these kinds of data can be accessed via their URL (i.e. their "Uniform Resource Locator", which we might otherwise know as their "web address"). You've no doubt seen URLs before – these are web addresses that may look something like `https://data.seattle.gov/` which if you type it into a web browser will take you to a webpage for the City of Seattle Open Data Portal. However, URLs can sometimes point towards things other than webpages – for instance, if an organisation makes its data available for open use (like the City of Seattle Open Data Portal does, hence the link above!), the data may be accessible via a URL that points to the dataset directly. When this is the case, we can call the URL where the data are stored (and accessible by us) the "end-point". Hence, the first thing we need to know when we're attempting to grab data is what the URL end-point of that dataset is – this can often be found by visiting the webpage in question and copying the information from there. Once you have the end-point, you can then plug that into Python (and associated libraries) and take things from there.

Reading from the web with `urllib.request`

The first way we'll look at reading data from the web is by using techniques from the `urllib.request` library to look at a dataset given by the URL end-point `https://data.seattle.gov/api/odata/v4/3xqu-vnum`.[2] For present purposes, we don't need to know much about what is actually in this dataset or what format it comes in – we'll get into those kinds of questions later. But for context, this dataset contains various bits of crime data from the city of Seattle. And if you put the URL end-point into a web browser, you should see a copy of what this dataset actually comprises – have a go at this for yourself, to get a rough familiarity with the kinds of things that this dataset could be used to do.

---

[2]There's a disclaimer to using these data that has to be repeated here, which goes: "The data made available here has been modified for use from its original source, which is the City of Seattle. Neither the City of Seattle nor the Office of the Chief Technology Officer (OCTO) makes any claims as to the completeness, timeliness, accuracy or content of any data contained in this application; makes any representation of any kind, including, but not limited to, warranty of the accuracy or fitness for a particular use; nor are any such warranties to be implied or inferred with respect to the information or data furnished herein. The data is subject to change as modifications and updates are complete. It is understood that the information contained in the web feed is being used at one's own risk." This information comes from the City of Seattle curators of the dataset, and is just something to bear in mind as we're working with the data they've made available.

The code that we can use to get a copy of this dataset is as follows:

```
1   from urllib.request import urlopen
2
3   url = "https://data.seattle.gov/api/odata/v4/3xqu-vnum"
4   response = urlopen(url)
5   data = response.read()
```

Taking this code line by line, we first import the relevant technique (urlopen) from its respective library (urllib.request). Then, we store the URL end-point in a variable called url. We then pass the url variable to the urlopen technique and store that in a variable called response – effectively, what we are doing here is requesting a copy of the information stored at the URL end-point (hence why we call it a "response") and opening it in Python. However, the content we grab is not yet readable in Python in any sensible way – this is evident if we do the following:

```
>>> type(response)
<class 'http.client.HTTPResponse'>
>>> print(response)
<http.client.HTTPResponse object at 0x02A91090>
```

Note here that the type of object stored in response isn't a string or a list or anything like that; it's an http.client.HTTPResonse object, which needs further decoding. We can do this decoding by reading the response object into Python using response.read(), which we store as another variable called data. From here, if we call data in the shell, the result should look like something that is perhaps more recognisable as the same data that we could see in our web browser when we followed the URL before.[3] However, although the data might be readable in the shell, some further work is perhaps still needed – let's check the type of information in data to see what kind of format we have them in:

```
>>> type(data)
<class 'bytes'>
```

So, we've still not got the data in the kind of format we might need in order to work with them further. Though we'll think more pointedly about decoding and formatting data shortly (e.g. when we get on to looking at specific data formats), one multi-purpose way of decoding data to a string is with the following command:

---

[3]It's worth noting that there's a *lot* of data stored at this end-point, and hence, your Python shell might take some while to print them all out - don't worry, this is normal, and you can always just close the shell if things start to plod too much. However, this is why, rather than call the dataset myself, I've simply checked its type. Perhaps if you want to see the dataset yourself, you could decode it to string format, then use techniques from previous chapters to write it to a text file which you can then open up and investigate yourself.

```
>>> string_data = data.decode()
>>> type(string_data)
<class 'str'>
```

This command turns "bytes" data into a string (as evidenced when we check the type of the variable we store the decoded version of data in). This can be quite handy in some contexts – for instance, if we want to save the data we've grabbed in a text file on our computers, Python won't let us write bytes to a text file, but it *will* let us write a string. So, at this point, we have a copy of a dataset grabbed from a URL and stored in a variable for us to work with later.

Reading from the web with requests

As noted above, we'll look at two ways of grabbing data with Python – the first of these is with urllib.request (which we do above), and the second is with the requests library (which we're doing right now). Here, we'll use the same dataset (and the same URL end-point), but just use a different set of Python commands to get hold of the information stored there:

```
1  import requests
2
3  url = "https://data.seattle.gov/api/odata/v4/3xqu-vnum"
4  response = requests.get(url)
```

Hopefully you can see that we're actually just doing much the same thing as before – importing a library (in this case requests), establishing a variable with the URL end-point details, then passing that variable to another variable (response) using a technique for grabbing the information at that end-point (in this case requests.get(url)). Let's explore this further to see what the differences are between this requests technique and the urllib.request method we looked at above. First, we can see in the code excerpt above that we don't have a separate line of code for reading in the data. However, let's see what happens when we try to call response here:

```
>>> type(response)
<class 'requests.models.Response'>
>>> print(response)
<Response [200]>
```

Clearly, there's an object stored in response, but it's not a type of object that can be printed out in a readable format. As in the previous method, we have to do some further work to turn it into something (like a string) which might be more useful to us:

```
>>> string_data = response.text
>>> type(string_data)
<class 'str'>
```

What we've done here is assign the text attribute of `response` (given by `response.text`) to a variable called `string_data`, and when we check the type of `string_data`, we can see it's a string.[4] And as before, now that the data are in string format, they can be played around with further – for instance, we can write them to a text file to be stored on our computer to work with later.

12.2 Show Me the Code! CSV Data

At this point, we can start to dig into the three different data formats we want to familiarise ourselves with. The first of these is CSV data, which stands for "Comma-Separated Values" – effectively, all this means is data where, if you open them as a text file, you would see that the individual values within each row of data are separated (or "delimited", as it is sometimes known) by commas. These data can be stored as a file with a `.csv` file extension. We'll see what these kinds of data look like when we pull some below. But for now, the URL end-point I have chosen (Northern Ireland Statistics and Research Agency, 2017)[5] directs us to an open dataset curated by the Northern Ireland government, which tells us about various measures of social deprivation (e.g. financial income, susceptibility to health risks, availability of high-speed broadband connections, infrastructural susceptibility to flooding, susceptibility to various types of crime including burglary, violent crimes and arson) taken in the year 2017, and breaks these down by the different parliamentary constituencies of Northern Ireland. As such, this CSV dataset could be used to understand how different locations there were more or less deprived than one another in 2017.

In order to really explore CSV as a data format, it's a good idea at this point to have a look at what some CSV actually looks like, so we can get a handle on what sort of things we will need Python to do to "decode" (i.e. make sense of, and work with) it. We can do this by cheating a little, and downloading the data file at the URL above manually and opening it up in a text editor to see what's going on. Figure 12.1 is a screenshot of what I can see when I open up this particular CSV file in a text editor.[6]

What we can see in this image is that line 1 of the data is the headings for each of the data "fields" – we're given labels like `AA2008code`, `AA2008name` and `Income_perc`, which indicate the names of the variables that have been collected here. Although it may be not so obvious what each of these labels actually means, we should note that there is also documentation accompanying this dataset that can help us resolve this (see OpenDataNI, 2017). If we consult the documentation, we can see that the `Income_perc` field presents data for the proportion of population living in households whose income is below 60% of the median for Northern Ireland (i.e. the middle value for household earnings), we can see that `Empl_perc` refers to the proportion of working-age population who are "employment deprived" (i.e. out

---

[4]The reason I check the type rather than call the dataset itself is that this is a massive dataset – it will almost certainly take ages to print out and will slow down your shell thereafter. So, I'm just trying to be smart about it!

[5]Source: NISRA (`www.nisra.gov.uk`).

[6]The text editor is Notepad++ (Notepad++, 2019) for anyone who's interested.

```
1   AA2008code,AA2008name,Income_perc,Income_child_perc,Income_65_perc,Empl_perc,PD_ratio,FB_ratio,Canc_ratio,EA_ratio,LBW_perc,Dental_ratio,Presc_ratio,LTHP_ratio,Pr_SEN_perc,Pr_abs_perc,PP_GCSE_perc,PP_
2   N06000001,Belfast East,10.3,14.2,4.5,18.4,110.7,92.1,101,115.8,4.9,95.3,93.8,102.8,10,5.37.1,2.4,68.9,9.7,6.6,32.5,1.6,1.2,15.5,25.2,3.3,83,4.2,127.8,3.7,3.1,13.9,3.7,7.6,1.8,8.8,2.5,24
3   N06000002,Belfast North,14.6,21.9,4.1,29.7,143.1,137.2,115.8,136.1,5.7,108.8,126.4,114.6,12.2,5.4,48.6,6,74,11.3,8,43.6,1.5,1.2,15.7,25.6,4.4,80.7,4.6,263.5,9.3,4.9,24.2,6.3,11.2,3.4,13.4,5.8,45
4   N06000003,Belfast South,9.9,13.7,4.9,14.5,101.3,79.2,97.8,89.2,4.4,78.2,92.6,92.9,9.9,4.6,25.2,2.5,59.4,8.3,5.9,23.3,0.5,1.8,17,27.3,4.5,85,5,137.2,3.9,1.8,20.6,7,14.7,4.5,10.4,2.7,36.3
5   N06000004,Belfast West,13.2,19.3,3.3,34.2,156.3,167.1,118.3,136.1,5.2,128.9,140.1,124.6,18.1,6,47.2,5.9,73.2,14.8,2,49.9,0.4,0.8,13.2,20.7,7.3,80.2,4.4,314.3,5.7,3.7,25.4,5,10.9,5.6,15.5,7.6,42.8
6   N06000005,East Antrim,11.1,16.0,5.7,17.4,91.5,83.8,101.9,96.9,3.9,83.9,96.1,98.9,7.5,4.1,35.5,4,68.6,7.1,6.6,31.5,7.7,2.2,14.9,27.4,2.1,84.9,2.5,83,3.1,3.5,9.7,2.7,4.5,0.9,6.3,21.8
7   N06000006,East London,18.1,22,7.3,21.7,91.7,95.2,94.7,88.7,4.8,92.6,90.3,96.8,8.6,4.1,35.9,3.1,63.4,8.3,5.6,35,11.2,2.4,15.9,28.3,5,88.2,1.5,60.8,4,1.2,16.9,3.1,6,4,9,4.2,8.2,9
8   N06000007,Fermanagh and South Tyrone,15,20.1,8.9,12.9,95.9,4.1,95,1.9,5.4,1.69.2,98.9,89.4,9.6,4.2,33.2,2.5,60.3,1.6,2.3,97.5,25.5,4.1,17,17.30.1,4.7,84.7,1,57,4.6,1,13.3,3.5,5.1,9.7,3.2,5,23.9
9   N06000008,Foyle,15.2,20.4,4.5,30.3,127.8,132.7,107.8,111.1,4.8,99.6,127.4,110.5,8.9,5.6,36.9,3.5,62.9,9.3,7.2,41.1,2,1.8,14.4,17.8,6,82.3,1,169,4.7,1.5,25.6,4.5,7.9,3.2,14,8.2,39.7
10  N06000009,Lagan Valley,10.5,16.4,5.5,14.6,76.8,73.4,91.6,87.3,3.8,95.3,83.4,93.8,8.2,4.1,29,1.6,60.5,7.8,5.3,29.2,8.1,2.1,14.8,26.5,2.6,65,1.2,2,131.8,4.6,2.4,11.6,3.4,4.8,1.5,5.5,1.2,21
11  N06000010,Mid Ulster,13.4,18.9,7.2,19.3,86.7,108.1,93.4,90.7,3.6,82.7,108.7,96.3,8.4,4.3,36.2,2.9,61.1,6.8,5.8,40.1,20.6,3.6,16.9,30.1,4.8,83.3,1,81,3.9,1.3,11.7,2,3.5,1.4,6.3,1.4,38.2
12  N06000011,Newry and Armagh,16.4,22.5,5,21.6,96.3,106.8,104.3,98,3.8,110.8,100.6,96.1,8.4,4.6,34.1,1.5,62.1,8.3,6.3,37.7,16.4,3.3,16.7,29.1,4.9,84.4,1.8,177,4.3,2.7,14.7,4.6,5.2,2.5,7.5,2.9,21.9
13  N06000012,North Antrim,13,18.9,7.6,18.2,86.1,86.4,93.4,86.9,4.8,94.3,94.2,93.1,6.9,4,38.2,2.6,64.2,6.5,5.8,36.9,16.7,3.2,16.7,39.4,3.3,84.7,1.8,81.5,4.1,2.2,11.3,2.9,5.7,1.1,6.4,1.9,22.3
14  N06000013,North Down,11.9,18.4,6.1,15.4,97.5,71.6,97,104.7,4.7,100.9,78.9,92.6,8.4,1.29,8.2,4,60.6,6.4,6.4,25.3,1.7,2.1,16.3,29,1.7,84.7,2.2,78.3,3.6,0.8,12.4,2.4,4.7,1.3,7.3,2.1,30.4
15  N06000014,South Antrim,10.4,15.5,8,15.7,96.4,83.4,109.3,95.9,4,75.3,95.4,95.8,8.4,4,35.7,2.5,63.9,7.8,6.2,31.8,9.9,2,14.4,26.1,2.6,84,2.1,8,86.9,4.1,2,9,10.8,3.4,5.7,1.8,7.2,2.8,32.3
16  N06000015,South Down,14.3,20.2,7.9,20.1,88.9,98.7,98.6,97.5,3.7,118.6,92.2,96.8,9.3,4,31.4,1.8,61.6,8.9,6.1,33,20.4,3.4,16.8,29.7,4.1,84.7,1.2,95.7,4.4,2.7,12.7,3.6,4.9,1.9,7.6,4.3,22
17  N06000016,Strangford,12.8,19.1,7.1,17.7,87.6,81.5,90.4,106.1,4.4,134.9,95.9,98.5,9.3,4.2,36.1,5,62.3,8.1,6.5,31.9,9.6,2.4,15.5,28.4,2.5,85.4,2.1,56,4.8,1.1,11.3,2.6,4.5,1.5,7.1,2.1,25.5
18  N06000017,Upper Bann,12.8,18.9,5.5,19.8,102,102.8,102.6,91.5,4.4,111.1,109.7,101.4,8.7,4.6,39.5,2.4,65.4,8.7,6.9,37,4.8,2.1,14.8,24.8,3.3,83.5,2.2,123,8.3,7.2,7.17,6,4.4,5.3,1.7,9.2,8,26.4
19  N06000018,West Tyrone,14.7,20.8,6.5,25.4,92.7,125.5,97.3,88.5,4.1,96.2,98.3,103.8,8.3,4.4,34.7,1.5,60.6,8,6.9,42.4,25.5,3.6,16.8,29.6,4.5,85,2.1,5,82.2,4.2,1.9,13.6,2.4,4.5,1.9,6.7,3,20.6
```

Figure 12.1 An excerpt from the `NIDeprivation.csv` dataset[7]

(*Source*: NISRA: http://www.nisra.gov.uk)

of work and in receipt of employment-related welfare), that `Unfit_perc` refers to the proportion of domestic dwellings that are unfit for habitation, and so on. Taken together, this range of measures is used to calculate an overall deprivation score for each area of Northern Ireland so that we can see which areas are least and most deprived, and by how much. However, for our purposes, the individual measures are actually quite interesting too, inasmuch as this dataset will help us break down different social problems by area of the country (e.g. we can talk about which areas of Northern Ireland are more prone to theft and burglary, which areas are more violent than others, which areas have the poorest household living conditions, and which areas have the poorest healthcare provision).

So, the headers (and the documentation that helps us read them) can show us what kind of thing we can expect to get from this dataset. The dataset itself is stored in lines 2–19, each of which shows one row of data, where a row represents data for specific areas of Northern Ireland – hence, we get a range of data fields for each of the areas of Northern Ireland (Belfast East, East Antrim, Foyle, Lagan Valley, etc.) which allows us to compare areas against each other.

That's a lot of really rich information about these different areas of Northern Ireland – now let's look at how this CSV dataset is packaged up. First thing to note is that we can see that each "value" of data (i.e. each entry in the dataset) is separated from other values by a comma. What this means is that when we load the data into Python, we'll need to tell Python to read them and split the values whenever it comes across a comma symbol, otherwise all the data will be read in as something like one enormous string including the commas – this is not very useful if we want to play around with the data. We should also note that each line of data ends with a CR and an LF, shorthand in my text editor for "carriage return" and "linefeed" – you might recognise these terms from when we've talked about string literals in previous chapters (cf. Chapter 10 on working with text files). So, each bit of data is separated by commas, until we get to the end of a row at which point we split the lines up with a carriage return and a linefeed – in string literal notation, this would look like \r\n. This means that in order for Python to make sense of the CSV data we'll need a way to tell Python to split the values in a line wherever it encounters a comma (as noted above), and split the lines from one another wherever it sees a \r\n.

---

[7]The headers displayed in line 1 trail off the end of the page, so it's really difficult to get an image together that displays all of them - this is just a taster of what the file looks like, to get us started thinking about CSV as a format.

Grabbing, reading and writing CSV data

Now we're prepped on what's actually in this CSV dataset, we're ready to pull it from the URL, store it as a .csv file on our computers, then do a little probing to pull out some information from it that may have some social scientific relevance.

The first step is to pull the data. In this case, we're going to use the requests library:[8]

```
1   import requests
2
3   url = "https://www.opendatani.gov.uk/dataset/e202fde9-7f0b-4d88-8711-\
4   e18a8817cff8/resource/887ad000-b6bf-4004-9ba8-3fb09372d432/download/nimdm2017\
5   ---aa2008.csv"
6
7   response = requests.get(url)
```

As before, we import the library we need (in this case, requests), input our URL end-point as a variable, then pass that URL to the relevant technique for getting the data stored in a variable to work with. Now, given that we know this is a CSV format dataset, we'll have to decode it and store it as a file on our computer with the following code, which draws on Python's in-built csv library:

```
1   import csv
2
3   with open("NIDeprivation.csv", "w", newline="") as csv_file:
4       writer = csv.writer(csv_file)
5       reader = csv.reader(response.text.splitlines())
6       for row in reader:
7           writer.writerow(row)
```

So what have we done here? First, we import the csv library – this is handy for when we want to use Python to make sense of CSV data as the specific data format at hand.

---

[8]The URL I've used is quite long here, hence it won't fit on one line and I have used "line breaks" (as denoted by the backslash symbol, \). If you want to follow along with the code, you should know, according to what you've already learned about "string literals" in earlier chapters, that the backslash in this context doesn't actually feature in the URL (inasmuch as if you put a URL including backslashes into a web browser, it won't work). Instead, these backslashes tell Python that although we need to break the URL across multiple lines due to its length, we still do want it to be treated as one object (i.e. a single string containing the URL end-point for the dataset). This is done purely so we can see the whole URL in one place, whereas if we didn't use line breaks in our script, the URL would just drift off the side of the page (which is not good in terms of readability!).

Next, we open a new file in write mode, called `NIDeprivation.csv`, as an object we call `csv_file`. Note also at this point that we set a parameter called `newline=""` – this is a parameter that tells Python that we want to open the file in such a way as to not add extra new lines in (since the default is for Python to *translate* extra line breaks into the data to separate rows, whereas our URL end-point is for a dataset that is already in CSV format and already has its own line breaks and doesn't need further processing at this stage).

With this file open (as an object called `csv_file`) in a way that we can write our CSV data to it, we then go on to establish a CSV `writer` object that we can use to write our CSV data to the file at `csv_file` – this is given by the line `writer = csv.writer(csv_file)` (e.g. an object called `.writer()` which comes from the `csv` library and which takes our file object `csv_file` as an argument). We do a similar thing to establish a CSV reader object, which we can pass our dataset to so it can be read into Python. This is given by the line `reader = csv.reader(response.text.splitlines())`, which we can unpack a little as follows: this is an object called `.reader()` which comes from the `csv` library and which takes some CSV data as its argument. Notably, though, our CSV dataset needs to be decoded, since it's still in an unreadable format – just as we did above when we were exploring the `requests` library, we need to take only the text attribute of our `response` variable (i.e. `response.text`) and we need to tell Python that, rather than read this dataset in as one huge string, we want to split it into different lines according to the line breaks that already exist in the dataset (which we saw above), which we do with `.splitlines()`. Then, for each row in the `reader` variable (where our readable CSV dataset now sits), we use the `writer` variable to write those rows into the data one by one. Once this operation is complete (and if you've been following along), you should see a new file in the same location as your script called `NIDeprivation.csv`. Open it up, and you should see a nicely formatted CSV file containing all the data you've just pulled.

Working with CSV data

Now we have a copy of the dataset that we can keep and use, let's load it into Python again and do some basic work to pull out some initial insights that might be of relevance to a social science project. Let's add this bit to the end of our data-pulling script:

```
1   import csv
2
3   f = open("NIDeprivation.csv", "r")
4   reader = csv.reader(f)
5   for row in reader:
6       print(row)
7   f.close()
```

Let's go through the code line by line to figure out what's happening here. First we import the `csv` module (since we'll need it to read in the data from our CSV file). Then we open our data file

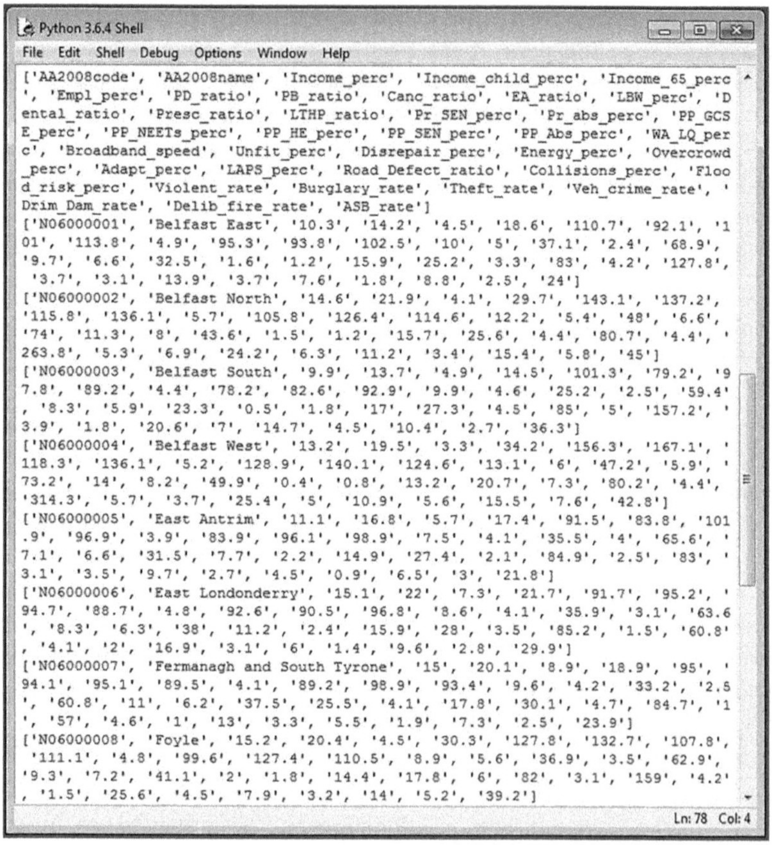

Figure 12.2 A really silly and difficult way to look at CSV data

(as f) in read mode, and use `csv.reader(f)` to establish a `reader` variable where our data are stored. Then we cycle through each row in the data with a for loop, printing out the row in full. If you have followed along with this code, what you should see is a rather messy output containing *all* the data in the dataset, with each row as an item in a list – Figure 12.2 shows how it looks.

However, we can tidy this up a bit by using a bit of clever string formatting – instead of printing out the entirety of each row in our for loop (with `print(row)`), try substituting in the following code:

```
1  for row in reader:
2      print(row[1] + " " + row[32])
```

Knowing that the data values for each row appear in lists (and that therefore each value is at the same index position in each row list), we can select only the bits of information we want to see and print them out in a way that we can easily visualise. Hence, the revised code above shows `row[1]` (i.e. the name of the area to which the data pertain) and `row[32]` (i.e. the index position at which a value is stored for the rate of violence in that area including

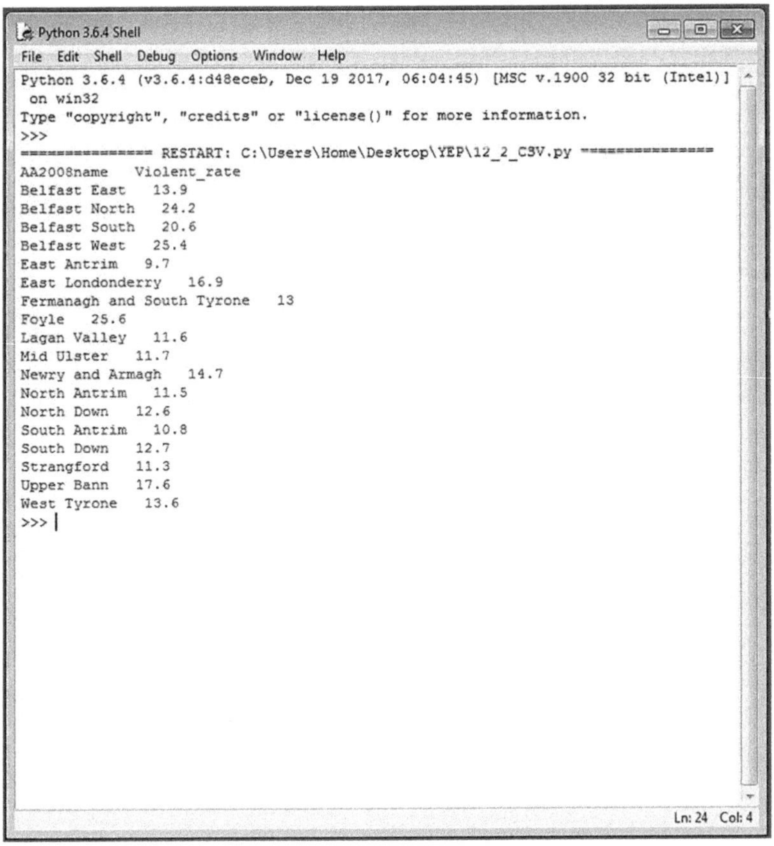

```
Python 3.6.4 Shell
File  Edit  Shell  Debug  Options  Window  Help
Python 3.6.4 (v3.6.4:d48eceb, Dec 19 2017, 06:04:45) [MSC v.1900 32 bit (Intel)]
on win32
Type "copyright", "credits" or "license()" for more information.
>>>
=============== RESTART: C:\Users\Home\Desktop\YEP\12_2_CSV.py ===============
AA2008name    Violent_rate
Belfast East    13.9
Belfast North    24.2
Belfast South    20.6
Belfast West    25.4
East Antrim    9.7
East Londonderry    16.9
Fermanagh and South Tyrone    13
Foyle    25.6
Lagan Valley    11.6
Mid Ulster    11.7
Newry and Armagh    14.7
North Antrim    11.5
North Down    12.6
South Antrim    10.8
South Down    12.7
Strangford    11.3
Upper Bann    17.6
West Tyrone    13.6
>>>
```

Ln: 24 Col: 4

Figure 12.3 A less silly and difficult way to look at CSV data

sexual offences, robbery and public order offences per 1000 population), separated by a few space marks for presentation purposes. And if we run this revised bit of code, we get the result shown in Figure 12.3.

Now we're getting somewhere! This shows us something we can easily look at – we can now compare individual areas in Northern Ireland to see which were more subjected to violent crimes in the year 2017. We can see that Foyle was the most violent area of Northern Ireland in 2017 (with 25.6 violent offenders per 1000 people living there), and East Antrim was the safest from violence (with only 9.7 violent offenders per 1000 people living there).[9] And, if you want to see a script where all of this stuff is put together (with a little documentation as a guide), here's one:

---

[9] It's worth noting that because of the way the CSV data are decoded, the numbers here are actually in string format - hence, if we want to do any numerical operations with them, we would have to store them in another variable and convert them with something like float (number).

```
1   import requests
2   import csv
3
4   #Data that go into calculating NI Multiple Deprivation Measures 2017
5   url = "https://www.opendatani.gov.uk/dataset/e202fde9-7f0b-4d88-8711-\
6   e18a8817cff8/resource/887ad000-b6bf-4004-9ba8-3fb09372d432/download/nimdm2017\
7   ---aa2008.csv"
8   response = requests.get(url)
9
10
11  with open("NIDeprivation.csv", "w", newline="") as csv_file:
12      writer = csv.writer(csv_file)
13      reader = csv.reader(response.text.splitlines())
14      for row in reader:
15          writer.writerow(row)
16
17  f = open("NIDeprivation.csv", "r")
18  reader = csv.reader(f)
19  for row in reader:
20      print(row[1] + " " + row[32])
21  f.close()
22
23  #AA2008name = Assembly area or parliamentary constituency name, stored at row[1]
24
25  #Violent_rate = rate of violence including sexual offences, robbery and public
26  #order offences per 1000 population, stored at row[32]
```

12●3   Show Me the Code! JSON Data

Having worked our way through CSV data as a relatively straightforward data format, we can now explore other richer formats that we might commonly find on the web. JSON, which stands for "JavaScript Object Notation", is one such format. JSON stores data as a collection of name and value pairs – this is similar in a way to dictionaries in Python, which we can consider as a way of collecting together objects that have a name (or "key") and a value associated with that name. We'll dig more into what that actually means when we take a look at some JSON data below – for now, all we need to know is that we can store this particular type as a file with a .json extension. Rather than grabbing the data by URL end-point as we did in Section 12.2, the example we're using here is the user data associated with a single Twitter account that we can pull through the Twitter API – the user in question is me, and these user data capture a lot of information associated with my own personal Twitter account (including my user ID, my biography, the number of followers I have, the number of people I follow, the date I created the account, the number of times I've favourited something, my last status and associated details such as the time and date it was posted, the tweet ID, the text content, any hashtags I used, and the device I used to tweet it). As such, although I've only collected the user data associated with my own personal Twitter account, we can perhaps also think about how these user data might be helpful to understanding any number of social science problems – for instance, we might be interested in the information around accounts that commonly tweet in support of current US president Donald Trump to see who those accounts belong to and if there are any patterns to them as a set of users (e.g. do they all tweet from a Russian location? Have their accounts all been created around the time Trump announced his presidential campaign or are they long-standing Twitter users?).[10]

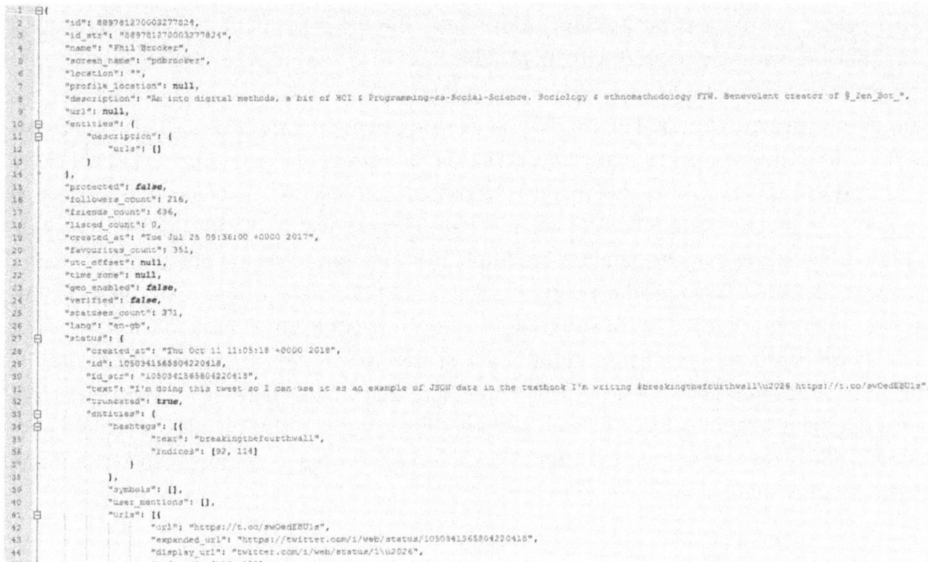

```
{
    "id": 889781270003277824,
    "id_str": "889781270003277824",
    "name": "Phil Brooker",
    "screen_name": "pdbrooker",
    "location": "",
    "profile_location": null,
    "description": "Am into digital methods, a bit of HCI & Programming-as-Social-Science. Sociology & ethnomethodology FTW. Benevolent creator of @_Zen_Bot_",
    "url": null,
    "entities": {
        "description": {
            "urls": []
        }
    },
    "protected": false,
    "followers_count": 216,
    "friends_count": 436,
    "listed_count": 0,
    "created_at": "Tue Jul 25 09:38:00 +0000 2017",
    "favourites_count": 351,
    "utc_offset": null,
    "time_zone": null,
    "geo_enabled": false,
    "verified": false,
    "statuses_count": 371,
    "lang": "en-gb",
    "status": {
        "created_at": "Thu Oct 11 11:05:18 +0000 2018",
        "id": 1050341565804220418,
        "id_str": "1050341565804220418",
        "text": "I'm doing this tweet so I can use it as an example of JSON data in the textbook I'm writing #breakingthefourthwall\u2026 https://t.co/swOedEBU1s",
        "truncated": true,
        "entities": {
            "hashtags": [{
                    "text": "breakingthefourthwall",
                    "indices": [92, 114]
                }
            ],
            "symbols": [],
            "user_mentions": [],
            "urls": [{
                    "url": "https://t.co/swOedEBU1s",
                    "expanded_url": "https://twitter.com/i/web/status/1050341565804220418",
                    "display_url": "twitter.com/i/web/status/1\u2026",
                    "indices": [116, 139]
                }
            ]
        },
```


Figure 12.4 Excerpt of Twitter user data in JSON format

Perhaps the best way to understand JSON data is to look at an excerpt from the example dataset we're going to use shortly (see Figure 12.4). As noted, this dataset contains my own Twitter user data. However, the interesting thing to note here is how such data are structured – although when we pull the data with Python they will appear as one long line of data, I have used a tool[11] to represent the data in a more visually readable format, so we can see and understand their structure.

[10] That's just one example of an interesting project that draws on Twitter user data - essentially, collecting and working with user data (in JSON format) could be valuable for any social science question where we might be interested in finding out more about a group of Twitter users and how they use Twitter.

[11] The JSTool plugin for the Notepad++ text editor (Notepad++, 2019), for anyone who is interested. This tool presents JSON data by breaking them up line by line.

In line 1 we can see that JSON objects are opened with a { symbol – although there's not room on the page for me to show the whole dataset, if we scrolled to the very bottom of the dataset we'd also see this "user" object being closed with a } symbol. And within these two curly brackets, we can see our "user" object, which itself has other hierarchies built into it. So, we can see various "sub-objects" that make up the larger "user" object – for instance, lines 2–9 show various different objects which each have a name/key (id, id_str, name, screen_name, location, profile_location, description and url) and a value associated with that name/key. However, we might also note that there are sub-hierarchies in this dataset, and we need to pay attention to how those are constructed with JSON syntax. Let's look at line 27 – here we can see a "sub-object" with the name/key status (i.e. the last status I posted on my Twitter account), but where the value seems to be a { symbol. This means that the value associated with the "sub-object" named status contains not just a single piece of information but a whole new set of "sub-sub-objects" – in this case, various details of the last status I posted on my Twitter account, including the time and date I posted it (created_at), the tweet ID (id), the tweet ID given as a string (id_str), the text of the tweet (text), and so on. We can also note that this set of "sub-sub-objects", having been opened with a { in line 27 (when the "status" object was first named), is closed in line 48 with a }.[12] What we can draw from this is that the data are structured in JSON format by the opening and closing of brackets – here we've focused on curly brackets ({ }) but we also note that the JSON format uses square brackets ([ ]) to structure bits of information in what is called an "array", which we can think of like a list in Python, where the information in an array is callable by virtue of its index position. We should also note here that where there are no sub-hierarchies to consider, name–value pairs can also broken up by a comma – this means that when we're looking at JSON data, if we see a comma we should know that it counts as the end of any particular name–value pair.

Grabbing, reading and writing JSON data

We've seen above how JSON data are structured, so we're a bit more familiar with what to expect when we're using Python to play around with this particular data format. Now we can pull some JSON data through the Twitter API, store them as a .json file on our computers, then navigate around the data in order to extract some potentially interesting information.

Let's look at how to pull the data – this was covered in the previous chapter when we looked at using social media APIs, so this will be a little recap on those techniques:

```
1   import tweepy
2   from AppCred import CONSUMER_KEY, CONSUMER_SECRET
3   from AppCred import ACCESS_TOKEN, ACCESS_TOKEN_SECRET
4
5   auth = tweepy.OAuthHandler(CONSUMER_KEY, CONSUMER_SECRET)
6   auth.set_access_token(ACCESS_TOKEN, ACCESS_TOKEN_SECRET)
```

---

[12]There are also several other hierarchies built into this status object along the way, but let's not go down this rabbit hole further by getting into "sub-sub-sub-objects" and so on!

```
7   api = tweepy.API(auth)
8
9   response = api.get_user("pdbrooker")
```

As in the earlier chapter, what we can see here is some code for importing in the tweepy module, and importing in our necessary authentication credentials from a separate file (which is called AppCred.py). Then we have a few lines of code for authenticating our access to Twitter's APIs with those credentials. This is followed by a Python command which will store the user details we want to grab in a variable called " response" – the api.get_user() method, which takes a Twitter username or ID as an argument, and which we covered briefly in the previous chapter about getting data through a social media API.

Now, given that we are working with the JSON format, we'll need to decode the data and store them as a file on our computer using Python's inbuilt json library – the code to do that looks like this:

```
1   import json
2
3   with open("UserData.json", "w") as json_file:
4       json.dump(response._json, json_file)
```

What we're doing here is importing the json library into our code as a way of making sense of JSON data as the format at hand. Next we open a file called UserData.json in write mode, as an object we're calling json_file. We then use the json.dump() command to put the data we've collected, in JSON format, into the file we've just opened. json.dump() takes two arguments here. First, we need to pass an argument which tells Python what data we want to dump in the file. Here, the argument is response._json, which refers to the user data we have previously stored in a variable called response, and specifically the JSON property of those data (._json).[13] The second argument denotes the place where we want to dump the data. Here, this is json_file, which refers to the file we have opened.

Working with JSON data

Now we have a copy of these data stored on our computer, let's load them into Python again and start to navigate our way around them to pull out some potentially interesting bits of information. Let's add the following code to the end of our data-pulling script:

---

[13] It's worth noting that not all JSON data will need to have this ._json bit on the end of the argument for json.dump() – it is used here because tweepy objects are themselves not "serialisable" (i.e. not readable) as JSON format, but they have a property (i.e. ._json) that does contain serialisable JSON data. So, all we're doing here is telling Python to dump the bits of the collected data that are in JSON format – if other data you're working with are already JSON serialisable, then this won't be necessary.

```
1    import json
2
3    f = open("UserData.json", "r")
4    data = json.load(f)
5    print("Screen Name: " + data["screen_name"])
6    print()
7    print("Blue Tick?: " + str(data["verified"]))
8    print()
9    print("Bio: " + data["description"])
10   print()
11   print("Total Tweets: " + str(data["statuses_count"]))
12   print()
13   print("Last Tweet: " + data["status"]["created_at"])
14   print(data["status"]["text"])
15   f.close()
```

Let's go through this code line by line so we can understand what's going on.

First, we import the json module since we're going to be using that to load in the data from our JSON data file. Then we open the file (as f) in read mode so that can we read in data from it. We then create a variable called data where we want to store the read-in (e.g. load) JSON data from our file – this is done in the line data = json.load(f). Next, we have a series of print statements which draw out bits of information from our JSON user dataset, with a little bit of fancy string formatting to make things more visually appealing in the printout. Here, I'm printing out the username in the data (given by data["screen_name"]), an indication of whether or not this account is a verified Twitter account (i.e. one held by a celebrity or not, given by data ["verified"]), the biographic details of the account (given by data["description"]), the number of tweets posted by the account (given by data["statuses_count"]) and the timestamp and text content of the last tweet posted by the account (given by data["status"] ["created_at"] and data["status"]["text"], respectively).

There are two things to note here. First, notice how I have to stringify certain bits of information so that I can print them out (e.g. the values given by data["verified"] and data["statuses_count"]). This is because those pieces of information are not already strings, and therefore Python will throw up an error if we try to print them out as strings – "verified" is given as a Boolean true/false value, and "statuses_count" is an integer. So, this serves as a reminder that the json library transfers JSON data to Python in ways which can sometimes mean they might *already* be treatable as integers or floats or other types of objects – compare this with the example CSV data we used above, where we stored all the data as strings, which meant that we would need to convert the numerical data to a float (using float()) if we wanted to perform any mathematical operations on them.

The second thing to note is the syntax through which we're pulling these bits of information out of the JSON dataset – we have a variable called data where the whole dataset is stored, and we can access different bits of it by calling on the keys/names with square brackets (e.g. data["screen_name"]). However, given that we know already that some of our dataset comes structured as sub-objects and sub-sub-objects and so on, how do we navigate our way around all those sub-hierarchies? You can see this in action when we're pulling details of the last posted status associated with this account – we start by saying we want to pull something from data (as the place where all our user data are stored), then specify that we want to pull some information from the status object (i.e. ["status"]), then further specify which bit of data we want to pull from the selection of objects stored with the status object (["created_at"] or ["text"]). When put together, the command for pulling information from our dataset that is contained within a hierarchy like this would be data["status"]["created_at"], where each subsequent set of square brackets denotes going one level deeper into the hierarchy.

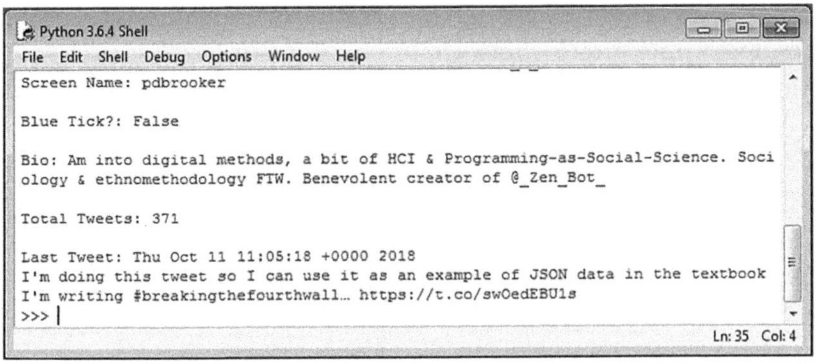

```
Python 3.6.4 Shell                                          □ ▣ ✕
File  Edit  Shell  Debug  Options  Window  Help
Screen Name: pdbrooker

Blue Tick?: False

Bio: Am into digital methods, a bit of HCI & Programming-as-Social-Science. Soci
ology & ethnomethodology FTW. Benevolent creator of @_Zen_Bot_

Total Tweets: 371

Last Tweet: Thu Oct 11 11:05:18 +0000 2018
I'm doing this tweet so I can use it as an example of JSON data in the textbook
I'm writing #breakingthefourthwall... https://t.co/swOedEBU1s
>>>
                                                          Ln: 35  Col: 4
```

Figure 12.5 JSON printout

When we run the code above, what results in the shell is shown in Figure 12.5. This presents a neat little selection of our JSON data – which otherwise might be too much information to take in, and not all of it relevant to our needs – such that we can see some potentially interesting information about the Twitter account in question. We can see my Twitter username, whether or not I'm a celebrity,[14] my biographical details, the number of tweets I've sent from this account, and the details of my last tweet.[15] And finally, if we want to put all of the above together in a script, it would look something like this:

```
1    import tweepy
2    from AppCred import CONSUMER_KEY, CONSUMER_SECRET
3    from AppCred import ACCESS_TOKEN, ACCESS_TOKEN_SECRET
4    import json
5
6    auth = tweepy.OAuthHandler(CONSUMER_KEY, CONSUMER_SECRET)
```

(Continued)

[14]I'm not.

[15]Am I now breaking the *fifth* wall? I'm starting to get a headache...

```
 7   auth.set_access_token(ACCESS_TOKEN, ACCESS_TOKEN_SECRET)
 8   api = tweepy.API(auth)
 9
10   response = api.get_user("pdbrooker")
11
12   with open("UserData.json", "w") as json_file:
13       json.dump(response._json, json_file)
14
15   f = open("UserData.json", "r")
16   data = json.load(f)
17   print("Screen Name: " + data["screen_name"])
18   print()
19   print("Blue Tick?: " + str(data["verified"]))
20   print()
21   print("Bio: " + data["description"])
22   print()
23   print("Total Tweets: " + str(data["statuses_count"]))
24   print()
25   print("Last Tweet: " + data["status"]["created_at"])
26   print(data["status"]["text"])
27   f.close()
30
31   #NOTE: for the purposes of printing, I've converted a Boolean True/False value
32   #for "verified" and an integer for "status_count" to strings. Useful to know,
33   #though, that if I hadn't done this, you could work with something like an
34   #integer as it is, no converting.
```

12●4 Show Me the Code! XML Data

On to another data format! This time, we'll look at some XML data, as another fairly common way of structuring data which we might want to use as social scientists. XML stands for "EXtensible Markup Language", and provides a way of structuring data with "tags" for the purposes of helping keep the data organised and making that information readily accessible (i.e. marking it up with "tags" which we can search for to call whichever bits of information we want). We'll see a bit more about what this particular type of data format looks like when we pull some below, but for now, the URL end-point I have chosen (Centers for Disease Control and Prevention, 2018) directs us to an open dataset curated by the National Center for Health Statistics containing death rates for the 10 leading causes of death in the United States[16] for each state, by year, between 1999 and 2016 (i.e. so we can compare the rates of various causes of death across states by year). This has the potential to be really useful for us if we want to look into something like inequalities between states in terms of the particular

---

[16]These are: heart disease, cancer, stroke, chronic lower respiratory disease, unintentional injuries, diabetes, influenza and pneumonia, kidney disease, suicide and Alzheimer's disease (source: https://www.cdc.gov).

conditions people are most at risk of dying from – for instance, we could look at which states (for any year between 1999 and 2016) had populations that were most at risk of dying from flu and pneumonia (which we might normally think of as preventable diseases) to start to understand which states have better healthcare provision as an issue of social scientific concern.

In order to explore XML as a data format, it's a good idea at this point to see what the dataset we've identified actually looks like, so we can figure out how Python can be used to decode and make sense of the data. Since we have a URL to look at (and since, quite handily, my web browser of choice will show me XML data in a pretty readable way), I've copied the URL endpoint into my web browser, Mozilla Firefox, and Figure 12.6 shows the result.

```
-<response>
  -<row>
    -<row _id="15029" _uuid="0E3080FB-5EF8-4BEF-834E-54B52DB8DFF3" _position="15029" _address="https://data.cdc.gov/resource/bi63-dtpu/15029">
      <year>2016</year>
      -<_113_cause_name>
        Accidents (unintentional injuries) (V01-X59,Y85-Y86)
      </_113_cause_name>
      <cause_name>Unintentional injuries</cause_name>
      <state>Alabama</state>
      <deaths>2755</deaths>
      <aadr>55.5</aadr>
    </row>
    -<row _id="15030" _uuid="5A6F1799-07FB-4C97-B6FC-A8BB792C5137" _position="15030" _address="https://data.cdc.gov/resource/bi63-dtpu/15030">
      <year>2016</year>
      -<_113_cause_name>
        Accidents (unintentional injuries) (V01-X59,Y85-Y86)
      </_113_cause_name>
      <cause_name>Unintentional injuries</cause_name>
      <state>Alaska</state>
      <deaths>439</deaths>
      <aadr>63.1</aadr>
    </row>
    -<row _id="15031" _uuid="50D8F132-BD59-4267-A3F9-7179EF5C2628" _position="15031" _address="https://data.cdc.gov/resource/bi63-dtpu/15031">
      <year>2016</year>
      -<_113_cause_name>
        Accidents (unintentional injuries) (V01-X59,Y85-Y86)
      </_113_cause_name>
      <cause_name>Unintentional injuries</cause_name>
      <state>Arizona</state>
      <deaths>4010</deaths>
      <aadr>54.2</aadr>
    </row>
    -<row _id="15032" _uuid="ED9700FE-F7EB-4B51-A5ED-3C8B710CA2E8" _position="15032" _address="https://data.cdc.gov/resource/bi63-dtpu/15032">
      <year>2016</year>
      -<_113_cause_name>
        Accidents (unintentional injuries) (V01-X59,Y85-Y86)
      </_113_cause_name>
      <cause_name>Unintentional injuries</cause_name>
      <state>Arkansas</state>
      <deaths>1604</deaths>
      <aadr>51.8</aadr>
    </row>
```

Figure 12.6 An excerpt example of XML data

What can we learn from this? The first thing to note is that we can see there are lots of what we might call "angled brackets" (< and >) which contain indications as to what type of information they contain and where that information begins and ends – for instance, in the fourth line of the data we can see `<year>2016</year>`. In XML, this means that we're opening a tag we want to call `year` for a piece of data (`<year>`), we're following that with the data value for `year` (2016), then we're closing that tag (`</year>`). In this way, we can identify that tags are opened with some kind of name/label contained in angled brackets, then some information is inserted into that tag, and the tag is closed by referring back to the named/labelled tag in another set of angled brackets with a forward slash before the name/label.

We can also see, like the JSON data as discussed above, that these XML data feature a hierarchy of information – in this case, our data seem to be all captured in a single <response> </response> tag,[17] and broken up into individual rows (<row></row>) that each contain various bits of information including the year the data refer to (<year></year>), the cause of death (<cause_name></cause_name>), the state the data refer to (<state></state>), the number of deaths (<deaths></deaths>) and the age-adjusted death rate (<aadr> </aadr>, which gives the number of deaths per 100,000 population adjusted for age).[18]

Grabbing, reading and writing XML data

So now we know what's in this dataset and how it's structured, we can use Python to grab it from the URL end-point we've found, store it in an .xml file on our computer, then use Python to investigate things further and pull out relevant bits of information that we can use for social scientific purposes.

The first thing we need to do is pull the data, and here we're going to use urllib.request (as covered in previous chapters):

```
1    from urllib.request import urlopen
2
3    url = "https://data.cdc.gov/api/views/bi63-dtpu/rows.xml?accessType=DOWNLOAD"
4    response = urlopen(url)
5    reader = response.read()
6    data = reader.decode()
```

This should, by now, be starting to look quite familiar – we're importing in the urlopen() method from urllib.request, then setting a URL in a variable (response) that we can use as an argument for urlopen(). We're then reading in the information stored in response (in a variable called reader), and decoding that information into a string using .decode() on our reader object so that we can store the data we've pulled as a string in a variable called data.

Next, we simply want to write our string of data to a file, as follows:

---

[17]Although we can't see it in the image, because the dataset is too big to fit on one page, if we scroll down in the browser to the end of the dataset we'll see the tag being closed at the end with </response>.

[18]You don't need to know what adjusting for age means here, but for interested readers, all that the "age-adjusted" bit of "age-adjusted death rate" means is that the figures given have been normalised across each of the 50 American states. For example, where particular states might have older populations (perhaps Vermont or Florida, which have large retirement-age communities), their death rates are weighted less in the dataset because the higher age of their population also means a higher risk of death. We use the age-adjusted death rate just so that we can make sensible comparisons between the states without worrying about which states have an older population than others.

```
with open("CDCDeaths.xml", "w") as xml_file:
    xml_file.write(data)
```

This code opens a file (CDCDeaths.xml) in write mode, as an object we call xml_file. Then, we write the data to xml_file using the techniques we've learned in previous chapters pertaining to working with text files (xml_file.write(data)).

Working with XML data

Now we have a copy of this dataset on our computer, we can load it back into Python to work with it and pull out some initial insights that can help us make sense of it. To do this, we'll need to get to grips with the lxml module (which, if you followed along with Chapter 8 when we were there, you should already have installed) and, specifically, its objectify command. Let's add the following into our script:

```
1   from lxml import objectify
2
3   #Load in the data.
4   xml = objectify.parse(open("CDCDeaths.xml"))
5
6   #start at the root of the data
7   root = xml.getroot()
```

This code first imports in the relevant commands from the lxml library. We then use the objectify functionality to apply the objectify.parse() method to our opened dataset file, to read the data into Python. Given that we know our XML data are in a hierarchical structure, we can then tell Python what is the root level of that structure – this is done with xml.getroot(), which we store as a variable called root, where the root is the base level on which other, increasingly specific elements in the hierarchy sit.

```
-<response>
  -<row>
    -<row _id="15029" _uuid="0E3080FB-5EF8-4BEF-834E-54B52DB8DFF3" _position="15029" _address="https://data.cdc.gov
    /resource/bi63-dtpu/15029">
      <year>2016</year>
      -<_113_cause_name>
        Accidents (unintentional injuries) (V01-X59,Y85-Y86)
      </_113_cause_name>
      <cause_name>Unintentional injuries</cause_name>
      <state>Alabama</state>
      <deaths>2755</deaths>
      <aadr>55.5</aadr>
    </row>
```

Figure 12.7 One full element of XML data

Unlike JSON data where we could call on hierarchical elements with series of square brackets, we need to access this information in a different way in XML. Now that we have established the root of the XML structure, we can look again at the first case in our dataset to ascertain which level of the hierarchy the interesting information is stored at (see Figure 12.7).

We can see that the <response> level is the root of our data (which we set for Python above with xml.getroot()). There is then a further level <row>, and *after* that we have another level of <row> within which the actual information we want (to do with years, causes of death, states, numbers of deaths and age-adjusted death rates) sits. Hence, once we've established the root, we can pull individual pieces of information as follows:

```
>>> print(root.row.row.year)
2016
>>> print(root.row.row.cause_name)
Unintentional injuries
>>> print(root.row.row.state)
Alabama
>>> print(root.row.row.deaths)
2755
```

However, this is quite limited – what if we want to pull details for all relevant rows of data (e.g. that aren't to do with this first row of data that deals only with deaths by unintentional injuries in the state of Alabama in 2016)? To do this, we need to tell Python which level of the hierarchy we want to pull information from, and this is done as follows:

```
1    children = root.row.getchildren()
```

What this means is that we're telling Python to start at the root (root.), go one row deeper (row.), then go another row deeper and take the "children" of *that* row as the level to work at (getchildren()). Here, the rows of rows are called children, and can be obtained in the line of code above.

Now that we have set the level of the hierarchy (e.g. the right set of "children") to work with, we can start to pull out some information that would be relevant to a social science question – perhaps we can investigate which states had the highest and lowest flu and pneumonia death rates in the year 2016. Let's add the following code to our script to help make some sense of the data:

```
1    flu_pneu_death_rates = []
2
3    for child in children:
4        if child.cause_name == "Influenza and pneumonia" and child.year == 2016:
5            flu_pneu_death_rates.append((child.state, child.aadr))
```

Line by line, what this code does is as follows. First, we set out an empty list we want to store some data in (`flu_pneu_death_rates = []`). Then, we construct a for loop to iterate through all the bits of data we've just stored in `children` – for each of those bits of data, if the `cause_name` is `Influenza and pneumonia` and the `year` is 2016, we add the name of the state and the age-adjusted death rate values to our `flu_pneu_death_rates` list as a tuple.[19] Now, we can print out everything in this list with the code shown in Figure 12.8.

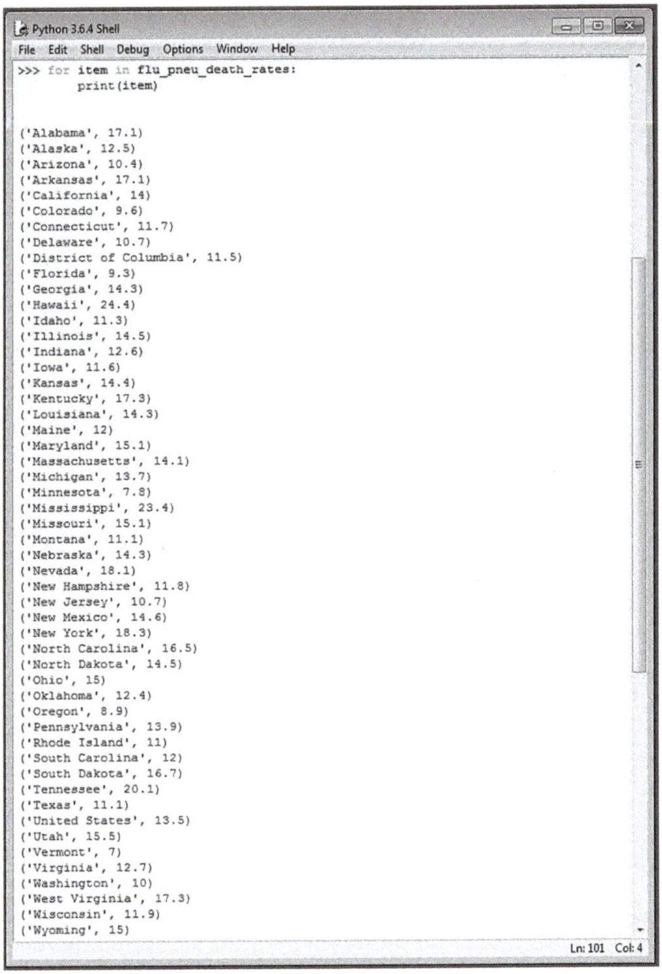

```
Python 3.6.4 Shell

File   Edit   Shell   Debug   Options   Window   Help
>>> for item in flu_pneu_death_rates:
        print(item)


('Alabama', 17.1)
('Alaska', 12.5)
('Arizona', 10.4)
('Arkansas', 17.1)
('California', 14)
('Colorado', 9.6)
('Connecticut', 11.7)
('Delaware', 10.7)
('District of Columbia', 11.5)
('Florida', 9.3)
('Georgia', 14.3)
('Hawaii', 24.4)
('Idaho', 11.3)
('Illinois', 14.5)
('Indiana', 12.6)
('Iowa', 11.6)
('Kansas', 14.4)
('Kentucky', 17.3)
('Louisiana', 14.3)
('Maine', 12)
('Maryland', 15.1)
('Massachusetts', 14.1)
('Michigan', 13.7)
('Minnesota', 7.8)
('Mississippi', 23.4)
('Missouri', 15.1)
('Montana', 11.1)
('Nebraska', 14.3)
('Nevada', 18.1)
('New Hampshire', 11.8)
('New Jersey', 10.7)
('New Mexico', 14.6)
('New York', 18.3)
('North Carolina', 16.5)
('North Dakota', 14.5)
('Ohio', 15)
('Oklahoma', 12.4)
('Oregon', 8.9)
('Pennsylvania', 13.9)
('Rhode Island', 11)
('South Carolina', 12)
('South Dakota', 16.7)
('Tennessee', 20.1)
('Texas', 11.1)
('United States', 13.5)
('Utah', 15.5)
('Vermont', 7)
('Virginia', 12.7)
('Washington', 10)
('West Virginia', 17.3)
('Wisconsin', 11.9)
('Wyoming', 15)

                                           Ln: 101  Col: 4
```

Figure 12.8   Readable output from our XML file

Here we've just used a for loop to iterate through every item in our newly created list and print it on its own line, and we can see that in the state of Vermont in 2016 only 7 people

---

[19] It's worth noting that the `aadr` values are given as floats already, and don't have to be converted if we want to perform numerical operations on them - handy!

in 100,000 died from flu and pneumonia, whereas in Hawaii the number was 24.4. In other words, in 2016 people in Hawaii were over three times as likely to die from these particular preventable diseases as people in Vermont. If we wanted to dig deeper into this dataset (e.g. compare other years or different causes of death), we might use this kind of information to piece together some really solid claims as to disparities in healthcare provision in different American states. If we put all this code together in one script, this is what it would look like:

```
1    from urllib.request import urlopen
2    from lxml import objectify
3
4    #Pulling the data from the web, decoding them.
5    url = "https://data.cdc.gov/api/views/bi63-dtpu/rows.xml?accessType=DOWNLOAD"
6    response = urlopen(url)
7    reader = response.read()
8    data = reader.decode()
9
10   #Saving the data to file.
11   with open("CDCDeaths.xml", "w") as xml_file:
12       xml_file.write(data)
13
14   #Loading in the data and working with them.
15   xml = objectify.parse(open("CDCDeaths.xml"))
16
17   #start at the root of the data
18   root = xml.getroot()
19
20   #The rows of rows are called children and can be obtained as follows:
21   children = root.row.getchildren()
22
23   flu_pneu_death_rates = []
24
25   for child in children:
26       if child.cause_name == "Influenza and pneumonia" and child.year == 2016:
27           flu_pneu_death_rates.append((child.state, child.aadr))
```

12●5 Some Possible Applications/Projects

In this chapter, we've focused primarily on grabbing a dataset and poking around in it to garner some initial exploratory social scientific insights. That is, of course, a very useful thing to be able to do, and, with this in mind, one thing you could do to extend your skills with Python and different data formats is replicate this kind of work by undertaking a small-scale research project on a different dataset. With the skills you already have, you could identify, grab, sort out and use a different dataset to explore a topic of your own research interest, whatever that may be. There are lots of open datasets available all across the web (and lots of different data available through things like social media APIs too, which you can tap into with the skills you've learned in this book), and undertaking a project like this is an ideal way to get some first-hand experience at dealing with different data formats for social scientific purposes.

However, we can also think about these techniques outside the confines of quantitatively oriented data explorations. For instance, you could add your own metadata to your (research) materials. Suppose you have a collection of written field notes from some ethnographic research, or interview transcripts, or notes taken on various pieces of academic literature you have read, or a collection of images (perhaps ones you've collected from Instagram? Or from a photo-elicitation research project?). Documents like this are really useful for research purposes, but often they are also difficult to make sense of – for instance, how are you sup- posed to identify things like patterns and repeated themes in a collection of images? One way to do this would be to use Python to "tag" the digitised versions of these images with extra metadata – perhaps you could build an XML dataset that is structured to contain details of the directory location of the image on your computer, the name of the person who took the picture, the time and date it was taken, the content of the picture (i.e. what is it a picture of?), and other details that might be relevant to your research interests. Having done this, you would be able to use Python to easily pull out sets of images that match whatever criteria you would find useful – images taken in a specified date range, images that contain a picture of a cat,[20] images taken by a specified person, and so on. So, one possible project would be to take and tag (or re-tag) an existing set of materials with extra information that can help you sort through the collection and see links that you might previously not have seen (whether those materials are research data, literature, notes taken in class, or whatever).

━━━━━━━━━━━━━━━ **Chapter summary** ━━━━━━━━━━━━━━━

- In this chapter, we explored how to grab information (e.g. datasets) from URL end-points using two libraries – `urllib.request` and `requests`.
- We then looked at the CSV data format, talking about it in general as well as working through an example of a CSV dataset in terms of how to grab it, how to decode it, and how to work with it in Python to make social scientific sense of it.
- We did the same for the JSON data format ...
- ... and then again for the XML data format.
- Finally, we noted some possible applications and projects which you could undertake in order to advance your skills and knowledge of data formats: this included both grabbing and working with new datasets related to your own interest, as well as *creating* data (and metadata) to help you do other types of (more qualitatively oriented) work.

───────────────

[20]Or perhaps something more social-science-relevant such as images of deprivation or family or deviance. I only mention cats because, from what I can see on the internet, 90% of images are of them.

13

Data Collection: Web Scraping

━━━━━━━━━━━━━━ **Chapter objectives** ━━━━━━

- Learn about how web-based information is structured as HyperText Markup Language (HTML).
- Use what we know about HTML to learn how to scrape information from webpages using the BeautifulSoup package.
- Think about what kinds of information we might want to scrape from the web as social scientists, and what we might do to make social scientific sense of it.

This chapter introduces the concept of web scraping – taking content directly from webpages – using Python, as a social scientific activity. This kind of activity has been on the horizon of social science for a number of years already, due to pioneering work by Marres and Weltevrede (2013) that has explored the idea of scraping webpages not only to get access to useful data for social science purposes, but also to pay more attention to the ways in which such data are structured and organised as a phenomenon to unpick in itself. As Marres and Weltevrede (2013: 317) note, web scraping "is not only a technique but equally involves a particular way of dealing with information and knowledge: it is also an *analytic practice*"; as such, the practice of web scraping itself requires an analytical focus on how and why webpages are constructed in the ways they are. So, web scraping can be understood as a way to dig into the information and information-sharing practices associated with the web. However, without the requisite programming skills, it's difficult for social scientists to tap into these data and data structures unless we rely on others to do the coding for us, and, unless we understand how the web works in code, this is going to put us quite some distance from a deep understanding of those data and data structures. To that end, this chapter looks at how information on the web comes packaged up as HTML, and will use Python (and the BeautifulSoup package) to pull some information from a webpage and turn it into a readable format. Using Python in this way will help us not only to get hold of data we might be interested in, but also to learn more about the ways in which such data are structured and organised for presentation as a webpage – therefore, this chapter is as much about learning some Python techniques as it is about reflecting on those techniques as *methodologies* for generating understandings of the social world.

13●1 Show Me the Code! Doing Detective Work in HTML

Before we dig into any scraping of information from the web, we need to understand the format in which that information is presented. HTML is the standard language for presenting information on the web via a browser – HTML code is the building blocks out of which a webpage can be made. So, whenever you're looking at a webpage, you're looking at the end result of some code written in HTML. However, for our purposes, we don't need to know too much about how to construct webpages with HTML – after all, this book is about teaching you Python, not other languages! What we *do* need to be aware of is how HTML elements – the individual bits of a webpage – appear in code, so that we can use that knowledge to scrape out the information we want from any given webpage.

The first thing to note is that HTML is a language that looks quite similar to something we've already seen: XML (see Chapter 12, Section 12.4). Just as with XML, HTML provides a way of structuring information with "tags" to keep various different elements organised and readily accessible. We don't need to know about all the different features available within HTML, but here's an example of some really basic HTML code that we can use to understand what sort of thing we're likely to find behind any given webpage:

```
<html>
<body>

<h1>This is the main title of the webpage</h1>

<h2>This is a sub-heading</h2>
<p>This is a paragraph of text.</p>

<h2>This is another sub-heading</h2>
<p>This is a paragraph of text with some words in bold.</p>
<img src="image.jpg" width="100" height="100">
<p>And that just above is an image.</p>

</body>
</html>
```

This is what a website looks like "behind the scenes" – just various bits of information tagged in different ways. What can we learn from this? From what we learned about XML in Chapter 12, we might already recognise the use of angled brackets (< and >) that sit around each piece of information and define what *type* of information it is. These sets of angled brackets always come in pairs – one set before the information to denote the start of it, and one set after the information to denote where it ends. For instance, we can see there's an <html> tag right at the beginning of this example which indicates where we're going to see some HTML code placed, and then an </html> tag right at the bottom to show where the code ends. Similarly, within that <html></html> pairing we can see that there is also a <body></body> pairing (which denotes where the "body text" of the HTML begins and ends). And there are various other elements within that body text – for instance, there are text headings (denoted with the <h1></h1> and <h2></h2> pairings) and text paragraphs (denoted with <p></p> pairings). The one thing in this example that *doesn't* come as a pair of tags is the image – this comes as a single set of angled brackets in which the image type is declared (img) and various parameters are set (the source/location of the image we want to see on this mocked-up webpage, and its dimensions in pixels) – so clearly sometimes the tags don't come in pairs, but the information required can instead be contained within the brackets of a single tag.

Exploring a real example of HTML

All of this is not intended as instruction in how to create a webpage out of raw HTML code – as I've said, this is a book about Python, not HTML. However, the thing we need to pay attention to for the purposes of web scraping in Python is that each piece of information in an

HTML script comes tagged as a specific type of content – hence, if we want to pull out certain types of information from a webpage, we'll need to know what type of content it is tagged as. Now we can look at a real webpage and see the code that constructs it to start working our way towards scraping it out with Python.

For this example, the information I'm interested in scraping is the text transcripts of (UK) Prime Minister's speeches, which are freely available via the UK government's official website – as social scientists, we might use this as material for thinking about the rhetoric that sits around various political ideologies on various topics. I have chosen one particular speech to work with here: a speech from June 2018 where Prime Minister Theresa May was speaking about the UK National Health Service (GOV.UK, 2018). So let's visit that webpage and do some detective work to see how that speech transcript looks in HTML.

Figure 13.1 shows what the webpage looks like when we visit it in a web browser. We might already be able to guess what we're going to find in the HTML code to some extent – alongside various other bits and bobs like links and clickable buttons, there are some

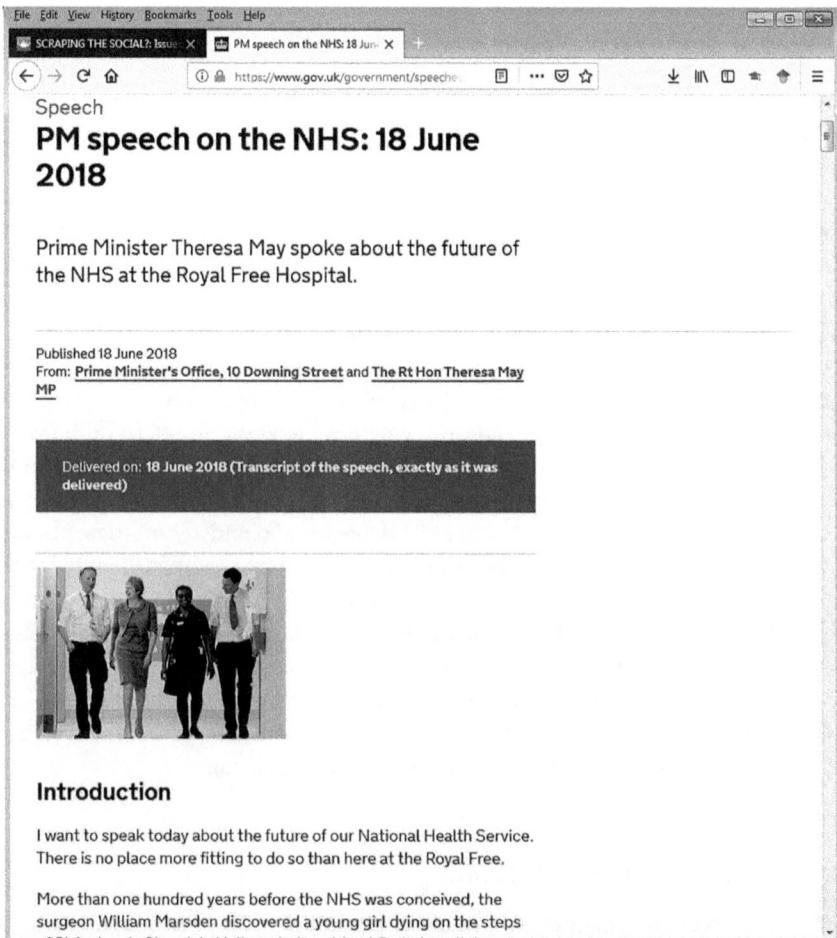

Figure 13.1 The speech we're scraping, in its webpage format

headings, there's an image, there are some paragraphs of text, and we've seen how they might look in HTML in the example above already. If I'm interested in pulling out the text of the speech (some of which is visible in Figure 13.1), I'm going to want to see what's in the paragraphs of body text rather than focus on things like the images and links and so on – this gives me a clue as to what to look out for in the HTML code.

Now comes the fun bit: let's get into the HTML! In my particular browser, going to the `Tools` menu and then the `Web Developer` option allows me to select to see the `Page Source` (i.e. the HTML code through which the website is constructed).[1] This is shown in Figure 13.2.

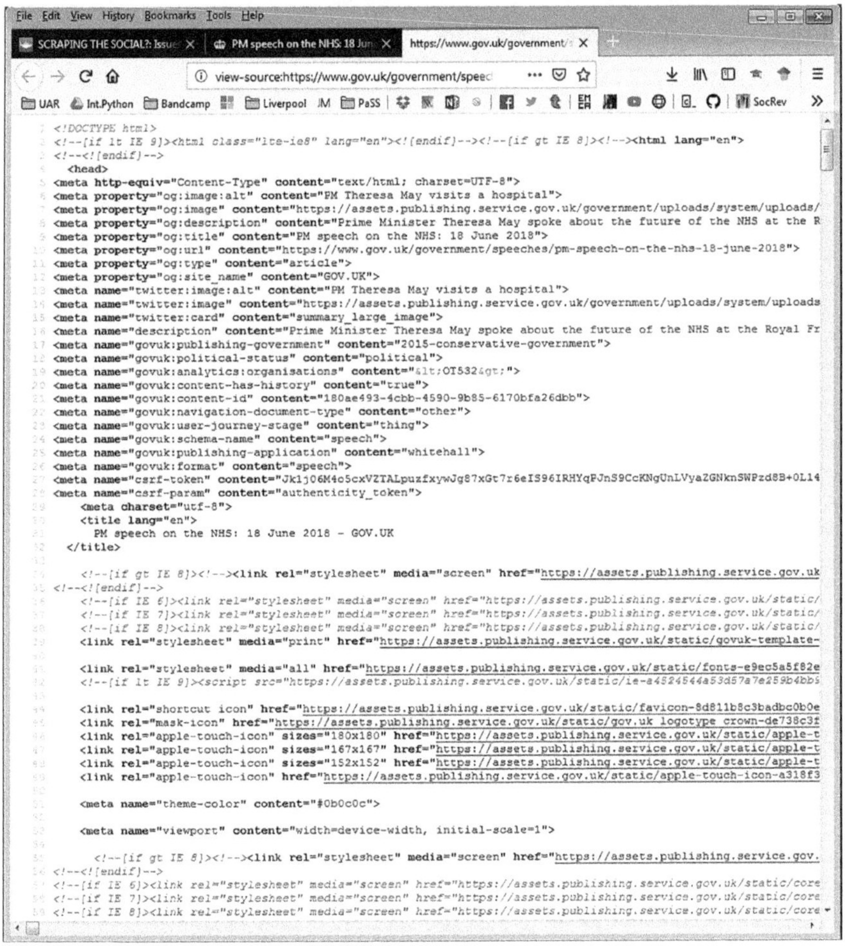

Figure 13.2 Some of the HTML code of the webpage we're scraping

---

[1] I use Mozilla Firefox rather than other browsers for various reasons - privacy, customisation, the warm fuzzy feeling of using open-source software - but you will be able to see the HTML behind websites using any popular browser of your choice. The commands to enable this might be different, though, so be aware of this if you're not using Firefox yourself.

Phew, that's a lot of stuff to look at! As noted already, though, we don't need to understand the ins and outs of this page – all we need to do is find the information we're interested in extracting from this webpage to see how it has been tagged. And to do that, we can do a bit of simple detective work to sift through the code to locate information relevant to us. Look back at Figure 13.1 – we can see that in the opening paragraph of text there's a line that begins "I want to speak today". Given we can see that on the webpage, we know that it must also therefore be present in the HTML code somewhere, and therefore we can search for this text to identify which bits of code to look out for in the whole script.[2] So, let's use this bit of text – "I want to speak today" – to try and identify the lines of HTML we're interested in and the tags that they come tagged with.

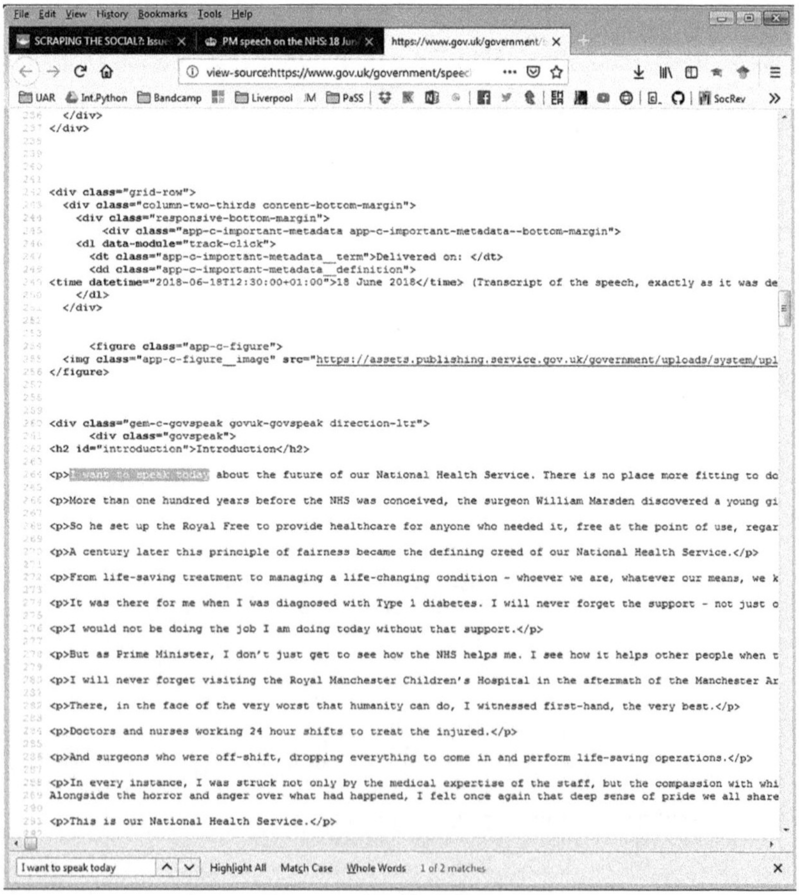

Figure 13.3 Searching for the text of the speech

---

[2]It's worth noting that searching for text is not *always* going to work for every potential case - for instance, what if the text we're actually interested in wasn't written into the HTML *as* text, but as an image or something else like that? In that case, the text *wouldn't* be available in the code to search and we'd have to do some more detective work to try to find it by another means. However, that's part of the fun of web scraping: figuring out the internal structure of the webpage and whatever it is you're looking for within it. And in fact, that's exactly what Marres and Weltevrede (2013) are trying to get us to pay attention to, as noted in the introduction to this chapter.

Right at the bottom of Figure 13.3 you can see I've opened up a `Find` dialog and typed in the phrase I want to search for ("I want to speak today")[3] – because HTML code is stored as text, it's possible to search through that text using text strings in this way, and we're taking advantage of this here. You can also see in Figure 13.3 that I've been able to locate the section of code where this opening line of the speech is stored – it looks like every paragraph of the Prime Minister's speech on this page is tagged as an individual paragraph (i.e. the bits of text I'm interested in are contained within a `<p></p>` tag pairing). Perfect! Now we have done enough digging around in this webpage to know that all the information we want is stored as paragraphs tagged with `<p></p>`, and we just need to tell Python to pull it out!

13●2 Show Me the Code! Web Scraping with BeautifulSoup

The first thing we need to do in our code is import in the libraries we're using, the URL of the webpage we want to pull data from, and get a copy of that information in Python-readable format – here's some code that will do that.

```
1   from requests import get
2   from bs4 import BeautifulSoup
3
4   url = "https://www.gov.uk/government/speeches/pm-speech-on-the-nhs-18-june-2018"
5   response = get(url)
```

Line by line, we've started by importing the `get()` method from a library called `requests` – this is what we need to grab the information from a specified URL. Second, we've imported the `BeautifulSoup` library which will give us all the web-scraping functionality we need. Then, we've stored a URL of the website we want to scrape from in a variable rather imaginatively named `url`.[4] Below this, we've then stored, in a variable called `response`, the information contained at that URL, by passing our `url` variable as a parameter to the `get()` method – this grabs the information we need. However, this information is not in any kind of readable format, nor do we especially want to treat *everything* on the website as data – there's a lot of junk we don't necessarily need to see in the HTML code, so now we can use BeautifulSoup to sift through and pull out the stuff we *do* want.

---

[3]On my browser of choice, Mozilla Firefox, you can do this by pressing Ctrl+F - this might apply to your browser of choice also, but if not, you should still be able to find a way to search a page for text information. If you can't, then I recommend you switch browsers, since web scraping is going to be unnecessarily difficult without such tools to help you do detective work on HTML code.

[4]I'm just being flippant here - we actually *shouldn't* use overly imaginative names for variables, otherwise nobody else will be able to understand what we mean by them. So, descriptive variable names FTW!

```
1   html_soup = BeautifulSoup(response.text, "html.parser")
2   speech_text = html_soup.find_all("p")
```

In the first line of this excerpt, we establish a variable called "html_soup" into which we place a BeautifulSoup object with some arguments. Effectively, we are passing two arguments into BeautifulSoup (i.e. the BeautifulSoup() bit, which you'll note has brackets ready to accept further arguments). The first argument is response.text, which says that we want to take the text from the information stored in our already declared response variable (see the first code excerpt in this section). The second argument is a string ("html.parser") which tells BeautifulSoup that we want to read in (or parse) this information as HTML code – here we're telling Python/BeautifulSoup which language to translate from.

In the second line of the excerpt, we declare a new variable, speech_text, in which we want to store a particular selection of information captured in our new html_soup variable – we want to apply the .find_all() method to html_soup, to search for all tags marked as "p" (and if we put it all together as Python code, this looks like html_soup.find_all("p")). The "p" comes from our prior detective work, where we identified that all the bits of the Prime Minister's speech were stored on this webpage in paragraphs tagged with a <p></p> pairing. Now, let's run this code as one script, and call speech_text to see what we get (see Figure 13.4).

OK, this is looking good! We can clearly see in Figure 13.4 that what is stored in our "speech_text" variable does include the paragraphs of the Prime Minister's speech! We can also see this information comes in the form of a Python list, where each individual entry is one of the things that was tagged with a <p></p> pairing in the original HTML code – as such, we can also call individual elements by using list index positions (e.g. speech_text[20] will give us the paragraph that sits at index position 20 in our list). However, we might also note that there are some other bits and bobs in there that we *don't* want to see – for instance, the first entry seems to be nothing to do with the Prime Minister's speech but a message about the website's policy on cookies for monitoring visitors' web usage. We can also see that every entry in our list has also retained the tags themselves – the <p> and </p> bits of HTML code that indicate where paragraphs begin and end. These things are not necessarily useful to us – however, knowing what we do about Python by this point, we're perfectly capable of cleaning up this information and just keeping the text transcript of the speech itself in our data.

Cleaning up web-scraped data

For the particular data that have been scraped, here's what we could do:[5]

---

[5]Some of this uses Python techniques that haven't been covered before in the relevant sections on string and list methods - specifically, we haven't yet seen the .replace() method as being applied to strings. That's not a problem for us, though, because by this point you should be comfortable enough with the idea of going and exploring new techniques and methods in the documentation for yourself. I'll of course walk us through the .replace() method here, but as a programmer in Python yourself, this data clean-up activity is nothing you couldn't learn to do yourself through independent exploration.

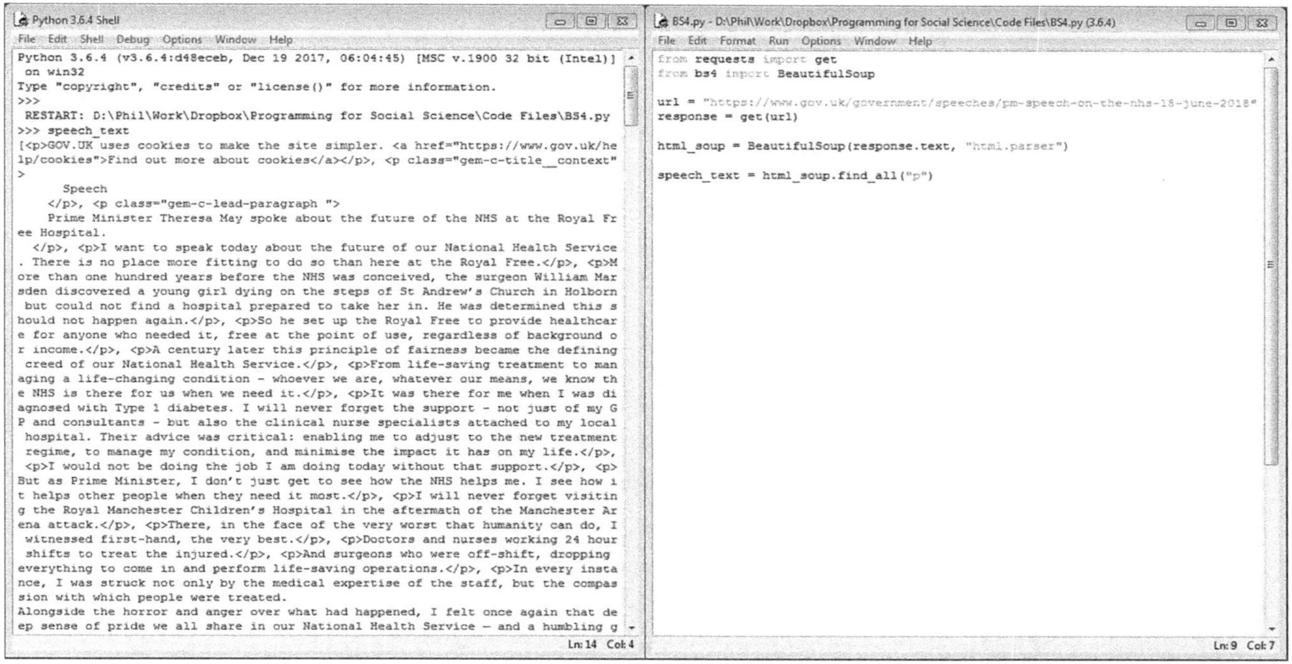

Figure 13.4 The web, scraped

```
1    del(speech_text[0:3])
2    del(speech_text[-1:-5:-1])
3
4    clean_speech_text = []
5    for item in speech_text:
6        item = str(item)
7        item = item.replace("<p>", "")
8        item = item.replace("</p>", "")
9        clean_speech_text.append(item)
```

If we look at the information contained in the speech_text list by calling the list to see what's in there, we can see that it's the first three entries and the last four entries that we want to delete – these are the bits to do with the cookie policy and other website-relevant information that isn't part of the Prime Minister's speech, and therefore the first two lines of code here are for deleting those bits of junk information (using the del method to delete a specified range of details from the start and end of the list).

Next, we'll need to remove the <p> and </p> tags from each item in our list – these are not part of the speech as such and they might confuse any analysis we might undertake on the speech itself, so now we've extracted the data from the web we no longer need the tags and should get rid of them. We can do this by first establishing a new empty list (clean_speech_text) for storing a cleaned-up version of our speech text in, and using a for loop to iterate through each item in the speech_text list, performing some clean-ups, and appending the clean data to our new list. Within the for loop, you should note that we start by making sure each item in our list is turned into a string (item = str(item)) – this is because BeautifulSoup hasn't pulled out these list entries as strings but as its own special kind of object class; if we run type(speech_text[0]), for instance, we'll get the result <class 'bs4.element.Tag'>, which is not the same as a string and therefore we won't be able to do any string formatting on those kinds of object. So, the first thing in our for loop is to turn each item into a string. Then we apply the .replace() method to each item – this method takes two arguments: first, a string of the thing we want to search for and replace (in our case, the <p> bit of the string we want to remove) and, second, the thing we want to replace it with (in our case, "", or an empty string, which is to say we want to replace <p> with nothing). The new version of the string without the <p> tag is then stored back in an updated version of item. We do exactly the same thing again in the next line of code, except this time replacing the </p> tag in the string with an empty string. Finally, once all that cleaning has happened, we append the fresh-as-a-daisy version of the string to our new clean_speech_text list. Let's call the first few entries in the list (see Figure 13.5).

As we can see in Figure 13.5, at this point we have a nice full list of the individual paragraphs of this particular speech by Prime Minister Theresa May. We started with just a URL and have ended up with a wealth of useful text data to help us understand the political rhetorics around healthcare – the world (wide web) is our oyster!

```
Python 3.6.4 Shell                                               [ _ ][ □ ][ x ]
File  Edit  Shell  Debug  Options  Window  Help
Python 3.6.4 (v3.6.4:d48eceb, Dec 19 2017, 06:04:45) [MSC v.1900 32 bit (Intel)]
 on win32
Type "copyright", "credits" or "license()" for more information.
>>>
 RESTART: D:\Phil\Work\Dropbox\Programming for Social Science\Code Files\BS4.py
>>> del(speech_text[0:3])
>>> del(speech_text[-1:-5:-1])
>>>
>>> clean_speech_text = []
>>> for item in speech_text:
        item = str(item)
        item = item.replace("<p>", "")
        item = item.replace("</p>", "")
        clean_speech_text.append(item)


>>> clean_speech_text[0:5]
['I want to speak today about the future of our National Health Service. There i
s no place more fitting to do so than here at the Royal Free.', 'More than one h
undred years before the NHS was conceived, the surgeon William Marsden discovere
d a young girl dying on the steps of St Andrew's Church in Holborn but could not
 find a hospital prepared to take her in. He was determined this should not happ
en again.', 'So he set up the Royal Free to provide healthcare for anyone who ne
eded it, free at the point of use, regardless of background or income.', 'A cent
ury later this principle of fairness became the defining creed of our National H
ealth Service.', 'From life-saving treatment to managing a life-changing conditi
on - whoever we are, whatever our means, we know the NHS is there for us when we
 need it.']
>>>
                                                                   Ln: 18  Col: 4
```

Figure 13.5 The web, scraped and polished

Some further reflections

There are a few things worth noting at this point, to round off our walkthrough of web scraping with BeautifulSoup. It should be mentioned that the website chosen for the example above is relatively simple, inasmuch as the HTML is relatively easy to deal with – everything we needed was contained in the <p></p> tag pairings, and there was relatively little junk we brought along with it just by doing a smash-and-grab search for that tag. Moreover, the small amount of junk that *did* come through with this technique was easily filtered out, by virtue of ts sitting only at the beginning and end of the information we collected. However, this is not going to be the case for every website, and the more complex the site you're dealing with, the savvier you'll have to be with spotting how to identify and extract the relevant stuff in a potentially messy and chaotic morass of HTML – in fact, the BeautifulSoup package takes its name from the idea of making beautiful order out of unreadable "tag soup".

One useful way of narrowing down the scope of stuff pulled out of a webpage is to do multi-level searches for tags – for instance, we can see in Figure 13.3 that there are lots of divider tags in the HTML for this website (i.e. sections of the website which may contain lots of different elements, but where the start and end are signified with a <div></div> pairing). Hence, if we wanted to narrow down our scope to just looking at one particular section of the website where our information was located, we could do the required detective work to find out which specific section our code was in and tell Python/BeautifulSoup to search only there. If we were doing this, we might want to insert the following lines of code in the right place in the script we've sketched out above:

```
1   text = html_soup.find("div", id="wrapper")
2   body_text = text.find_all("p")
```

The first line of this code finds a specific <div></div> pairing that's given an id of wrapper in its native HTML – we don't really need to know what wrapper refers to, only that the speech text paragraphs are contained within this particular division of the website (which we can identify by looking through the HTML as we've been doing already). Then the second line of code is what we've seen already with a slight twist – now we're applying the .find_all() method to only that particular division (the one with an ID of wrapper) rather than the whole html_soup contents. So, detective work plus multi-level or layered searches can help keep the information tidy as it comes in rather than having to spend more time tidying it up afterwards.

But really, the general point to make here is that exactly how you approach the web scraping for any particular webpage is completely dependent on the webpage itself and what you hope to get out of it. It's important to note that HTML is not written necessarily to be easily readable or extractable by web-scraping programmers – some websites are not written with clearly structured HTML at the top of the priority list, and just because a website looks good in a browser doesn't mean it's not a hideously terrifying pile of garbage when you lift the lid and a have a poke about in it. Hence, more so than the actual Python, it's the detective work of unpicking the internal structure of a webpage that is probably the most vital skill here. The more you dig into the idiosyncrasies of an individual webpage, the more you'll understand how it is structured and organised, and that inside knowledge is what you'll need in order to make any kind of sense of that information. It also gets us to pay close attention to what we're doing when we're doing web scraping as social researchers – in doing this detective work, we repeatedly come up against methodological decisions about what is and what isn't relevant and have to reason through strategies of how to pull that information out of the page at hand. This is, in fact, one of the values of programming as a social scientist in a general sense (more on that in the final chapter), but, as Marres and Weltevrede (2013) remind us, this is made especially relevant in the work of web scraping where we have to become intimately acquainted with the inner structures and orders and organisation of the web. As such, as with any programming activity, web scraping provides an opportunity for methodological reflection, as an often valuable practice when learning and doing new research activities.

13●3 Some Possible Applications/Projects

In this chapter, we've focused on exploring HTML code as the language of the web, and then using BeautifulSoup to translate that language into Python as something we're now more familiar with. We've done this with regard to a specific project around extracting a single UK Prime Minister's speech from a government website and turning it into something that can, in principle, be worked with further as part of social scientific work. However, the fact that these web-scraping techniques could be extended to capture information contained on *pretty much any website in existence* should indicate that there is an infinite array of work that might be done here. Practising these skills in different contexts is the way to build your skills further, and working to get different types of information out of different webpages will help you do this. Here are a few examples of potentially interesting applications to kickstart some thinking around how to take your skills further:

- *Building further on what we've done.* Using the techniques we've learned throughout the book to this point, we could extend the work we've done and use Python to assist in an analysis of the words used around healthcare in the current political climate. So, using the example worked with above, once we have our clean list of paragraphs from the Prime Minister's June 2018 speech on the National Health Service, we could join together all the individual strings in the list into one big string, break it back up into individual words, remove common words with a stop list (i.e. delete all words such as "and", "the", "to") then count up all the remaining words to see what kinds of topics were most prominent in the speech. This would give a flavour of the particular rhetoric around healthcare, which we might then compare against other Prime Minister's speeches by applying these exact same techniques to different URLs on the gov.uk website.
- *Grabbing data for qualitative analysis.* We could look at different sites altogether, to gather data that we might want to then approach in very different ways. For instance, we could scrape the user-generated comments from an online news article about a topic of interest (e.g. politics, technology, health, crime – effectively, anything that is reported on in the news), which would give us really rich attitudinal insight into what people think about the topic at hand. We could then read through these data qualitatively, as meaningful opinions and attitudes on socially relevant issues.[6]
- *Grabbing data for quantitative analysis.* Web scraping is a multi-purpose tool, so you can do whatever kind of research you like with the available data – this is because the "available data" effectively consist of pretty much the whole of the internet. Some webpages store readily available numerical information that might be of relevance to a social scientist. For instance, Worldometers (2019) features a full list of countries in the world by population (including other relevant statistics such as total area of the country and yearly population change) – you could extract this information and use a measure of population density (e.g. population divided by land area) and see what correlations there might be between population density and other data such as those collected as part of the United Nations *World Happiness Report*. Tables are just another type of tagged information, so all you'd need to do here is the detective work required to find the right tag within which the information you need is stored.

---

[6]This is exactly the approach taken in some of my own research – see Brooker et al. (2017a) for further details.

Chapter summary

- In this chapter, we first looked at the concept of web scraping – what it is, and why social scientists might be interested in it, both as a technique for grabbing data and as a way of attuning ourselves to the underlying structure of information as it is presented on the web.
- We explored how to do "detective work" on a webpage, by inspecting the HTML at the source of a page and searching for relevant details within it.
- We then used Python and BeautifulSoup to extract those details from a webpage as data.
- Following on from this, we did a few clean-up jobs on the data to wrangle them into a more usable shape.
- At that point, we also reflected on how web scraping is very much a contextually dependent task which depends on the specific nature of the webpage you're scraping and the way it has been structured in HTML.
- Finally, we outlined some further ways in which these techniques can feed into other projects of social scientific interest.

14

Visualising Data

■■■■■■■■■■■■ Chapter objectives ■■■■■■

- Learn how to use the `pandas` library to create series and dataframes through which you can make visual sense of data.
- Learn how to use the `matplotlib` library to visualise data in graphic format.
- Learn how Python can help us reflect, social-scientifically, on the practice of producing (visual) representations of data.

So far, we've covered lots of Python code for grabbing and working with data in various ways – visualising such data is the next logical step in many regards. As the datasets we're dealing with get larger in volume and richer in content, it becomes imperative to have some way to see what is going on in them if we are to articulate any kind of story from them. This becomes all the more important if we're dealing with datasets that originate outside the social sciences (such as open government datasets, data drawn from social media platforms, etc.), since such datasets are not primarily *intended* to have a social science relevance, and therefore they may contain lots of information that obscures the stuff that *is* relevant to our concerns. In these cases, we can make different kinds of (visual) representations of data in order to help us cut through the noise and draw out social science accounts of the data more clearly and explic- itly. To that end, this chapter will walk you through using two Python libraries, `pandas` and `matplotlib`, which can help produce exactly these kinds of (visual) representations of data. And along the way, we can use this to 'unpack the black box of visualisation' more widely and ask social science questions around what sense it makes to look at data in some ways and not others. As such, using Python to 'get under the hood' of visualisation in this way can not only help us construct visual materials to help us analyse and display data, but also help us to be more reflexive about our methodological practice as social science researchers.

14●1 Show Me the Code! Pandas

`pandas` is an add-on library for Python which is designed to provide user-friendly functional- ity around data manipulation and analysis. For instance, one major feature of Pandas is that it can be used to read in data and present them in a rows-and-columns type of format – although it's potentially possible to do this kind of work with some fancy list/dictionary methods and for loops and string formatting (as we have done in previous chapters), using something like Pandas can produce neater (and therefore more readable) results in terms of both the outputs produced and the lines of code used to produce them. There are lots of things you can do with Pandas which you might find useful for social scientific projects – however, this chapter will take a relatively small-scale look at some of the more basic Pandas concepts: reading in data in different ways, visualising data as a series and visualising data as a dataframe (we'll define terms like "series" and "dataframe" as we arrive at them).

Pandas series

A series in Pandas is a way of looking at a single type of data alongside its labels – a series is often described as a "one-dimensional array", which just means that the representation we produce (i.e. the series) is dealing with one particular dataset and its labels. What this means will become clearer if we jump straight into the code:

```
1   import pandas as pd
2
3   violent_rate = {"Belfast East": 13.9,
4                   "Belfast North": 24.2,
5                   "Belfast South": 20.6,
6                   "Belfast West": 25.4
7                   }
8
9   vrni_series = pd.Series(violent_rate)
```

Line by line, what we're doing here is first importing in the pandas module but calling it by a shorthand name, pd – we *could* just import the pandas library without giving it this shorthand and still use it (which means wherever it says "pd" in the code we'd just have to type out pandas in full), but the shorthand is useful in two respects. First, it's (ever so slightly) quicker to type out, which might become important if we're writing lots of bits of code that use lots of bits of the pandas library. However – and arguably this is much more important – the shorthand pd is a widespread convention among Python users using Pandas, which means that most people using Pandas do it this way too. If we want to do things like make our code readable to others, or even use code ourselves that other people have written and integrate it with our own, sharing their code-writing conventions prevents errors and confusion along the way.

Next, what we do in the code excerpt above is declare a variable called violent_rate in which we store a small dictionary of data: there are keys in this dictionary which refer to different constituencies we have collected data for, and the values associated with those keys indicate levels of violent crimes that happened in those constituencies in the year 2017. These data come from the Northern Ireland deprivation data we used as an example of CSV data in Chapter 12. For clarity, this is a small selection of that original dataset, taking the four political constituencies of Belfast and the number of violent crimes (including sexual offences, robbery and public order offences) occurring per 1000 people in the year 2017.[1]

We have some data and we've stuck them in a variable: so far, so familiar. The next line is where we invoke pandas to format the data into a Pandas series – we do this by declaring a variable called "vrni_series" and using the pandas library series method (pd.Series()) into which we pass an argument (the violent_rate dictionary). Figure 14.1 shows what this looks like when we print it.

---

[1] If you're following along with the code excerpts and working through these techniques by yourself (and you *should* be!), you *could* just copy these data across into a script of your own - but I think that would be cheating. Why not try to go back to the CSV dataset and the techniques covered in Chapter 12 to derive these data for yourself using Python techniques? That'd be a really nice way to practise skills you've already learned and see how discrete programming activities (like getting data and visualising data) can be joined up as part of a cohesive whole project. So, do that!

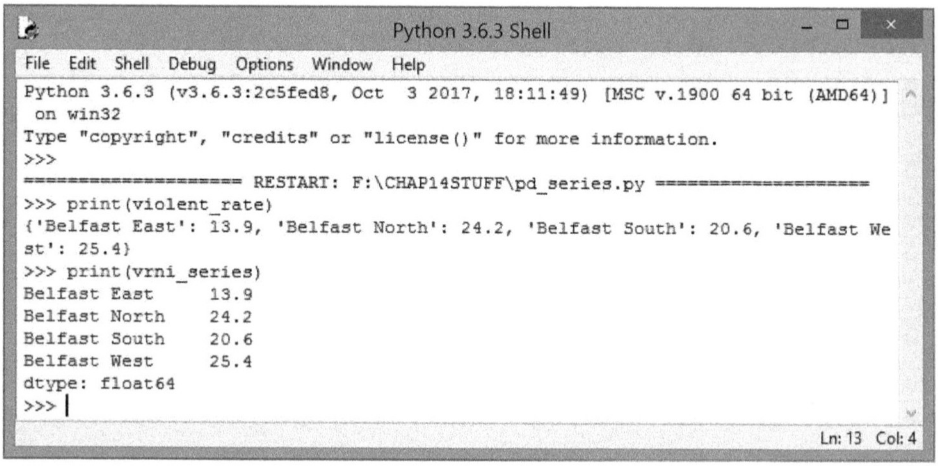

```
Python 3.6.3 Shell                                             –  □  ×
File  Edit  Shell  Debug  Options  Window  Help
Python 3.6.3 (v3.6.3:2c5fed8, Oct  3 2017, 18:11:49) [MSC v.1900 64 bit (AMD64)]
on win32
Type "copyright", "credits" or "license()" for more information.
>>>
==================== RESTART: F:\CHAP14STUFF\pd_series.py ====================
>>> print(violent_rate)
{'Belfast East': 13.9, 'Belfast North': 24.2, 'Belfast South': 20.6, 'Belfast We
st': 25.4}
>>> print(vrni_series)
Belfast East      13.9
Belfast North     24.2
Belfast South     20.6
Belfast West      25.4
dtype: float64
>>>
                                                              Ln: 13  Col: 4
```

Figure 14.1 Two ways to view our Belfast violence rate data

What we can see is that though our information is all contained in a dictionary (with keys and values) and we can print that out in its dictionary form, it's not necessarily very easy to look at – imagine trying to do this with 1000 dictionary entries and having to make sense of *that* mess! However, when we print out the Pandas series version, we can see that it has reformatted the dictionary keys and values into nice neat rows and columns such that we can now see each constituency of interest and the number of violent offences committed per 1000 in that constituency in the year 2017 side by side, for easy visual comparison.

There are also various things we can do with this series now we have it stored in Python's memory – here are some useful commands that we can use to probe our way around the data:

```
>>> vrni_series[0]
13.9
>>> vrni_series[0:3]
Belfast East      13.9
Belfast North     24.2
Belfast South     20.6
dtype: float64
>>> vrni_series[-1]
25.4
>>> vrni_series[[1,3]]
Belfast North     24.2
Belfast West      25.4
dtype: float64
>>> print(vcuk_series["Belfast South"])
20.6
```

Let's go through each of these commands in turn to unpick what's happening. First, we can see that `vrni_series[0]` gives us the value of the piece of data in the series at index position 0. We can also see that list slicing techniques work with a Pandas series – when we call `vrni_series[0:3]`, for instance, we are given the data stored at index positions 0, 1 and 2. It's worth flagging here that, as with slicing by index in the way we've covered in previous chapters, 3 is *not* included and the value stored at index position 3 is not shown.[2] We can apply other types of list slicing techniques to a series like this too. For instance, when we call `vrni_series[-1]`, we are given the last value in the series. And if we want to print out (or store in a variable, or use in other ways) the values associated with individual keys, we can call them by their key as we do with `print(vrni_series["Belfast South"])`. This is just a little snapshot of the kinds of things you can do with data as stored in a Pandas series, and as you start to use these techniques in projects for yourself, you will find creative ways to extend these techniques to do useful things in your social scientific work).

Pandas series can also be used to collate together different data structures. For instance, in the example above we had a nice neat dictionary which stored values alongside keys and that formed the basis of the series, but what about if we have two separate lists of information which we would like to put together? Pandas can do this. The following example uses information stored in two separate lists – one a list of the political constituencies of Belfast, and one a list of numbers representing the amount of violent offences committed in those constituencies in 2017[3] – to compute a Pandas series that combines them:

```
1  constituency_names = ["Belfast East", "Belfast North", "Belfast South",
2                        "Belfast West"]
3
4  violent_rates = [13.9, 24.2, 20.6, 25.4]
```

The information we might be interested in is the entries in the `violent_rates` list, whereas the entries in the `constituency_name` list are the labels we would like to apply to those entries. We *could* just run the series on the information in `violent_rates` in the same way we did with the violent crimes dictionary above (i.e. storing the data a series in a variable, then printing out that variable) – Figure 14.2 shows how that looks.

Shoehorning just the data values into a series and printing it out *does* give us the relevant numbers, but the labels (0, 1, 2 and 3) aren't especially useful – all they tell us is which index position the values are at, whereas it would be more helpful if we could see which constituency each label refers to. Handily for us, Pandas lets us put keys and values from different places together in a series, as you can see in Figure 14.3.

---

[2] Just for completeness, it's also worth noting that the `dtype: float64` statement that is tacked onto the end of the series just refers to the type of data that is being represented in the series - in this case, each datapoint is a 64-bit float (though for our purposes, just knowing it is a float is plenty).

[3] Again, I'm using the same Northern Ireland data here, but just presented in a different format this time so we can practise building the series in a different way.

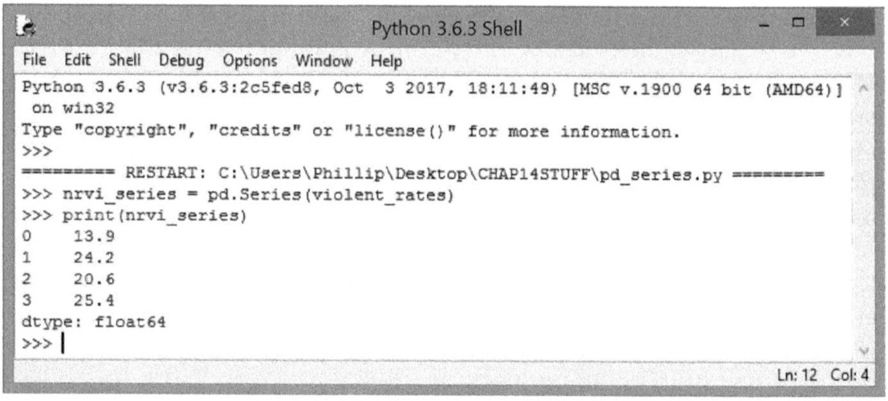

```
Python 3.6.3 Shell                                        -  □  ×
File  Edit  Shell  Debug  Options  Window  Help
Python 3.6.3 (v3.6.3:2c5fed8, Oct  3 2017, 18:11:49) [MSC v.1900 64 bit (AMD64)]
on win32
Type "copyright", "credits" or "license()" for more information.
>>>
========= RESTART: C:\Users\Phillip\Desktop\CHAP14STUFF\pd_series.py =========
>>> nrvi_series = pd.Series(violent_rates)
>>> print(nrvi_series)
0     13.9
1     24.2
2     20.6
3     25.4
dtype: float64
>>> |
                                                          Ln: 12  Col: 4
```

Figure 14.2 Printout of `nrvi_series` data

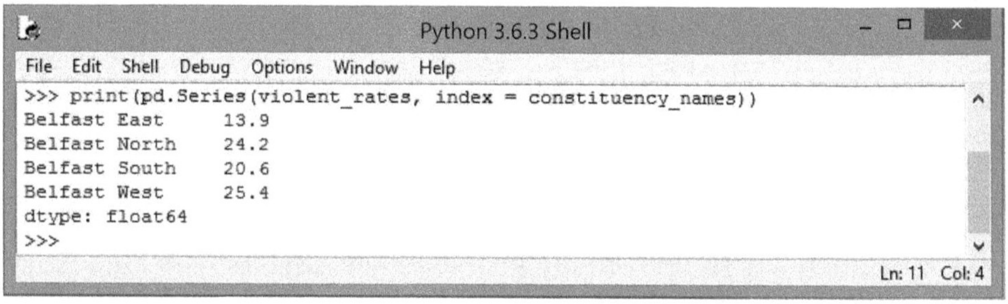

```
Python 3.6.3 Shell                                        -  □  ×
File  Edit  Shell  Debug  Options  Window  Help
>>> print(pd.Series(violent_rates, index = constituency_names))
Belfast East      13.9
Belfast North     24.2
Belfast South     20.6
Belfast West      25.4
dtype: float64
>>>
                                                          Ln: 11  Col: 4
```

Figure 14.3 Values and keys, together at last!

You can see that I've given an instruction to print the `violent_rates` data using `constituency_names` in place of the index (index = `constituency_names`), and it's given us the labels and data together – great! We can even go one step further and permanently fix the data labels we want to our series (rather than having to pass them to that series as a separate parameter in an argument), using the following code to create the series using the `violent_rates` list as data, then fixing the `constituency_names` to it as an index:

```
>>> nrvi_series = pd.Series(violent_rates)
>>> nrvi_series.index = constituency_names
```

This little code excerpt makes it so that when you print out the series you'll see the same fully labelled table as in Figure 14.3.

There are also other methods and descriptive statistics we can draw out from a Pandas series, which might be helpful depending on the work you are trying to do with them. Here are just some:

```
>>> nrvi_series.count()
4
```

This command counts up all the non-null (i.e. not missing) pieces of data in the series. Note that this is similar to doing something like `len(nrvi_series)`, although the `len()`

method will give you the full length of the series *including* missing values (e.g. where no data were given, or the data type isn't the same as the rest of the data in the series), whereas the `.count()` method only gives values that aren't missing (and hence may sometimes produce a value less than the length of the series, if there are missing values in the data).

```
>>> nrvi_series.sum()
84.1
```

This command produces the sum of the data (i.e. it adds all the values together and gives you the result). Note that the values must be integers or floats for this to work (and this applies also to the other descriptive statistics Pandas allows for below too). It's also worth noting that, given we're looking at amounts of violent crimes per 1000 people across four different constituencies, the actual *relevance* of adding all the numbers together is questionable here. Which is to say, though it's possible to add all these numbers together with `.sum()` (and this is a valid thing to do for certain types of analysis), it's not an especially sensible thing to do here except for the purposes of showing you the `.sum()` method, and for reminding you that as with anything in Python, we need to carefully think through the methodological reasoning and implications of why we're doing the things we're choosing to do – with great power comes great responsibility, and all that! And with that thinking in mind, I'll now look dispassionately at some other methods.

```
>>> nrvi_series.mean()
21.025
```

This command gives the mean (or average) value of the data series (i.e. it adds all the values together, then divides that number by the length of the series).

```
>>> nrvi_series.median()
22.4
```

This command gives the median value of the data series (i.e. the middle value when all the bits of data in the series are sorted into order).

```
>>> nrvi_series.mode()
0      13.9
1      20.6
2      24.2
3      25.4
dtype: float64
```

This commands give the mode value(s) of the data series (i.e. the value(s) which occur(s) most frequently in the series). Note that since each of the values in `nrvi_series` appears once (and, hence, they all appear in the data as many times as each other), this command returns all of them.

```
>>> nrvi_series.describe()
count      4.000000
mean      21.025000
std        5.169381
```

```
min        13.900000
25%        18.925000
50%        22.400000
75%        24.500000
max        25.400000
dtype: float64
```

This command gives a range of descriptive statistics for the data series, including the count and mean (which we've seen an alternative way of drawing out above) as well as the standard deviation (i.e. the amount of variation in the data series), the minimum and maximum values, and the quartiles of the series (i.e. a value for the lower quartile below which 25% of the data lie, the middle value (or median) below which 50% of the data lie, and a value for the upper quartile below which 75% of the data lie). These types of descriptive statistics can be really useful if you're interested in using Python to undertake quantitative research,[4] but even if you're just looking to get a quick sense of any kind of dataset without it becoming a project in social statistics, drawing on the descriptive statistics that can be derived from a Pandas series can be a useful way of doing so.

Pandas dataframes

However, what if we want to do stuff that's slightly more complex than looking at one series of data at a time? Pandas has us covered there too, with dataframes. As with Pandas series, we can read in various types of data in different ways – let's look at one of those ways now, building a dataframe out of a dictionary of lists:

```
1    import pandas as pd
2
3    constituency_names = ["Belfast East", "Belfast North","Belfast South",
4                          "Belfast West"]
5    violent_rates = [13.9, 24.2, 20.6, 25.4]
6    theft_rates = [7.6, 11.2, 14.7, 10.9]
7    veh_crime_rates = [1.8, 3.4, 4.5, 5.6]
8
9    data = {"Name": constituency_names,
10           "Violence Rate": violent_rates,
11           "Theft Rate": theft_rates,
12           "Veh Crime Rate": veh_crime_rates}
13
14   data_df = pd.DataFrame(data)
```

---

[4] I appreciate these are not necessarily the fullest descriptions of any of these statistical concepts, but this is not a quantitative methods book - all I'm intending to do here is outline what's available in Pandas. Feel free to complement your Python and Pandas knowledge with other quantitative methods learning if that's what you're into!

Line by line, what is happening here? First we're importing the pandas library as pd (as we did before to work with series). Next up is the dataset we're using – four lists, each containing four entries relating to different bits of data about the four political constituencies of Belfast and various types of rates of criminal offences (counts per 1000 people).[5] Note here that there are different types of data at play – constituency_names contains strings representing the four different constituency names, and violent_rates, theft_rates and veh_crime_rates are floats that represent occurrences of different types of crimes (violent offences, thefts and vehicle crimes, respectively) per 1000 population. But we could also have other data types in our dataframe – for instance, alongside strings and floats we could have integers or Boolean True/False values. However, since we don't have those in the original Northern Ireland deprivation data, we'll just be working with strings and floats for now. Once the four lists are declared and structured, they are compiled into a big dictionary (data) which stores each list under a descriptive key (Name, Violence Rate, Theft Rate and Veh Crime Rate). Finally, we create a Pandas dataframe out of this new dictionary (with pd.DataFrame(data)) and store it as a variable called data_df. When we print out data_df, we get the output shown in Figure 14.4.

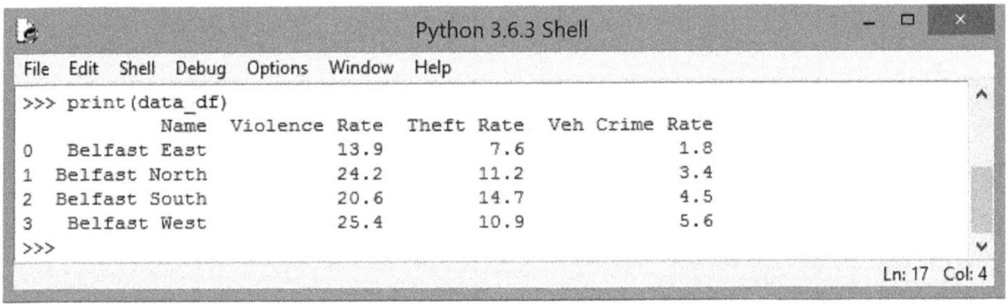

```
                                Python 3.6.3 Shell                    _ □ ×
File  Edit  Shell  Debug  Options  Window  Help
>>> print(data_df)
            Name   Violence Rate   Theft Rate   Veh Crime Rate
0    Belfast East            13.9          7.6              1.8
1   Belfast North            24.2         11.2              3.4
2   Belfast South            20.6         14.7              4.5
3    Belfast West            25.4         10.9              5.6
>>>
                                                              Ln: 17  Col: 4
```

Figure 14.4 A tidy dataframe

You can see that the dataframe takes the keys of the data dictionary as headers for a table view of all the data (whereas a series would only be able to accommodate one header/data source at a time). You can also see that the index positions of the rows are given (which is helpful if we want to refer to them for such purposes as iterating through them, plucking individual cases out for scrutiny, or other list slicing tasks). This dataframe provides a nice easy way of looking at what could otherwise be a complex mess of information.

There are, as I suggested above, a few different ways of collating information for a dataframe which are worth knowing (e.g. in case we receive data in other formats). For instance, we can create a dataframe from a list of tuples, as follows:

---

[5]Again, these data are drawn from the Northern Ireland deprivation dataset we used in Chapter 12 and in our discussion of Pandas series above.

```
1    import pandas as pd
2
3    data = [("Belfast East", 13.9, 7.6, 1.8),
4             ("Belfast North", 24.2, 11.2, 3.4),
5             ("Belfast South", 20.6, 14.7, 4.5),
6             ("Belfast West", 25.4, 10.9, 5.6)]
7
8    data_df = pd.DataFrame(data)
```

Here we're importing pandas as pd again, but instead of using a dictionary of lists, we're using a list of tuples to build the dataframe – each tuple contains all the relevant information for each constituency, and the same Pandas method as before (pd.DataFrame()) to take that set of information and store it as a variable which we can then print out. However, you might have spotted that we no longer have the benefit of having the keys of a dictionary to label each column as we did before, and so this version of the dataframe prints as shown in Figure 14.5. With this code, we only get a further set of index positions to denote what each column refers to rather than header titles which indicate what the numbers actually mean. But at least this gives us a rough-and-ready way to make sense of our data even if presented to us as a list of tuples.

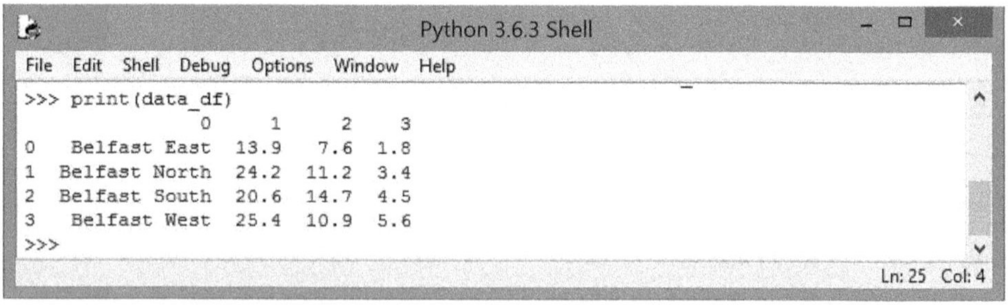

```
Python 3.6.3 Shell                                        –  □  ×
File   Edit   Shell   Debug   Options   Window   Help
>>> print(data_df)
          0     1     2    3
0    Belfast East   13.9   7.6   1.8
1    Belfast North  24.2  11.2   3.4
2    Belfast South  20.6  14.7   4.5
3    Belfast West   25.4  10.9   5.6
>>>
                                                    Ln: 25  Col: 4
```

Figure 14.5 A slightly less tidy dataframe (but still OK)

One other way of reading data into a dataframe is as a list of dictionaries, which would look something like this:

```
1    import pandas as pd
2
3    data = [{"Name": "Belfast East",
4             "Violence Rate": 13.9,
5             "Theft Rate": 7.6,
6             "Veh Crime Rate": 1.8},
7
8             {"Name": "Belfast North",
9              "Violence Rate": 24.2,
```

```
10            "Theft Rate": 11.2,
11            "Veh Crime Rate": 3.4},
12
13         {"Name": "Belfast South",
14            "Violence Rate": 20.6,
15            "Theft Rate": 14.7,
16            "Veh Crime Rate": 4.5},
17
18         {"Name": "Belfast West",
19            "Violence Rate": 25.4,
20            "Theft Rate": 10.9,
21            "Veh Crime Rate": 5.6}]
22
23  data_df = pd.DataFrame(data)
```

We use the same method as before (pd.DataFrame()) to store the list of dictionaries in a variable as a dataframe. You can see the results in Figure 14.6, and might also note that rather than repeat the different fields in the order they feature in each dictionary, they are presented alphabetically (so instead of Name/Violence Rate/Theft Rate/Veh Crime Rate as in Figure 14.4 we get Name/Theft Rate/Veh Crime Rate/Violence Rate).[6] This is not *necessarily* a problem (though it could be if, for instance, the field that we want to display in the leftmost column does not come first alphabetically), but just something interesting to be aware of when we're thinking about how to construct a dataframe for analytic purposes.

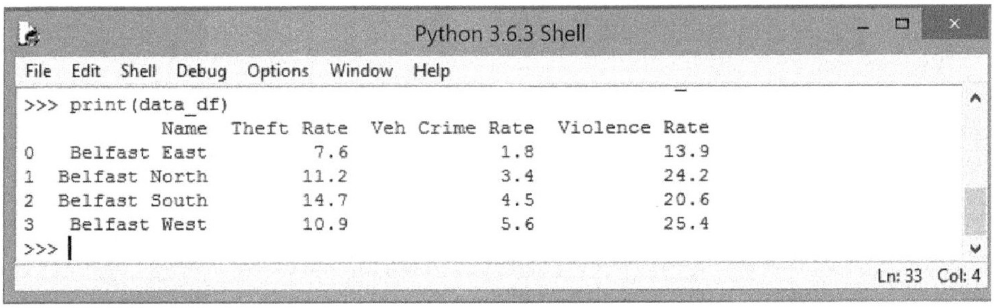

```
                        Python 3.6.3 Shell                          —  □  ×

File  Edit  Shell  Debug  Options  Window  Help

>>> print(data_df)
            Name   Theft Rate   Veh Crime Rate   Violence Rate
0    Belfast East        7.6              1.8            13.9
1   Belfast North       11.2              3.4            24.2
2   Belfast South       14.7              4.5            20.6
3    Belfast West       10.9              5.6            25.4
>>> |
                                                     Ln: 33  Col: 4
```

Figure 14.6 Another tidy dataframe

The code above prints out the same dataframe as we were able to get from the dictionary of lists method (apart from the reordering of the fields as discussed above), but you can see that we've constructed this using a different data storage technique (i.e. storing the data as a list of

---

[6]It's an interesting Python thought-experiment to think about why this might happen - can you have a guess at that (before reading the next sentence where I give the answer)? It's because in this way of constructing a dataframe we're now working with dictionaries as the "unit" of data (i.e. each constituency is its own dictionary and we're reading in information from those dictionaries), and dictionaries do not order fields in fixed index positions in the same way that lists or tuples do. Hence, the dataframe sorts the information alphabetically rather than by index position (because for a dictionary, there is no index). The more you know!

dictionaries) – quite handy to know we can build dataframes in these various ways depending on what data structures we have at our disposal!

Now let's look at some commands for navigating around dataframes – although these are new to you (if you've never used Pandas before), they draw on various Python conventions (such as list slicing, finding things by index positions, applying methods to objects), which you should be very familiar with by now. So, try following along with these commands as we go through them (perhaps by building you own little mock dataframe to play around with), to see how they work for you.

One thing we can do to keep working with dataframes is to use their keys and/or index positions to pull out sections to look at – for instance:

```
>>> print(data_df["Name"])
0        Belfast East
1        Belfast North
2        Belfast South
3        Belfast West
Name: Name, dtype: object
```

This command prints out the values associated with a specified key of the dataframe where they are available – in this case, all the values associated with the key called Name. We can even print out multiple columns of data according to what we might be interested in looking at:

```
>>> print(data_df[["Name", "Veh Crime Rate"]])
            Name Veh Crime Rate
0    Belfast East            1.8
1   Belfast North            3.4
2   Belfast South            4.5
3    Belfast West            5.6
```

This command prints out the values for two selected keys alongside one another (as well as the headers for their columns) – note also that the syntax for this command requires a double square bracket ([[ ]]). This is useful if we have lots of data but we actually only want to look at some selected fields (i.e. columns in the dataframe table) to answer a specific question we might have. Similarly, if we only want to look at a selected range of rows, we can use index-based list slicing techniques as follows:

```
>>> print(data_df[2:4])
            Name   Violence Rate   Theft Rate   Veh Crime Rate
2  Belfast South          20.6          14.7            4.5
3   Belfast West          25.4          10.9            5.6
```

Many of the standard list slicing techniques would apply here (and as with any of these techniques, the value is in their usage not just to print things out to the shell, but to slice up and store relevant bits of data elsewhere, for use in other structures and in other ways).

We can also replace the numerical index position with something more descriptive, as follows:

```
>>> constituency_initials = ["BE", "BN", "BS", "BW"]
>>> data_df.index = constituency_initials
>>> print(data_df)
```

		Name	Violence Rate	Theft Rate	Veh Crime Rate
BE	Belfast East		13.9	7.6	1.8
BN	Belfast North		24.2	11.2	3.4
BS	Belfast South		20.6	14.7	4.5
BW	Belfast West		25.4	10.9	5.6

In this case we have introduced two-letter "constituency codes" that we can use to identify each constituency as a shorthand. It's worth noting, however, that even having changed the index in this way, we can't then pull the whole row of information for a country by its index, and we still need to use its (numerical) index position value, like this:

```
>>> print(data_df[0:1])
```

		Name	Violence Rate	Theft Rate	Veh Crime Rate
BE	Belfast East		13.9	7.6	1.8

Note that we still have to use a list range (i.e. `[0:1]` instead of just `[0]`) to select an individual row of data – this is simply a quirk of how Pandas operates, and is due to the fact that Pandas uses individual index numbers to try to find columns of data, whereas that functionality changes when dealing with slices, whereupon Pandas uses the index range to search for rows. So, if we tried `print(data_df[3])`, we would get an error, since there is no column in this dataframe labelled 3.

This idea of pulling information out can also be done in quite smart ways. For instance, we can build conditions into our code to select certain pieces of information that fit the criteria we set out:

```
>>> print(data_df[data_df["Veh Crime Rate"] > 4])
```

		Name	Violence Rate	Theft Rate	Veh Crime Rate
BS	Belfast South		20.6	14.7	4.5
BW	Belfast West		25.4	10.9	5.6

This can be quite useful – if we have quite a lot of rows of data, we can pluck out a range of those that are relevant to us for whatever purpose (e.g. we might only be interested in constituencies with a particularly high vehicle crime rate, and can pull them specifically out without having to wade through other data).

Although we can't use our newly fixed index of country codes to pull rows of data, we *can* use the index to pull single pieces of information, for example:

```
>>> print(data_df["Name"]["BE"])
Belfast East
```

And in a similar way to how we've changed the index numbers for labels that are more descriptive, we can also edit the column names if we wish:

```
>>> cols = ["Name", "Violence", "Theft", "Vehicle Crime"]
>>> data_df.columns = cols
>>> print(data_df)
            Name   Violence    Theft   Vehicle Crime
BE    Belfast East      13.9      7.6             1.8
BN    Belfast North     24.2     11.2             3.4
BS    Belfast South     20.6     14.7             4.5
BW    Belfast West      25.4     10.9             5.6
```

As before when we were looking at series in Pandas, we can also draw out various descriptive statistics as and when appropriate.[7] Figure 14.7 shows the same set of information as we looked at previously in our Pandas series example, but we should note that we're only getting descriptive statistics for three of the columns – "Violence", "Theft" and "Vehicle Crime". This is because these are the only data fields that *support* such statistical descriptions, on the basis that they contain numerical data (either integers or floats), whereas the "Name" column and the information within it (strings of constituency names) do not.

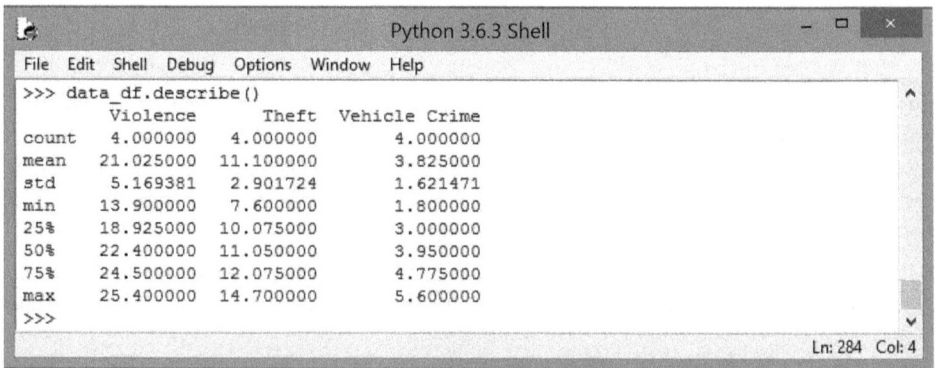

```
>>> data_df.describe()
            Violence       Theft   Vehicle Crime
count      4.000000    4.000000        4.000000
mean      21.025000   11.100000        3.825000
std        5.169381    2.901724        1.621471
min       13.900000    7.600000        1.800000
25%       18.925000   10.075000        3.000000
50%       22.400000   11.050000        3.950000
75%       24.500000   12.075000        4.775000
max       25.400000   14.700000        5.600000
>>>
```

Figure 14.7 Descriptive statistics for data_df

Pandas also allows you to edit and otherwise play around with existing dataframes. Let's add in a new row of data:

```
>>> new_row = [{"Name": "East Antrim",
               "Violence": 9.7,
               "Theft": 4.5,
               "Vehicle Crime": 0.9}]
>>> new_row_df = pd.DataFrame(new_row)
>>> data_df = data_df.append(new_row_df, ignore_index = True)
>>> print(data_df)
```

---

[7] And what makes a statistical description appropriate is something you should decide on the basis of quantitative methods training and literature - I allude to it above in a bit more detail when I'm talking about similar concepts as applied to Pandas series which might give you a head start at least.

```
1                Name    Theft   Vehicle Crime   Violence
2   0    Belfast East     7.6             1.8       13.9
3   1    Belfast North    11.2            3.4       24.2
4   2    Belfast South    14.7            4.5       20.6
5   3    Belfast West     10.9            5.6       25.4
6   4     East Antrim      4.5            0.9        9.7
```

Here we first set out the information for our new row of data as a list of dictionaries (though we don't actually have to have more than one dictionary in the list of course). Then we put this information in its own dataframe (new_row_df) and append it to the existing data_df – we could put the new dataframe in a new variable altogether, but here we overwrite the data_df variable with a new version of data_df with the information about another constituency, East Antrim, appended (which has the benefit that we can still call data_df in the shell and see this new information). It's also worth noting that we have to tell Pandas to ignore the index position that East Antrim has in new_row_df – this is because by default the new dataframe will give East Antrim an index position of 0, and data_df already has something at index position 0 (i.e. information for Belfast East). Hence, we want to append *everything but* the index position for this new information about East Antrim to data_df, and the ignore_index parameter lets us do that – we can see that the index position that is given instead is 4. And one final thing to note – even though we had previously set the indexes for data_df to be constituency initials (BE, BN, etc.), because we didn't provide a constituency initial for East Antrim, data_df has reverted instead to using the numerical index positions. If we want to set the constituency initials as indexes again, we could do so using the commands outlined above, but of course we would have to make sure that *each* row of information has a constituency initial in order for this to work properly.

And just to round off our discussion of adding new things to dataframes, we can also delete them. For instance, we can delete a column of information as follows:

```
>>> data_df.drop(["Violence"], axis = 1)
                Name    Theft   Vehicle Crime
0    Belfast East     7.6             1.8
1    Belfast North    11.2            3.4
2    Belfast South    14.7            4.5
3    Belfast West     10.9            5.6
4     East Antrim      4.5            0.9
```

Here we use a method called .drop() to delete a specified column. The axis parameter can be set to either 0 or 1, where 0 will drop labels from the index (i.e. it will take out a row of information by its index position), and 1 will drop labels from a column. With this in mind, let's now also drop a full row of information from this table:

```
>>> data_df.drop([4], axis = 0)
                Name    Theft   Vehicle Crime   Violence
0    Belfast East     7.6             1.8       13.9
1    Belfast North    11.2            3.4       24.2
2    Belfast South    14.7            4.5       20.6
3    Belfast West     10.9            5.6       25.4
```

You should see from this information that we've presented the dataframe without the information that sat at index position 4 (i.e. the stuff we recently added relating to East Antrim), which is what we expected, but also that the `Violence` column has come back, which perhaps we didn't expect. What this tells us is that the `.drop()` method is a way of *temporarily* dropping out bits of information for the purpose of visualising the table. It doesn't actually edit or alter the information contained in the dataframe – if we wanted to make a permanent change, we could write the dropped version of the dataframe to a new variable, or simply overwrite the original dataframe with the new edited version in the same way we did above when adding the East Antrim entry in.

And that about wraps up our working with series and dataframes – there are, of course, *loads* of other things you can do with Pandas and lots of commands that I haven't covered here. Rather than attempting the impossible and providing a comprehensive account of everything it's possible to do with Pandas series and dataframes (which would be a book in itself, and likely to age quickly) and other functionality Pandas offers, this has instead been a very brief crash course to get you started in thinking about how to use this tool to work with data. The next step is, as with any of the chapters in this book, to do some further reading (in this case, the Pandas documentation would be an ideal place to start), and work on projects yourself to practise and further develop your skills.

14.2 Show Me the Code! Matplotlib

As above, we're going to use an add-on library – `matplotlib` – as a means of improving our capacity to use Python to engage with data we might want to feed it. We can think of `matplotlib` as a library of techniques for helping us *visualise* data in various ways. The simplest ways we can demonstrate this visualisation process employ techniques you probably already know about and have worked with before, such as line graphs and bar charts, which you might encounter not only in the context of social science (e.g. in quantitative research reporting) but also in everyday life via news articles and so on. Although these types of visualisation can be useful for certain social scientific purposes, there is much more we can do with Python and Matplotlib to take things further – however, all this chapter aims to do is give you a head start on these more advanced visualisations by getting you acquainted with the basic concepts and techniques. To that end, we'll explore how to build a line graph and a bar chart using the XML dataset we looked at in Chapter 12, on the topic of the 10 leading causes of death across different US states from 1999 to 2016 (which is useful for thinking about things like healthcare inequalities across different states and across time). These are the most basic things you can do in Matplotlib, but will stand you in good stead as you develop your skills further and start to envision (and construct) more complex and sophisticated visualisations in Python to suit your analytic needs. Indeed, part of what this chapter is intending to do is emphasise the idea that as a Python programmer you are now in a position where you have a great deal of power and control over how you construct your analyses and findings – the creative application of a library like `matplotlib` can assist in that in many different ways, and you might go on to develop some really innovative and new ways of looking at social phenomena through Python programming. But, as with anything, we have to start by learning the basics and work from there – so, let's do exactly that!

Line graphs in Matplotlib

One of the simplest things we can do in Matplotlib is look at numerical data on a line graph. All we mean by a line graph is a plot with an *x*- and *y*-axis (i.e. two lines starting from a single point of origin, one going from left to right/horizontal, and one going from bottom to top/vertical), onto which we can place various "datapoints" (i.e. individual bits of data) and see if there are any patterns we might identify by looking at this collection of datapoints as an object of analysis. If that description of what a line graph is sounds a little abstract, don't worry – let's do some coding that will make a line graph emerge that we can then map that description back onto:

```
1   import matplotlib.pyplot as plt
2
3   NY_flu_death_rates = [(1999, 28.4), (2000, 26.5), (2001, 25.5), (2002, 26.6),
4                         (2003, 26.1), (2004, 26.6), (2005, 26.3), (2006, 23.0),
5                         (2007, 20.5), (2008, 21.0), (2009, 20.5), (2010, 20.6),
6                         (2011, 21.4), (2012, 18.8), (2013, 20.5), (2014, 19.5),
7                         (2015, 20.0), (2016, 18.3)]
8
9   values = [item[1] for item in NY_flu_death_rates]
10
11  plt.plot(values)
12  plt.show()
```

The code above, when executed (i.e. when you run the script), will produce an image of a line graph. However, let's take this code line by line to see how exactly that happens. First, we import the `matplotlib` library into Python as `plt` (as we did with `pandas`, when we imported it as `pd`); this is just a conventional shorthand that Matplotlib users generally use so that they don't have to constantly type out `matplotlib.pyplot`, and it's quite helpful to be aware that this is what other programmers might be familiar with if you're ever sharing your own code or using code written by others. Next, we establish some data to actually graph out – here, I've taken the original full XML dataset and extracted all the values for the age-adjusted number of deaths by flu and pneumonia per 100,000 population, from 1999 to 2016 and specifically within the state of New York.[8] So, we might expect that this is going to tell us something about how healthcare has changed in New York between 1999 and 2016, which itself could be the start of an analysis of different governments' approaches

---

[8]We discuss what exactly these numbers and terms like "age-adjusted" mean in Chapter 12, where the original XML dataset is first introduced. And again, although it's possible to simply copy over the data I've used here into your own shell, it'd be a much more valuable endeavour to go back into the XML dataset and practise pulling it from the web and sorting it out to use Python to derive a list of all flu and pneumonia deaths by year in the state of New York, as I've done here. You should be seeking out any opportunity to flex your Python skills by now; this is one of those opportunities.

to healthcare and social welfare. This dataset is stored in a variable called NY_flu_death_rates, in a list-of-tuples format (where the tuples each contain an integer indicating the year the data represent, and a float representing the number of flu/pneumonia deaths per 100,000 in New York in that year).

In order to graph out the death rates, however, we need to do some further work to extract them from the tuples they are currently in – in short, we need a list that *just* contains the numbers (i.e. the data) and not the dates (i.e. the labels). So, to do this I have set up a list comprehension which iterates through each item in NY_flu_death_rates and stores the thing that is at index position 1 in a list called values.[9] So, values contains just the data which we want to put into our graph.

The last two lines in the code above are where the Matplotlib magic happens: first, we can use the plt.plot ("command (which takes one argument, namely the data we want to plot (i.e. values)) to put each datapoint on a plot, and then plt.show() to display an image of what we have just plotted, which is shown in Figure 14.8.

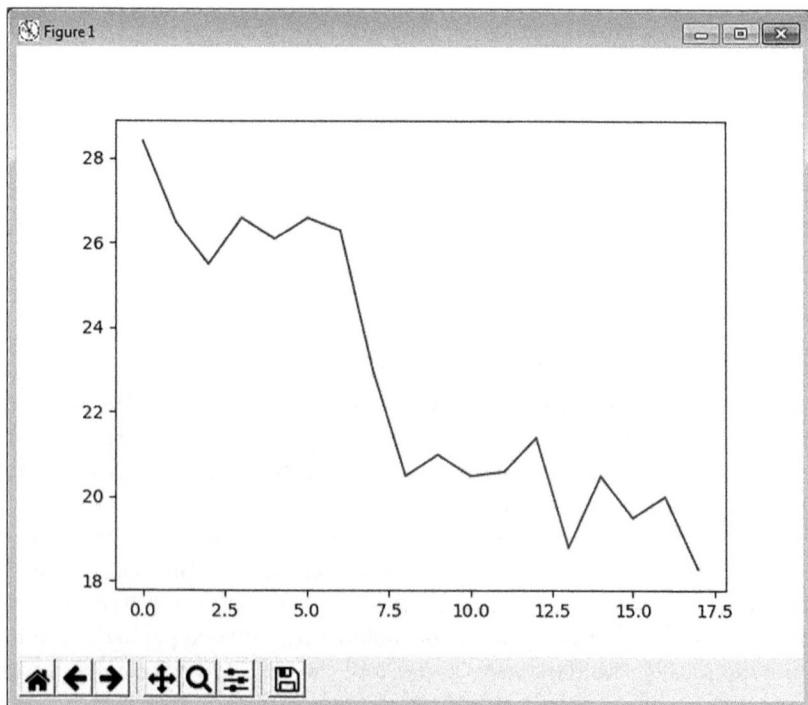

Figure 14.8 An incredibly basic line graph

---

[9]This is why list comprehensions are handy - sometimes list comprehensions can be a bit tricky to read because there's a lot going on in a short line, but as in this instance, they're worth knowing as a technique so you can quickly and dynamically create new useful lists. If you're struggling with how this list comprehension works, it'd be good at this point to have a quick refresher of the material in Section 6.2.

Let's just take a minute to review what we can see in this line graph. First, each of the data-points in our list is given a position on the *x*-axis according to its index position in the list called `values` – hence, on the (horizontal) *x*-axis, we can see labels going in steps of 2.5 from 0 to 17.5, which tell us the index position of the datapoint we're looking at.[10] We can also see that each datapoint is given a position on the (vertical) *y*-axis in relation to the numerical value stored in `values`. This is why the line goes up and down on the graph: the piece of data at index position 0 in the list gives a value of 28.4, and that translates onto the plot as an *x*-axis value of 0 and a *y*-axis value of 28.4. And this is repeated for each of the datapoints stored in `values`, so that we can now see the data, and (in the context of flu/pneumonia death rates in New York from 1999 to 2016) start to make some sense of what these data reflect in social science terms – we can now see which years had more flu/pneumonia deaths than others, and start to think about why this might be (changing political leadership, intro-duction of new healthcare systems, etc.).

However, what we might also note is that this image of the graph is very basic and would be difficult for anybody to read outside of the present context. We've already noted that the labels on the *x*-axis are really very misleading – they give index positions in increments of 2.5, which is *very* unhelpful, but also those index positions don't actually tell us which year the datapoint represents. So, we have to use our knowledge of how the data were constructed (i.e. where "0.0" represents the data stored at index position 0, which represents the year 1999) in order to say anything sensible about the graph. For somebody viewing the graph who *doesn't* have that knowledge, this graph is basically completely unreadable. Aside from this major issue, there are other things we could do to make the graph more visually intuitive/readable too. For instance, we might want to put a title on the graph to say what it is about, and we might want to have titles for both the axes to indicate what data we are actually graphing out – and we'll come to those important presentational aspects later. But for now, that's a line graph!

Bar charts in Matplotlib

What we're going to do here is simply graph out another slice of the data from the XML dataset on leading causes of death across states in the United States from 1999 to 2016, but in a different form of visualisation – as a bar chart. The focus of this book being Python and not quantitative methods, I don't want to get too deep into the differences between these two ways of looking at data (line graphs and bar charts). But in a nutshell, we might use a bar chart to represent datapoints on an *x*-axis which we *could* use to look at in terms of how those display a broader trend, but which can also be used to visualise data in groups/categories which don't necessarily have to represent any kind of trend. For example, we'd use a line chart to visualise something like the population of a single country by year, where the *x*-axis would represent a year of data and the *y*-axis would give the number of people in the country in that year. With a line graph, we'd be able to see how the population of

---

[10]Obviously index positions can never be anything other than integers, so, the fact that this graph shows us numbers like 2.5 is problematic in terms of readability. But we'll get on to formatting and making graphs more readable in due course.

that country *changes* over time. In contrast, we'd use a bar chart if we wanted to graph out the population of different countries in a given year with *y*-axis values representing population figures and *x*-axis values representing the different countries. This is a case where it wouldn't make sense to think of population as a "trend" between countries (because it doesn't make sense to think of one category as a continuation from the previous one in the same way as it did in the line graph alluded to above, where we're looking at years on the *x*-axis), but we could still use the graph to make useful comparisons *between* countries. Let's see how a bar chart looks in code:

```
1    import matplotlib.pyplot as plt
2
3    flu_death_rates = [('Alabama', 17.1),('Alaska', 12.5),('Arizona', 10.4),
4                       ('Arkansas', 17.1),('Cali.', 14.0),('Colorado', 9.6),
5                       ('Conn.', 11.7),('Delaware', 10.7),('Florida', 9.3),
6                       ('Georgia', 14.3),('Hawaii', 24.4),('Idaho', 11.3),
7                       ('Illinois', 14.5),('Indiana', 12.6),('Iowa', 11.6),
8                       ('Kansas', 14.4),('Kentucky', 17.3),('Louisiana', 14.3),
9                       ('Maine', 12.0),('Maryland', 15.1),('Mass.', 14.1),
10                      ('Michigan', 13.7),('Minnesota', 7.8),
11                      ('Miss.', 23.4),('Missouri', 15.1),('Montana', 11.1),
12                      ('Nebraska', 14.3),('Nevada', 18.1),
13                      ('New Hamp.', 11.8),('New Jer.', 10.7),
14                      ('New Mex.', 14.6),('New York', 18.3),
15                      ('N. Carolina', 16.5),('N. Dakota', 14.5),
16                      ('Ohio', 15.0),('Oklahoma', 12.4),('Oregon', 8.9),
17                      ('Penn.', 13.9),('Rhode Isl.', 11.0),
18                      ('S. Carolina', 12.0),('S. Dakota', 16.7),
19                      ('Tennessee', 20.1),('Texas', 11.1),('Utah', 15.5),
20                      ('Vermont', 7.0),('Virginia', 12.7),('Washington', 10.0),
21                      ('W. Virginia', 17.3),('Wisconsin', 11.9),('Wyoming', 15.0)]
22
23   values = [item[1] for item in flu_death_rates]
24
25   plt.bar(range(0,len(values)), values)
26   plt.show()
```

Lots of the code are pretty much the same as in the line graph example. We import the same library,[11] we've got some data to plot (this time, it's a list of tuples called flu_death_rates containing individual states and the flu/pneumonia death rate per 100,000 for the

---

[11]If you're following your bar chart code on from within the same script as the line graph example alluded to above, then you won't need to re-import in the library at this point. However, if you're building the bar chart code in a new script, then you will.

year 2016),[12] a list comprehension to pull out just the datapoints (`values`), and (once we've set the plot up) we make the plot with the `plt.show()` method.

However, the key difference is that we have a different method for doing the plotting. We use `plt.bar()`, which takes two arguments. The second argument, `values`, is the list where the data are stored. The first argument (`range(0,len(values))`) is the scale of the x-axis. Whereas with the line graph the `plt.plot()` method took the index position of the data in the list as the default scale, we need to set this scale manually when we're using `plt.bar()`. We could do this in a few different ways – for instance, given that I know there are 50 states in the United States (and therefore 50 datapoints in my `values` list) I *could* set the scale of the axis by explicitly establishing a range of 0 to 50 going in steps of 1 (i.e. `range(0,50)`) which would give one bar per piece of data. However, there are two problems there. First, we might not always know how many datapoints to expect in a list – here we know it's 50, but what about if we have a huge dataset where we *don't* know how many datapoints there are? How would we check that? In a case like that, our code would have to be a little smarter, and more dynamic in terms of how we identify the number of datapoints (i.e. the length of the list) – which is why I set the scale of the x-axis with `range(0,len(values))`. This uses a property of the list called `values` – namely, the length of (i.e. the number of items in) the list. Of course, this still gives a value of 50, but it doesn't require us to know that there are 50 items in advance, which is helpful.

The second issue with setting the x-axis scale like this (and which referring to the length of the list *doesn't* solve either) is that we still won't end up with a usefully descriptive set of labels for our x-axis categories – we'll still effectively only see the index positions of each datapoint as we saw before, and these don't do much to tell us what each bar actually relates to. This is problematic when each bar refers to a state. However, this is something we can address when we come on to formatting and adding some presentational tweaks to the code below. For now, let's just run this code excerpt and look at the graph that results (Figure 14.9).

As before, we can see the shape of the data in this bar chart – each entry in `values` is visually represented with a bar along the x-axis, and the size of the bar (i.e. how tall it is) is given by the value of that entry (i.e. the number of flu/pneumonia deaths per 100,000 population in 2016) on the y-axis. The problem is that, even though this visualisation represents the data, it's still really quite unreadable – we can't easily see which bar refers to which state, nor do we have other features (a title, axis labels, etc.) which might help us resolve those confusions. Which tees me up to talk about …

Taking visualisations further – formatting

What we've done so far is produce some perfectly serviceable but not especially good look-ing or analytically intuitive visualisations. The insights we can draw from the visualisations might be perfectly valid inasmuch as they give us a way to look at large volumes of data in a

---

[12] Again, the best way to follow along with this would be to go back to the XML data and derive this list of tuples for yourself, rather than just copying it across to your own script or typing it out again. However, for full disclosure, I've "manually" edited the text of some of the longer state names to shorten them a little, just so they more easily fit on a visualisation image.

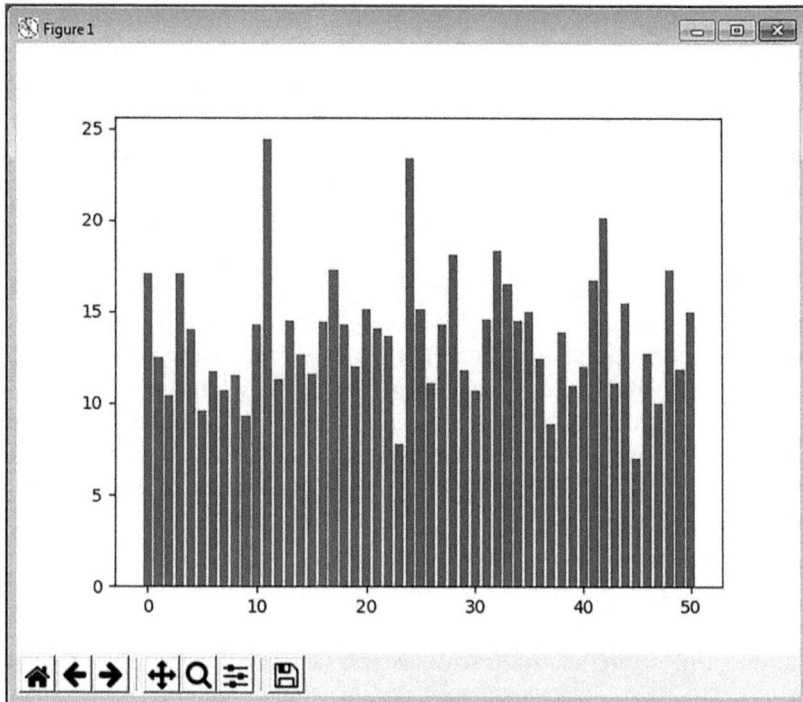

Figure 14.9 An incredibly basic bar chart

more easily digestible format, but there are still some problems here. Mainly, what if we want to show other people the work we've done – can we expect them to understand a bar chart like that in Figure 14.9? Look at it from the point of view of somebody seeing the graph for the first time. What would they think this graph is *about*? There are no titles, no labels for the *x*- and *y*-axes, nothing but some fairly uninformative numbers on the "ticks" of each axis to mark key reference points – in short, no information that might help them make sense of the graph at all. To them it would just be a picture of some rectangles attached to some numbers, and impossible to make any actual *sense* of this and use it to say anything meaningful about the social world. In order to turn this picture into a visualisation, we need to therefore help viewers view it, and we can do this by formatting the graph in various ways to give viewers a bit more information.

So let's return to the code for our bar chart as we outlined it above, but add in some new techniques from the matplotlib library to turn this image into something we can use. Here is the full script for you to have a look at before we get into a line-by-line discussion:

```
1    import matplotlib.pyplot as plt
2
3    flu_death_rates = [('Alabama', 17.1),('Alaska', 12.5),('Arizona', 10.4),
4                       ('Arkansas', 17.1),('Cali.', 14.0),('Colorado', 9.6),
5                       ('Conn.', 11.7),('Delaware', 10.7),('Florida', 9.3),
```

```
6          ('Georgia', 14.3),('Hawaii', 24.4),('Idaho', 11.3),
7          ('Illinois', 14.5),('Indiana', 12.6),('Iowa', 11.6),
8          ('Kansas', 14.4),('Kentucky', 17.3),('Louisiana', 14.3),
9          ('Maine', 12.0),('Maryland', 15.1),('Mass.', 14.1),
10         ('Michigan', 13.7),('Minnesota', 7.8),
11         ('Miss.', 23.4),('Missouri', 15.1),('Montana', 11.1),
12         ('Nebraska', 14.3),('Nevada', 18.1),
13         ('New Hamp.', 11.8),('New Jer.', 10.7),
14         ('New Mex.', 14.6),('New York', 18.3),
15         ('N. Carolina', 16.5),('N. Dakota', 14.5),
16         ('Ohio', 15.0),('Oklahoma', 12.4),('Oregon', 8.9),
17         ('Penn.', 13.9),('Rhode Isl.', 11.0),
18         ('S. Carolina', 12.0),('S. Dakota', 16.7),
19         ('Tennessee', 20.1),('Texas', 11.1),('Utah', 15.5),
20         ('Vermont', 7.0),('Virginia', 12.7),('Washington', 10.0),
21         ('W. Virginia', 17.3),('Wisconsin', 11.9),('Wyoming', 15.0)]
22
23   values = [item[1] for item in flu_death_rates]
24   labels = [item[0] for item in flu_death_rates]
25
26   plt.bar(labels, values)
27
28   plt.title("Bar chart to show US 2016 flu/pneumonia death rates by state")
29   plt.xlabel("States")
30   plt.ylabel("Deaths per 100,000")
31   plt.xticks(rotation=90)
32
33   plt.tight_layout()
34
35   plt.show()
```

This code snippet, if you run it, would produce a decent-looking bar chart with plenty of information to help a viewer make sense of what was going on (and when you do run this code, be sure to maximise the resulting image to make it as visually intuitive as possible). As a first step, copy all this code across into a script for yourself, run it, and see what happens – we'll unpick the differences between this version of the bar chart and the earlier more basic one as we go. Let's dig into it line by line to see what's been added and discuss things further.

The first thing to note is that we're importing matplotlib in as plt just as before, and we have the same list-of-tuples data we used before, stored in flu_death_rates. We also have the same list comprehension as before, to pull out all the numbers we want to use as data-points and store them in a list called values. Then we have a new line of code – a similar list comprehension, but one which pulls out the names of the US states from flu_death_rates and stores *them* in a list called labels. This iterates through each tuple in the list of flu_death_rates and pulls out a piece of information from it (this time, the piece of information stored at index position 0 in each tuple, i.e. the name of the state) and puts it in a list format. Why are we doing this? Well, if we're now wanting to add information into our bar chart of flu/pneumonia death rates by state, it'd be handy to be able to label each bar in our chart with the state each datapoint represents – for that, we need a list of those state names, and I'm using this list comprehension statement to generate that list. So, type out the list comprehension code yourself and call labels to see what results – is this what you expected?

The next line is something we've already seen: `plt.bar()` takes two sets of data – our new `labels` list and our existing `values` list – and plots them on the *x*- and *y*-axes (respectively) of a bar chart.

The next four lines are new, but also quite intuitive. We start with a command, `plt.title()`, into which we can pass a string to give a title to our chart. Next, we have a command, `plt.xlabel()`, into which we can pass a string that we want to appear as a label for our *x*-axis. And somewhat predictably, we then have a command, `plt.ylabel()`, into which we can pass a string that we want to use for our *y*-axis label. This is then followed by a command, `plt.xticks()`, which can take various arguments, but the one we focus on here is a parameter that governs the rotation of the text of all the different tick labels (i.e. the names of the US states) as they appear on the plot. The reason why we do this will become apparent when you see the visualisation, but in essence the default rotation is 0 degrees (i.e. text reads from left to right across the page just as it does in this book), and I have set the rotation instead to be at 90 degrees (i.e. text reading vertically, bottom to top). If we leave the rotation at 0/default and we have a large amount of labels close together (i.e. if they all read left to right), they will end up overlapping – try this for yourself in your own version of the script by deleting or "commenting out" (i.e. turning a line of code into a comment so it won't be executed when the script runs) the `plt.xticks(rotation=90)` line of code. Can you see what's happened? All the information in labels is now overlapping and impossible to read – urgh! So let's "uncomment" that line of code again and rerun the script – the difference should be immediately visible to you, inasmuch as we again have a version of the chart in which the rotation of the *x*-axis tick labels makes it possible to read them all individually.

There is also another new line of code which is *really* useful when visualising stuff in Matplotlib – `plt.tight_layout()`. This little command ensures that the plot area (i.e. the white space where all the graphing is done and all the axes, titles and labels are placed) is large enough to accommodate all the formatting we're trying to do. So, typing `plt.tight_layout()` after any formatting code and before we display (or save – see next section) the visualisation solves most problems to do with information going off the end of a page. To see this in action, "comment out" the `plt.tight_layout()` command and run the script – you should see in the resulting image that many of the names of the US states are chopped off the bottom of the image, and we also can't see the title of the *x*-axis (because that too gets chopped off). Running the script with `plt.tight_layout()` ensures that none of this information gets chopped off and our plot area is always big enough to fit in everything we want to see. So, this is probably a command you'll use in pretty much every Matplotlib visualisation you produce – worth keeping it handy, for sure!

Finally, we display the plot with the `plt.show()` command. When you run this code (and stretch out the resulting image a little to help distinguish between bars), you will see a bar chart that looks like Figure 14.10. Now we have a bar chart that we can actually *use* to tell us about the different levels of flu/pneumonia deaths by state in 2016 – we can see, for instance, that Hawaii, Mississippi and Tennessee have particularly high death rates, whereas Vermont,

Minnesota and Oregon have particularly low death rates. We might want to then start questioning what is happening differently across each of these states that might produce such a disparity in a cause of death which we might normally assume to be an easily preventable disease – there's a social science research question here in which we could then go on to look at the levels of poverty or the demographic make-up of each state and see if there are any correlations between these things and access to healthcare in the United States. So a visualisation like this can be the start of something really important!

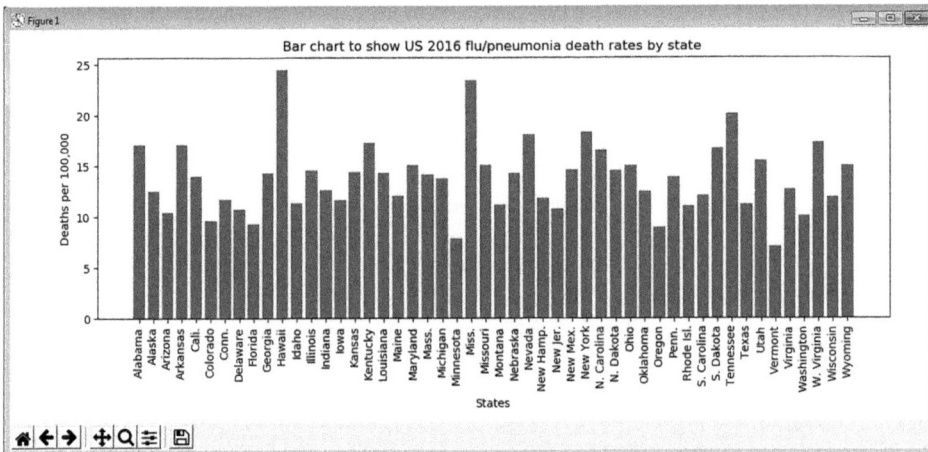

Figure 14.10   Still a bit basic, but a *slightly* funkier (and much more useful) bar chart

The formatting techniques demonstrated here (and others) will work across various different types of plot, so it's very useful to have an awareness of them as a basic starting-point for formatting your visualisations. If you want to dig deeper and extend your skills, consulting the Matplotlib documentation (Matplotlib, 2019) or even trying out other visualisation libraries for Python like Seaborn (Seaborn, 2018), ggplot (ggplot, 2014) or geoplotlib (Cuttone, 2018) will switch you on to new techniques to try out and new ways to produce representations of data of many different kinds. There are lots of alternative libraries out there, and matplotlib is (and has hopefully been) a great one to start with since it offers a nice easy way into the basics.

Taking visualisations further – saving

This would be an appropriate point in our discussion of coding in Matplotlib to go over how to save in a usable format the visualisations you generate. You might have seen already that when we use plt.show() to display a plot, it pops up with some buttons, one of which pertains to saving the image as a file[13] – so it's easy enough to save your image that way, but

---

[13]The "floppy disk" button, if people still know what floppy disks are?

we can also write this into code to further automate the process. This is done with a single command, `plt.savefig()`, which takes as its argument a string detailing the file directory (including filename) to which you want to save the image. So, for completeness, let's return to the line graph we started working on earlier in the chapter, add in some formatting to make it as readable as we can (which will also mean learning a new technique for formatting line graphs – handy to know!), and save it to a file:

```
1   import matplotlib.pyplot as plt
2   import os
3
4   NY_flu_death_rates = [(1999, 28.4), (2000, 26.5), (2001, 25.5), (2002, 26.6),
5                         (2003, 26.1), (2004, 26.6), (2005, 26.3), (2006, 23.0),
6                         (2007, 20.5), (2008, 21.0), (2009, 20.5), (2010, 20.6),
7                         (2011, 21.4), (2012, 18.8), (2013, 20.5), (2014, 19.5),
8                         (2015, 20.0), (2016, 18.3)]
9
10  values = [item[1] for item in NY_flu_death_rates]
11  labels = [item[0] for item in NY_flu_death_rates]
12
13  plt.plot(values)
14
15  plt.title("Graph to show NY flu/pneumonia death rates by year")
16  plt.xlabel("Year")
17  plt.ylabel("Deaths per 100,000")
18  plt.xticks(range(0,len(labels)), labels, rotation=90)
19
20  plt.tight_layout()
21
22  file_dir = os.getcwd()
23  plt.savefig(file_dir + "\\Flu_Deaths_US_2016.png")
```

What we have here is pretty much the same line-graph-generating script as before, with a few differences/additions worth paying attention to. First of all, note that we've imported a library of techniques called `os` (which we met in Chapter 10 and which offers various commands and methods to do with the operating system of our computer); this becomes relevant when we're saving the image file, since we need to tell Python where on our computer to save the file.

As with the formatted bar chart, in order to generate a list of labels for the x-axis (i.e. the years that each datapoint represents), we've extracted those from their tuples with a list comprehension called `labels`. Then there are lines of code we've seen before for plotting the datapoints and adding various formatting bits and bobs (titles and labels). For a line graph, however, in order to add "tick" labels (i.e. give each datapoint a label to represent the year), we have to add some more arguments to `plt.xticks()`. Here, we're giving `plt.xticks()` three arguments. First, we need to provide information that sets the *locations* of the ticks, and I use something similar to what we've already seen in the bar chart script to do this, `range(0,len(labels))`, to tell the command that I want there to be as many ticks as there are labels. Second, I pass in the *content* of the ticks – I give the argument `labels` to say where to pull the information from. And third, I pass in another argument to say that I want the text of those labels to be rotated at a 90-degree angle (which we've seen before). After this, I use `plt.tight_layout()` to make sure that all this information will be visible in the resulting plot, as before.

At this point, however, there is a new variable called `file_dir` in which we use the `os.getcwd()` method store a string representing the current working directory – this is something we encountered earlier in Section 10.1 in Chapter 10, so if you're unsure as to what this is doing, check back there. Then we add in a line of code to save the image – `plt.savefig(file_dir + "\\Flu_Deaths_US_2016.png")` – and there are two things to note about this. First, we're using a smart way to identify the current working directory, by automatically identifying the current working directory and adding on details of a filename to the end. The reasons why we might want to do this are discussed more fully in Section 10.1, but it's also worth noting that in our filename we get to choose what kind of file extension we want to save our image as. Matplotlib supports saving data as certain types of format, `.png` being one which is particularly common as a format for storing images (which is why I use it here), but you can also store these image data in other formats – for instance, as a `.pdf` file, which will work just fine too. However, `.png` will likely be fine for most (if not all) purposes. And if you run this script, you will then see a new `.png` file containing an image of this line graph, created in the same directory as the script is currently located (see Figure 14.11).

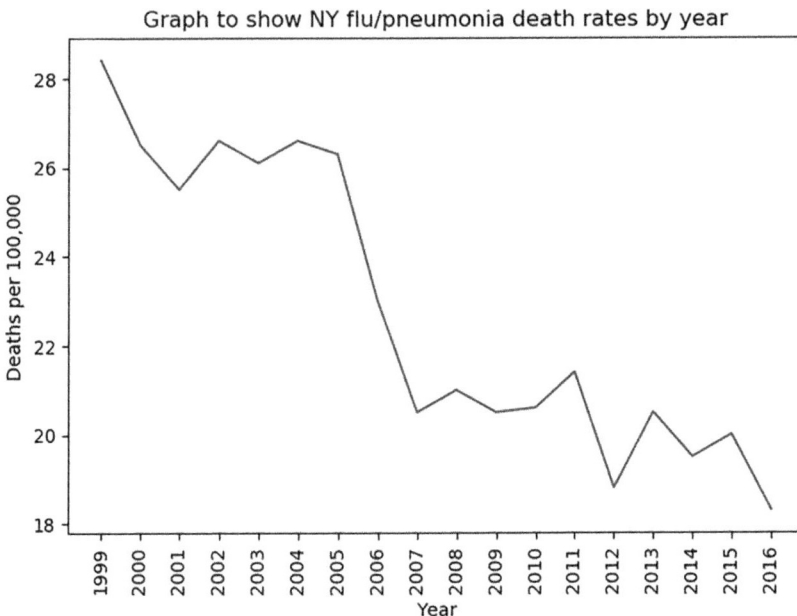

Figure 14.11 We did it! A formatted, saved, useful visualisation!

Nice! There is perhaps a bit more we could do in terms of making the title and axis labels bold, or overlaying other states over the NY graph with different-coloured lines, but here we have a graph that's really useful analytically – we can use this as a starting-point for understanding what's gone on in New York from 1999 to 2016 in terms of healthcare provision (e.g. why the sudden drop in flu/pneumonia deaths in 2005–2007? Why do death rates not seem to improve much in the early 2000s?). Again, some relatively simple techniques have opened up plenty of social scientific possibilities here in terms of thinking about and understanding what goes on in the social world, even on the basis of just about the simplest visualisations we can think to do (e.g. a line graph and bar chart). This gives you a great starting-point to get deeper into thinking about visualisations and building your own in ways that support the work you are doing.

One final note on saving images using Python and Matplotlib: you should use *either* `plt.savefig()` *or* `plt.show()`, but not both in the same script. Using both can cause problems due to how Matplotlib handles the opening and closing of plots – problems like empty image files or no image files being saved at all, and so on. So, best to make a decision on whether you want your script to show *or* save an image and build the code accordingly.[14]

Data visualisation as a sociological activity

Why have we spent a lot of time going over the line-by-line detail of how to construct some relatively basic forms of visualisations? Perhaps the most obvious reason is that this is a good way to learn about the code required to do the work. But there's much more to it than this. One key thing we've done here is pay some really close attention to data visualisation as an active process which is not just about representing numbers with code, but about constructing interpretations of the social world by making design choices with code – in other words, reflecting on data visualisation as a methodological issue.

Aside from just giving you the details of which commands to use to build the various visualisations, going line by line through the code helps us see and understand the fine detail of what we're doing in Python. What we've seen is that a visualisation library like pandas or matplotlib offers a range of ways to visually represent data, and for the most part we actually have to do very little in the code to choose between them. Sometimes, it can just be a case of slightly tweaking one little line of code to produce something that can look quite different (e.g. changing `plot` to `bar`), and therefore ends up saying quite different things about the world. However, as a social scientist, this should raise an eyebrow – it's not good enough to just unthinkingly produce a picture of the social world without questioning how that picture has come to be (in terms of the contexts and motivations that are implicated in and by its generation). Worse still, visualisations can in principle be constructed in such a way that they *obscure* the social world, either accidentally through careless thinking or on purpose for political or ideological ends. For instance, imagine a graph showing the number of immigrants coming into a country year by year over the last 200 years – this graph may show that there

---

[14]You could even construct an IF/ELSE statement that asks you if you want to apply a function that saves the visualisation or one that shows the visualisation and then performs the relevant operations – why not?

are increasing levels of immigration through history, and some right-wing interpreters might treat this as evidence of a social problem.[15] However, if we constructed that visualisation differently, perhaps taking into account rising levels of populations in the country (i.e. visualising migrants as a *percentage* of the total population year on year) then we might get a very different and far less drastic picture. We might also want to overlay gross domestic product (a common measure of economic activity in a country) to help demonstrate that as migration levels rise, so do the living standards of everybody in that country – this could be used as a starting-point to give us a better angle on the benefits that increased migration brings, and (hopefully) preclude right-leaning interpretations that would use the data to cast fear and doubt over migration as a social issue.

Hence, the general point here is that we need to think about not only how to get our code to work, but also how to construct visual accounts of the social world that are useful, descriptive, explanatory and transparent with regard to their methods of production. As a Python programmer with a knowledge of Matplotlib, you can now control the choice of visualisation you want to produce; as social scientists we have a responsibility to construct those visualisations in (a) a sensible way that reflects what is going on behind the data (i.e. not just the numbers, but the people's stories that generate those numbers), (b) a socially responsible, moral, ethical and/or critical way, and (c) a clear, transparent, appropriate and readable way.

All of which makes building visualisations far more powerful a tool than just turning data into pictures!

14.3 Some Possible Applications/Projects

In this chapter we've focused primarily on exploring some of the core concepts and techniques of pandas and matplotlib, as ways of playing around with data and shaping them in different ways. The skills you've learned here are useful in their own right, but, as with any of the techniques presented in this book, this shouldn't be seen as the end of the story. In order to keep building on your skills and developing as a programmer, you'll need to practise these techniques and learn new ones as part of genuine projects relevant to social science. Here are a few examples of potentially interesting things you might want to try in this regard.

"Reverse-engineer" a visualisation. With the skills you already have, you could find a data visualisation in someone else's work (where their data for producing the visualisation is also available) and try to recreate the original graph from the data. This may be from other researchers' work (e.g. in a journal article), from government reports based on open datasets, or newspaper articles that use data to make their points. In doing this, you have a great opportunity to reflect on how difficult it might be to get the graphs looking the same (if they are) and the reasons why you might be seeing differences in the original graph and yours (i.e. are you and the original authors working with the same data in different ways and with different assumptions? What different interpretations do your respective visualisations seem to naturally lead to?).

---

[15] I would disagree with them entirely, of course, but that's how a right-leaning person might take that graph.

Critical data visualisation. Perhaps using the same data as noted in the point above, *intentionally* produce a very different visualisation of data used for another purpose (e.g. in a journal article or government report or newspaper article) that offers a more critical perspective on the data than the original visualisation did. Use your own visualisation to produce a counter-argument to the original work. This also gives you an opportunity to think about such things as how existing theory and literature can be factored in as ways to elaborate on visualisations – seeing the connections between visualisations and literature/ existing research is no insignificant task, and this is an ideal opportunity to practise those skills to genuine social scientific effect.

Generating more sophisticated visualisations. As noted above, there are lots of things in the `matplotlib` library that we've not had room to discuss here, and there are lots of different visualisation libraries (e.g. `Seaborn`, `ggplot` or `geoplotlib`) that offer different features and functionalities altogether: explore these! Is there anything in `matplotlib` or other libraries that you think looks particularly interesting? Different types of visualisations that would be relevant to some work you're involved in? If so, use the skills you already have as a platform to learn how to do those new things, and apply them to your work. The documentation for each of these libraries will be helpful here, alongside what you know already about how to grab, work with and make a visual sense of data.

Chapter summary

- In this chapter we first looked at `pandas` as a library for reading in data and presenting them in various table-like formats. We looked specifically at constructing Pandas series and dataframes (and ancillary techniques around editing and formatting those things).
- We then looked at the `matplotlib` library, taking two simple visual formats - a line graph and a bar chart - and using those as a vehicle for digging into the types of coding that are relevant to producing visualisations.
- This was then complemented by a discussion of how visualisation is an activity of much social scientific interest - if it's possible to design visualisations to produce different understandings of the social world, then how should *we* (as social scientists) engage with that process?
- Finally, we looked at a small selection of possible applications of the skills you possess, in projects of genuine social science relevance - these are of course not the *only* things you can do with the skills you have so far, but might be a good starting-point for you.

Summary of Part Three

- In Part Three, we took our core knowledge of Python one step further by starting to think about how it might be applied to a range of tasks relevant to social science.

  o Chiefly, this followed a (loose) narrative of thinking about designing research to suit social scientific needs, grabbing and working with various different types of data in various different ways, and visualising such data in various different formats so that we can understand/analyse them.

- We pitched the idea of "design" as being a bridge between programming and social science that we can leverage in various ways to undertake methodologically robust work.
- We looked at various Python techniques for working with text files, using social media APIs (e.g. Twitter) to collect data, how to decode/encode data in popular web formats (e.g. CSV, JSON and XML), how to scrape data from the web, and how to visualise data in various ways (e.g. in tabular form using Pandas, and in graphic form using Matplotlib).
- Each of these topics also indicated ways to extend your learning as you dig into your own projects and work using Python to undertake social scientific study, as a way of connecting the skills and techniques learned back to PaSS as the approach that underpins our motivation for programming in the first place.

The point here is dual: first, to learn how to do tasks relevant to social science in Python; and second, to give you a means to explore how your skills can be taken further and applied to your own projects and interests.

PART FOUR

Part Four contents

PROGRAMMING-AS-SOCIAL-SCIENCE

Part Four objectives

- To review in general what you have learned by this point in the book.
- To further explore and solidify PaSS as a particular approach to programming (in Python).
- And finally, to thank you for getting this far!

15

Conclusion: Using Your Programming-as-Social-Science Mindset

━━━━━■ **Chapter objectives** ■━━━━━

- To start wrapping up the book by briefly recalling what you've learned so far.
- To point towards how to take your Programming-as-Social-Science (PaSS) work further by sharing and writing about your code for social science purposes.
- To reflect on what PaSS means, in part by referring back to a previous exercise (the "dictionary of you") to highlight some of the salient issues.
- Finally, to make sure that when you close this book, you're confident and comfortable enough with Python to start doing PaSS for yourself!

Phew! We made it! Here's the conclusion! I'd like to start it simply by saying thank you. Thank you for taking the time to read this far and get to grips with what I think is an enormously powerful and exciting tool for social science. I really do hope you've enjoyed learning the things on offer in this book, and that you've got something out of it. As these skills trickle more and more into the core methods of social science research (as I hope they will), I personally can't wait to see what the social science research community ends up doing with Python in our work. To that end, do use the web resources associated with this book to communicate and share ideas with other readers and PaSS practitioners, and please do feel free to get in touch with me directly to tell me about it too, genuinely.

We've learned *a lot* of stuff by this point. If you turned to page 1 knowing absolutely nothing about Python programming, by this point you've taught yourself about the underlying ideas and purposes of computer programming, why it might be a valuable thing for a social scientist to do, how social science might undertake programming work in its own unique way, you've learned the core concepts of Python code (in terms of how to build and work with things like variables, IF/ELSE type logic, various objects such as lists, dictionaries and strings, functions, loops and classes), as well as how to extend the basic Python functionality with things like add-on modules and automated scripts, and from there you've gone on to look at design as a key concept for integrating Python into the work of social science, and explored a variety of relevant techniques including working with text files, using social media APIs, unpicking various data formats (CSV, JSON and XML), web scraping and unpicking HTML information, and then turning data into various types of visualisation. You should be really proud of making it this far; this is by no means an insignificant achievement, and you now have lots of skills and techniques under your belt that you didn't have before. So, go you!

However, perhaps the most important thing you've learned (and which this chapter is really about) is *how to learn more* about PaSS with Python. Each chapter has been constructed so as to give you a head start on a key concept and/or technique, but they have all also been explicitly pitched to say "this is not the full story, and if you want to take things further, you'll need to use what you've learned here to go on and find out more as part of your own personal projects". If you've taken that advice and gone on to play around with Python as part of your own work, you should now be at least fairly comfortable with the idea of how to do things with Python that *aren't* captured in this book – a single book is *never* going to be able to capture the full range of stuff you might want to do,[1] but if you

---

[1] After all, social science is a broad and diverse grouping of disciplines and practices, and so is Python programming.

can see how to apply these lines of thinking to your own work going beyond the concepts and techniques that it is possible to put down on a page in a book, you've cracked it. And, as with anything, this needs plenty of practice – if it still seems a bit daunting to put your programming skills to use in projects of your own, really the only way to tackle this is head-on, by diving right into it and getting to work. Hopefully what this book has shown you is that doing exactly that can be incredibly valuable, and maybe even a little fun and/or interesting too.

15●1 A Few Final Points

As you're close to putting this book down and going on to do some work with Python for yourself, it is also worth making a few final comments on how to present PaSS projects to others. It should be no surprise that not every social scientist knows programming,[2] and even if we're speaking to others who *can* read Python code, we need to consider how best to tell people about the PaSS work we've done (e.g. in essays, papers or presentations). Inherently, we're going to be operating in an interdisciplinary space here (see Section 1.3 in Chapter 1), where our programming and code need to be shown as situated within a wider socio-technical research assemblage (see Section 1.2 in Chapter 1), and there are several things to consider here.

Sharing your code

The first thing to note is that whatever work we've done with Python, it'll be useful to be able to share that code with others so they can see and even use it for themselves. Hence, we need to make our code available. One thing to think about here is where we should put our code so that it can be accessed by others. There are various platforms that help do this job already and are worth exploring (though such explorations are outside of the remit of the present book). I feel like I have to (begrudgingly) mention GitHub (GitHub, 2019) as one such platform where you can set up an account to host, share and collaborate on coding projects.[3] Another (perhaps preferable) option is storing code in Jupyter Notebook format developed by Project Jupyter (Project Jupyter, 2019), which is an open-source not-for-profit tool for sharing and collaborating on coding projects that supports Python alongside over 40 other programming languages.[4] The building and sharing of code via platforms such as these

---

[2] - yet! But I'mma work on that ☺.

[3] This is a begrudging mention because GitHub presents a bit of an ethical/moral dilemma. While it is perhaps the single most popular code-sharing platform, it is also routinely used as a way of recruiting many hours of unpaid labour and is a for-profit business owned by Microsoft. As with anything in the social sciences, we're all navigating a moral maze.

[4] The open-source and not-for-profit aspect make this preferable for me ideologically, but as a tool it's also just very good. However, it is worth noting that Jupyter Notebooks is a spin-off development of the IPython (Interactive Python) command shell tool which itself is stored in ... the GitHub repository ☹ (cf. previous footnote). It's a moral maze!

are good practice for transparency of your work in a number of ways. As noted, it's useful to share our code with others so they can see, check and use it for themselves – this is how academic research fundamentally operates, especially in the social sciences where we need to be reflective and reflexive about the claims we're making and how our methods support those claims. However, as Somers (2018) notes, tools like these, where research is represented in, by and with software such that readers can see how a research project develops (as opposed to just seeing the finished polished output in an essay or paper as a text-heavy document or a fixed-in-stone PDF file), offer new and useful ways to represent research. So, learning how to use tools to share your work and bring readers/users along for the ride with you is definitely a very useful and interesting to do.

Related to this, but also important in a much more general sense, is the need to document your code effectively (see Section 8.5 in Chapter 8). It should be noted that in the code excerpts and files associated with this book, I haven't done much of this myself, purely because I've had to keep things looking relatively clean on the page – the documentation for the code in this book is within the text of the book itself, though of course it needs to be acknowledged that supplementing a code with a book is absolutely not standard practice for the purposes you'll be putting your Python knowledge to (unless you're also writing a text-book aiming to teach Python to social scientists, in which case *get off my patch!*). However, when you're presenting your own coding work to other readers/users, you'll need to think carefully about what to incorporate into your code to help them understand/use it. If you're sharing your code on a public platform, where in principle anybody could access and use it, you also need to consider a few other things. Aside from making your code as readable as possible (via commenting and user/reader-focused decisions on things like how to name variables), you might want to include some identifying details that link the code specifically back to you as a header for a script – your name, your affiliation (e.g. the university you study at/work for), contact details, version number of the script, the date it was released, and a one-liner on the purpose of the code and any other such details, where relevant. All these details will help a reader/user understand more about who you are, what this code is for and how to work with it, as well as allowing you to take credit for your code (which is important too in itself). The code files associated with Part Two of this book show what these kinds of headers might look like (though not with all the details I've mentioned in this paragraph), and, as noted, previous sections also explore more fully the idea of building readable code – both of these things are worth revising before you make public any code of your own.

One further (and also related) thing that is *very* important to consider when sharing your code is the idea of keeping private information private. This was explored already in the con-text of access credentials for using social media APIs (see Chapter 11), but in a more general sense, where we stored our Twitter access credentials in a separate script and imported in that private information to a data collection script such that we could then show the data collection script to others without giving up our Twitter passwords and other private details. As such, if you're going to upload your code to any public space, you will need to first review that code to see if you actually *want* everything in it to be publicly available – if not, you should consider "modularising" the code (i.e. taking out private bits and writing a few lines of extra code to import those bits in from elsewhere when necessary, as we did in the Twitter example above). Even aside from the (very important) issues of privacy and security, modu-larisation of code is just good practice and quite useful too. As you start doing more and more programming, you're likely to end up with files full of useful scripts which might overlap in functionality – for instance, you might have a script for grabbing data from Reddit, and a range of different separate scripts for doing different types of data visualisation of Reddit data. Clearly it would be a waste of time and potentially quite unreadable to have multiple copies of your data collection script set within the data visualisation scripts themselves – instead, you could import in your data collection methods to your visualisation scripts so that everything looks a lot cleaner (and any changes you might want to make to your data collection script would also then automatically apply to any visualisation script that draws on them, which is arguably just as handy, if not more so). Keeping an eye out for how to organise your code files for use and reuse can end up being a massive time-saver as well as keeping your coding work streamlined and readable.

It's also important to consider that, as a social scientist, your code might be of interest to other social scientists who don't necessarily have the same coding skills you now have (or perhaps even just the same *level* of skills you have). If you're sharing your code with others, you have to design the code and its method of sharing so that the intended audience can access and use it – this recalls our earlier thinking on design (see Chapter 9) as well as the techniques you learned about building interfaces to help others use the tools you build (see Section 8.4 in Chapter 8). Of course, all of the above is important, but so is being sensitive to the skills and tools your intended readers/users have at their disposal, and some of your coding effort might be directed towards not just making your tools work, but making them accessible too. If you *are* going to consider accessibility, and if you're designing tools where readers might benefit from some instruction in how to use those tools, uploading the code with a supplementary README.txt file (which would contain further details and instructions) is never a bad idea. As with documenting and commenting on your code effectively, considering accessibility is not a chore to be done grudgingly; it actually benefits you too. For instance, when you share your code with others and have others use it for their own purposes, this can be a perfect opportunity to get valuable insight into the sense others can make of your code and how useful it really is – in other words, users who give you comments on your code can tell you more about how to keep improving your skills and the things you build. So, considering accessibility and the needs of the intended audience for your code is not only good and nice in general, but also mutually beneficial.

Writing about your code

Part of disseminating your code and the social scientific work that it is situated within will, almost inevitably, involve writing. However, there's a perennial problem of interdisciplinarity here, in that it's potentially quite difficult to explain what might be very complex work in a way that is clear for people who don't share the same skills and knowledges that your work is premised on. The outputs of social scientific work (e.g. essays, papers, conference talks) require methodological transparency (i.e. a good clear account of how you did what you did), and if we're talking about work that involves skills and knowledges that we might expect our audience to be unfamiliar with, we'll need to do extra work to maintain clarity in how we present our work. Your writing up of PaSS projects should enable a user who doesn't have much (or even any) experience of Python to understand what your code is doing without necessitating that they check the code itself (though the code should, of course, be available to them as well, for methodological transparency). What I hope to have shown you throughout this book, in all the times I've gone line by line through excerpted sections of code (i.e. as transparently as I could), is that it is possible to write descriptively and clearly about what any given piece of code is doing without relying on technical terms or esoteric language/concepts. I did this in the hope that it could stand as good practice for you to follow, so hopefully you have read a lot of examples of this already such that you can apply the model to your own writing. And of course, this is best supported by also having good readable code at the outset – it is impossible to write clearly about a spaghetti mess of code, so readability is at the core of everything we do from the beginning. Laying things out clearly means you can then go on to write about them clearly; hence the focus on design and planning earlier (e.g. Chapter 9). As with the practice of writing code, writing *about* code is something that can (and should) be practised, so the more opportunities you give yourself to do it (e.g. in essays, papers, presentations, blogs, even just in emails), the quicker you will become adept at it.

As I have also tried to do throughout, in your own writing you should also take care not only to *describe* your code in terms of what it does, but also to *explain* why you have designed things to work in that way. It is incredibly helpful for readers to be party to your decision-making process as a way of understanding your work, and explaining why you have done things in one way and not another (and even what other ways might look like) affords a reader insight into the role of the construction of code in whatever project you are writing about. Again, clarity and transparency are key, as is the integration of code into the social science research process more widely, so making those connections and considering the audience (i.e. designing your writing *for* them) is a useful skill to work on.

15●2 Reflecting on What We're Doing When We're Doing Programming-as-Social-Science

That brings me neatly on to my own reflections on what Programming-as-Social-Science, as pitched in this book, is all about. What we've been doing here is not just learning how to code in Python (though that is of course a part of it), but learning how to pay attention to *why* we're coding; figuring out *just what we're doing when we're doing coding* from our social science perspective. Just as one example of what I'm referring to here, recall when we were building a "dictionary of you" for an exercise in Section 5.3 in Chapter 5. We were, of course, at that point primarily interested in figuring out and practising skills with dictionaries and dictionary methods, but now we can also reflect more generally and social-scientifically on what we were doing there. One thing we might note is that in building a "dictionary of you", we were trying to find a way to organise information about ourselves – the exercise asked you to build a dictionary containing your date of birth, place of birth, favourite TV show and favourite film. Later in the exercise, you were also asked to replace the date of birth with your current residence, and generate a new dictionary of your favourite albums by your favourite bands/artists (and within that dictionary, also store details of those favourite albums such as their year of release and number of tracks). In doing all that, we learned about the grammar and syntax and practicalities of working with dictionaries and dictionary methods. But as social scientists, what else can we say about this exercise?

We might argue that in boiling ourselves down to a set of attributes (date of birth, current residence, favourite albums, etc.) we're "dataifying" ourselves – cramming our complex and unique social lives into a limited standardised structure that we also (implicitly) assume applies universally and not just to us. What does it mean to capture human life as data/metadata? Is it possible to standardise things like this (i.e. does it make sense to describe everybody in terms of their date of birth, current residence, favourite albums, etc.)? What sort of potentially useful things are missing from this "dictionary of you"? What is important to *you* and your identity that this dictionary *didn't* capture (political opinions, employment status/occupation, favourite foods, hobbies and interests, etc.)? If we're building a "dictionary of you", in effect what we're doing is designing a structure within which all the information about ourselves can be contained. However, in doing so, we're inevitably also placing constraints on what our self and our identity might be conceptually – how we code the dictionary determines the kinds of ways in which we might think and talk about our identity (i.e. as a particular combination of attributes that are shared across all humans universally). This is, of course, inherently problematic – whoever is in charge of coding this dictionary is also by default in charge of defining what it means to be human, and there's no reason to assume that a Python dictionary can ever capture something as rich as that in a finite set of formalised attributes. Hence, we have to *decide* what's relevant and what's not, and in doing so, *design* "self" and "identity" in code. Following on from this, the way we design/construct the dictionary is something that we need to consider as social scientists – could it be done differently? *Should* it be done differently? What kind of visions of ourselves could we create (and what would the implications be)? Is it possible to even "dataify" ourselves in this way at all, and what might the limitations of this way of thinking about the world be? Does thinking about how humans can be boiled down to data and metadata in this rather crude way help us understand what's going on when companies like Facebook or Fitbit or Amazon do the same when they're forcing the data they have on us into highly organised structures which are not necessarily rich or meaningful as descriptors of ourselves and our lives? And does it help us understand the problems that arise when companies like Facebook, Fitbit and Amazon collect these bits of data and find "creative" ways to use them to make money out of us? This is what PaSS is all about for me – programming is a tool not just for doing stuff with computers, but for inspiring social scientific thinking about the broader contexts within which our coding activity is embedded and implicated.

You can apply this kind of PaSS thinking and go back through *any* chapter in this book and use the exercises and code we've worked with to think about the social world in a similar way. For instance, when we're collecting data from Twitter (as we did in Chapter 11) we're *coding, designing and constructing an image of the world* (and reflecting how Twitter constructs images of the world for us) in a very particular way, and we need to question and reflect on what that means and what's happening when we do that. When we're visualising information (as we did in Chapter 14) we're *constructing* an account of the world that's designed to be persuasive in some way, and we need to think about why we should be pushing the particular argument we are instead of some other way of looking at the world, and how the visualisations themselves feed into the rhetorical process of doing so. When we're looping through a list of things and applying a function to each of them (as we did in Chapter 6) we're working on the assumption that all of those things can be treated identically (even if they're something like a word list where every word has its own individual context and distinct practices around its usage) and thereby *constructing an image of a phenomenon* whereby these things are standardised and directly and unproblematically comparable with one another. Given that we've designed the idea of comparability into our code, we need to ask some careful questions as to what makes these particular things comparable, whether they could be constructed otherwise, and what we want to do in comparing them (and is comparing them going to be a *valuable* thing to do? How? Why?)

Being able to see all of these things in the code itself, as you now can, offers a way to look at the mechanisms by which social research provides accounts of the world in general, not just in terms of computational and digital stuff, but also in terms of broader questions about the ontologies and epistemologies of social research (i.e. questions around what sort of stuff exists in the world, and how can we learn things *about* that stuff). Having Python programming skills can be a way of getting us to pay closer attention to crucial questions (such as those outlined above) that are rooted in the cores of our disciplines, but which have not yet been answered. Of course, there is no reason to expect that skill in Python programming could be the thing that's been missing all along – I'm by no means calling Python programming a social science silver bullet or anything like that – but it's one more tool in our toolbox by which we can draw attention to such issues when, more often than not, they get glossed over. In this sense, programming in Python can give us a means of asking and working on new social science questions, as well as revisiting old ones from different angles, thereby extending the reach of social science in a hitherto uncharted way.

Exciting, no?

REFERENCES

Anderson, C. (2008) The end of theory: The data deluge makes the scientific method obsolete. *Wired*, 23 June. Available at: https://www.wired.com/2008/06/pb-theory/ (accessed 3 May 2018).

Bardzell, J. and Bardzell, S. (2013) What is critical about critical design? *Proceedings of the SIGCHI Conference on Human Factors in Computing Systems CHI'13*, Paris, France. New York: ACM, pp. 3297–3306.

Baym, N.K. and Markham, A.N. (2009) Introduction: Making smart choices on shifting ground. In A.N. Markham and N.K. Baym (eds), *Internet Inquiry: Conversations about Method*. London: Sage, pp. vii–xix.

BBC News (2015) The Twitter bot that "corrects" people who say "illegal immigrant". *BBC News*, 3 August 2015. Available at: http://www.bbc.co.uk/news/blogs-trending-33735177 (accessed 25 May 2018).

Bjögvinsson, E., Ehn, P. and Hillgren, P.-A. (2012) Design things and design thinking: Contemporary participatory design challenges. *Design Issues*, 28(3), 101–116.

Bogost, I. (2007) *Persuasive Games: The Expressive Power of Videogames*. Cambridge, MA: MIT Press.

Brooker, P. (2019) My unexpectedly militant bots: A case for Programming-as-Social-Science. *The Sociological Review [Online First]*. Available at: https://doi.org/10.1177/004912411772970310.1177/0038026119840988.

Brooker, P., Barnett, J. and Cribbin, T. (2016) Doing social media analytics. *Big Data & Society*, 3(2), 1–12.

Brooker, P., Barnett, J., Cribbin, T. and Sharma, S. (2015) Have we even solved the "first big data challenge"? Practical issues concerning data collection and visual representation for social media analytics. In H. Snee, C. Hine, Y. Morey, S. Roberts and H. Watson (eds), *Digital Methods for Social Science: An Interdisciplinary Guide to Research Innovation*. Basingstoke: Palgrave Macmillan, pp. 34–50.

Brooker, P., Barnett, J., Vines, J., Lawson, S., Feltwell, T. and Long, K. (2017a) Doing stigma: Online commenting around weight-related news media. *New Media & Society*, 20(9), 3201–3222.

Brooker, P., Dutton, W. and Greiffenhagen, C. (2017b) What would Wittgenstein say about social media? *Qualitative Research*, 17(6), 610–626.

Bryman, A. (2012) *Social Research Methods* (4th edition). Oxford: Oxford University Press.

Bucher, T. (2018) *If … Then: Algorithmic Power and Politics*. Oxford: Oxford University Press.

Burrows, R. and Savage, M. (2014) After the crisis? Big Data and the methodological challenges of empirical sociology. *Big Data & Society*, 1(1), 1–6.

Button, G., Coulter, J., Lee, J.R.E. and Sharrock, W. (1995) *Computers, Minds and Conduct*. Cambridge: Polity Press.

Centers for Disease Control and Prevention (2018) *NCHS Leading Causes of Death: United States*. Available at: https://data.cdc.gov/api/views/bi63-dtpu/rows.xml?accessType=DOWNLOAD (accessed 2 May 2019).

Cuttone, A. (2018) *geoplotlib*. Available at: https://github.com/andrea-cuttone/geoplotlib (accessed 2 May 2019).

Di Salvo, C. (2012) *Adversarial Design*. Cambridge, MA: MIT Press.

Garfinkel, H. (1967) *Studies in Ethnomethodology*. Englewood Cliffs, NJ: Prentice Hall.

Gaver, W. (2002) Designing for Homo Ludens. *I3 Magazine*, 12, 2–6.

Gaver, W., Bowers, J., Boucher, A., Gellerson, H., Pennington, S., Schmidt, A., Steed, A., Villars, N. and Walker, B. (2004) The Drift Table: Designing for ludic engagement. *Proceedings of the SIGCHI Conference on Human Factors in Computing Systems CHI'04*, Vienna, Austria. New York: ACM, pp. 1–16.

Gehl, R.W. and Bakardjieva, M. (2017) Socialbots and their friends. In R.W. Gehl and M. Bakardjieva (eds), *Socialbots and Their Friends: Digital Media and the Automation of Sociality*. Abingdon: Routledge, pp. 1–16.

ggplot (2014) *ggplot from ŷhat*. Available at: http://ggplot.yhathq.com/ (accessed 2 May 2019).

Gitelman, L. and Jackson, V. (2013) Introduction. In L. Gitelman (ed.), *"Raw Data" Is an Oxymoron*. Cambridge, MA: MIT Press, pp. 1–14.

GitHub (2019) *GitHub*. Available at: https://github.com/ (accessed 2 May 2019).

González-Bailón, S. (2013) Social science in the era of Big Data. *Policy and Internet*, 5(2), 147–160.

GOV.UK (2018) *PM Speech on the NHS: 18 June 2018*. Available at: https://www.gov.uk/government/speeches/pm-speech-on-the-nhs-18-june-2018 (accessed 2 May 2019).

Guzman, A.L. (2017) Making AI safe for humans: A conversation with Siri. In R.W. Gehl and M. Bakardjieva (eds), *Socialbots and Their Friends: Digital Media and the Automation of Sociality*. Abingdon: Routledge, pp. 47–68.

Hallett, R.E. and Barber, K. (2014) Ethnographic research in a cyber era. *Journal of Contemporary Ethnography*, 43(3), 306–330.

Housley, W., Procter, R., Edwards, A., Burnap, P., Williams, M., Sloan, L., Rana, O., Morgan, J., Voss, A. and Greenhill, A. (2014) Big and broad social data and the sociological imagination: A collaborative response. *Big Data and Society*, 1(2), 1–15.

Kozinets, R.V. (2010) *Netnography: Doing Ethnographic Research Online*. London: Sage.

Langlois, G. (2011) Meaning, semiotechnologies and participatory media. *Culture Machine*, 12. Available from: https://culturemachine.net/wp-content/uploads/2019/01/7-Meaning-437-890-1-PB.pdf (accessed 25 July 2019).

Lazer, D., Pentland, A., Adamic, L., Aral, S., Barabási, A.L., Brewer, D., Christakis, N., Contractor, N., Fowler, J., Gutmann, M., Jebara, T., King, G., Macy, M., Roy, D. and Van Alstyne, M. (2009) Computational social science. *Science*, 323(5915), 721–723.

Lupton, D. (2014) *Digital Sociology*. London: Routledge.

Lupton, D. (2018) Towards design sociology. *Sociology Compass*, 12(1), e12546.

Lynch, M. (2000) Against reflexivity as an academic virtue and source of privileged knowledge. *Theory, Culture & Society*, 17(3), 26–54.

Malpass, M. (2013) Between wit and reason: Defining associative, speculative, and critical design in practice. *Design and Culture*, 5(3), 333–356.

Marres, N. and Weltevrede, E. (2013) Scraping the social? Issues in live social research. *Journal of Cultural Economy*, 6(3), 313–335.

Matplotlib (2019) *Overview*. Available at: https://matplotlib.org/contents.html (accessed 2 May 2019).

Mills, C.W. (2000 [1959]) *The Sociological Imagination* (40th anniversary edition). Oxford: Oxford University Press.

Mozilla Foundation (2019) *Firefox*. Available at: https://www.mozilla.org/en-US/firefox/new/ (accessed 2 May 2019).

Muller, M.J. (2003) Participatory design: The third space in HCI. In A. Sears and A. Jacko (eds.), *Human-Computer Interaction: Development Process*. Boca Raton, FL: CRC Press, pp. 165–185.

Nagy Hesse-Biber, S. and Leavy, P. (2011) *The Practice of Qualitative Research* (2nd edition). London: Sage.

Neff, G. and Nagy, P. (2016) Talking to bots: Symbiotic agency and the case of Tay. *International Journal of Communication*, 10, 4915–4931.

Nelson, L.K. (2017) Computational grounded theory: A methodological framework. *Sociological Methods & Research*. Available at: https://doi.org/10.1177/0049124117729703 (accessed 30 April 2019).

Northern Ireland Statistics and Research Agency (2017) *Northern Ireland Multiple Deprivation Measures 2017*. Available at: https://www.opendatani.gov.uk/dataset/e202fde9-7f0b-4d88-8711-e18a8817cff8/resource/887ad000-b6bf-4004-9ba8-3fb09372d432/download/nimdm2017---aa2008.csv (accessed 2 May 2019).

Notepad++ (2019) *Notepad++*. Available at: https://notepad-plus-plus.org/ (accessed 2 May 2019).

OpenDataNI (2017) *NIMDM2017 – Variables*. Available at: https://www.opendatani.gov.uk/dataset/northern-ireland-multiple-deprivation-measures-2017/resource/a73471bf-7047-4d34-9542-8d7eea92ae46?inner_span=True# (accessed 2 May 2019).

Perez, S. (2016) Microsoft silences its new A.I. bot Tay, after Twitter users teach it racism [Updated]. *TechCrunch*. Available at: https://techcrunch.com/2016/03/24/microsoft-silences-its-new-a-i-bot-tay-after-twitter-users-teach-it-racism/ (accessed 24 May 2018).

Project Jupyter (2019) *Jupyter*. Available at: https://jupyter.org/ (accessed 2 May 2019).

Python Software Foundation (2013) *PEP 8 – Style Guide for Python Code*. Available at: https://www.python.org/dev/peps/pep-0008/ (accessed 2 May 2019).

Python Software Foundation (2017) *Python2orPython3*. Available at: https://wiki.python.org/moin/Python2orPython3 (accessed 3 May 2018).

Python Software Foundation (2019a) *Python*. Available at: https://www.python.org/ (accessed 2 May 2019).

Python Software Foundation (2019b) *Download the Latest Version of Python*. Available at: https://www.python.org/downloads/ (accessed 2 May 2019).

Python Software Foundation (2019c) *Python Package Index*. Available at: https://pypi.org/ (accessed 2 May 2019).

Python Software Foundation (2019d) *Python Module Index*. Available at: https://docs.python.org/3/py-modindex.html (accessed 2 May 2019).

Python Software Foundation (2019e) *15.3. time – Time Access and Conversions*. Available at: https://docs.python.org/2/library/time.html (accessed 2 May 2019).

Python Software Foundation (2019f) *datetime – Basic Date and Time Types*. Available at: https://docs.python.org/3/library/datetime.html (accessed 2 May 2019).

Raspberry Pi Foundation (2019a) *About Us*. Available at: https://www.raspberrypi.org/about/ (accessed 2 May 2019).

Raspberry Pi Foundation (2019b) *Scheduling Tasks with Cron*. Available at: https://www.raspberrypi.org/documentation/linux/usage/cron.md (accessed 2 May 2019).

Robertson, T. and Simonsen, J. (2012) Challenges and opportunities in contemporary participatory design. *Design Issues*, 28(3), 3–9.

Savage, M. and Burrows, R. (2007) The coming crisis of empirical sociology. *Sociology*, 41(5), 885–899.

Savage, M. and Burrows, R. (2009) Some further reflections on the coming crisis of empirical sociology. *Sociology*, 43(4), 765–775.

Schutz, A. (1972) *The Phenomenology of the Social World*. Evanston, IL: Northwestern University Press.

Seaborn (2018) *Seaborn*. Available at: http://seaborn.pydata.org/index.html (accessed 2 May 2019).

Sengers, P., Boehner, K., David, S. and Kaye, J.J. (2005) Reflective design. *Proceedings of the 4th Decennial Conference on Critical Computing: Between Sense and Sensibility*, Aarhus, Denmark. New York: ACM, pp. 49–58.

Sengers, P. and Gaver, B. (2006) Staying open to interpretation: Engaging multiple meanings in design and evaluation. *Proceedings of the 6th Conference on Designing Interactive Systems DIS2006*, University Park, Pennsylvania, USA. New York: ACM, pp. 99–108.

Sharma, S. (2013) Black Twitter? Racial hashtags, networks and contagion. *New Formations*, 78, 46–64.

Sharma, S. and Brooker, P. (2017) #notracist: Exploring racism denial talk on Twitter. In J. Daniels, K. Gregory and Y. McMillan Cottom (eds), *Digital Sociologies*. Bristol: Policy Press.

Somers, J. (2018) The scientific paper is obsolete: Here's what's next. *The Atlantic*, 5 April. Available at: https://www.theatlantic.com/science/archive/2018/04/the-scientific-paper-is-obsolete/556676/ (accessed 4 January 2019).

Tweepy (2019) *Tweepy Documentation*. Available at: http://docs.tweepy.org/en/v3.5.0/ (accessed 2 May 2019).

Twitter (2019a) *Docs*. Available at: https://developer.twitter.com/en/docs.html (accessed 2 May 2019).

Twitter (2019b) *Twitter*. Available at: https://twitter.com (accessed 2 May 2019).

Twitter (2019c) *Developers*. Available at: https://developer.twitter.com (accessed 2 May 2019).

Wilkie, A., Michael, M. and Plummer-Fernandez, M. (2015) Speculative method and Twitter: Bots, energy and three conceptual characters. *Sociological Review*, 63(1), 79–101.

Winch, P. (1990) *The Idea of a Social Science, and Its Relation to Philosophy*. London: Routledge & Kegan Paul.

Wittgenstein, L. (1958) *The Blue and Brown Books*. Oxford: Blackwell.

Wittgenstein, L. (2009 [1953]) *Philosophical Investigations* (translated by G.E.M. Anscombe, P.M.S. Hacker and J. Schulte). Chichester: Wiley-Blackwell.

Worldometers (2019) *Countries in the World By Population* (2019). Available at: http://www.worldometers.info/world-population/population-by-country/ (accessed 2 May 2019).

INDEX